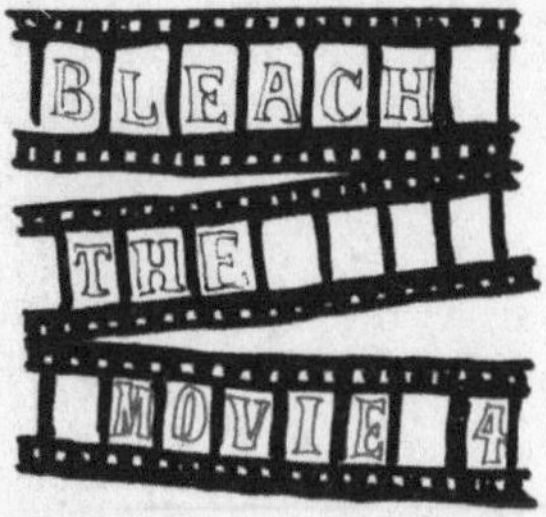
BLEACH
THE
MOVIE 4

The fourth movie will be in theaters the day after this volume is released in Japan. Hell over there, hell over here, it's hell for me too. I hope you enjoy all of them.

-Tite Kubo

BLEACH is author Tite Kubo's second title. Kubo made his debut with *ZOMBIEPOWDER.*, a four-volume series for *WEEKLY SHONEN JUMP*. To date, *BLEACH* has been translated into numerous languages and has also inspired an animated TV series that began airing in the U.S. in 2006. Beginning its serialization in 2001, *BLEACH* is still a mainstay in the pages of *WEEKLY SHONEN JUMP*. In 2005, *BLEACH* was awarded the prestigious Shogakukan Manga Award in the *shonen* (boys) category.

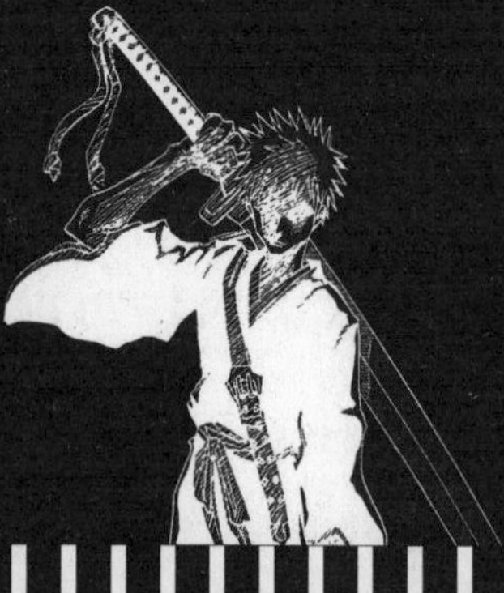

BLEACH
Vol. 48: GOD IS DEAD
SHONEN JUMP Manga Edition

STORY AND ART BY
TITE KUBO

English Adaptation/Lance Caselman
Translation/Joe Yamazaki
Touch-up Art & Lettering/Mark McMurray
Design/Kam Li
Editor/Alexis Kirsch

Printed in the U.S.A.

Published by VIZ Media, LLC
P.O. Box 77010
San Francisco, CA 94107

10 9 8 7 6 5 4 3 2 1
First printing, October 2012

People are all imitations of monkeys
Gods are all imitations of humans

BLEACH 48 GOD IS DEAD

Shonen Jump Manga

STARS AND

黒崎一護

Ichigo Kurosaki

-plot-

When high school student Ichigo Kurosaki meets Soul Reaper Rukia Kuchiki his life is changed forever. Soon Ichigo is a soul-cleansing Soul Reaper too, and he finds himself having adventures, as well as problems, that he never would have imagined. Now Ichigo and his friends must stop renegade Soul Reaper Aizen and his army of Arrancars from destroying the Soul Society and wiping out Karakura as well.

As the final showdown approaches, Ichigo must face a seemingly unstoppable Aizen who continues to gain power with every battle. Now Aizen and Gin head for Karakura to create the Oken, which will seal the Soul Society's doom. Unbeknownst to them, Ichigo has been training in the Dangai, where time is condensed, to learn the Final Getsuga Tensho. But will even that be enough to overcome Aizen's godlike powers?

BLEACH ALL

市丸ギン

Gin Ichimaru

Sôsuke Aizen

藍染惣右介

STORIES

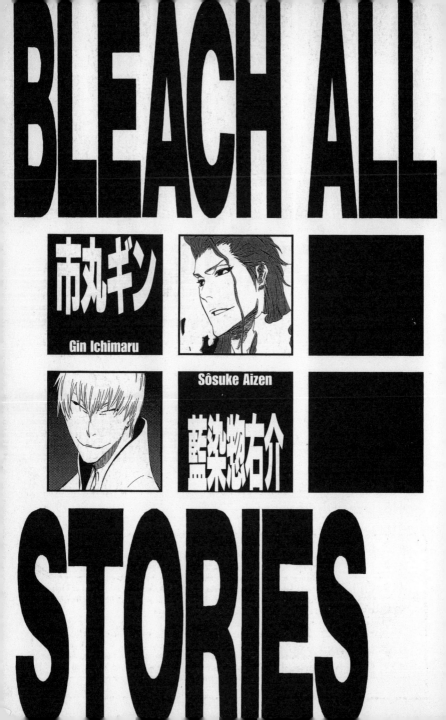

BLEACH48

GOD IS DEAD

Contents

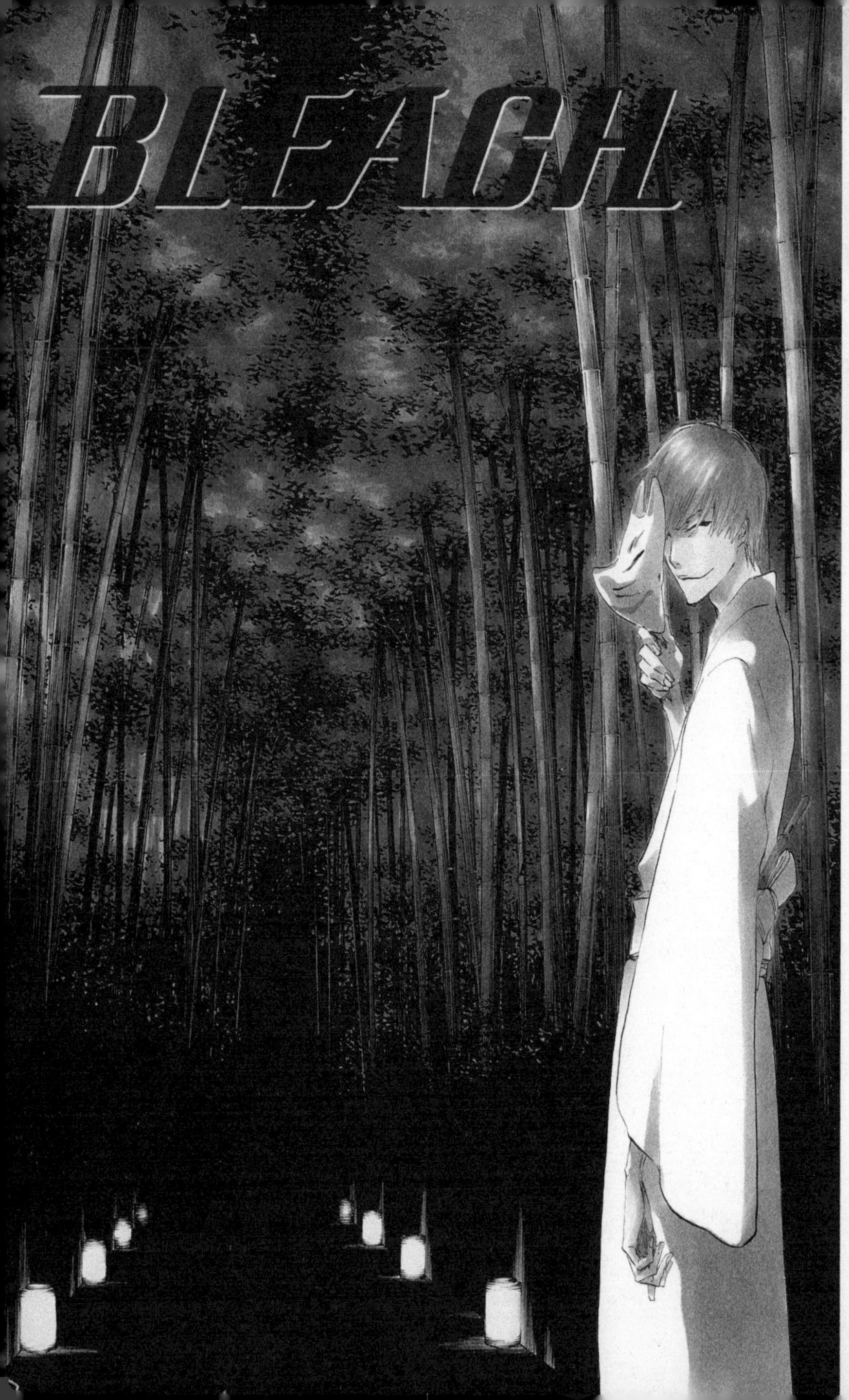
BLEACH

BLEACH

ブリーチ

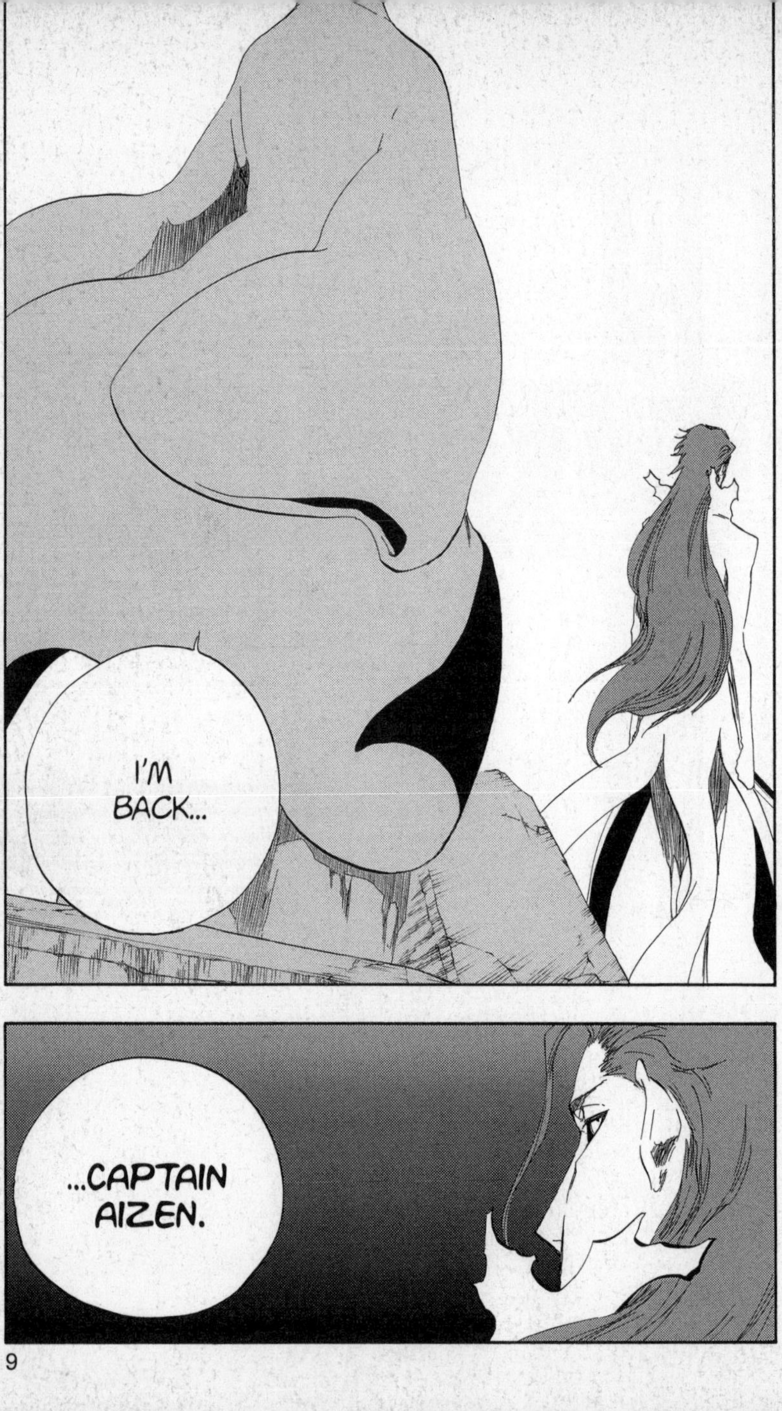
I'M BACK...
...CAPTAIN AIZEN.

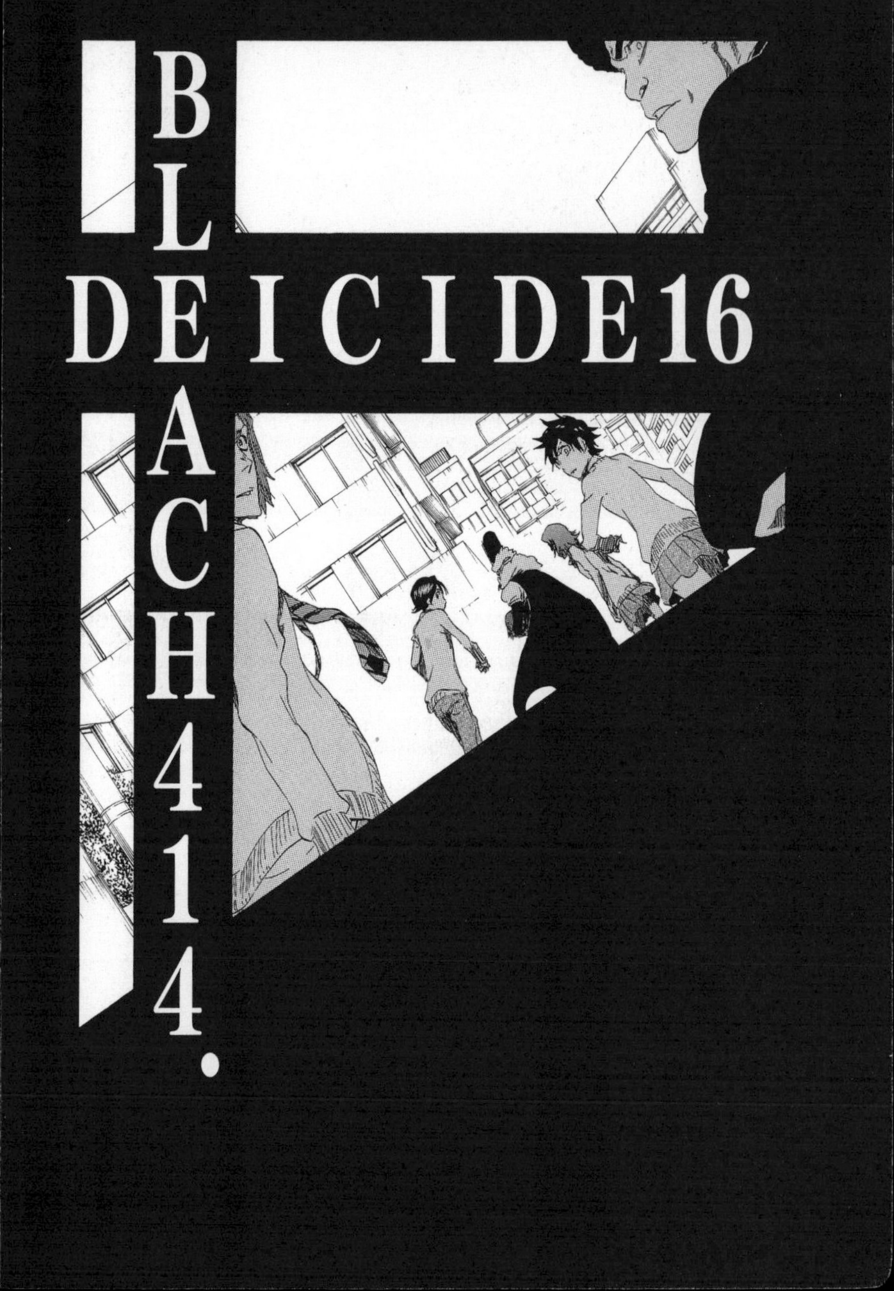
BLEACH 414.
DEICIDE16

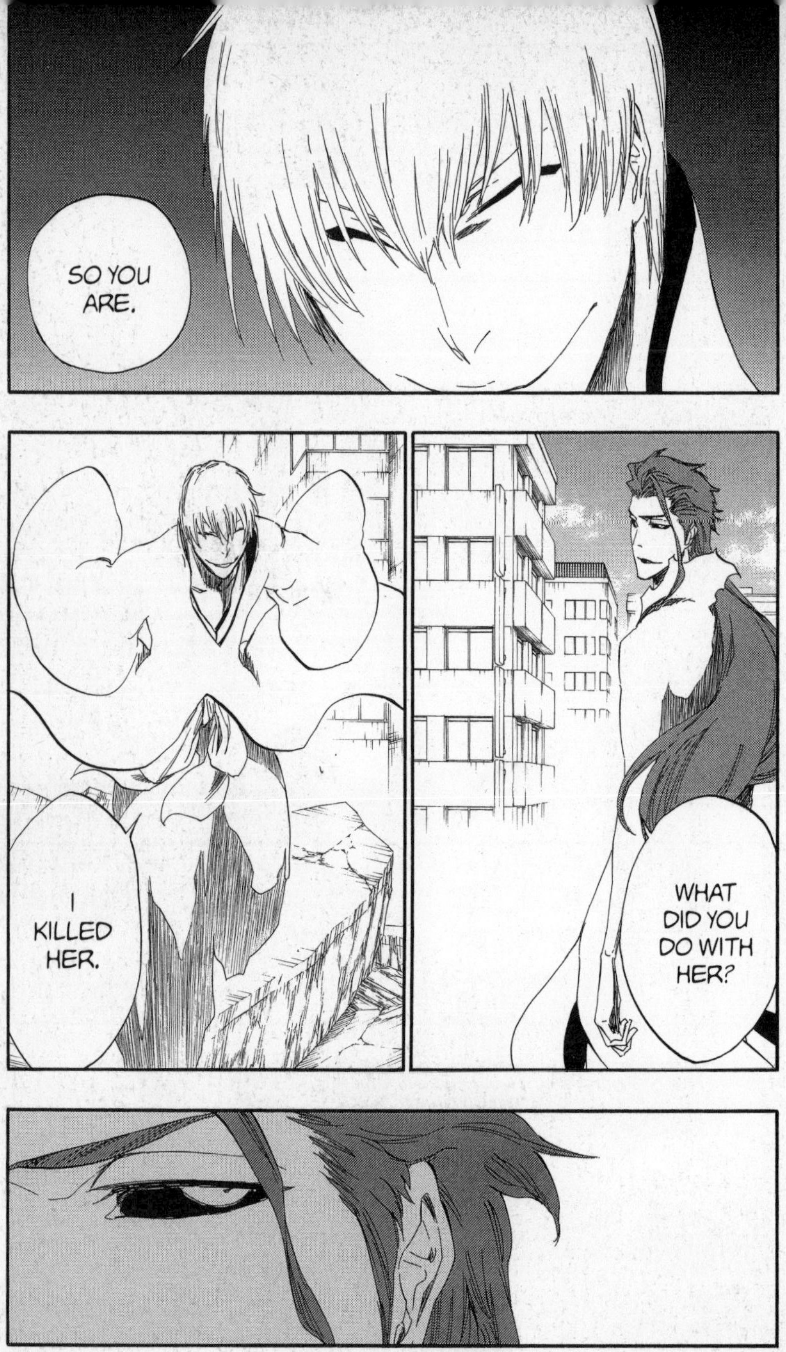
SO YOU ARE.
WHAT DID YOU DO WITH HER?
I KILLED HER.

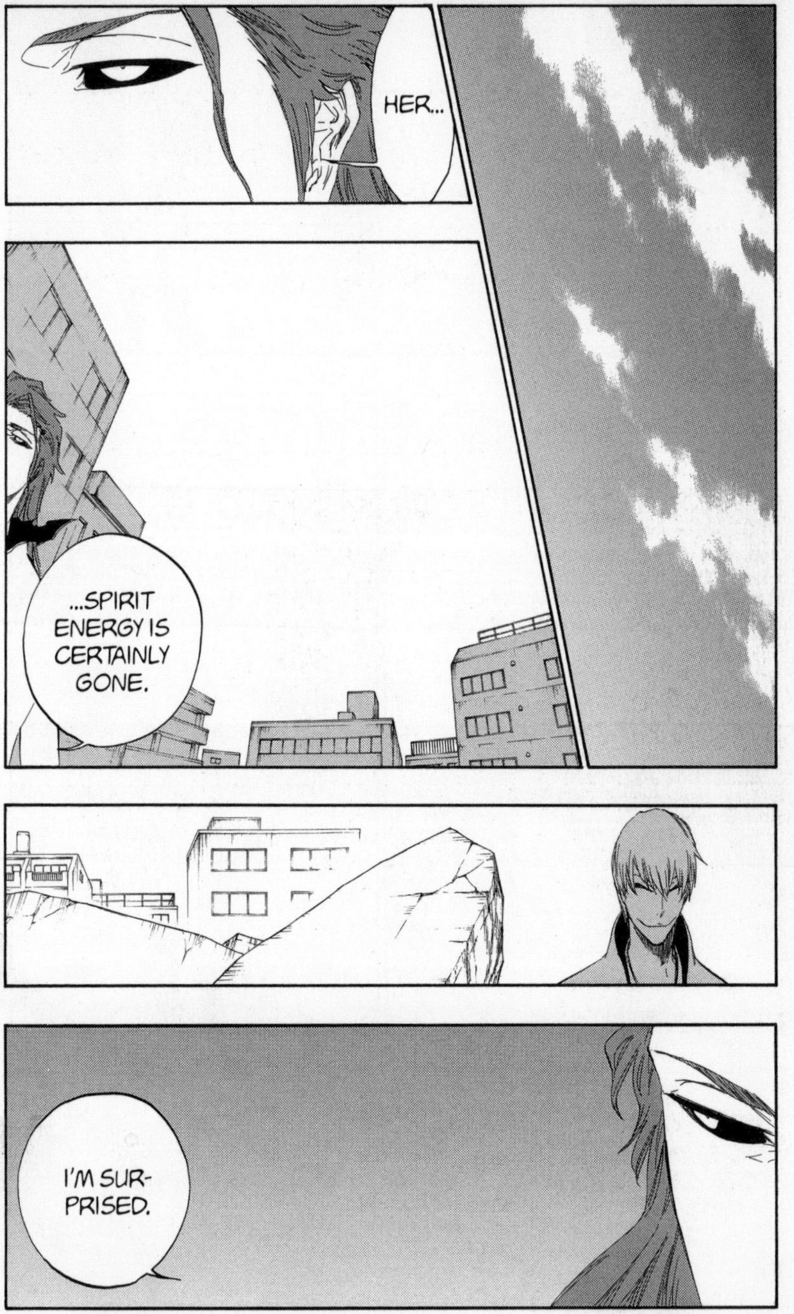
HER...
...SPIRIT ENERGY IS CERTAINLY GONE.
I'M SUR- PRISED.

READ THIS WAY

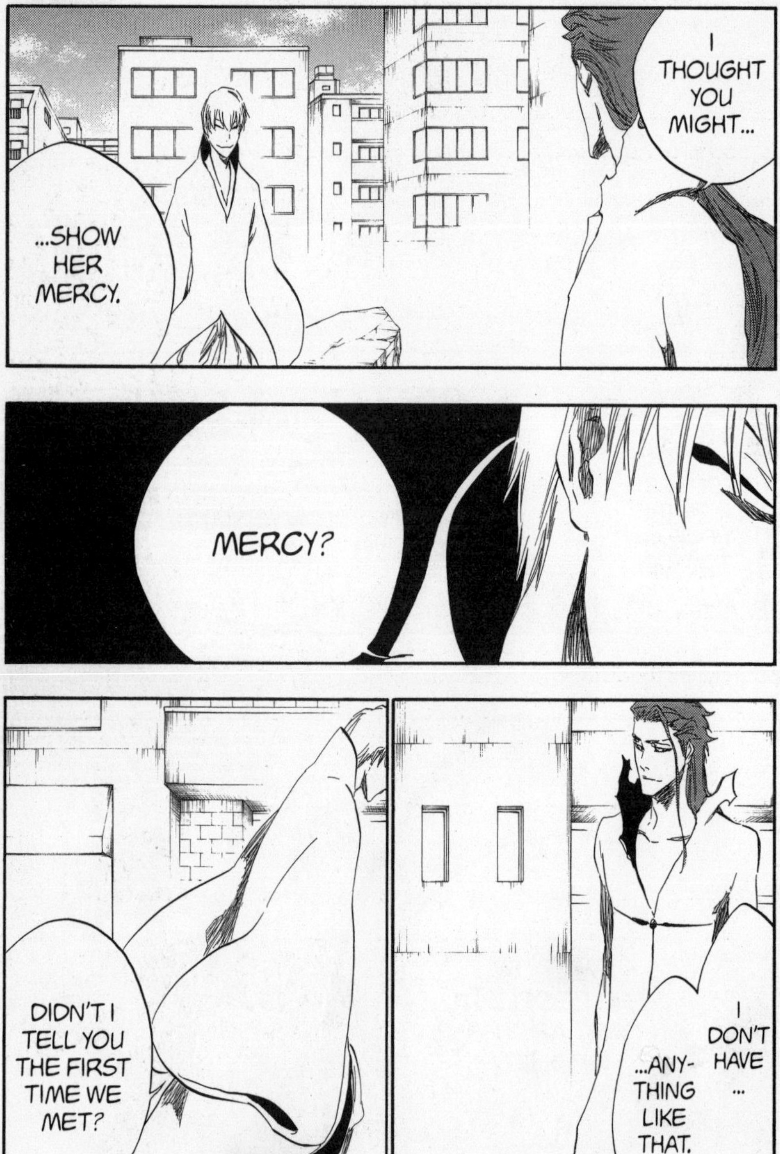
I THOUGHT YOU MIGHT...
...SHOW HER MERCY.
MERCY?
I DON'T HAVE ...
...ANY-THING LIKE THAT.
DIDN'T I TELL YOU THE FIRST TIME WE MET?

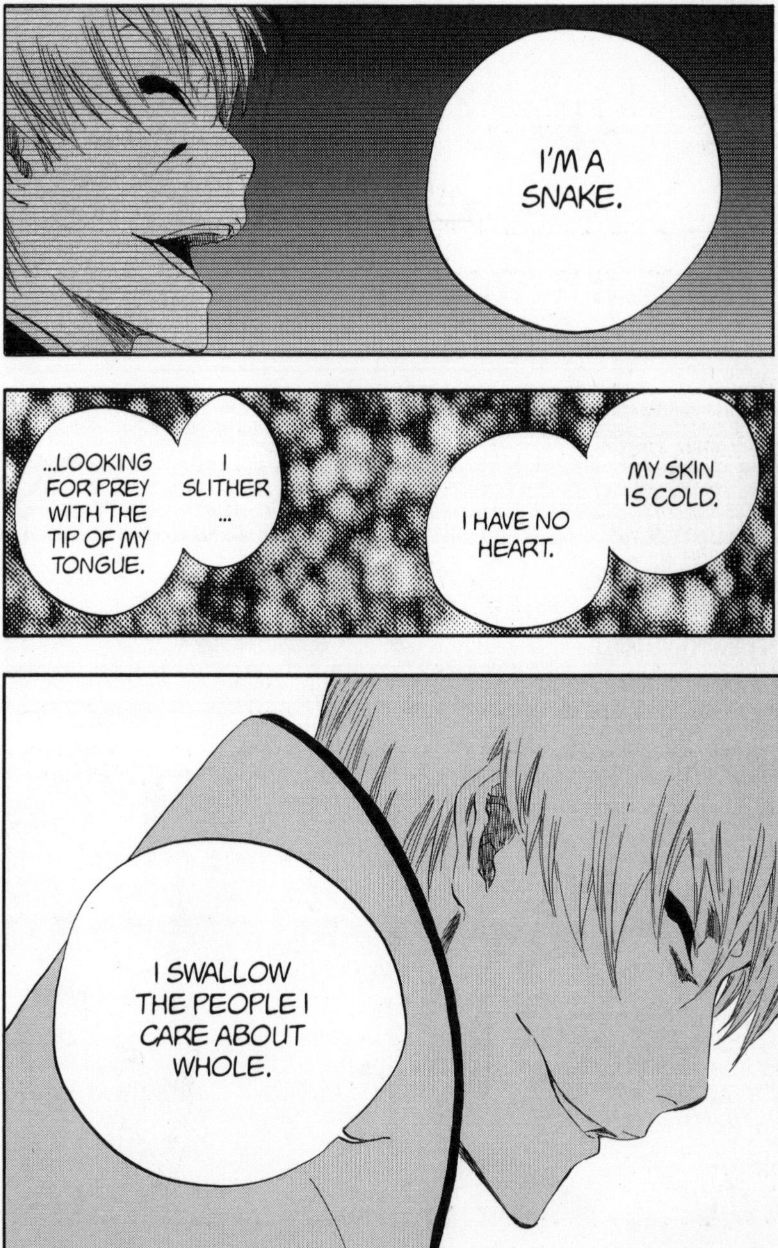
I'M A SNAKE.
MY SKIN IS COLD.
I HAVE NO HEART.
I SLITHER ...
...LOOKING FOR PREY WITH THE TIP OF MY TONGUE.
I SWALLOW THE PEOPLE I CARE ABOUT WHOLE.

READ THIS WAY

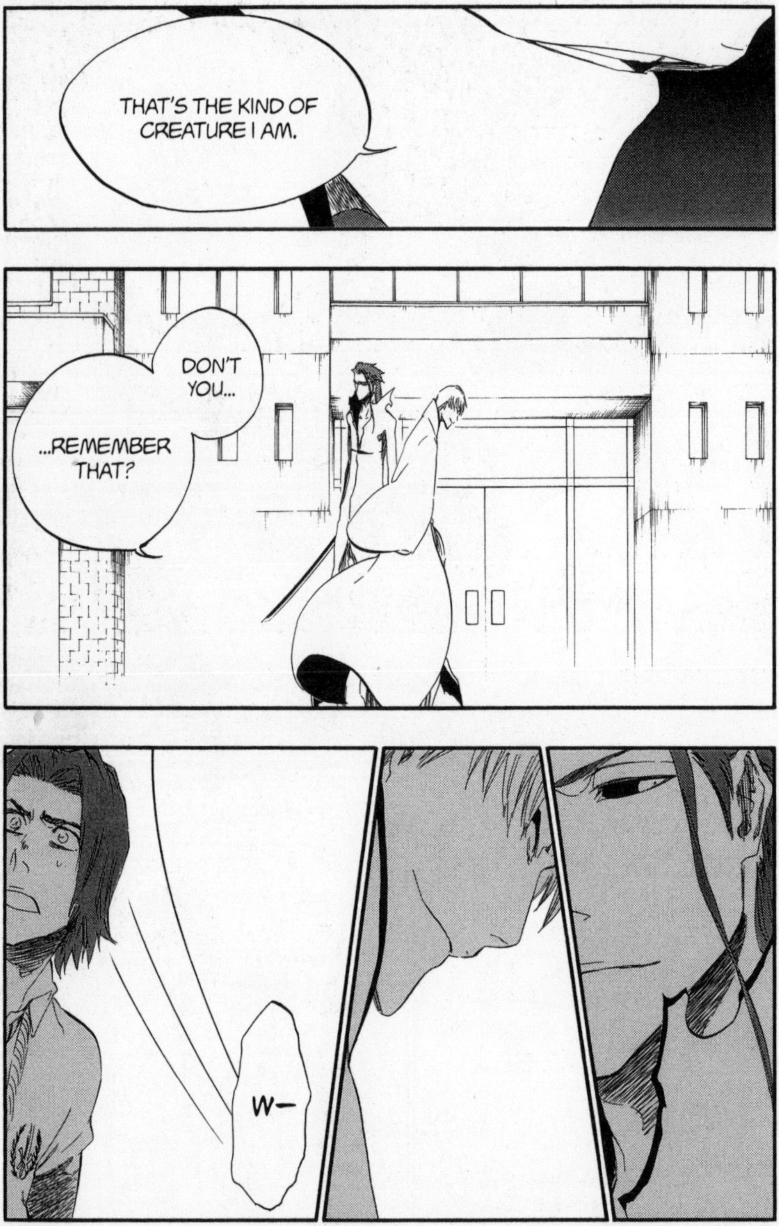
THAT'S THE KIND OF CREATURE I AM.
DON'T YOU...
...REMEMBER THAT?
W—

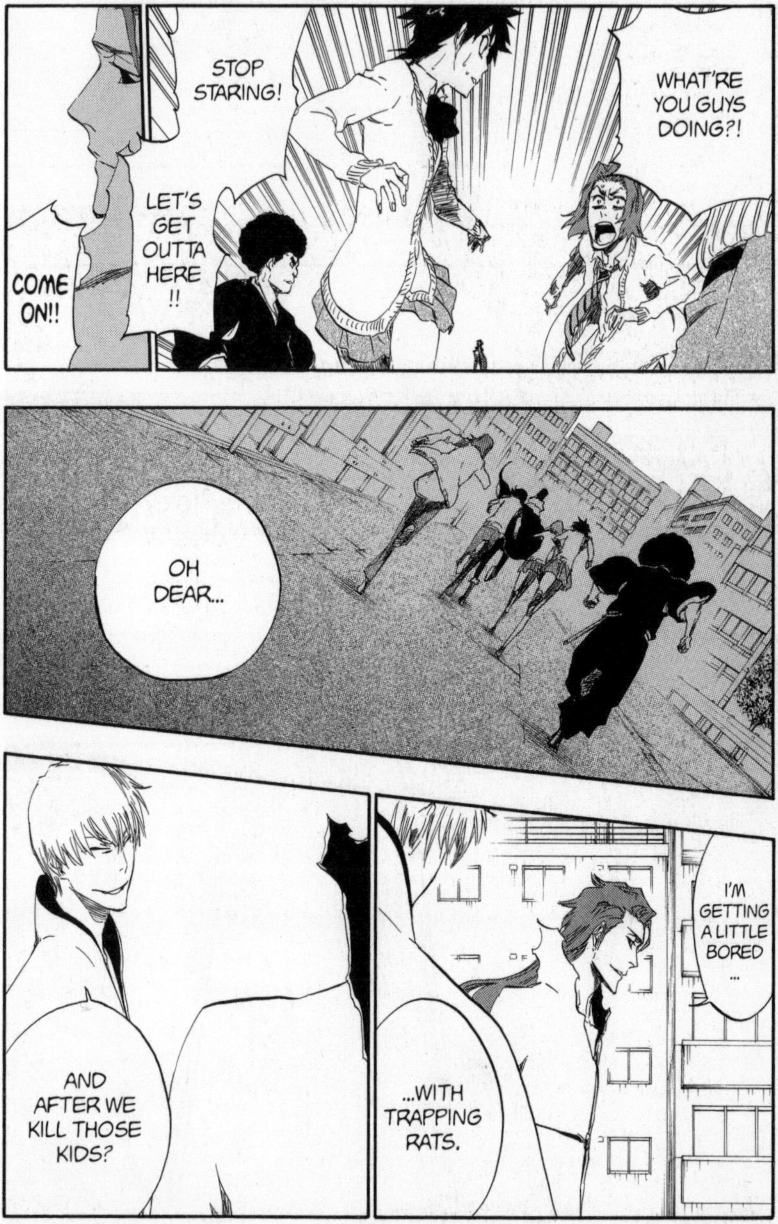
WHAT'RE YOU GUYS DOING?!
STOP STARING!
LET'S GET OUTTA HERE!!
COME ON!!
OH DEAR...
I'M GETTING A LITTLE BORED ...
...WITH TRAPPING RATS.
AND AFTER WE KILL THOSE KIDS?

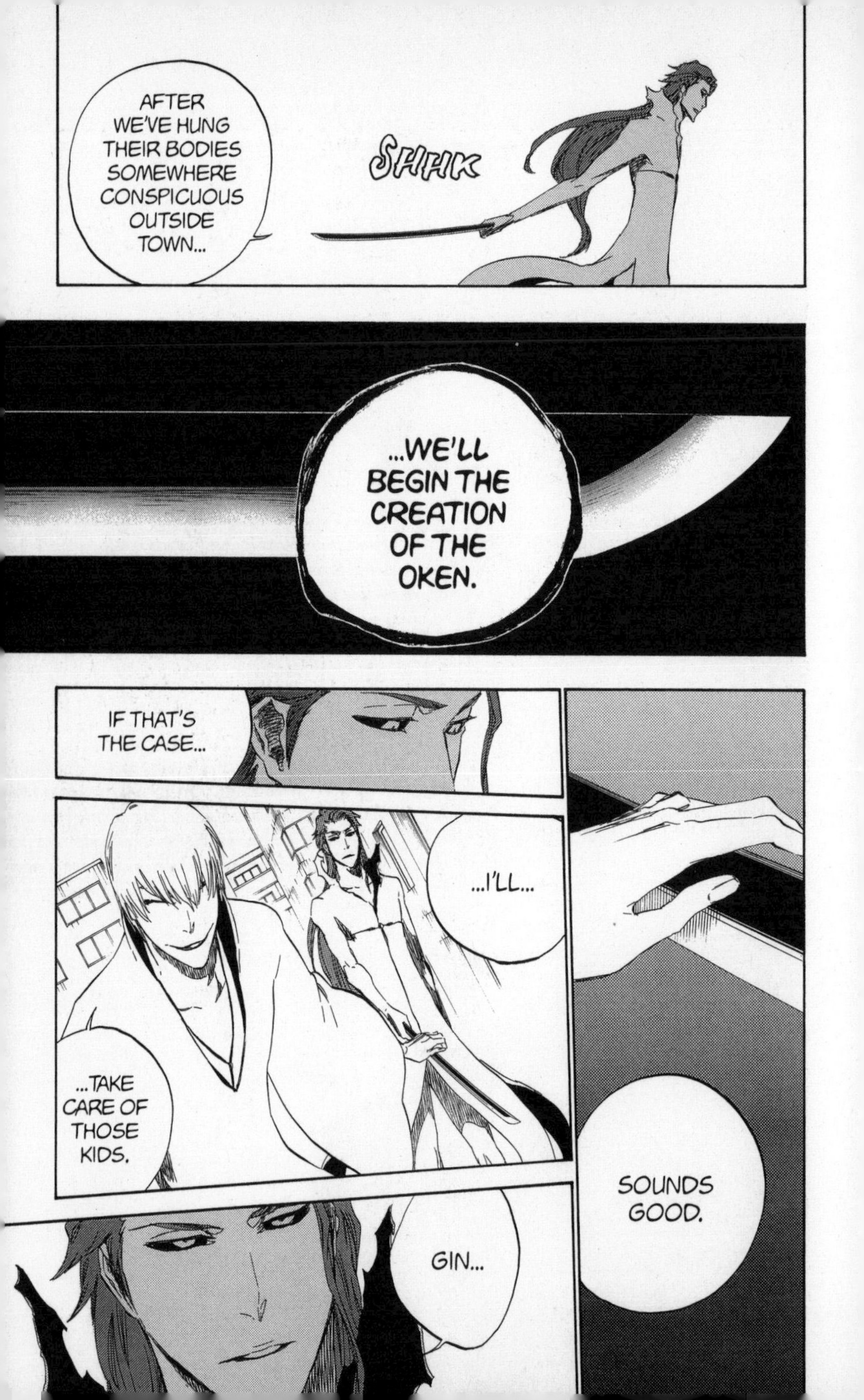
AFTER WE'VE HUNG THEIR BODIES SOMEWHERE CONSPICUOUS OUTSIDE TOWN...
SHHK
...WE'LL BEGIN THE CREATION OF THE OKEN.
IF THAT'S THE CASE...
...I'LL...
...TAKE CARE OF THOSE KIDS.
GIN...
SOUNDS GOOD.

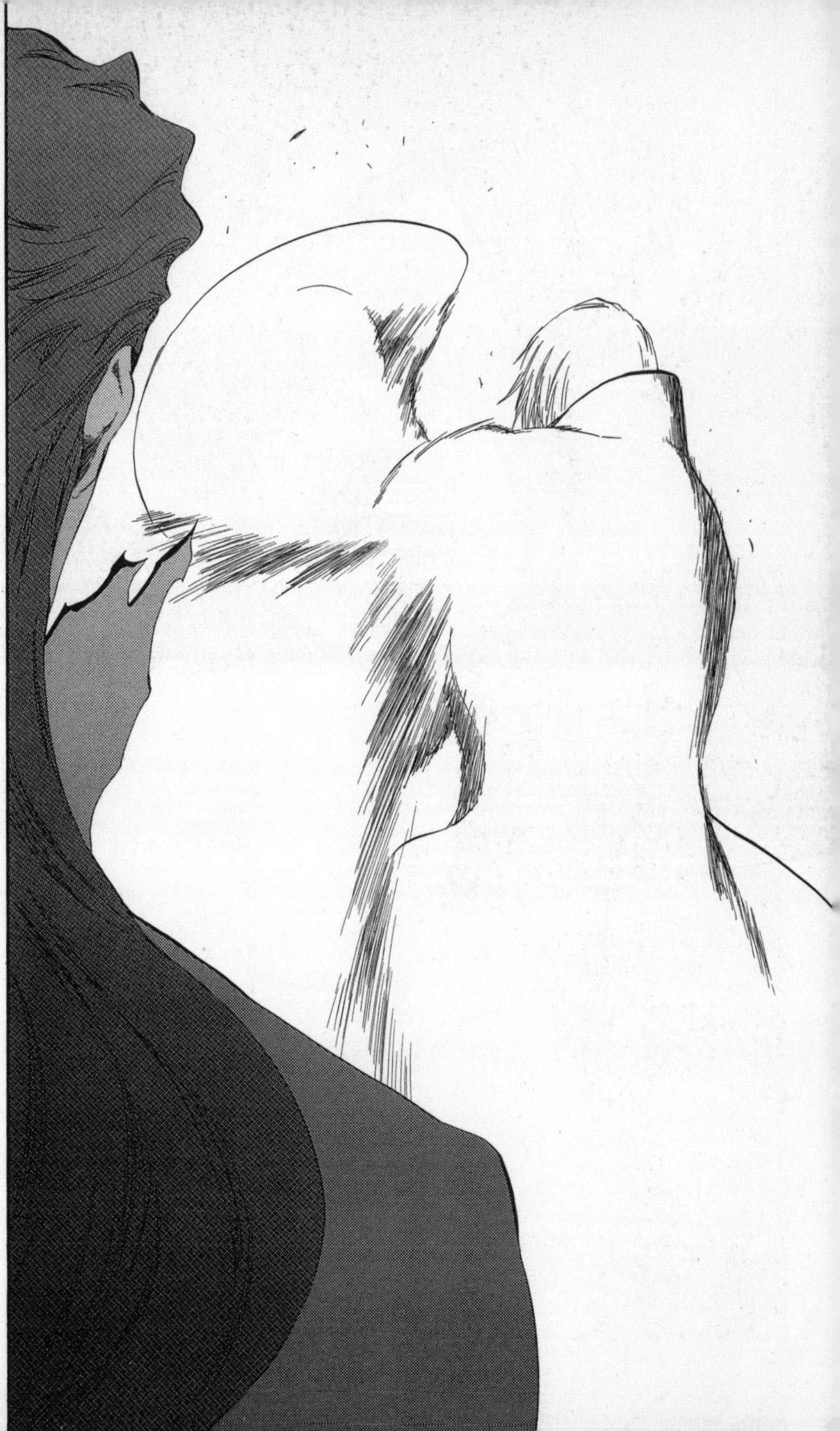

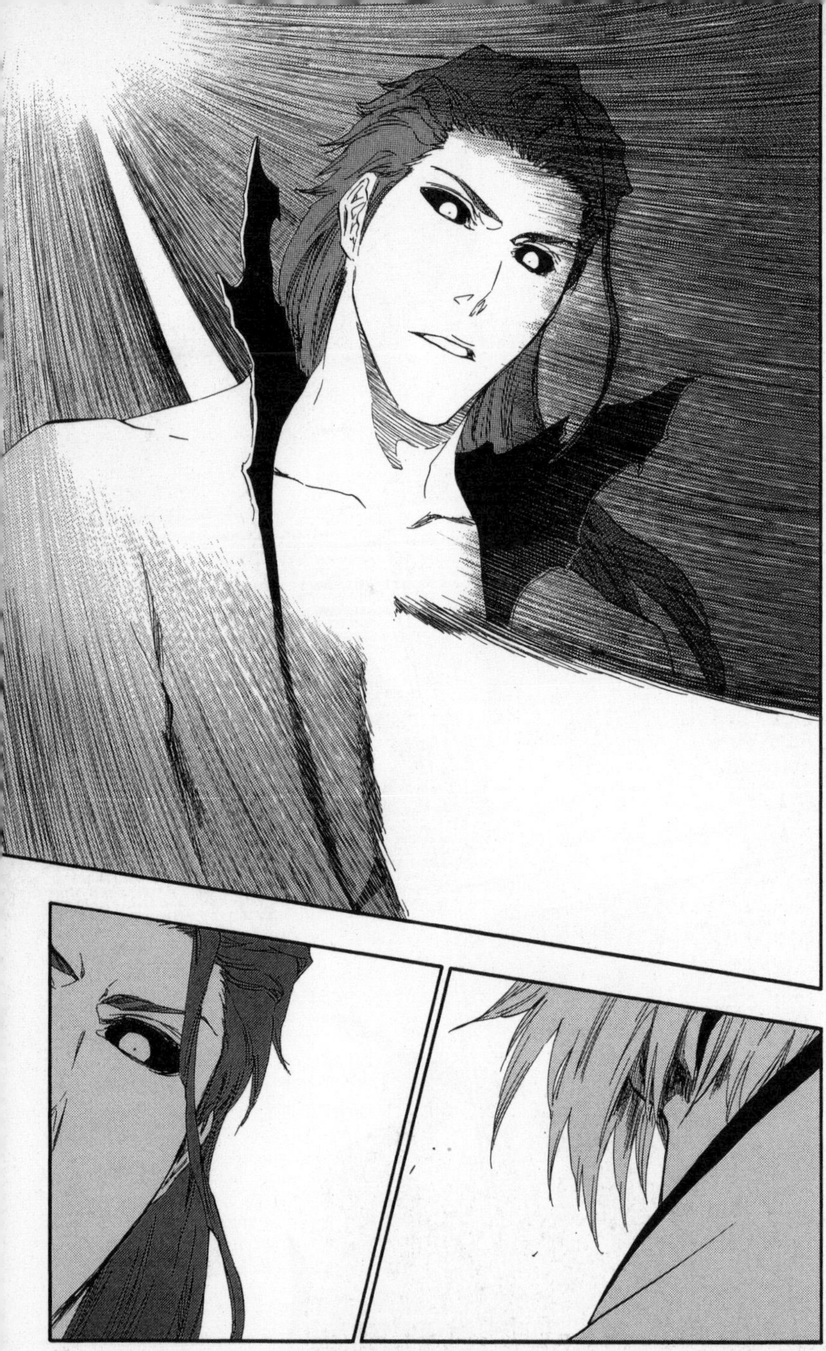

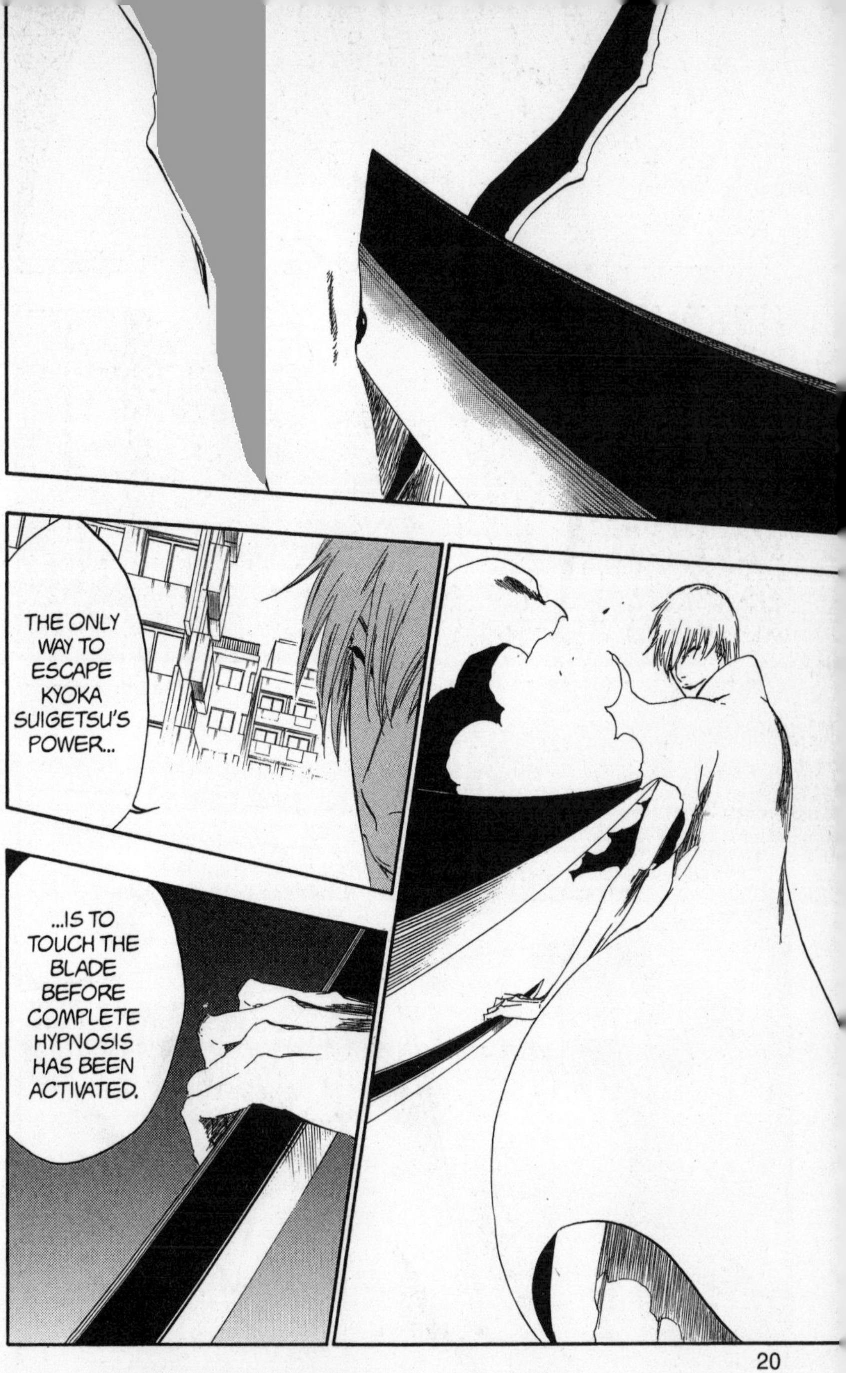
THE ONLY WAY TO ESCAPE KYOKA SUIGETSU'S POWER...
...IS TO TOUCH THE BLADE BEFORE COMPLETE HYPNOSIS HAS BEEN ACTIVATED.

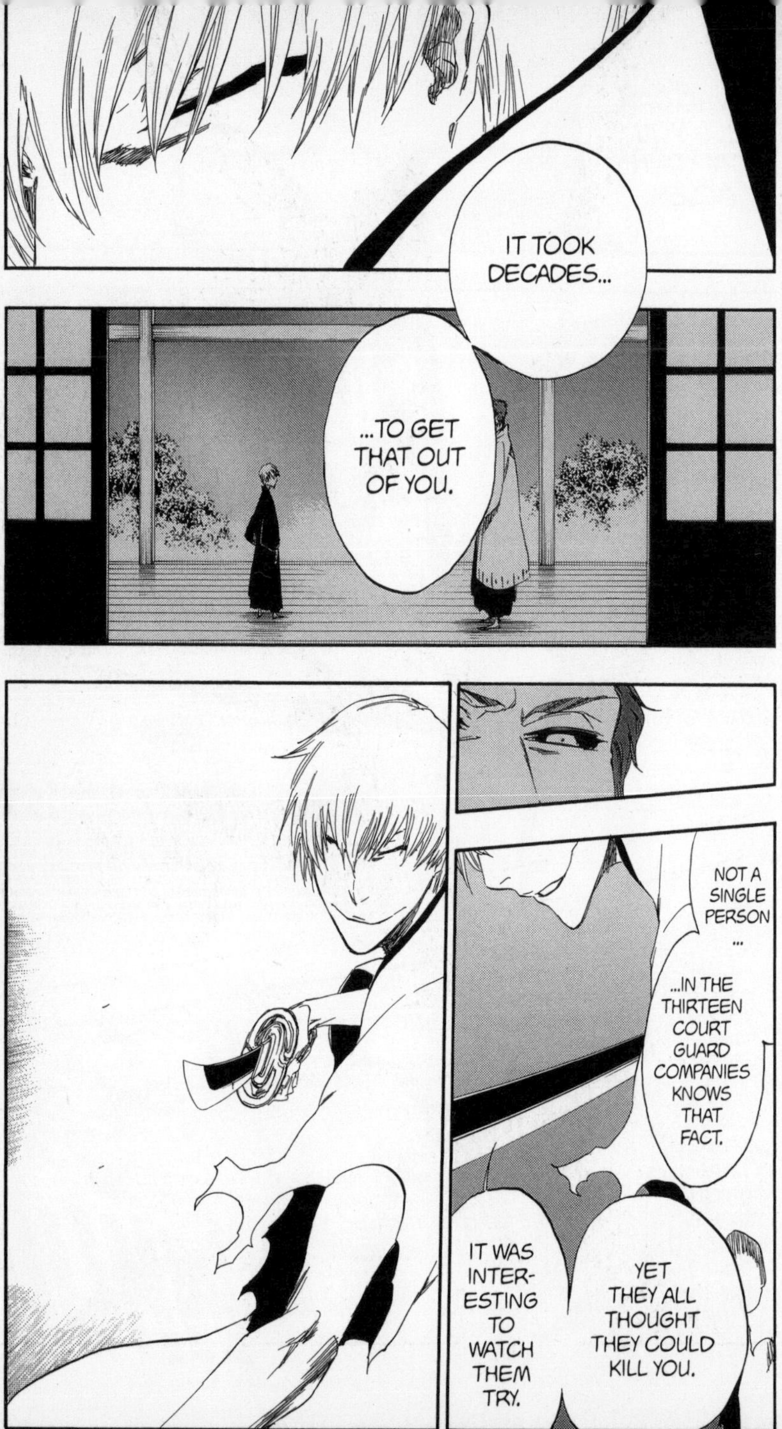
IT TOOK DECADES...
...TO GET THAT OUT OF YOU.
NOT A SINGLE PERSON ...
...IN THE THIRTEEN COURT GUARD COMPANIES KNOWS THAT FACT.
YET THEY ALL THOUGHT THEY COULD KILL YOU.
IT WAS INTER-ESTING TO WATCH THEM TRY.

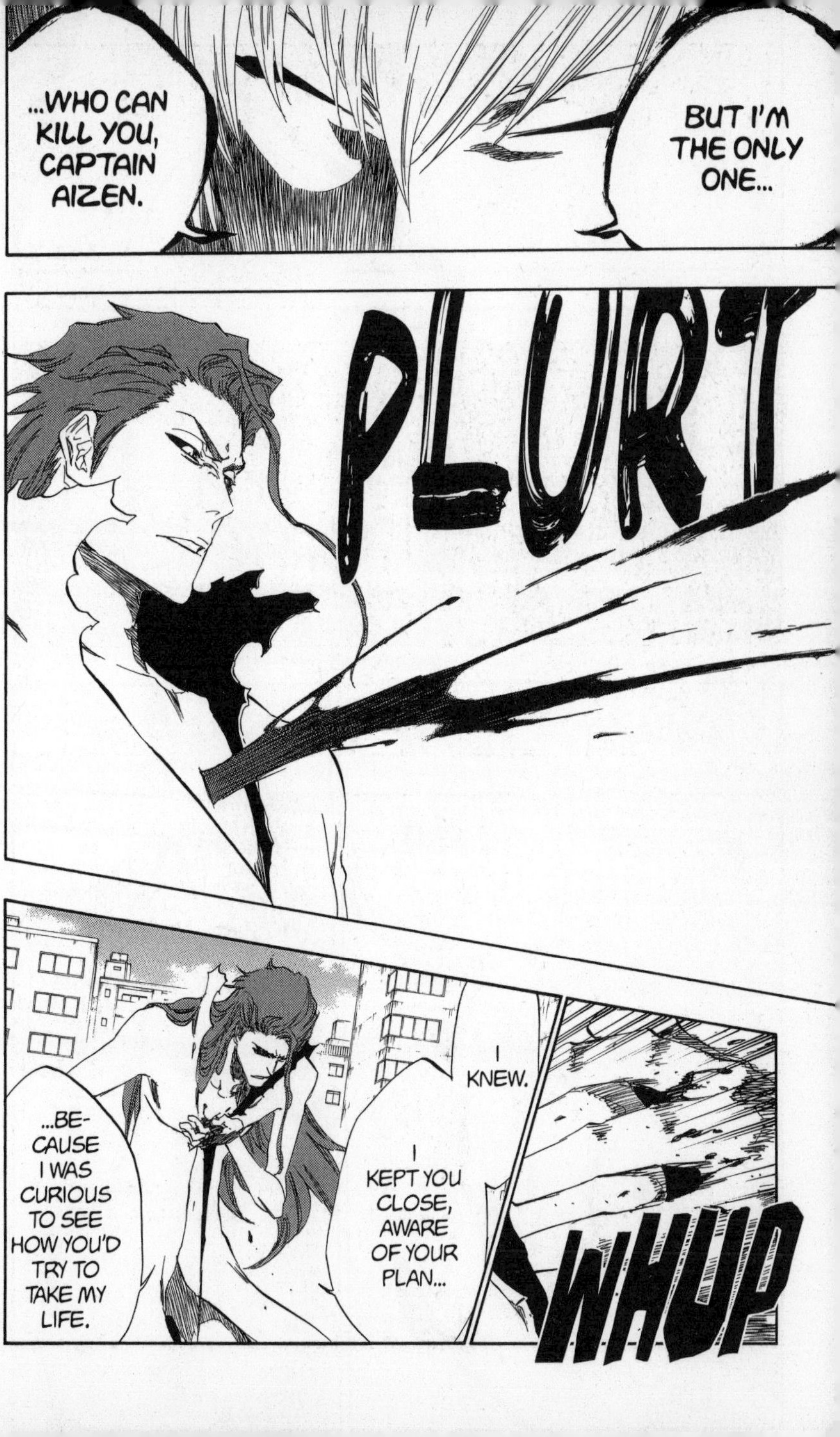
BUT I'M THE ONLY ONE...
...WHO CAN KILL YOU, CAPTAIN AIZEN.
PLURT
WHUP
I KNEW.
I KEPT YOU CLOSE, AWARE OF YOUR PLAN...
...BE-CAUSE I WAS CURIOUS TO SEE HOW YOU'D TRY TO TAKE MY LIFE.

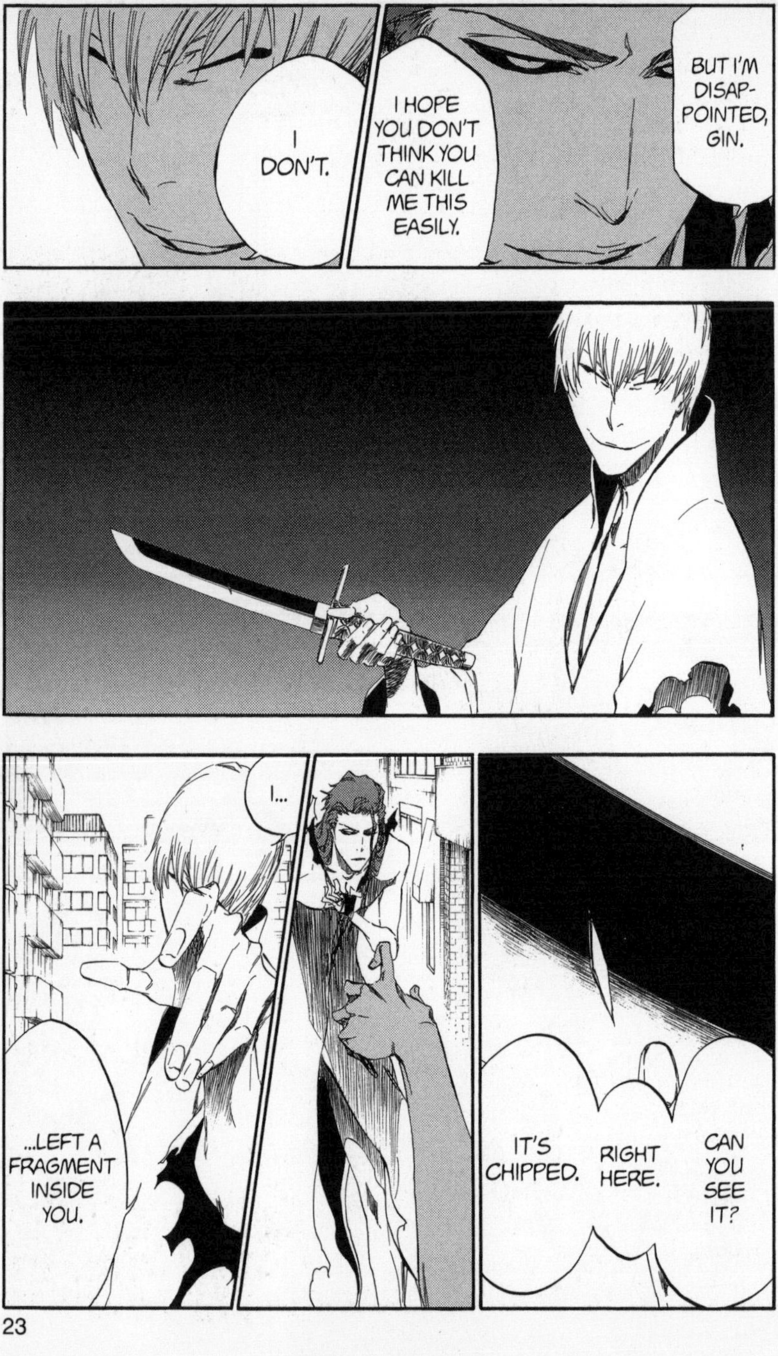
BUT I'M DISAP-POINTED, GIN.
I HOPE YOU DON'T THINK YOU CAN KILL ME THIS EASILY.
I DON'T.
CAN YOU SEE IT?
RIGHT HERE.
IT'S CHIPPED.
I...
...LEFT A FRAGMENT INSIDE YOU.

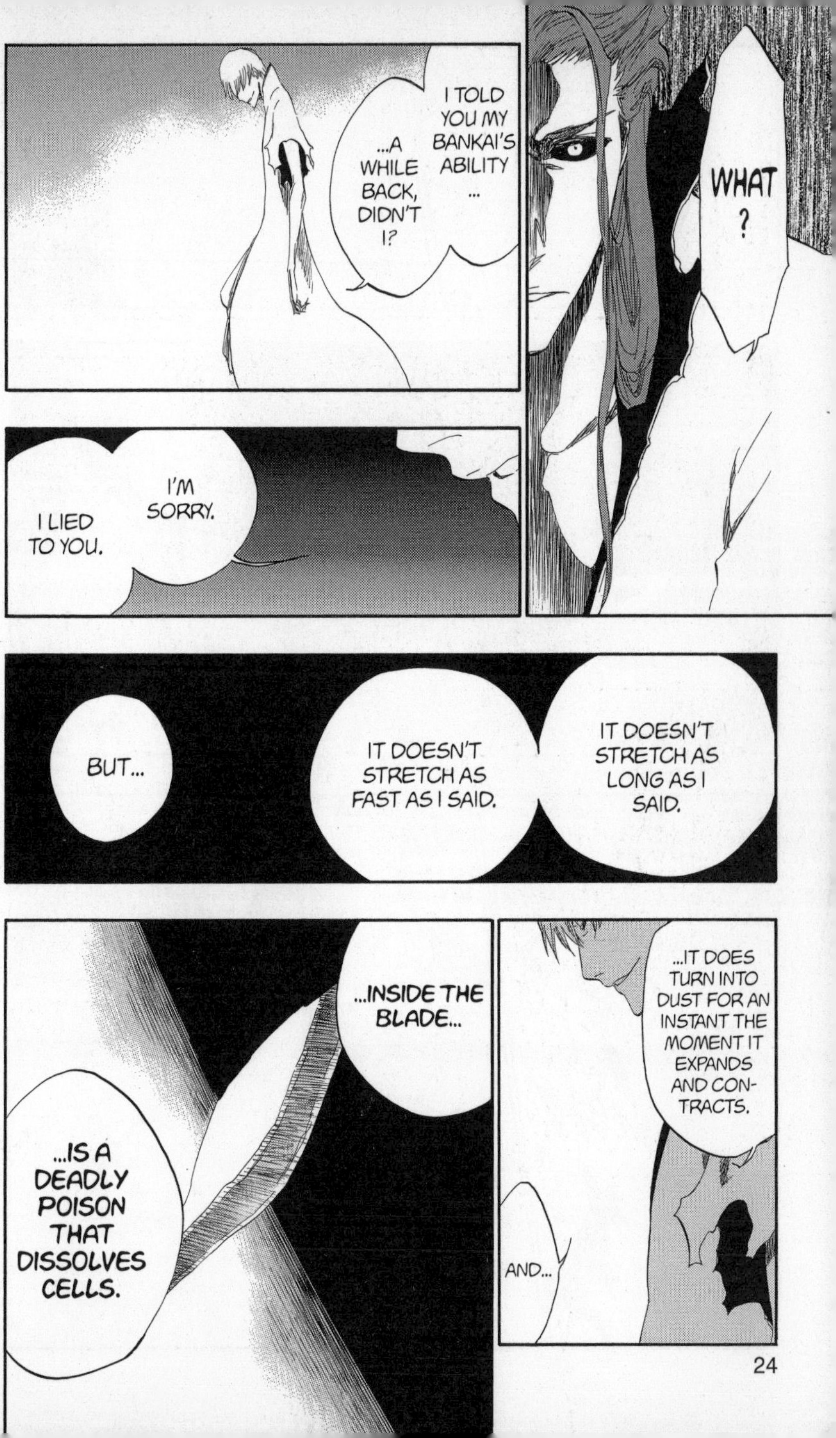
WHAT?
I TOLD YOU MY BANKAI'S ABILITY...
...A WHILE BACK, DIDN'T I?
I'M SORRY.
I LIED TO YOU.
IT DOESN'T STRETCH AS LONG AS I SAID.
IT DOESN'T STRETCH AS FAST AS I SAID.
BUT...
...IT DOES TURN INTO DUST FOR AN INSTANT THE MOMENT IT EXPANDS AND CON-TRACTS.
AND...
...INSIDE THE BLADE...
...IS A DEADLY POISON THAT DISSOLVES CELLS.

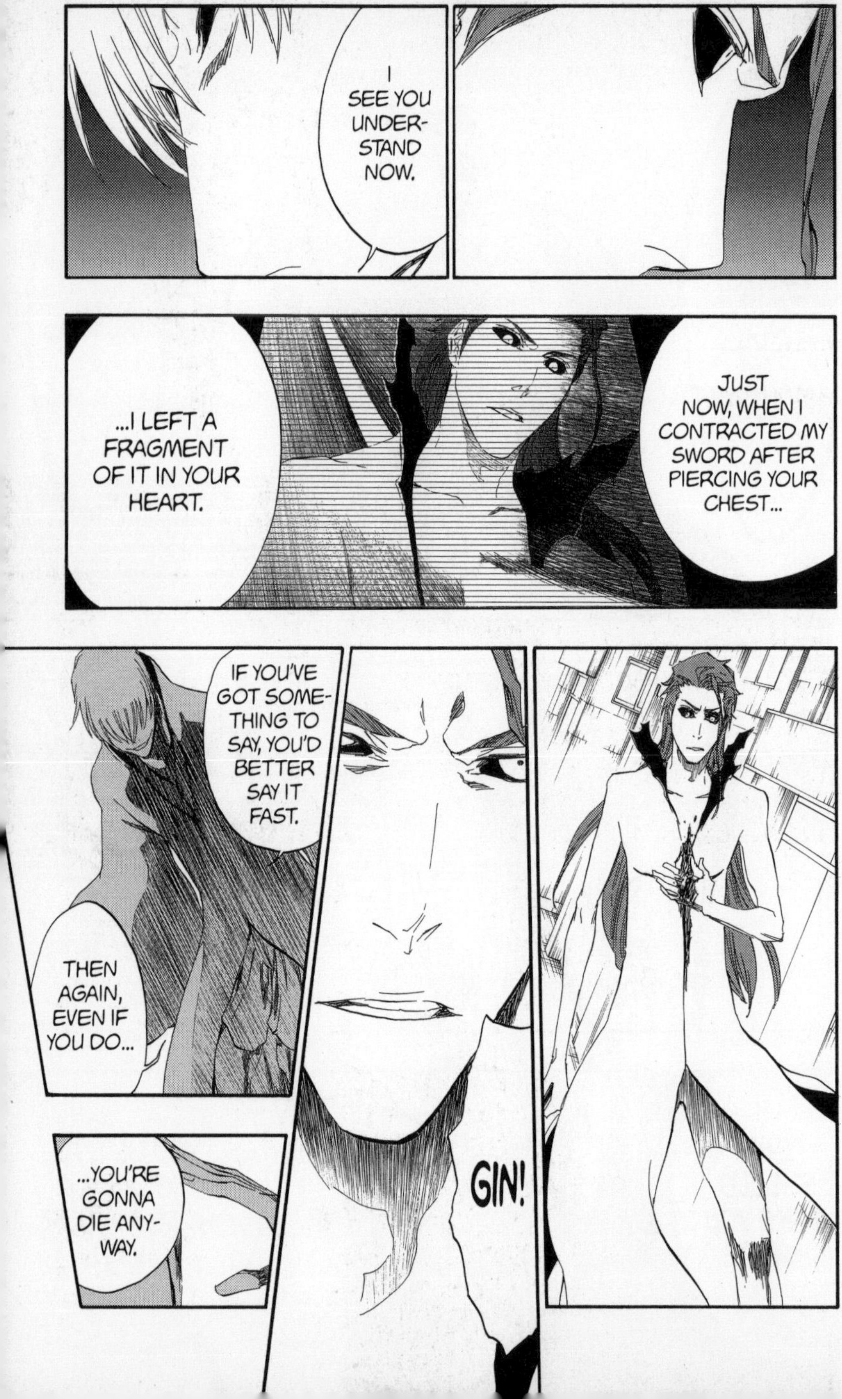
I SEE YOU UNDER-STAND NOW.
JUST NOW, WHEN I CONTRACTED MY SWORD AFTER PIERCING YOUR CHEST...
...I LEFT A FRAGMENT OF IT IN YOUR HEART.
GIN!
IF YOU'VE GOT SOME-THING TO SAY, YOU'D BETTER SAY IT FAST.
THEN AGAIN, EVEN IF YOU DO...
...YOU'RE GONNA DIE ANY-WAY.

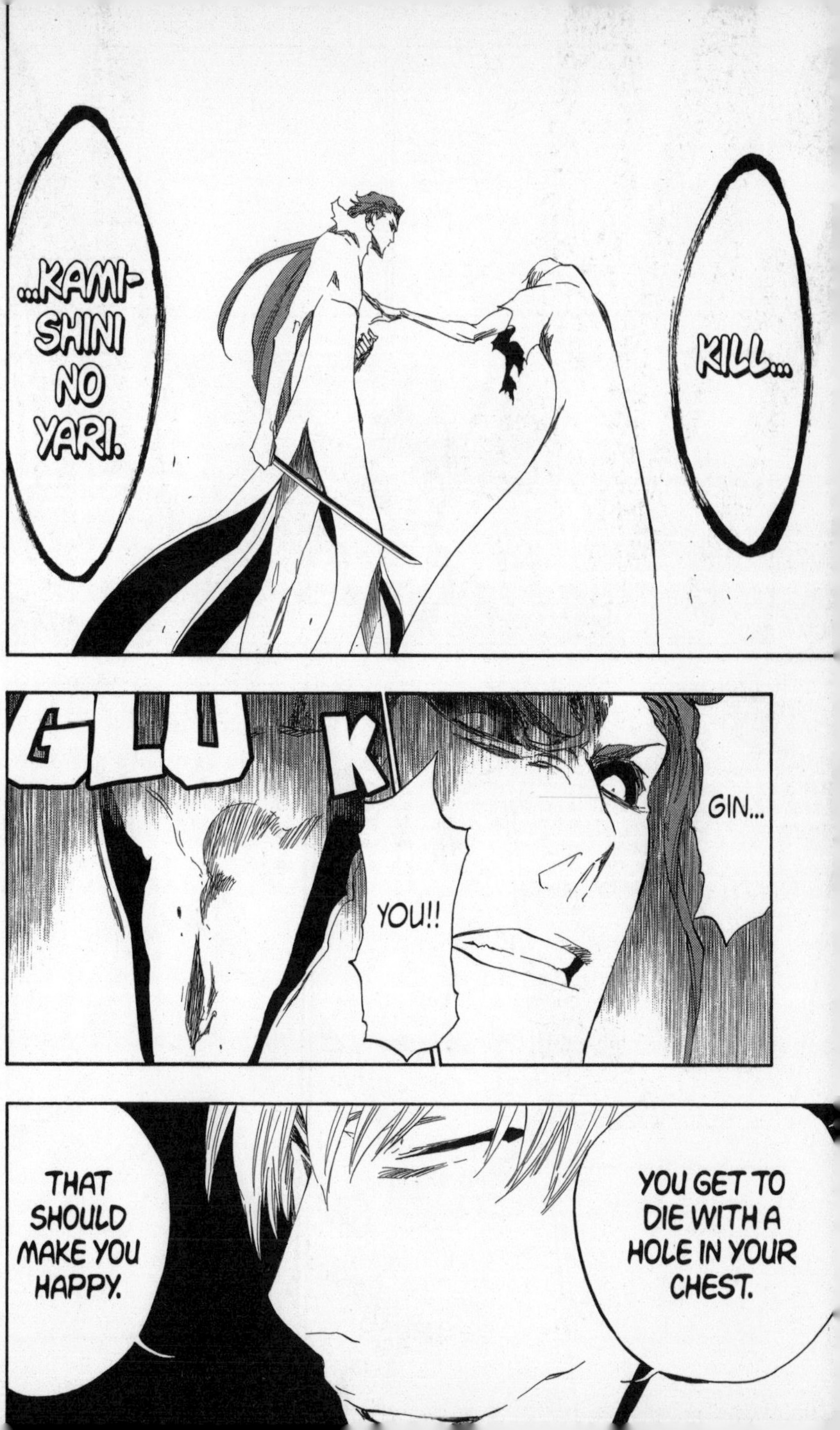
KILL...
...KAMI-SHINI NO YARI.
GLUK
GIN...
YOU!!
YOU GET TO DIE WITH A HOLE IN YOUR CHEST.
THAT SHOULD MAKE YOU HAPPY.

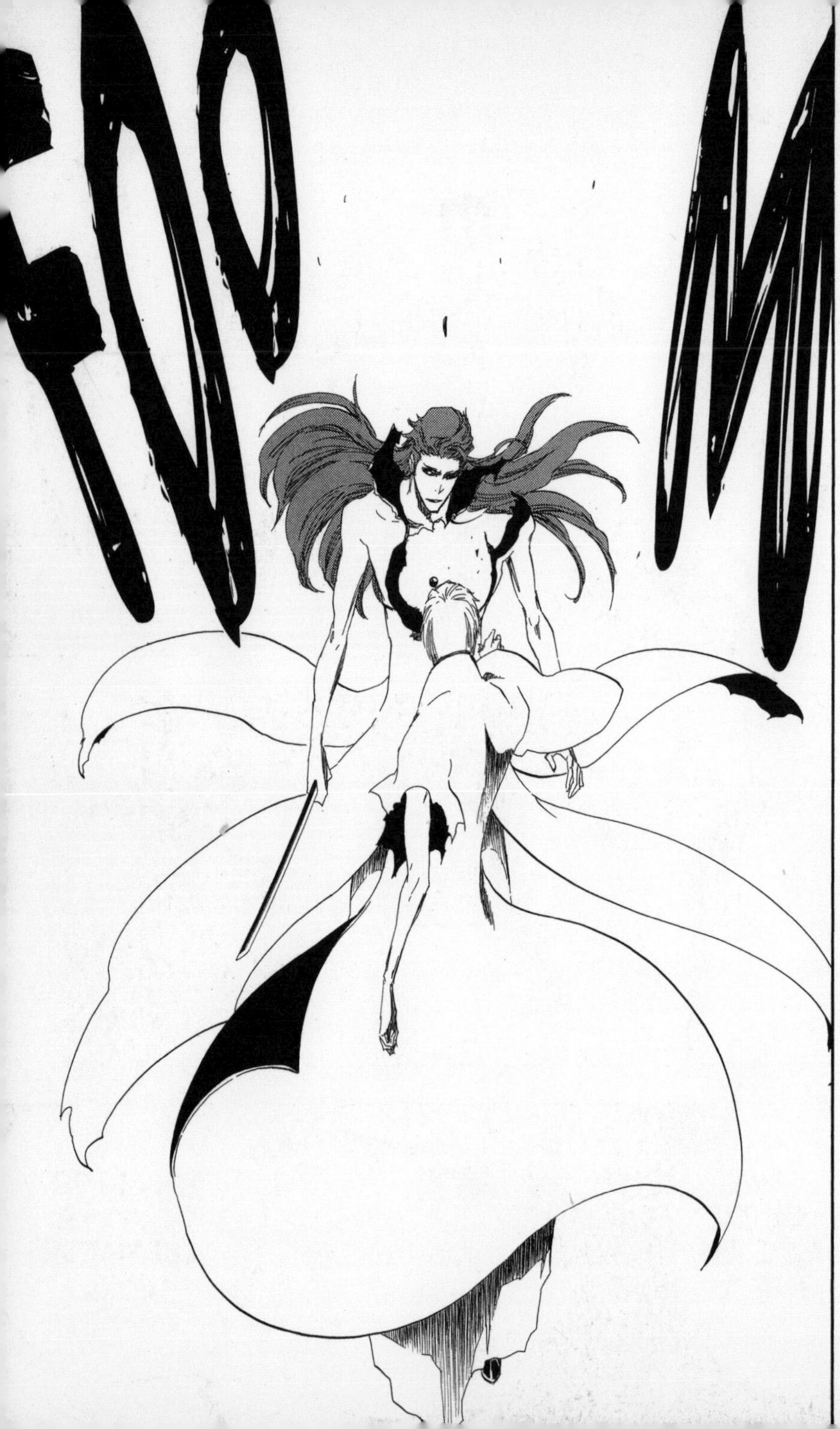

415. DEICIDE 17

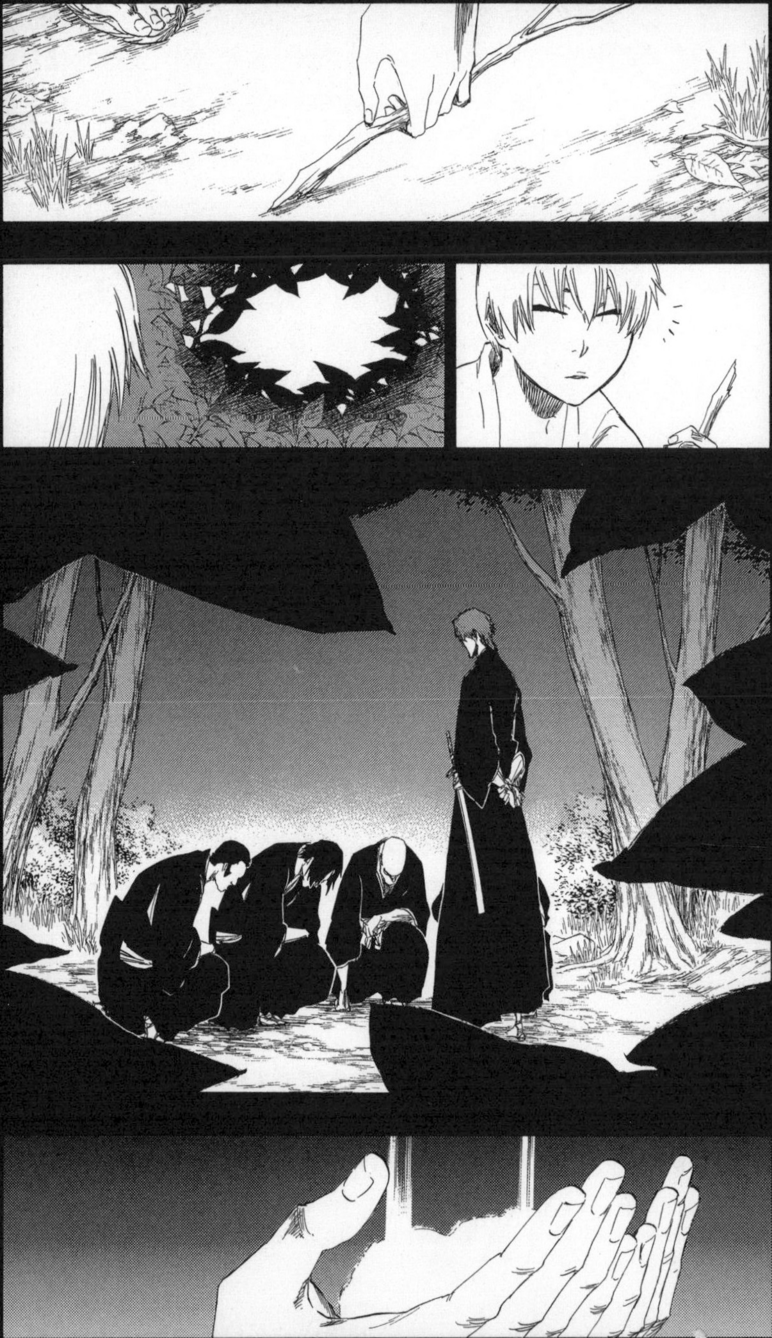

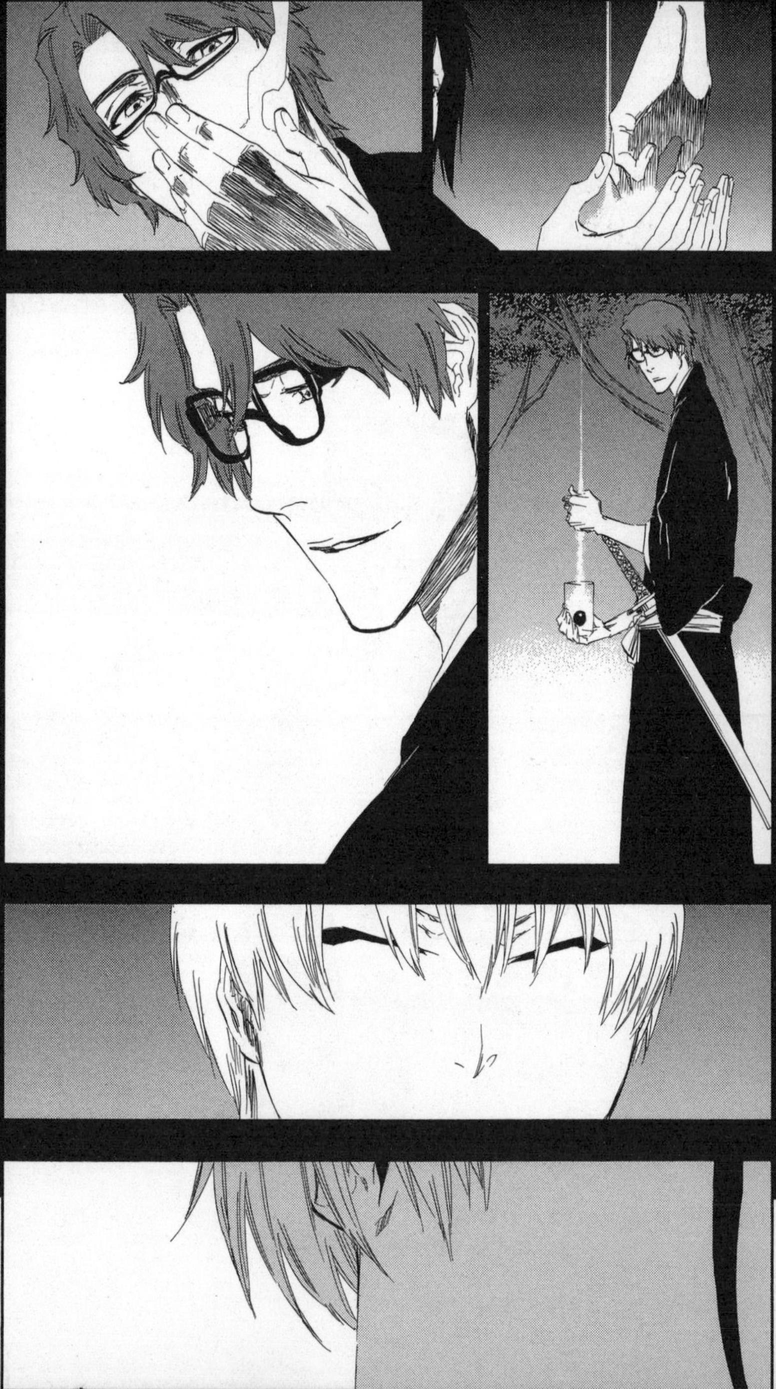

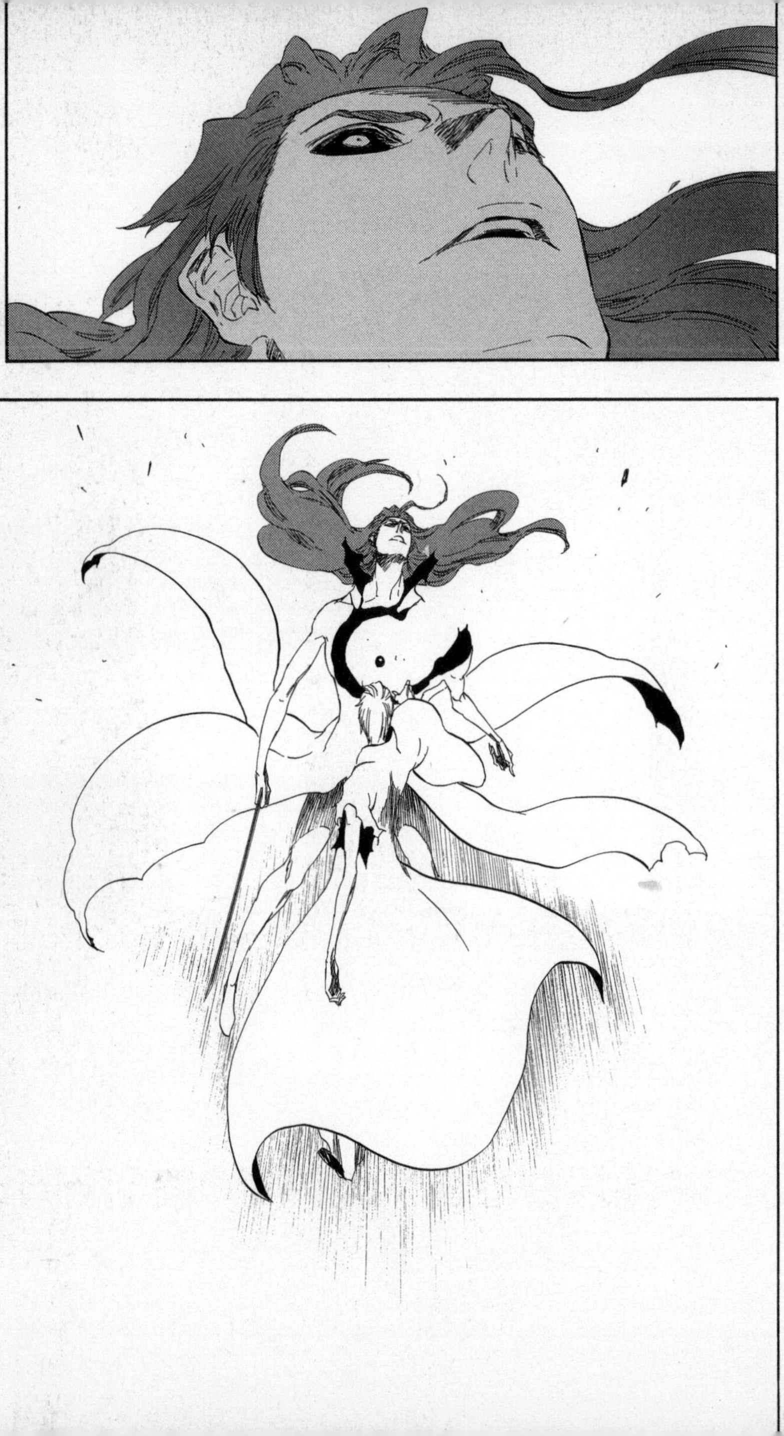

BLEACH415.

deicide17

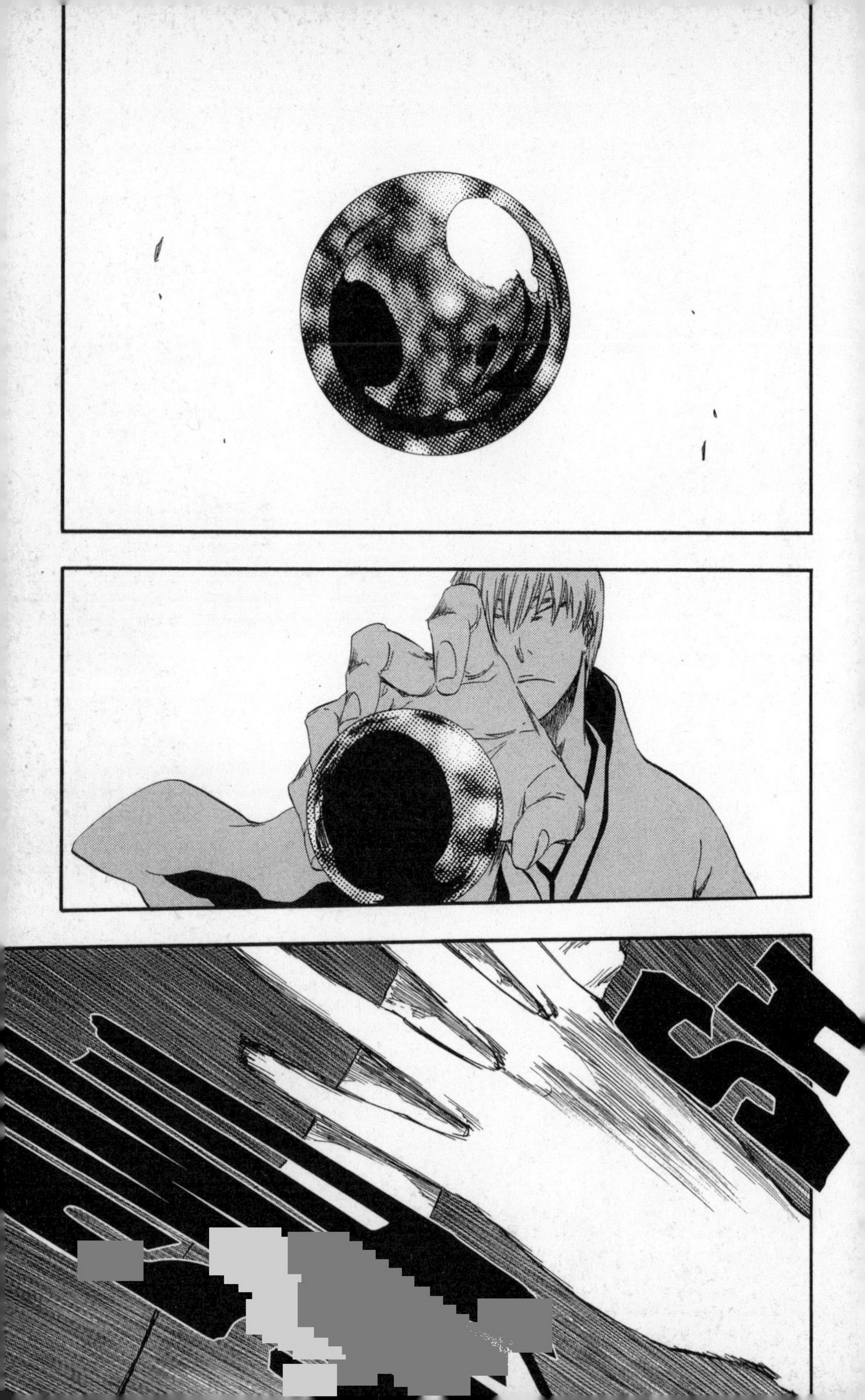
SH

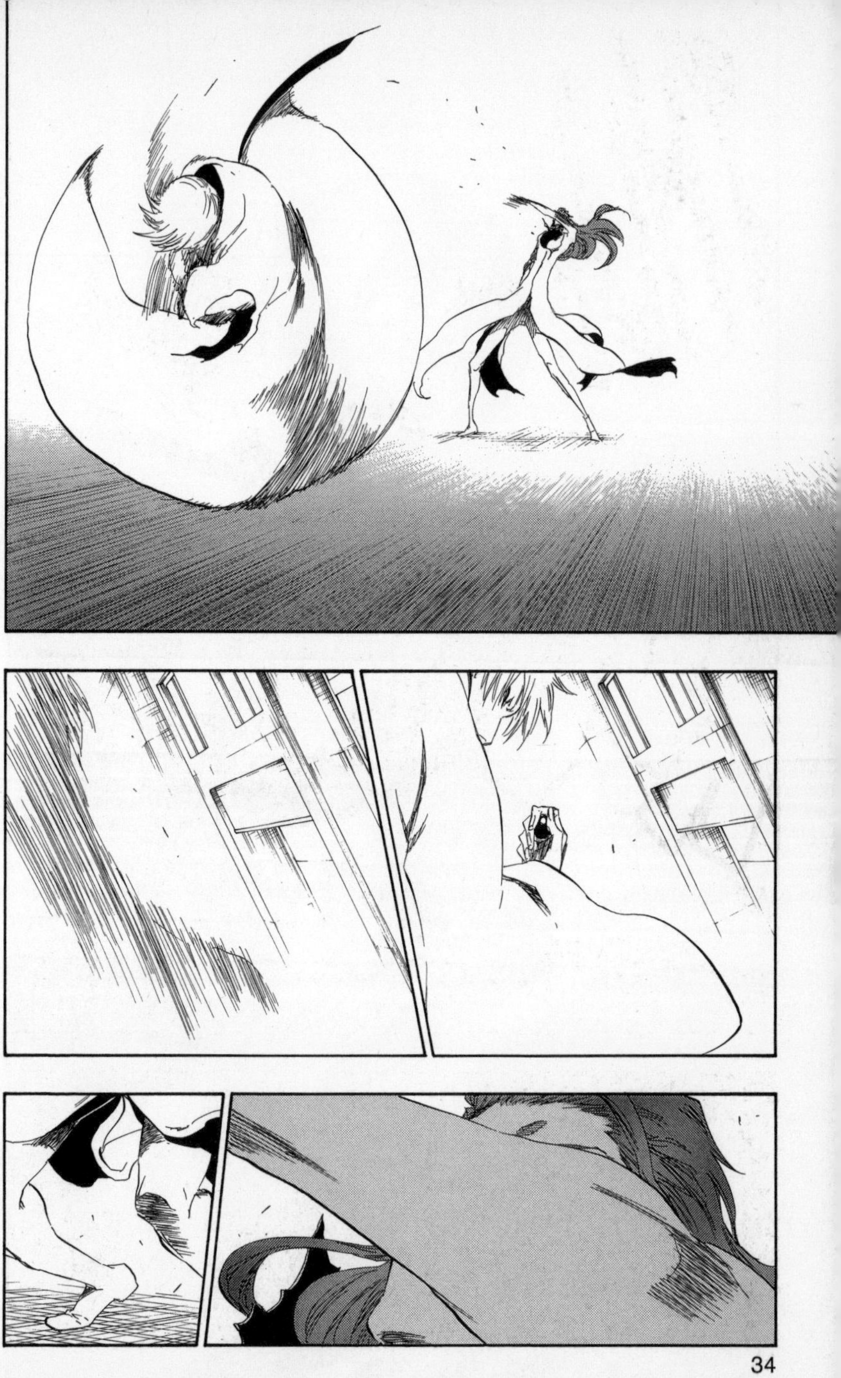

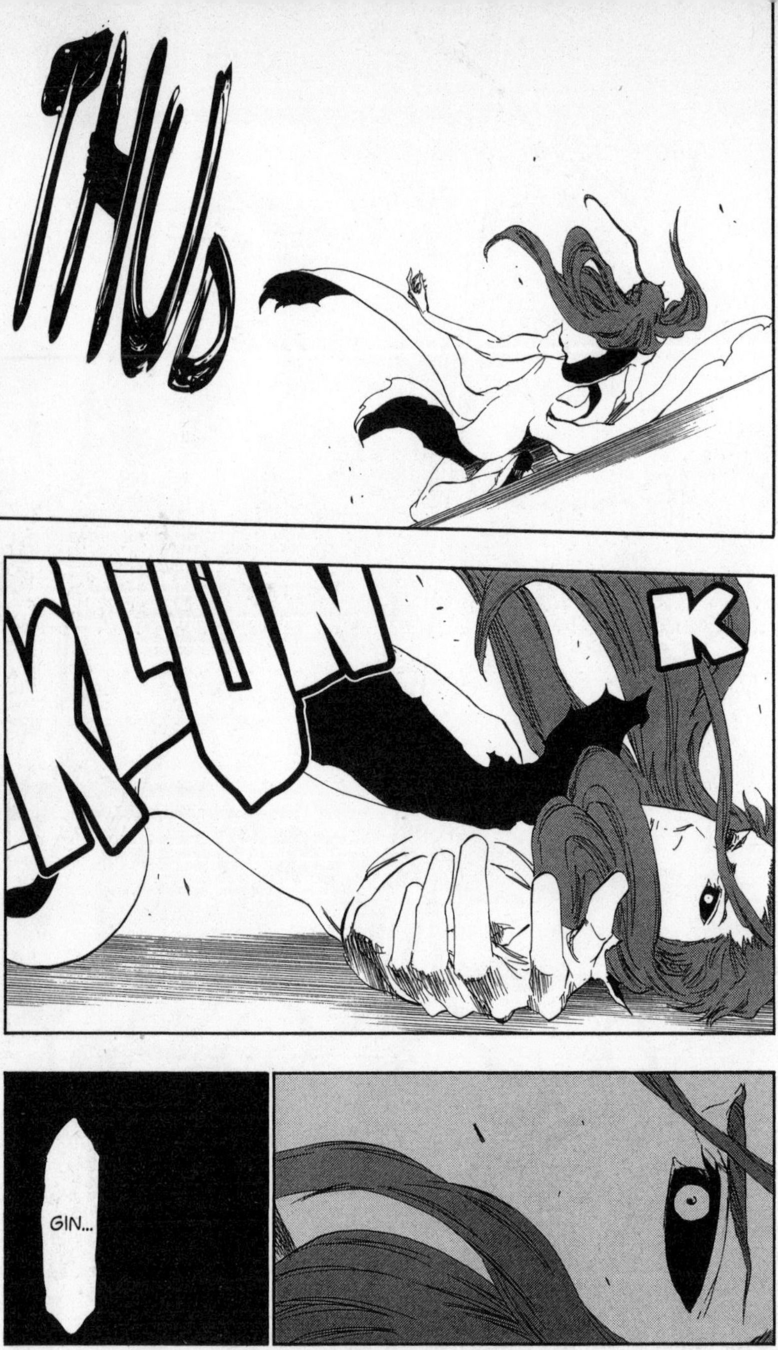
THUD
KLUNK
GIN...

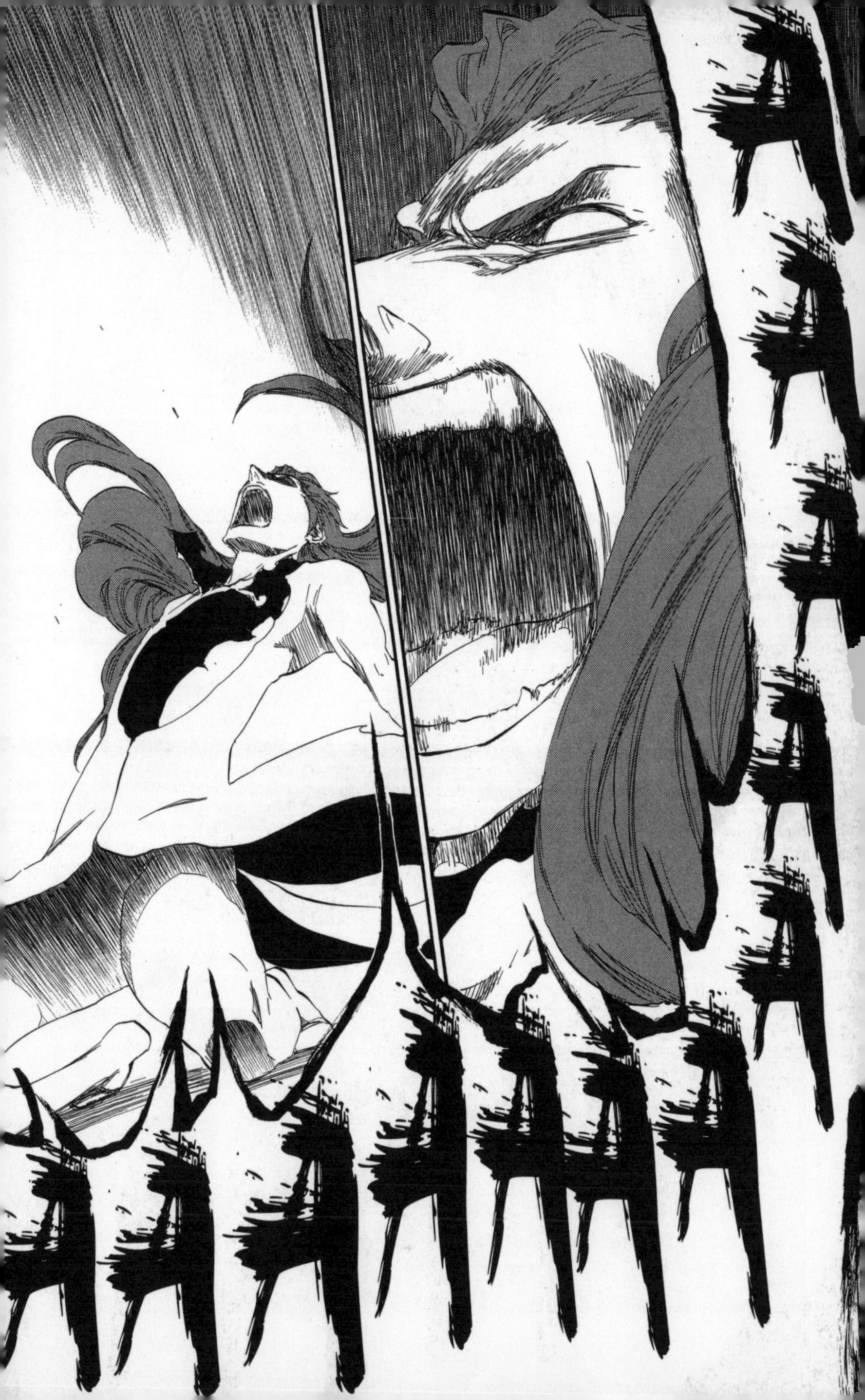
AAAAAAAAAAAA

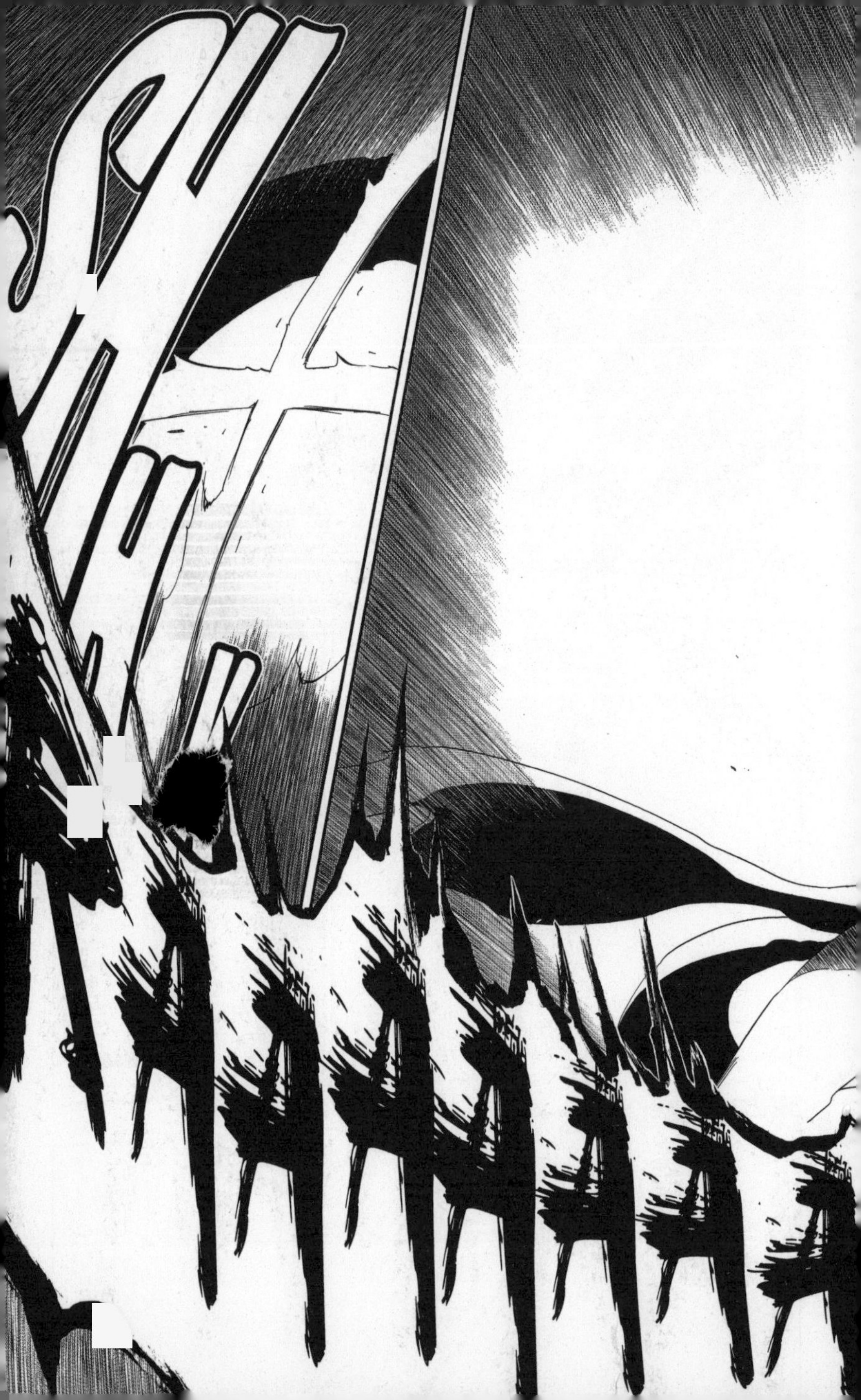
SHAAAAAAA

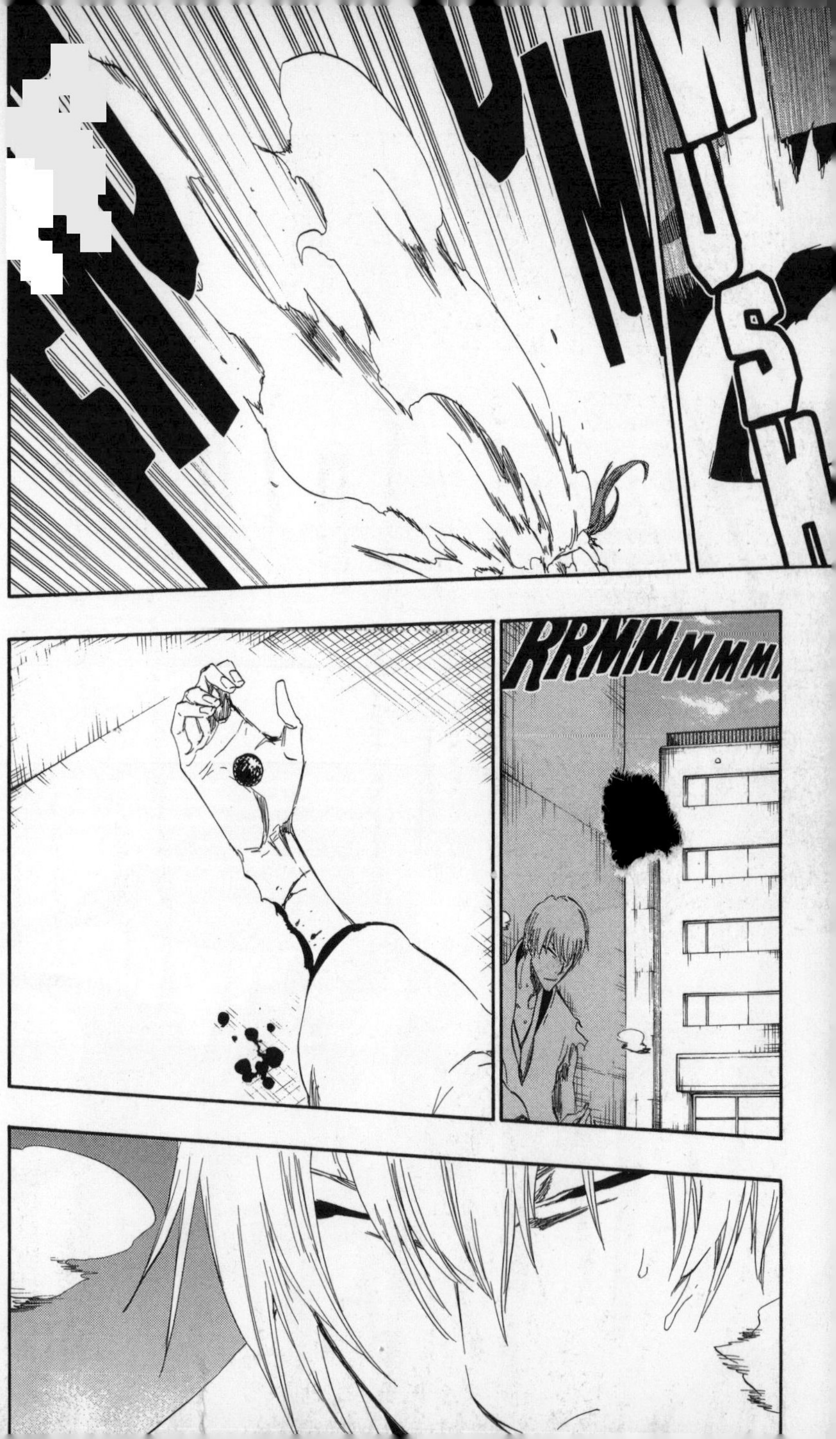
RRMMMMMM

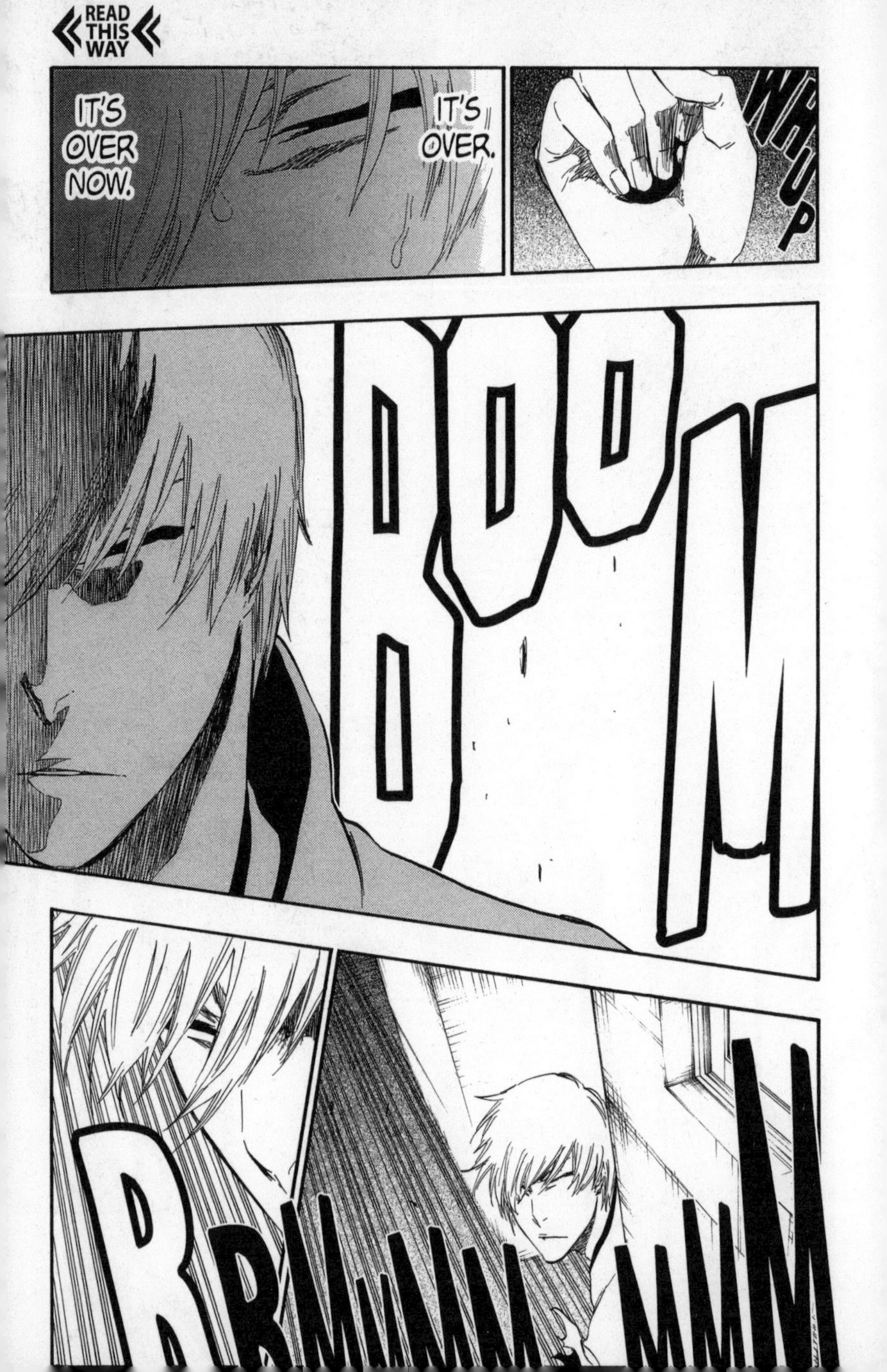
READ THIS WAY
WHUP
IT'S OVER.
IT'S OVER NOW.
BOOM
BRMMMMMMMMMM

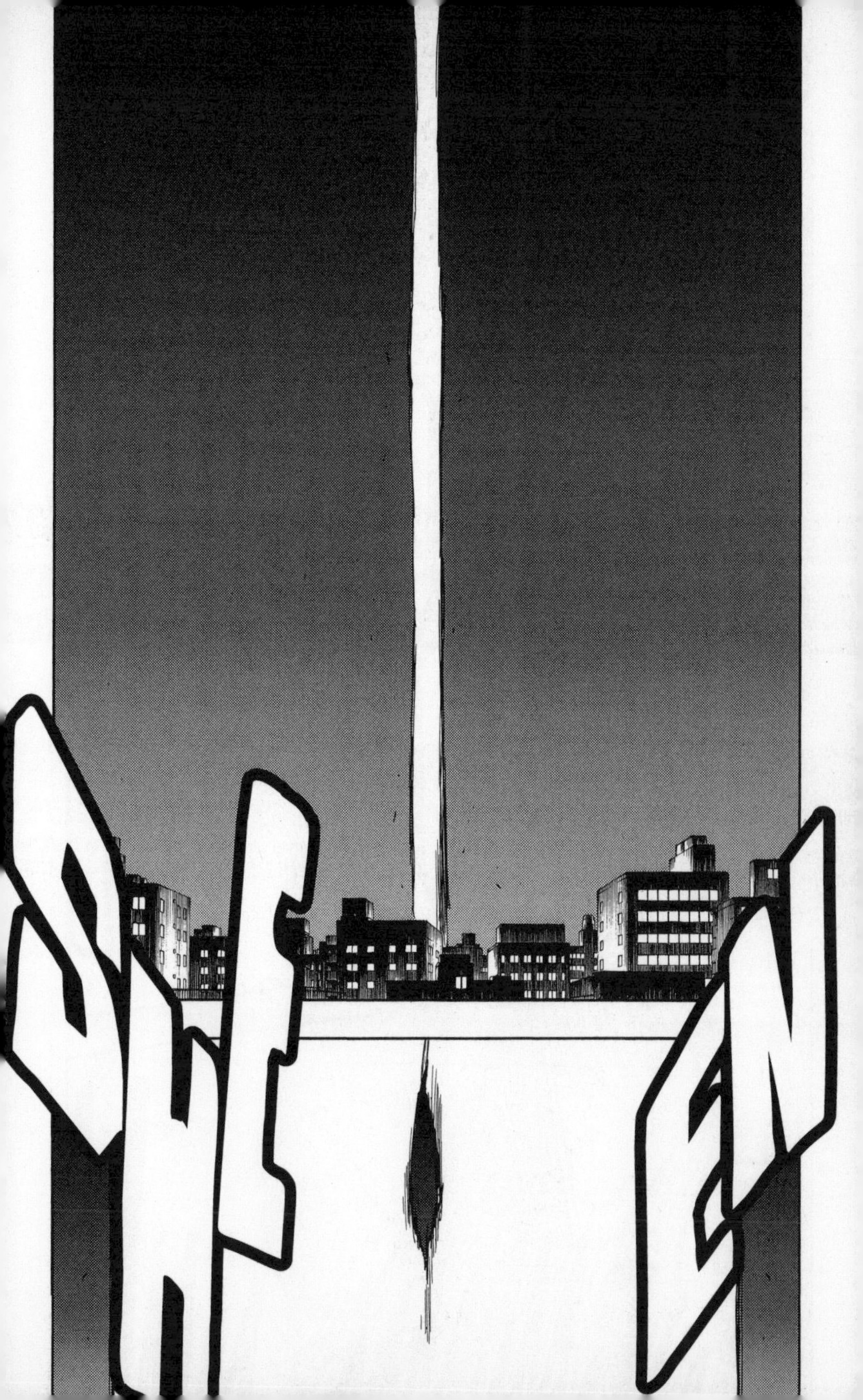

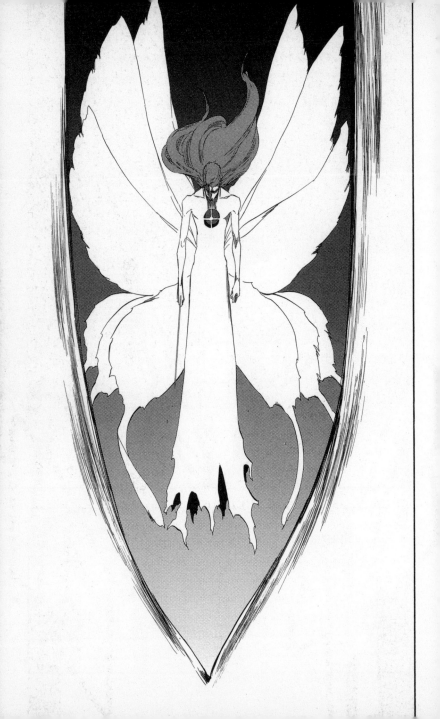

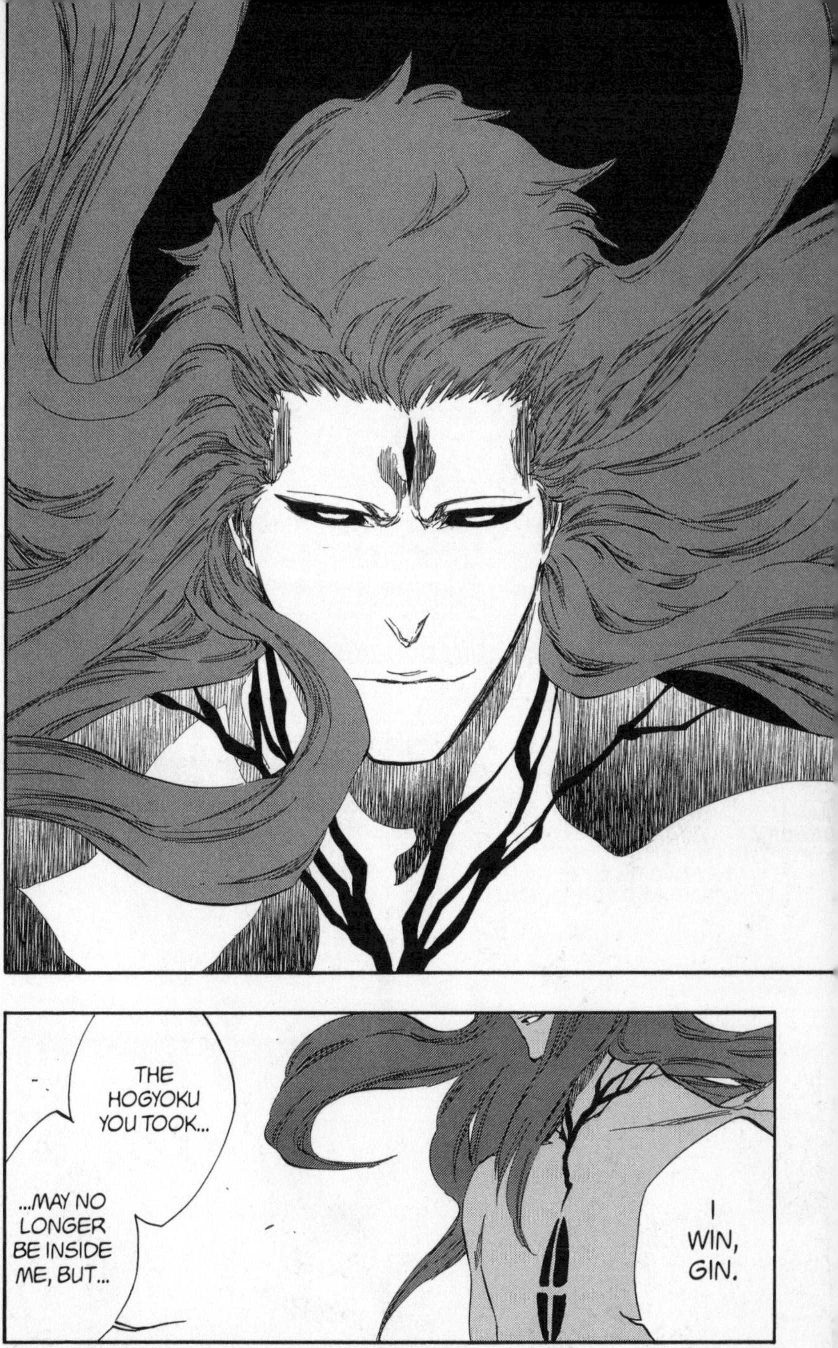
I WIN, GIN.
THE HOGYOKU YOU TOOK...
...MAY NO LONGER BE INSIDE ME, BUT...

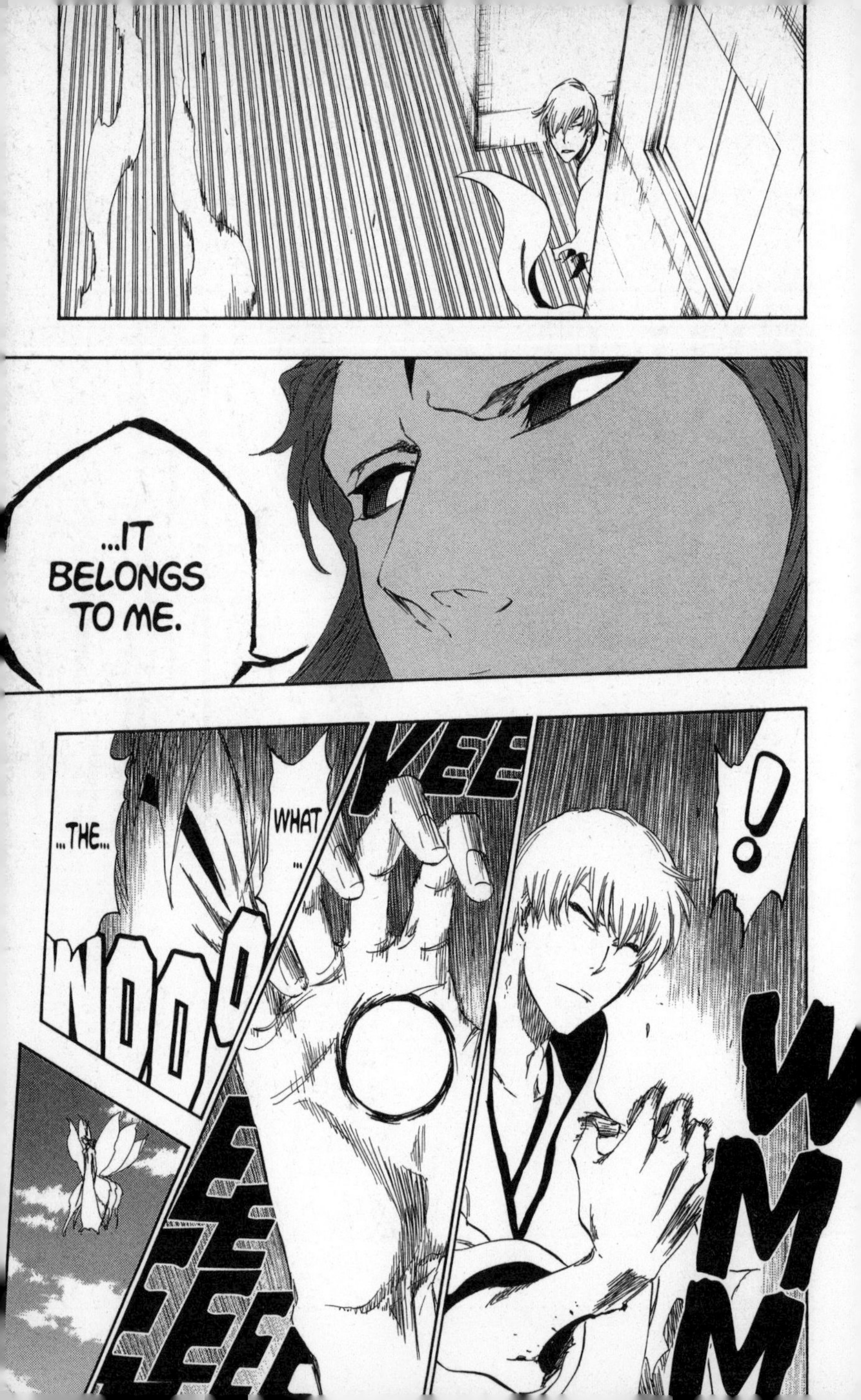
...IT BELONGS TO ME.
!
WMMM
VEE
WHAT ...
...THE...

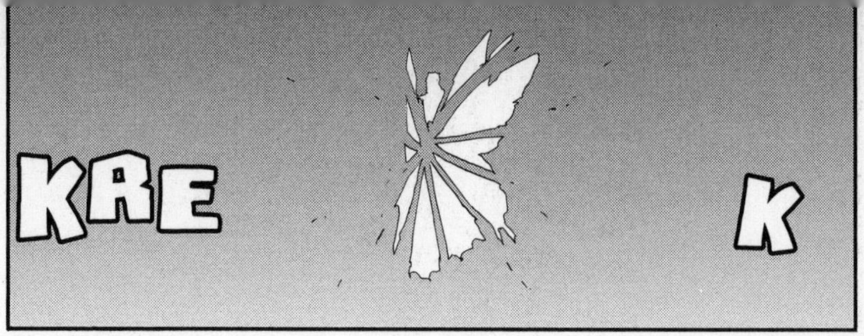
KRE
K

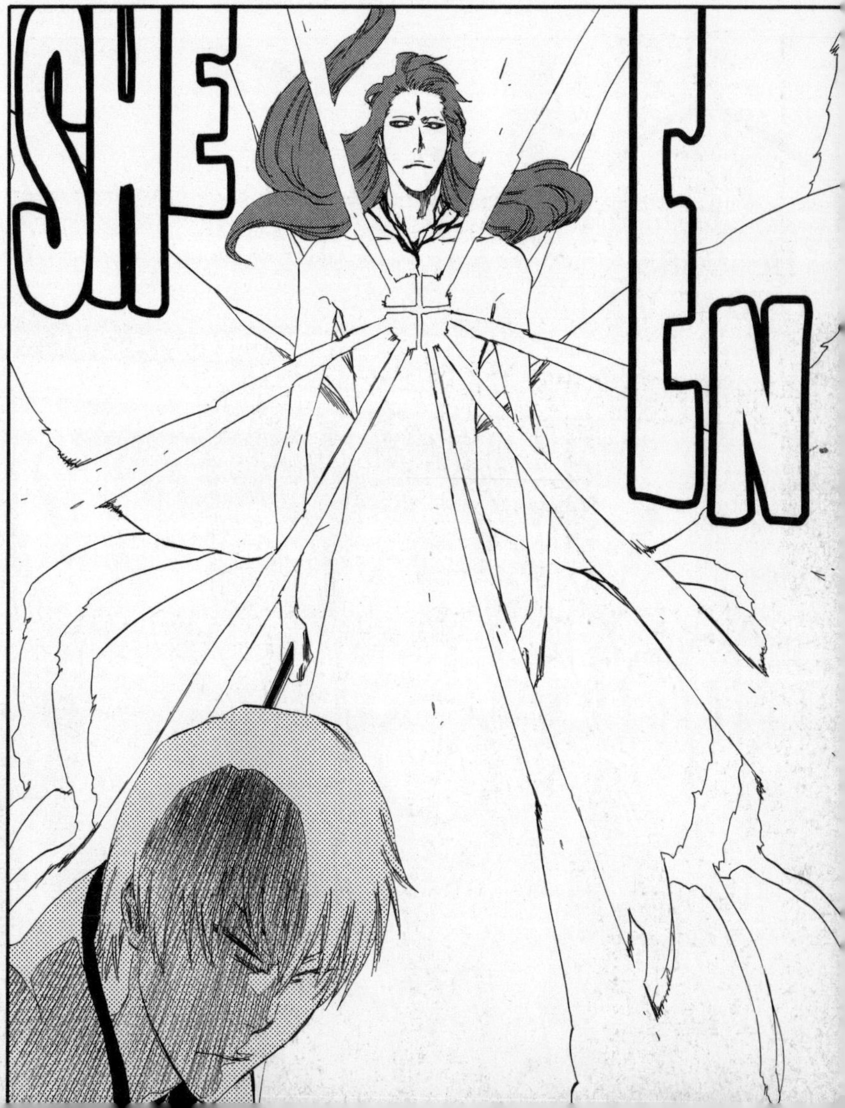
SHE
EN

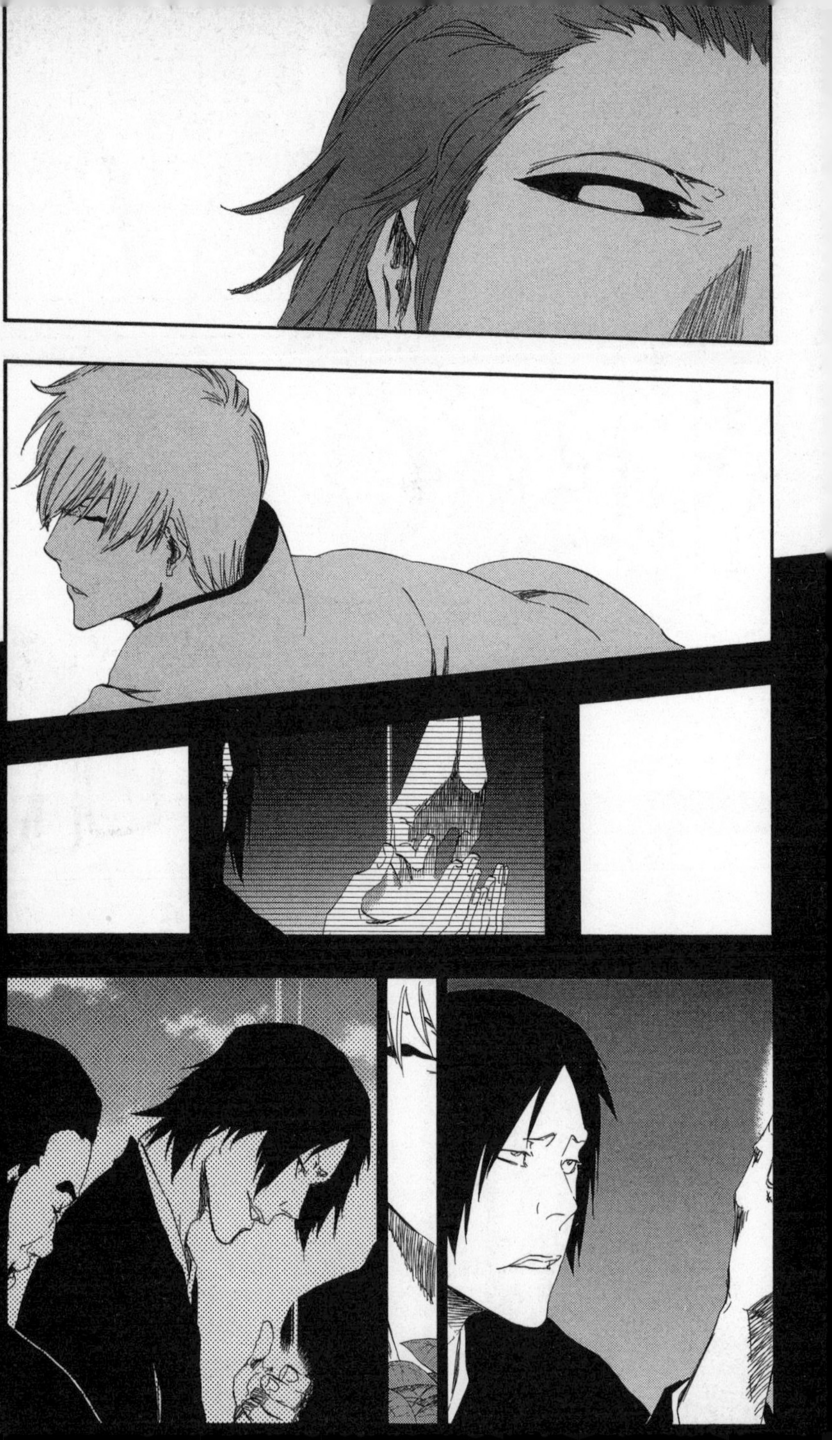

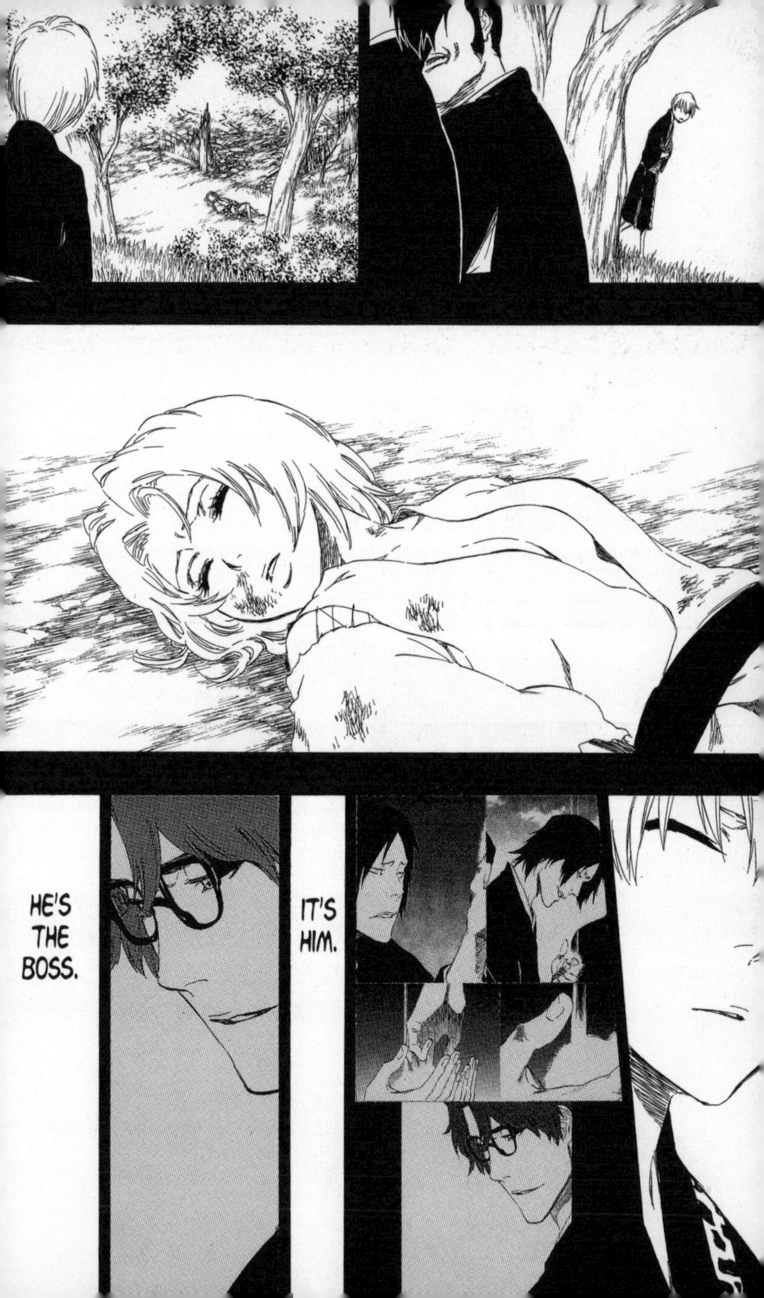
IT'S HIM.
HE'S THE BOSS.

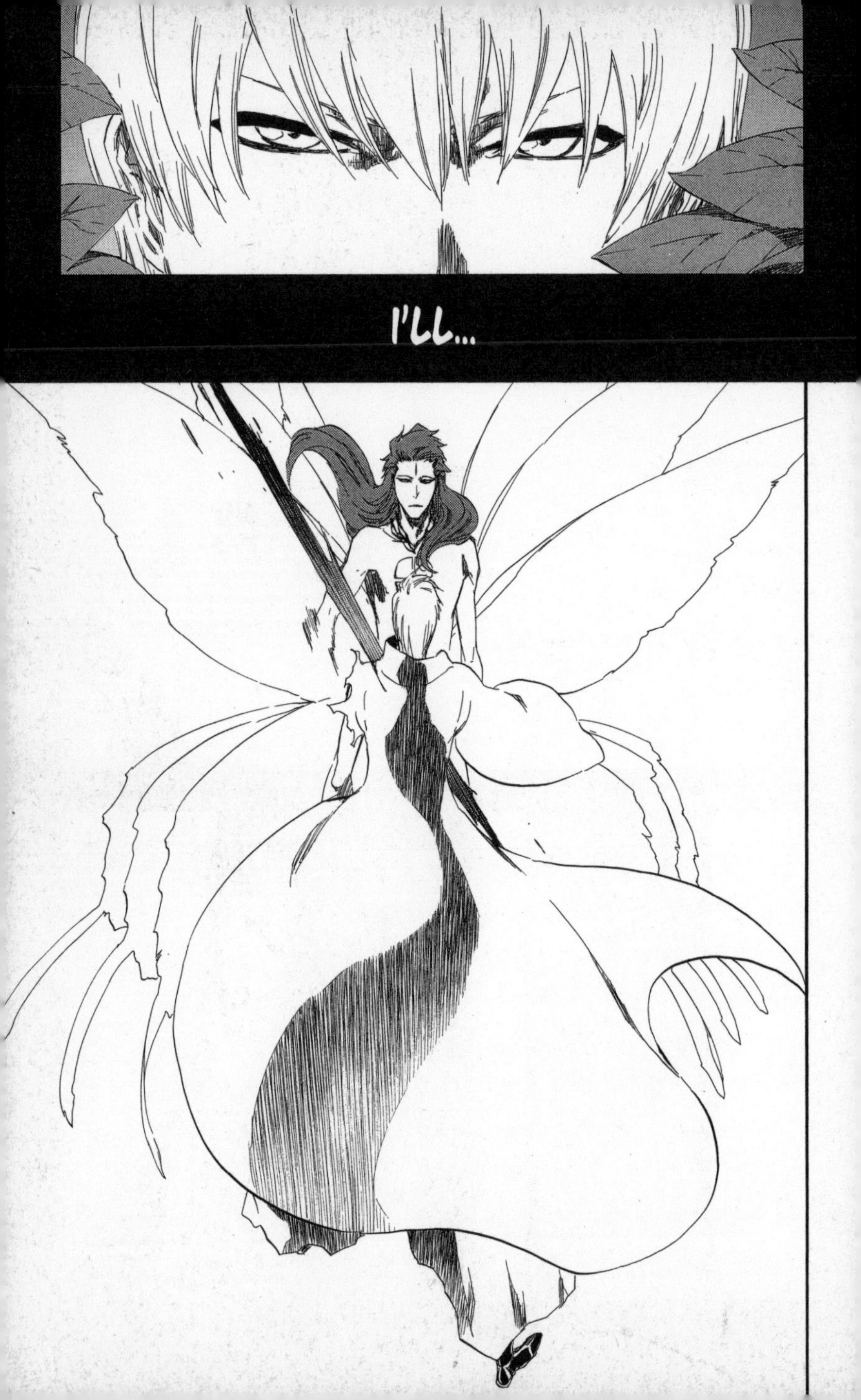
I'LL...

416. DEICIDE 18 [THE END]

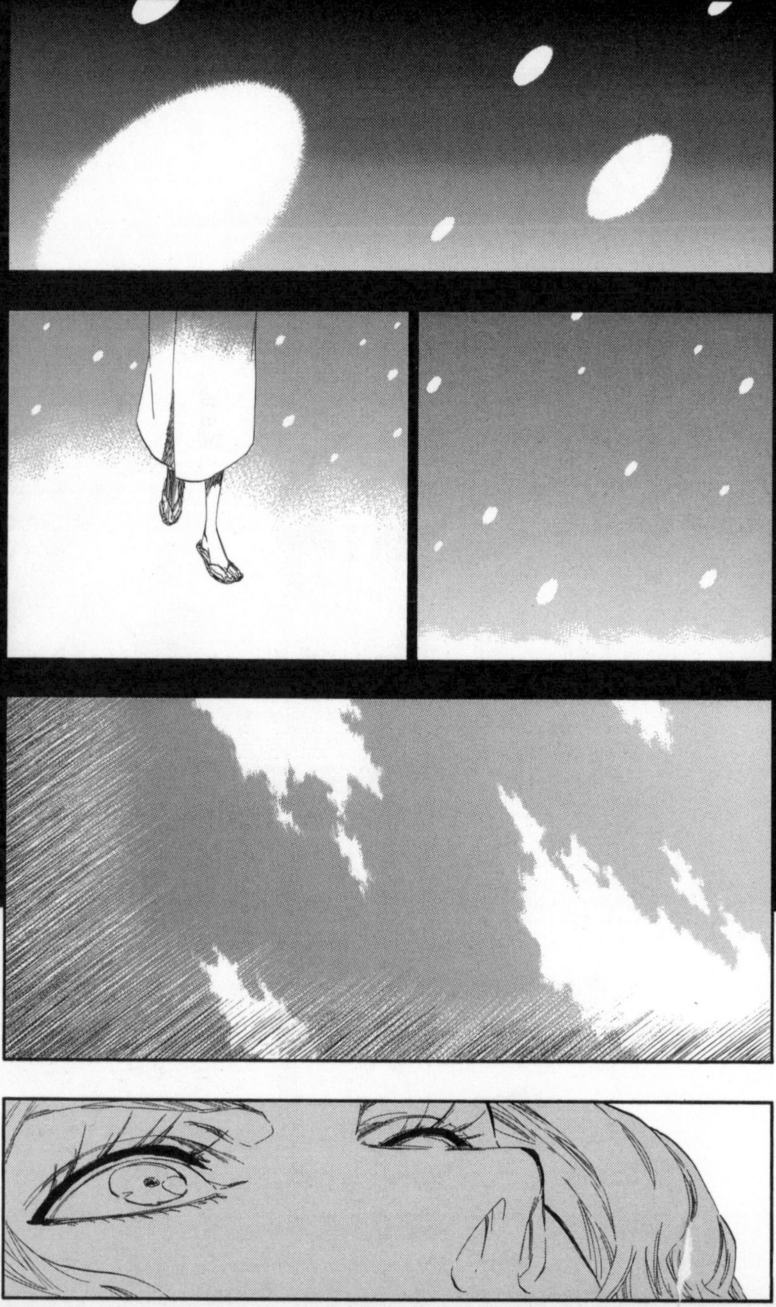

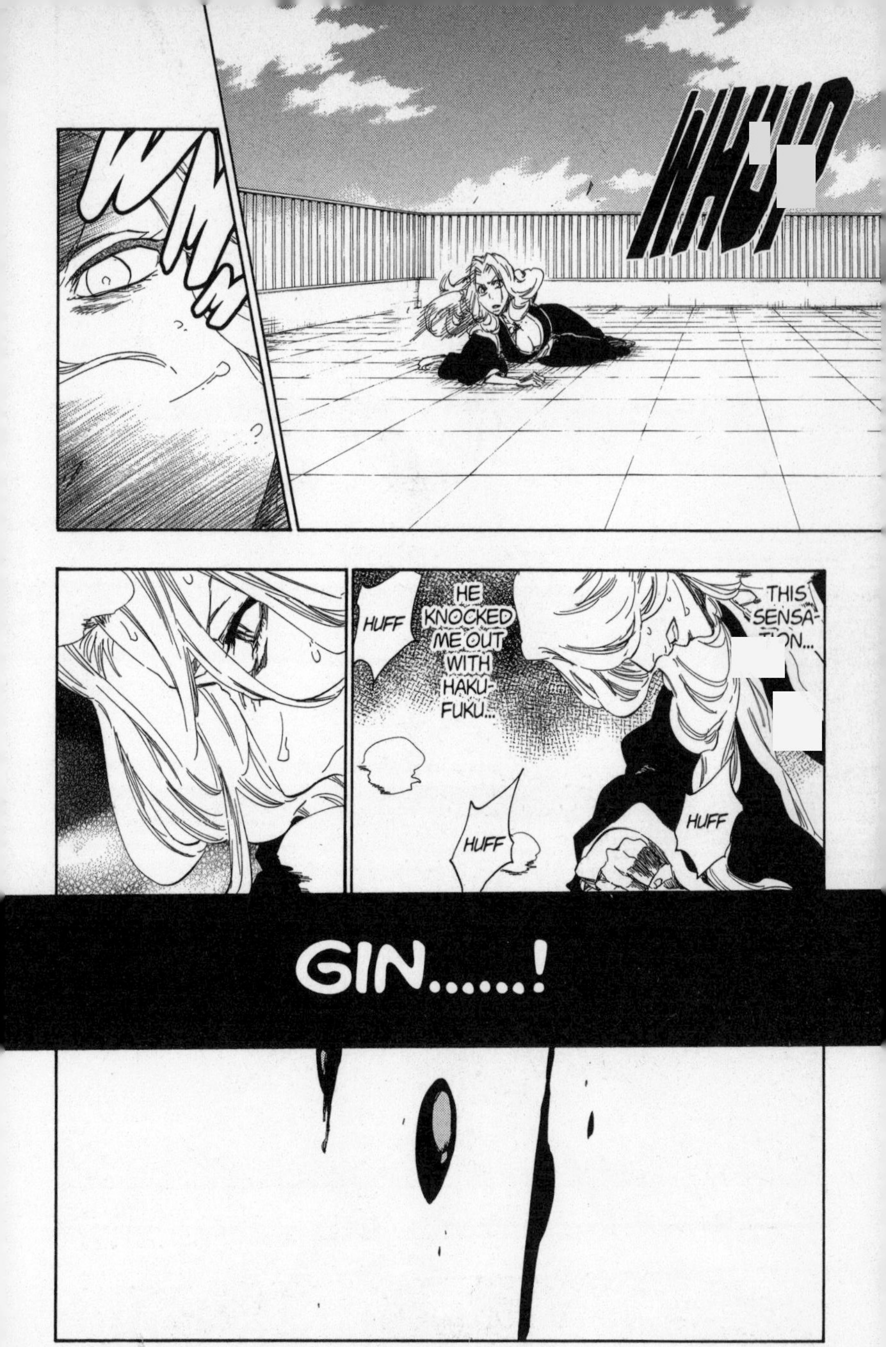

THIS SENSATION...
HE KNOCKED ME OUT WITH HAKUFUKU...
HUFF
HUFF
HUFF
GIN......!

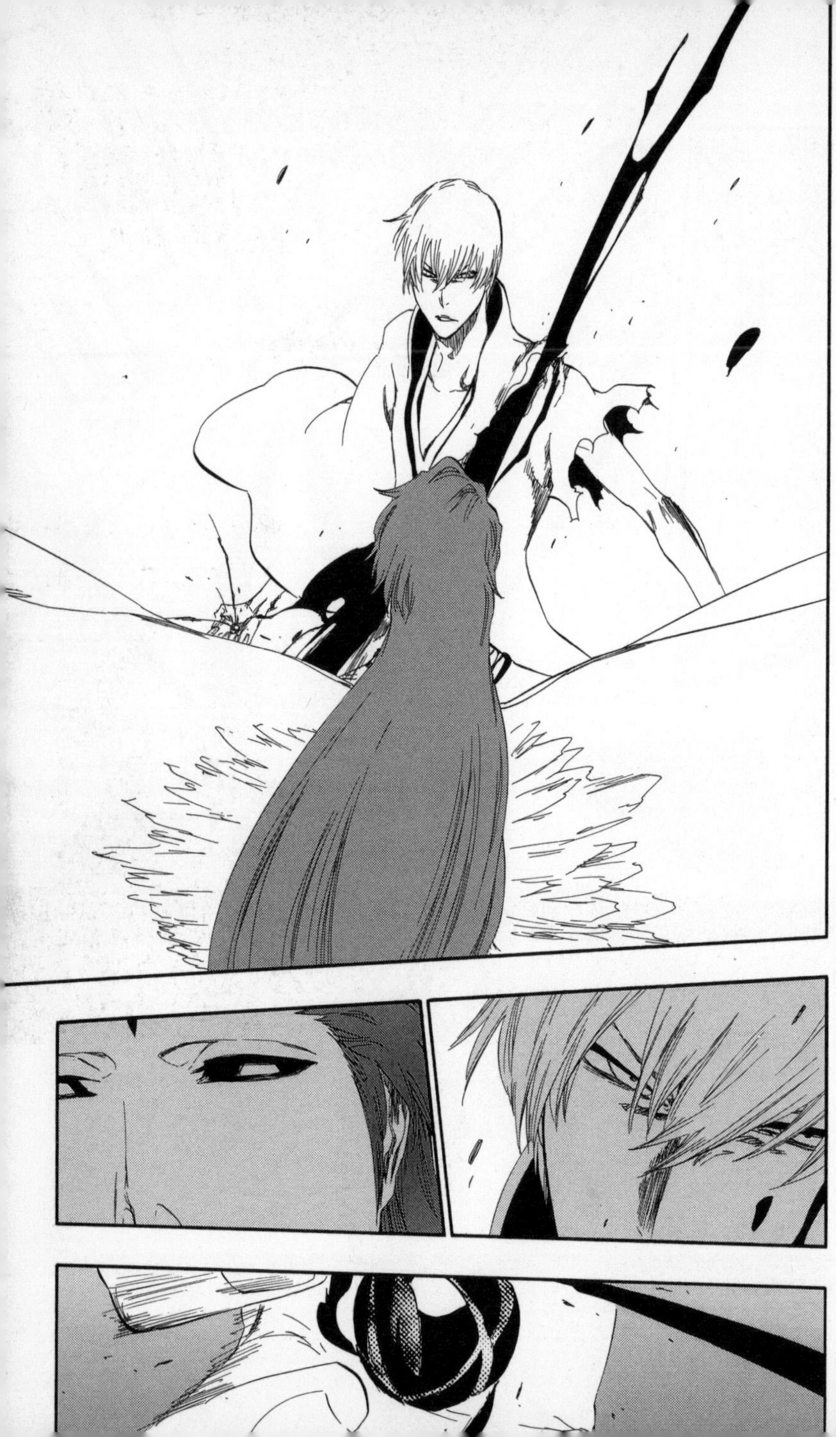

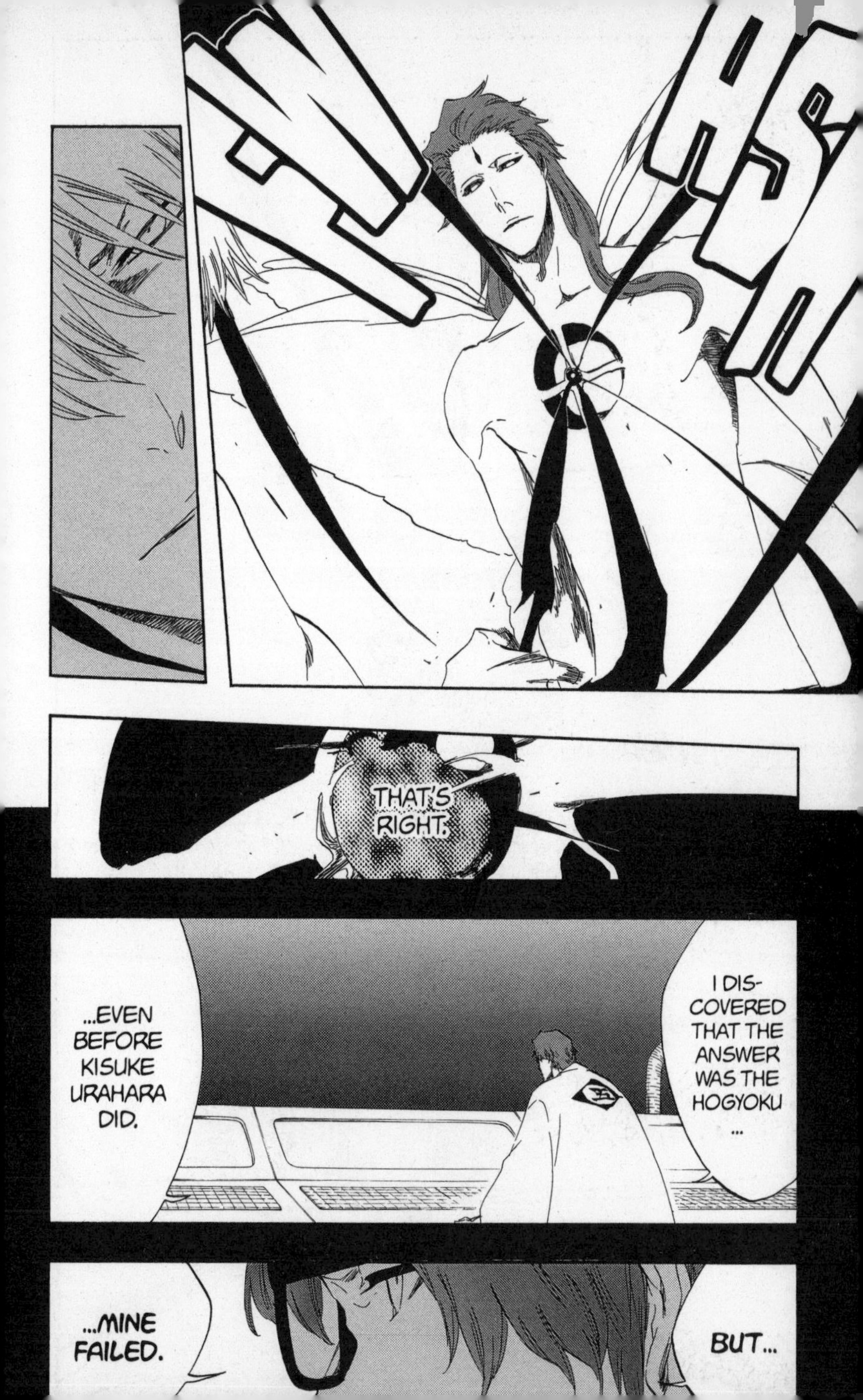
THAT'S RIGHT.
I DISCOVERED THAT THE ANSWER WAS THE HOGYOKU...
...EVEN BEFORE KISUKE URAHARA DID.
BUT...
...MINE FAILED.

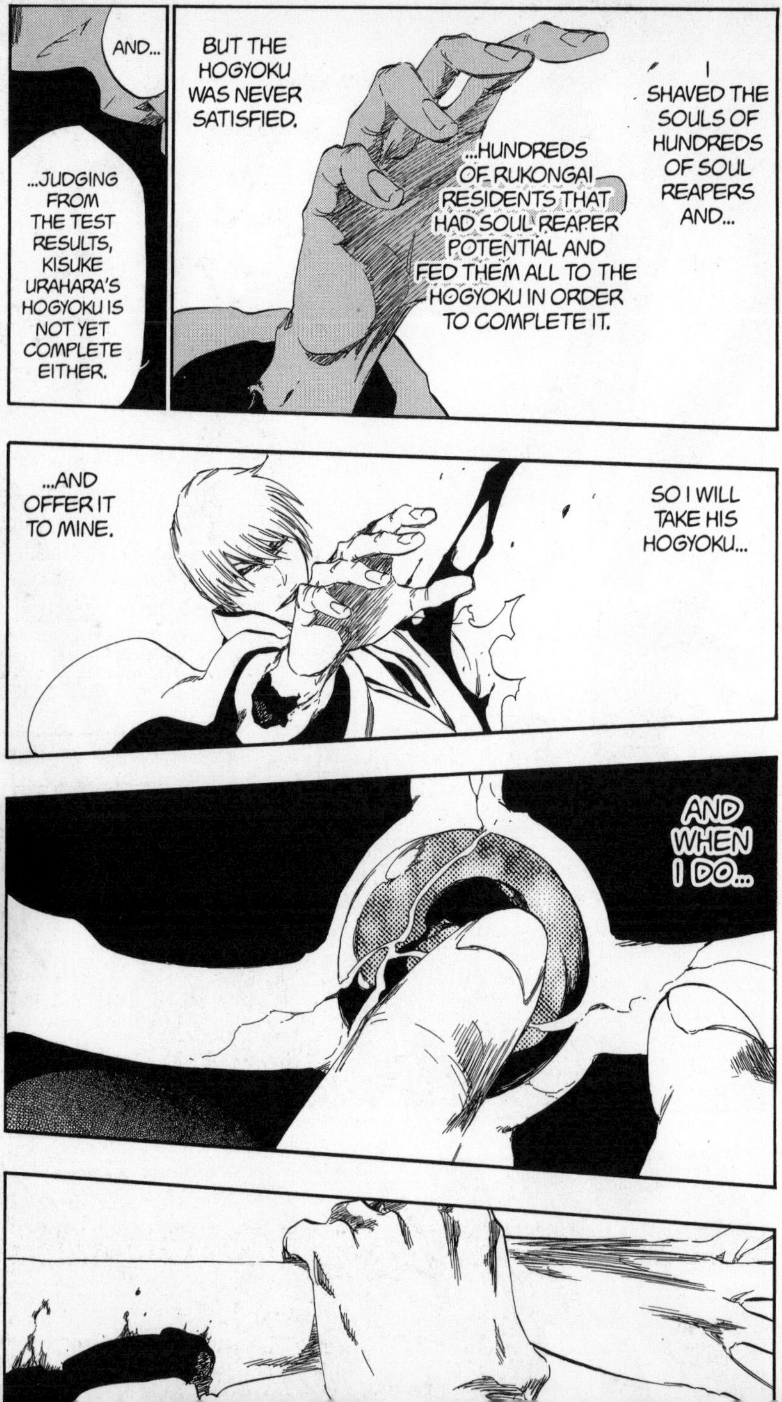
I SHAVED THE SOULS OF HUNDREDS OF SOUL REAPERS AND...
...HUNDREDS OF RUKONGAI RESIDENTS THAT HAD SOUL REAPER POTENTIAL AND FED THEM ALL TO THE HOGYOKU IN ORDER TO COMPLETE IT.
BUT THE HOGYOKU WAS NEVER SATISFIED.
AND...
...JUDGING FROM THE TEST RESULTS, KISUKE URAHARA'S HOGYOKU IS NOT YET COMPLETE EITHER.
SO I WILL TAKE HIS HOGYOKU...
...AND OFFER IT TO MINE.
AND WHEN I DO...

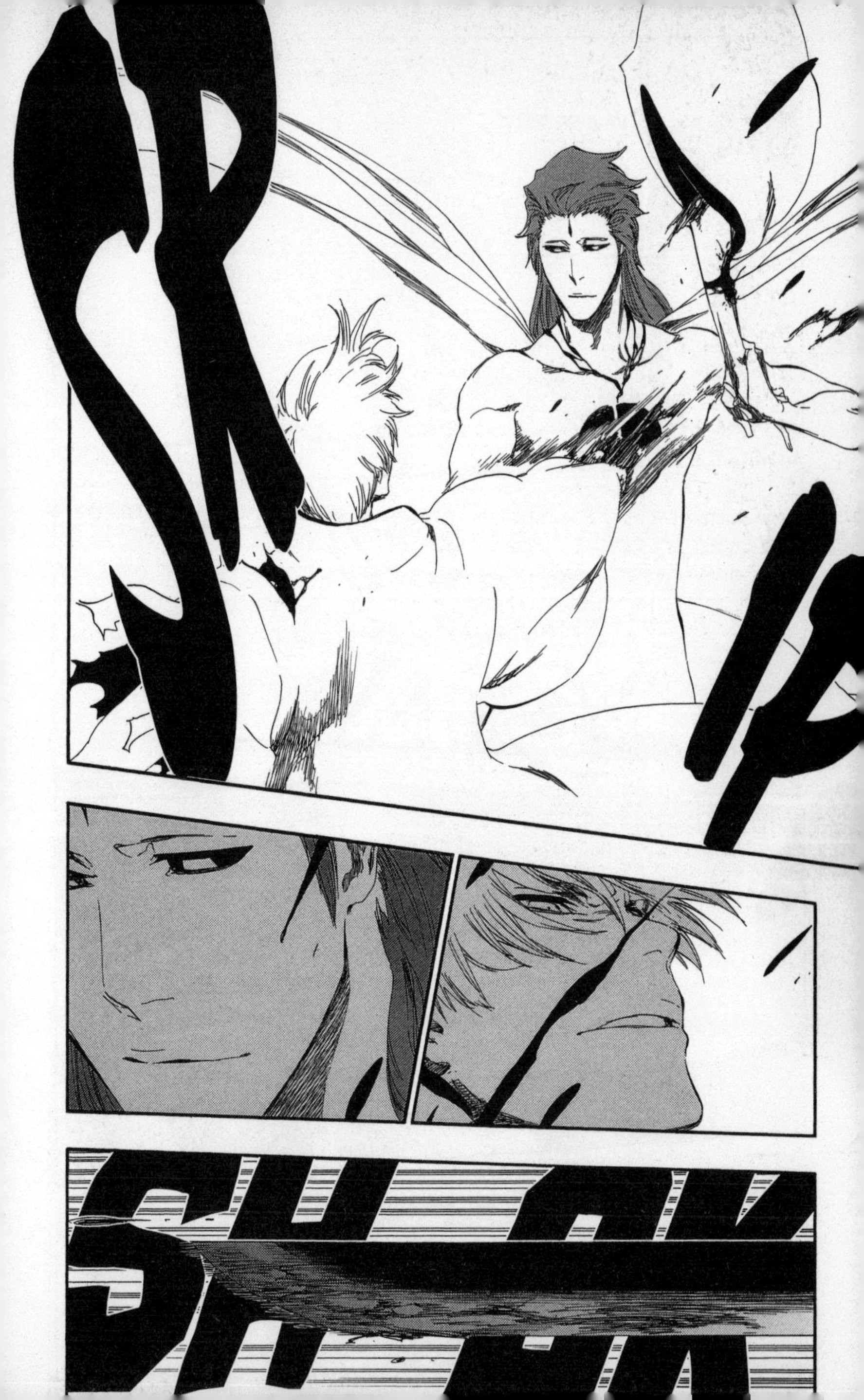

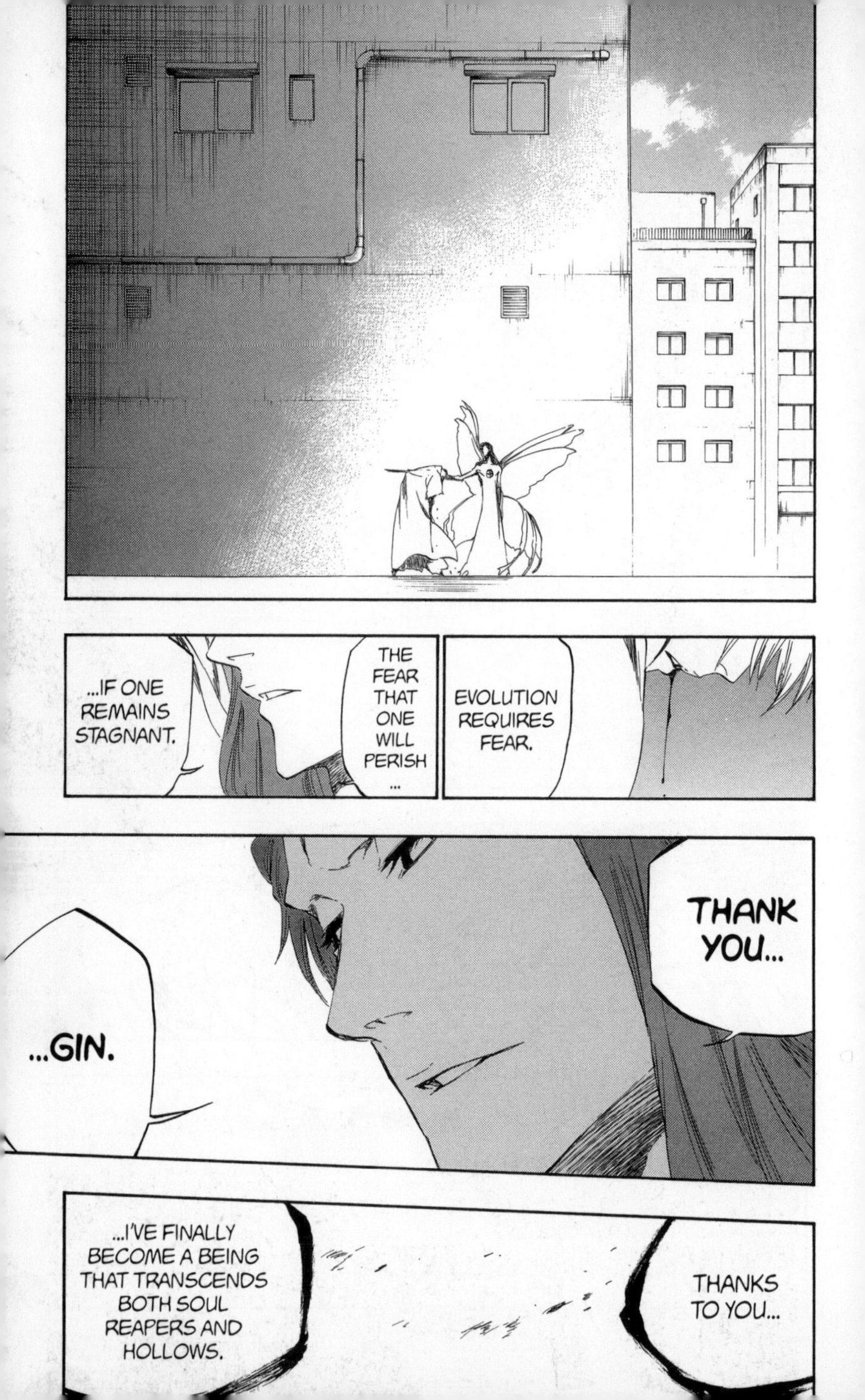
EVOLUTION REQUIRES FEAR.
THE FEAR THAT ONE WILL PERISH...
...IF ONE REMAINS STAGNANT.
THANK YOU...
...GIN.
THANKS TO YOU...
...I'VE FINALLY BECOME A BEING THAT TRANSCENDS BOTH SOUL REAPERS AND HOLLOWS.

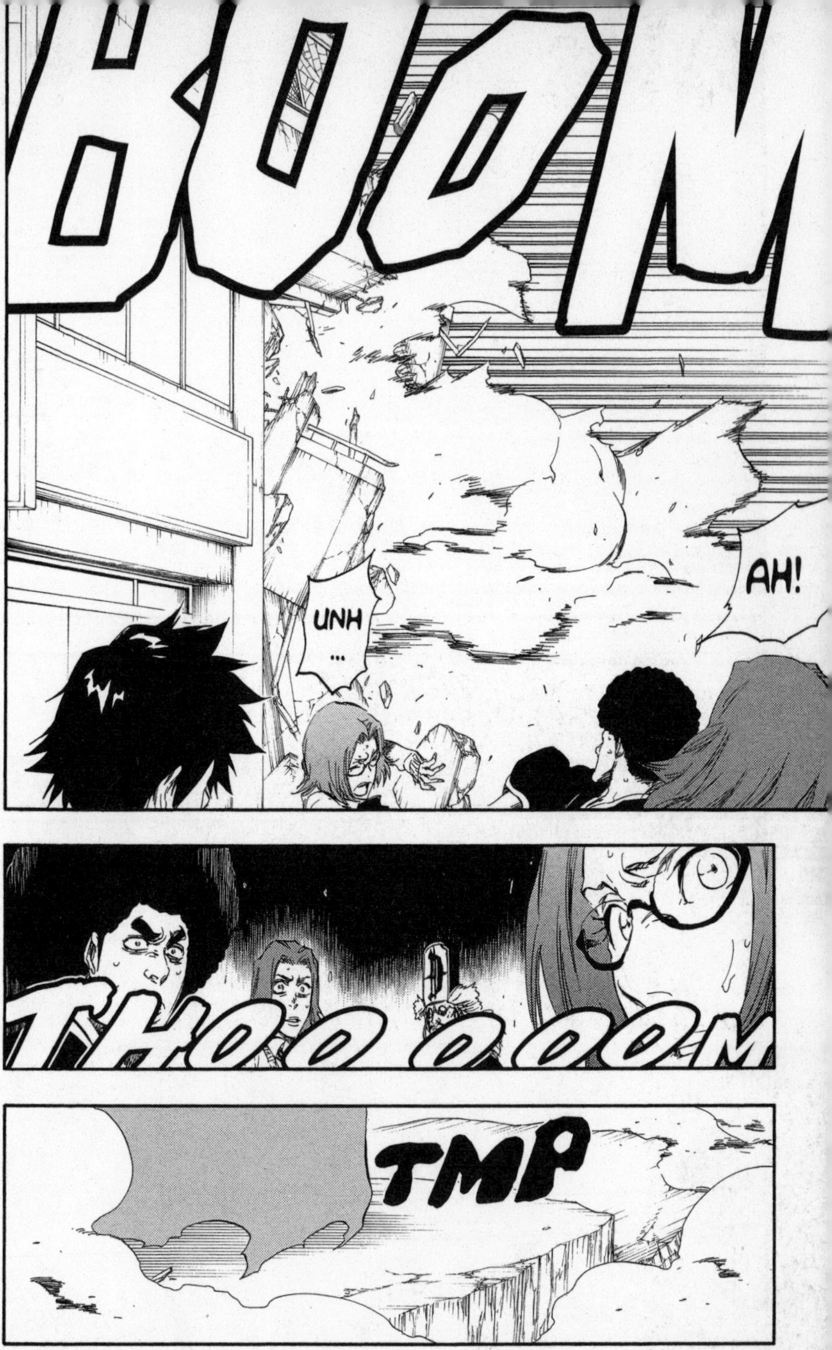
BOOM
AH!
UNH ...
THOOOOOM
TMP

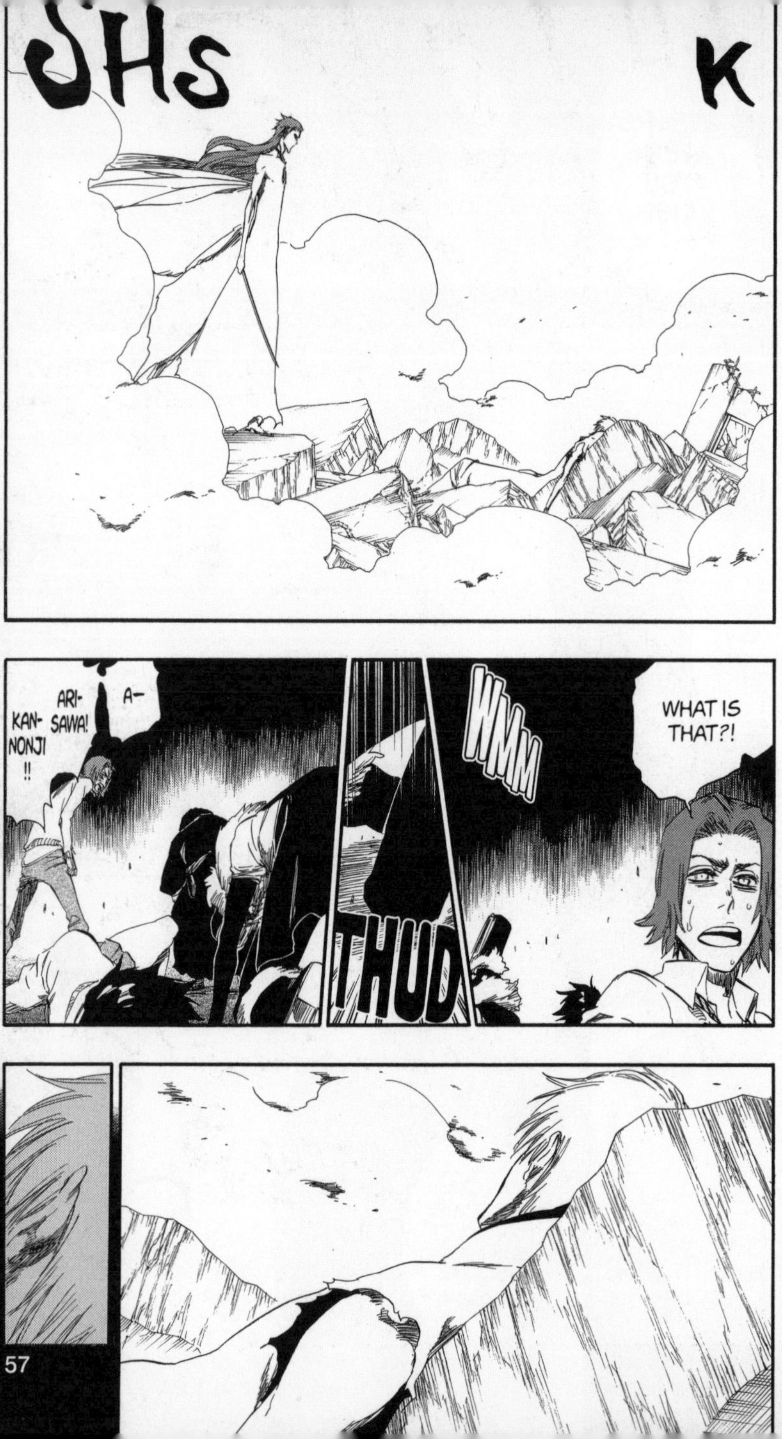
SHS
K
WHAT IS THAT?!
WMM
THUD
A-
ARI-
SAWA!
KAN-
NONJI
!!

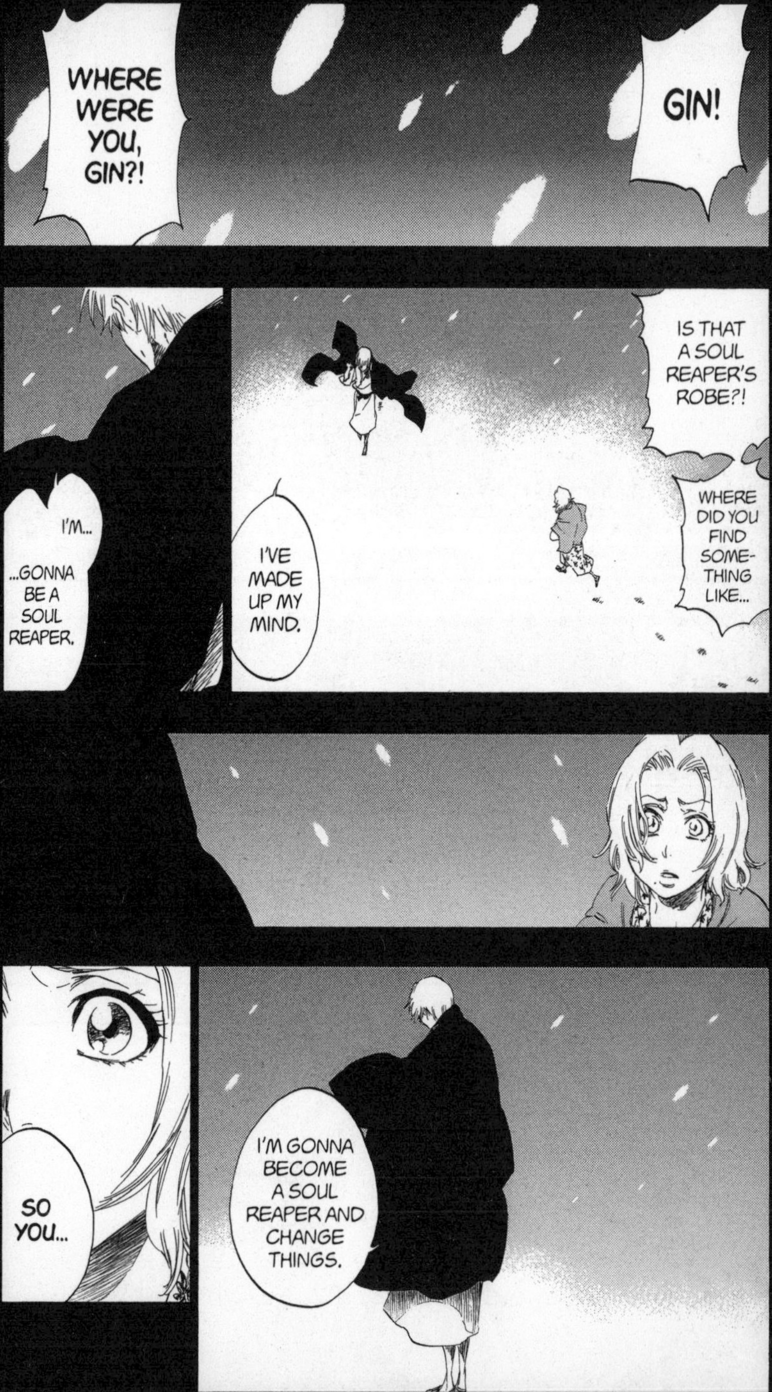
GIN!
WHERE WERE YOU, GIN?!
IS THAT A SOUL REAPER'S ROBE?!
WHERE DID YOU FIND SOME-THING LIKE...
I'VE MADE UP MY MIND.
I'M...
...GONNA BE A SOUL REAPER.
I'M GONNA BECOME A SOUL REAPER AND CHANGE THINGS.
SO YOU...

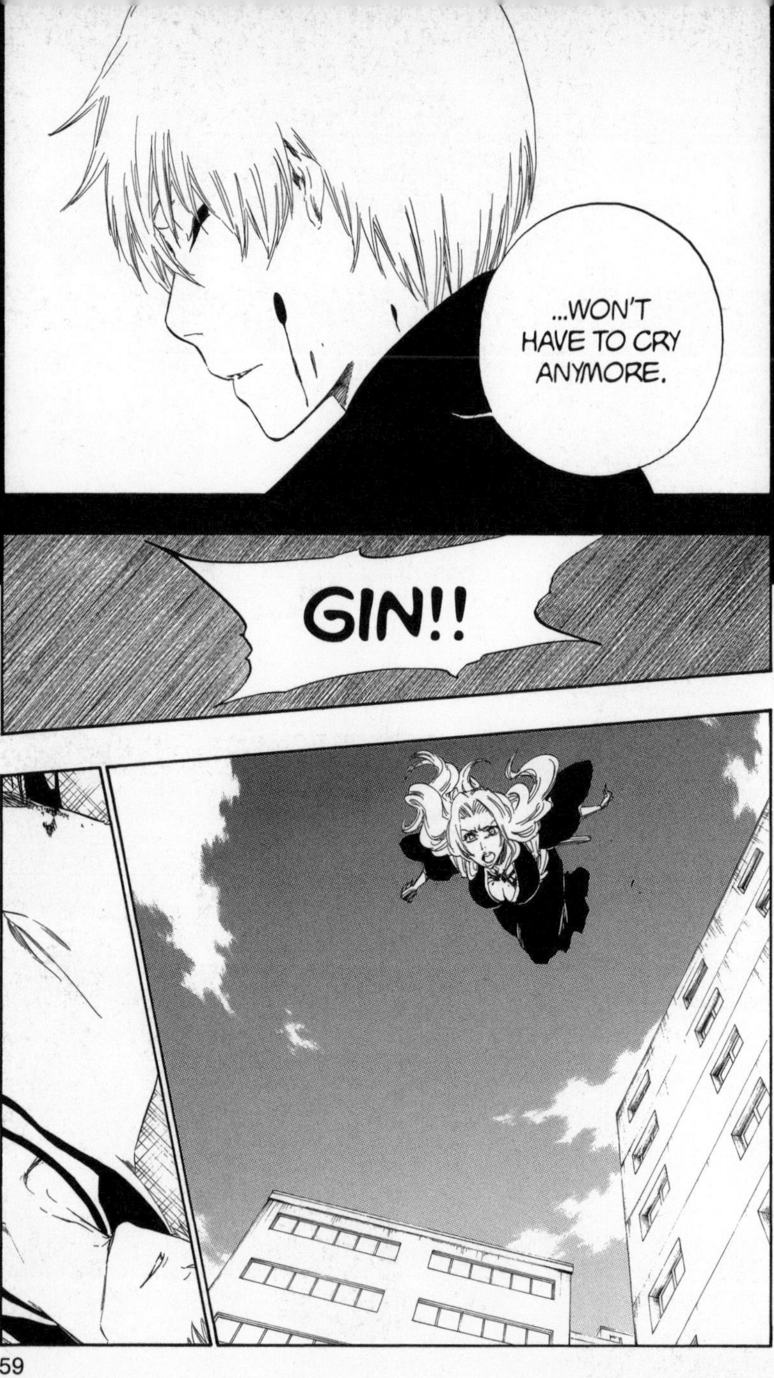
...WON'T HAVE TO CRY ANYMORE.
GIN!!

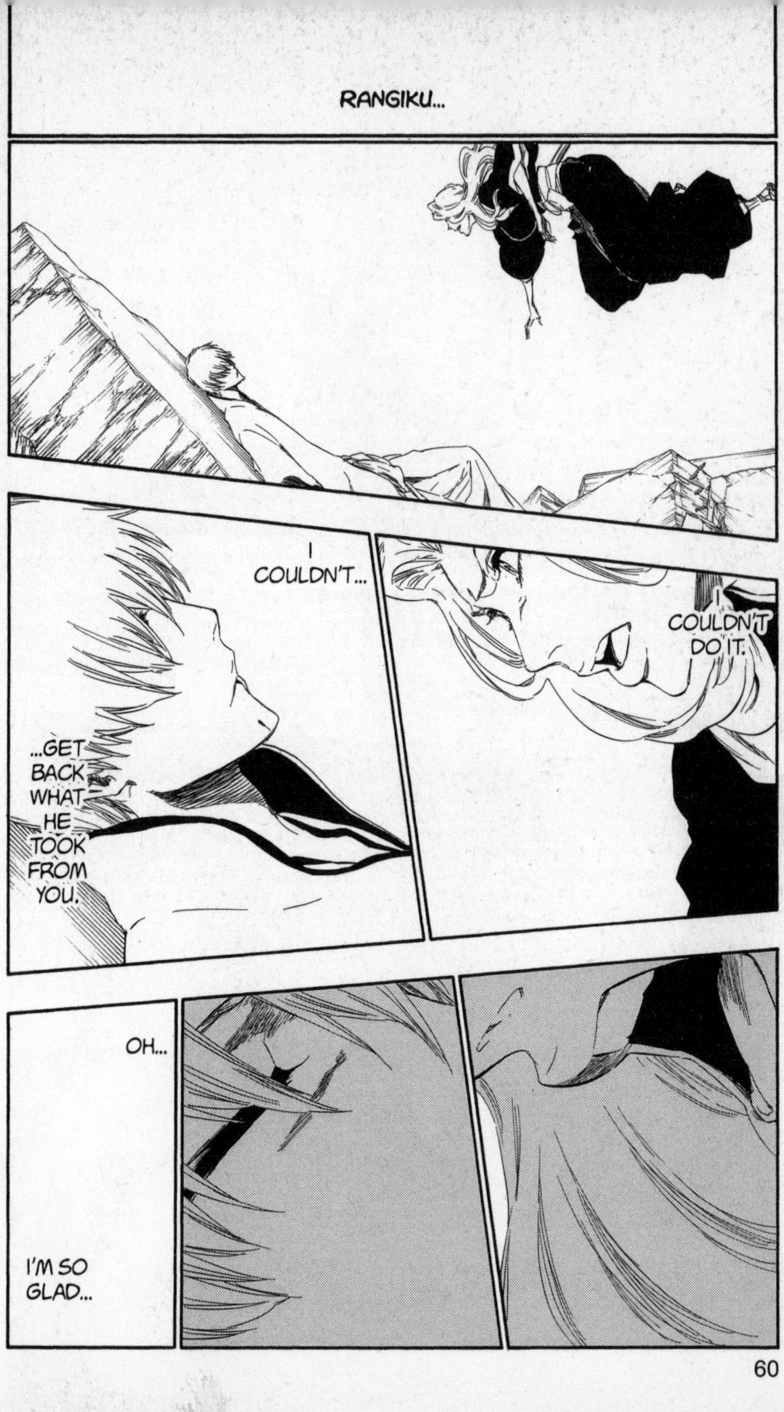
RANGIKU...
I COULDN'T DO IT.
I COULDN'T...
...GET BACK WHAT HE TOOK FROM YOU.
OH...
I'M SO GLAD...

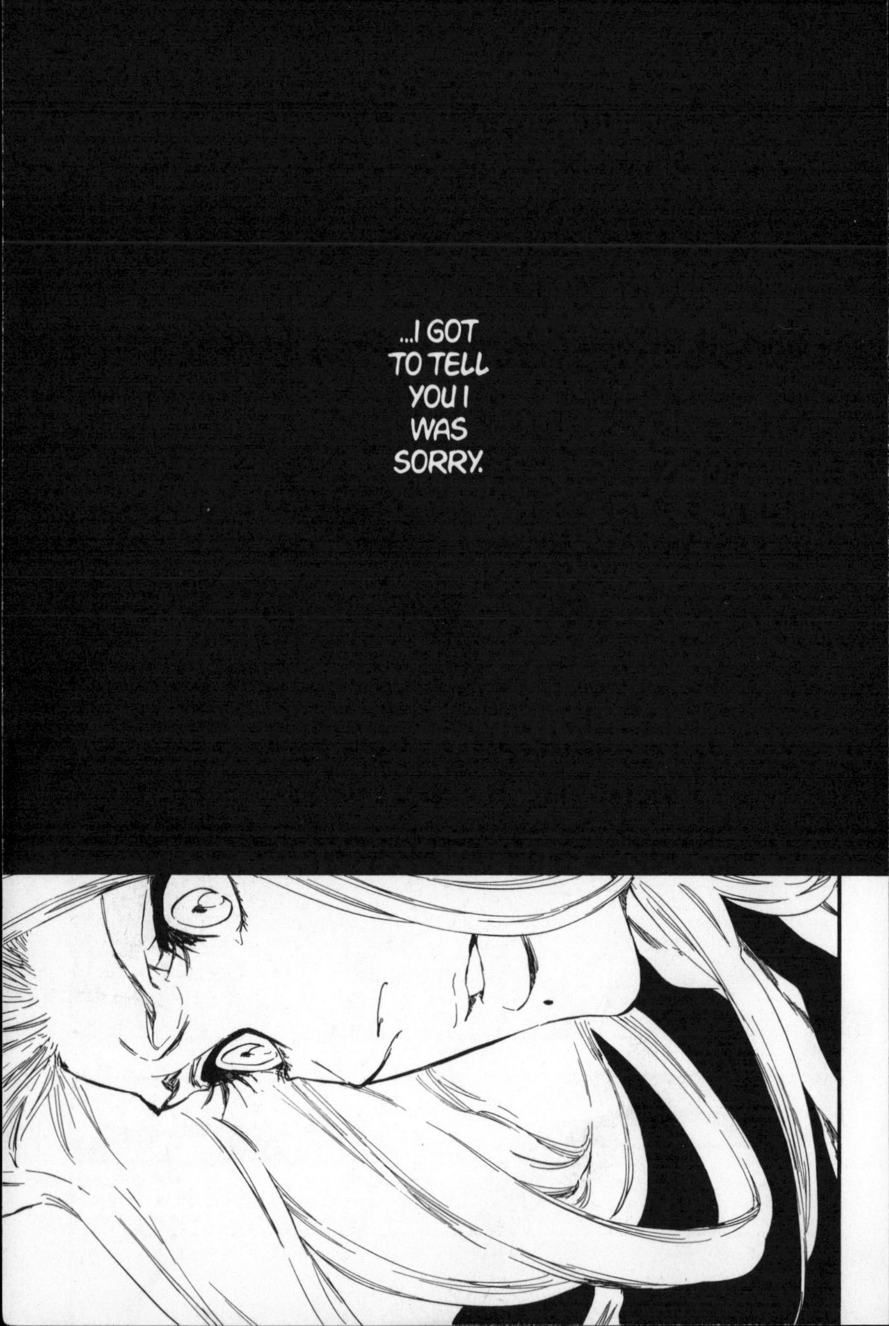
...I GOT TO TELL YOU I WAS SORRY.

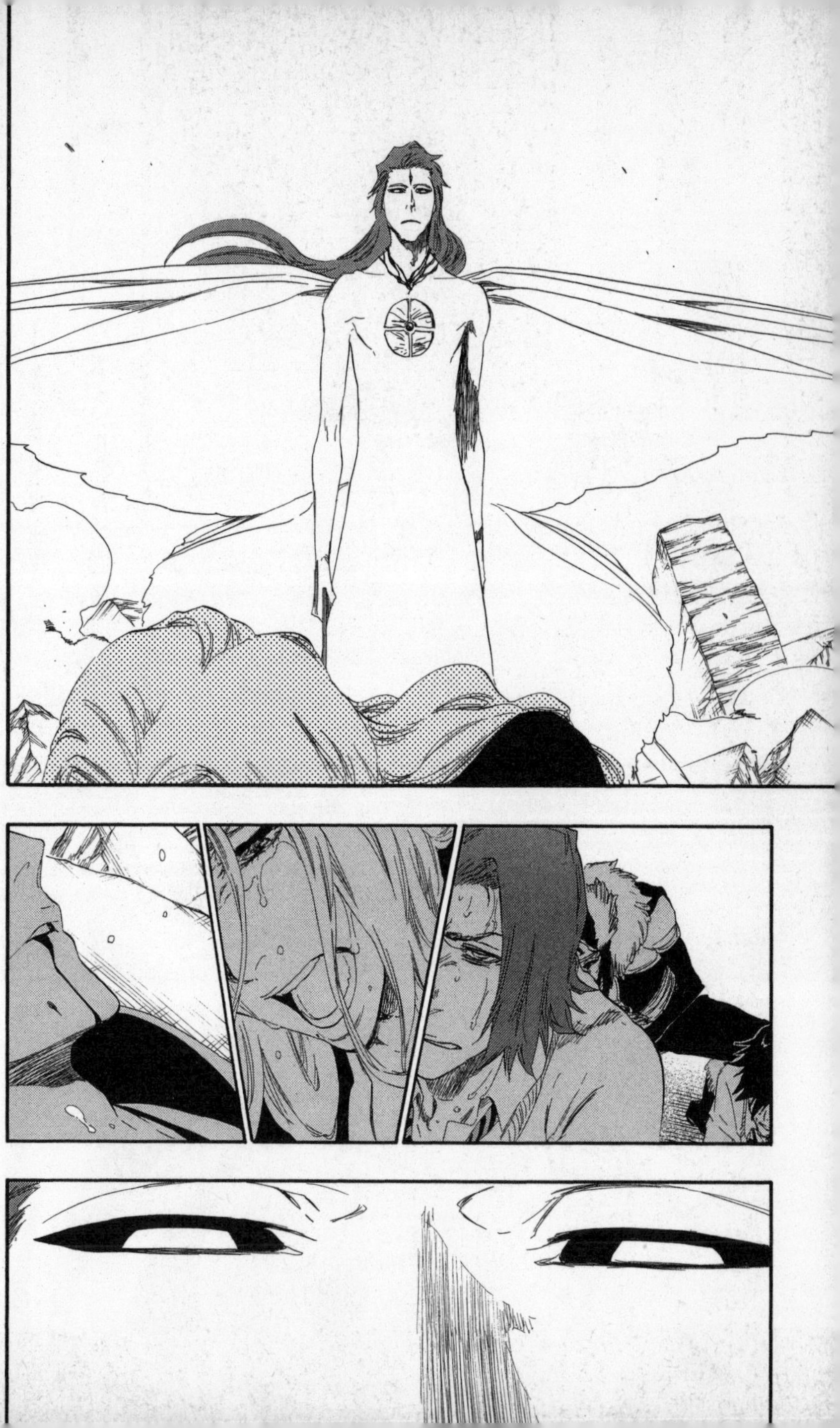

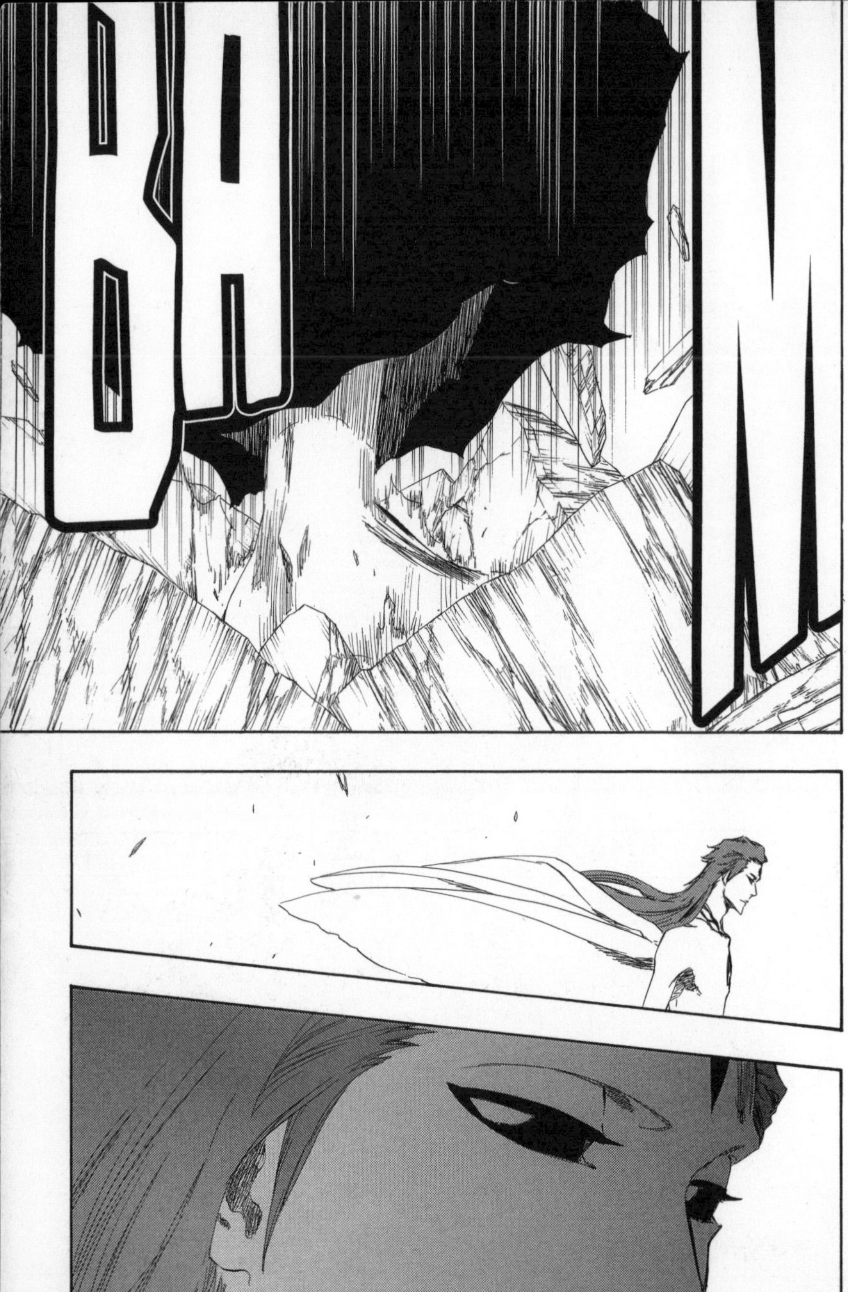

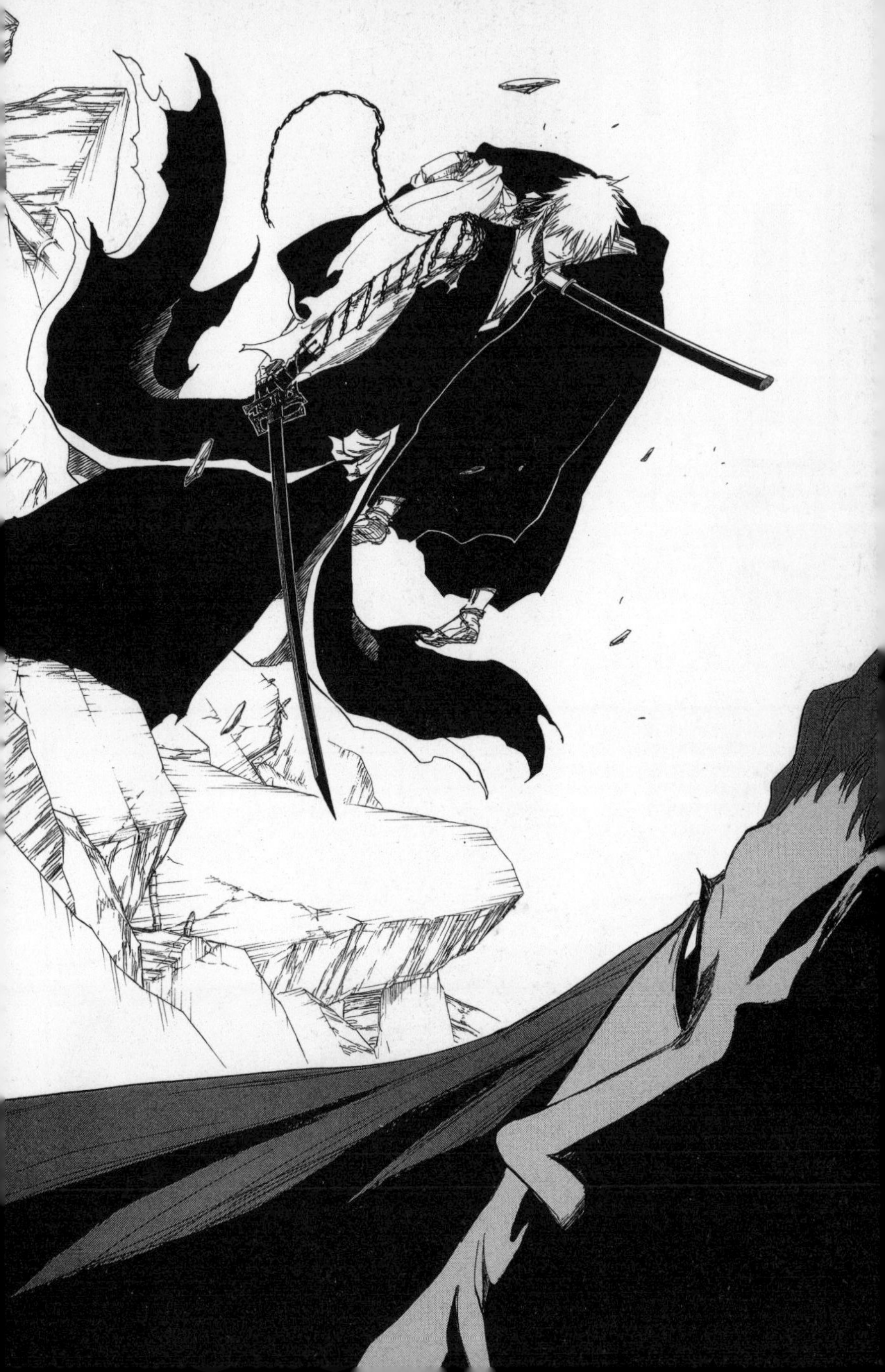

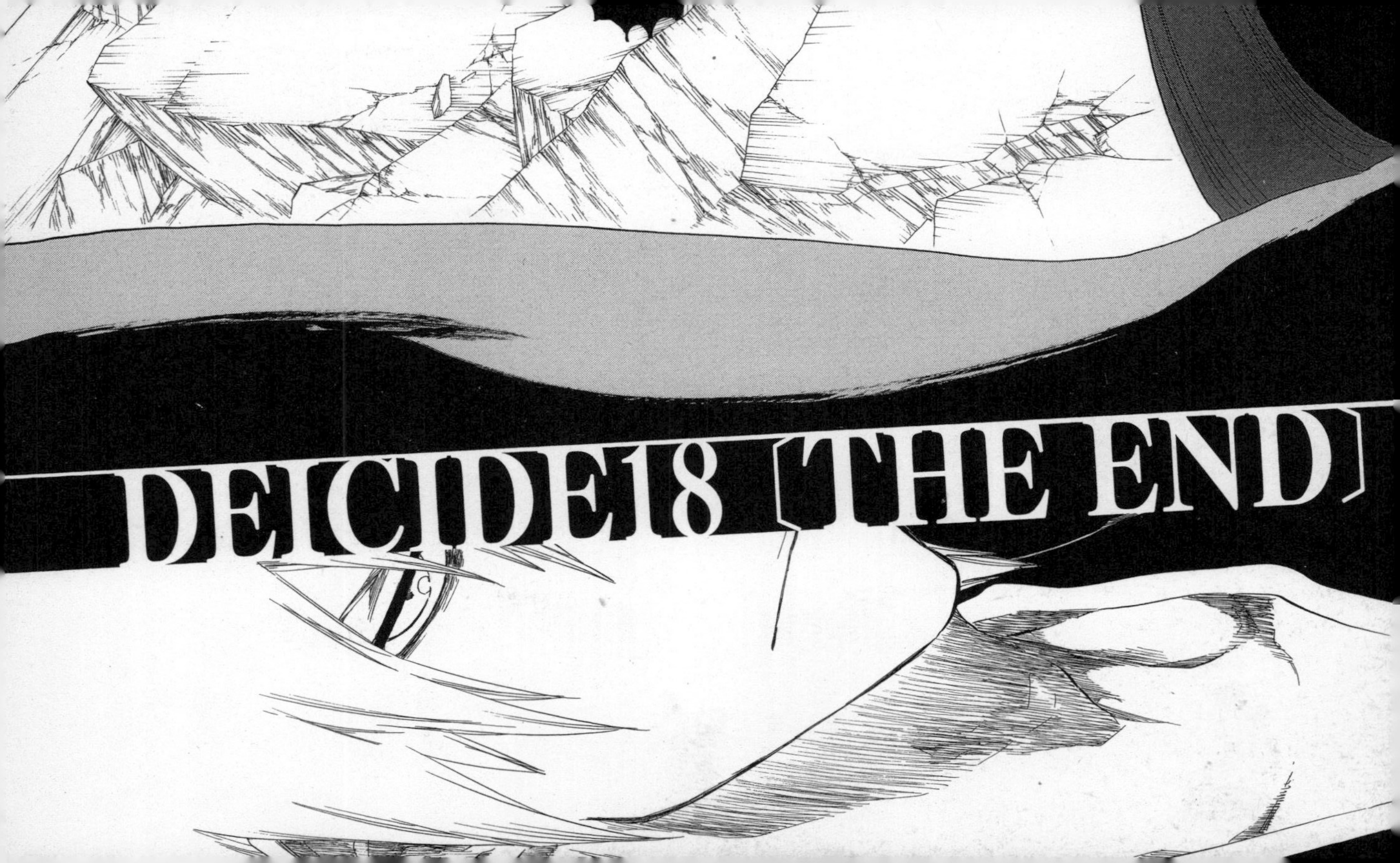
DEICIDE18 [THE END]

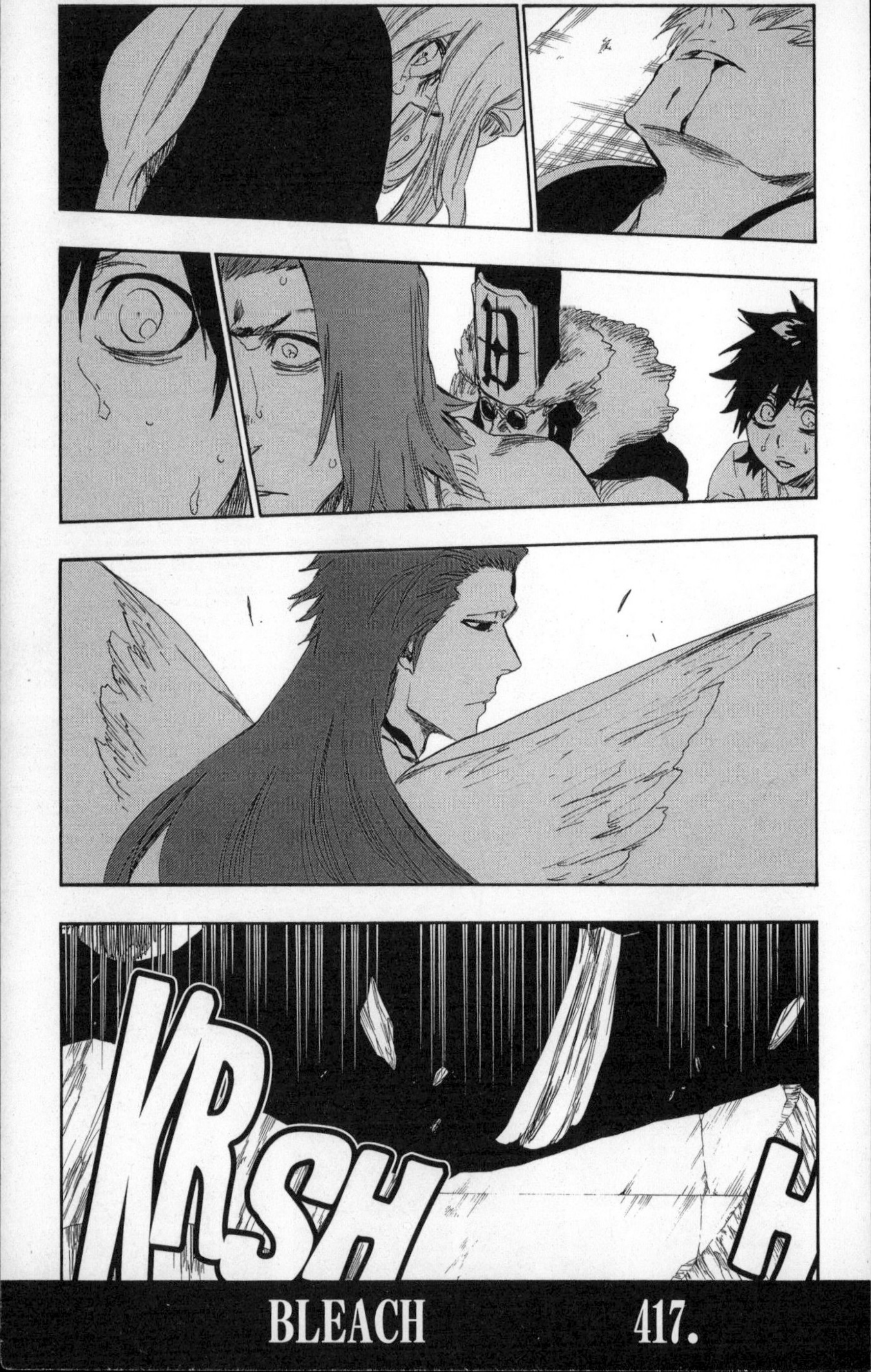
KRSH

BLEACH 417.

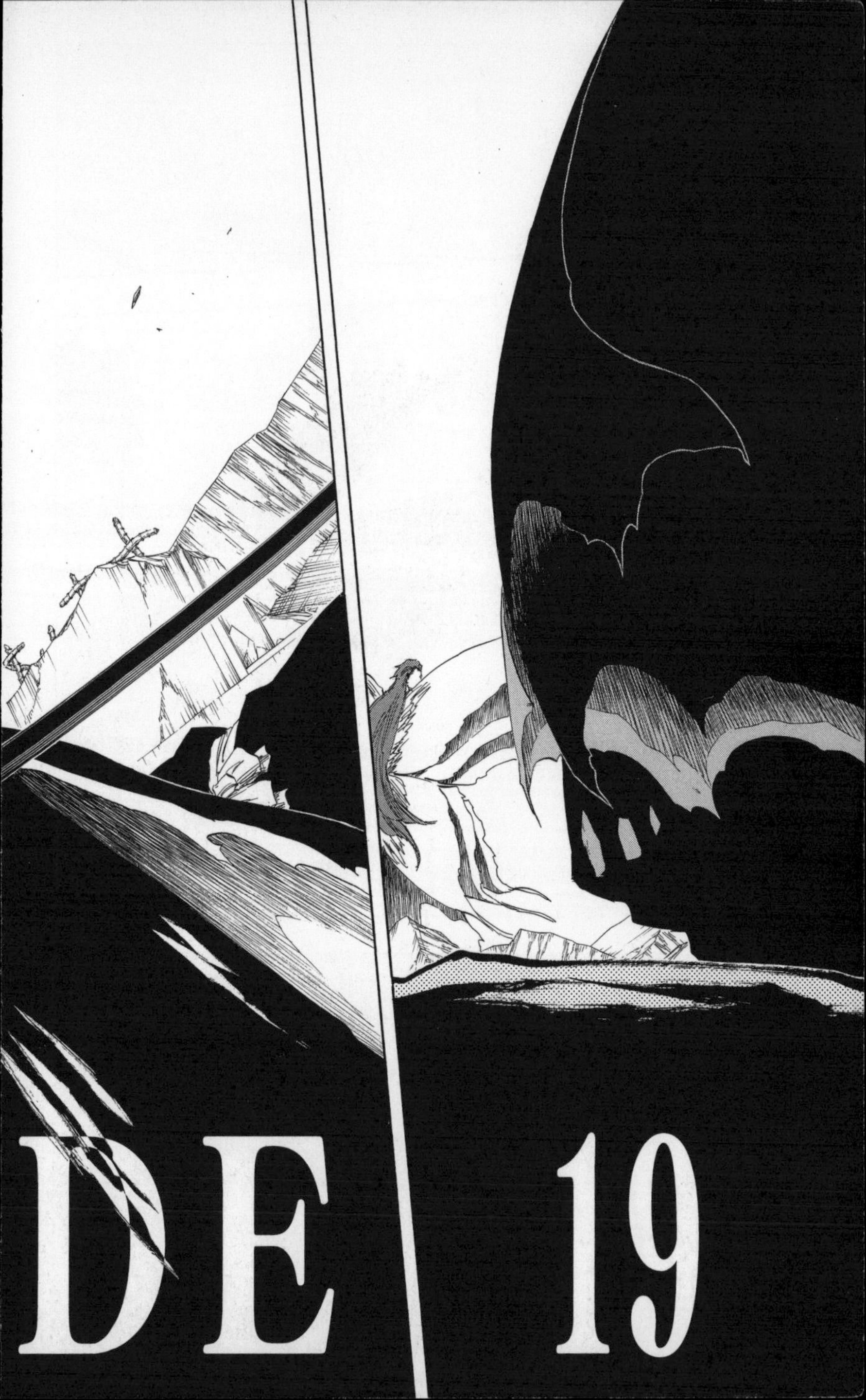
DE
19

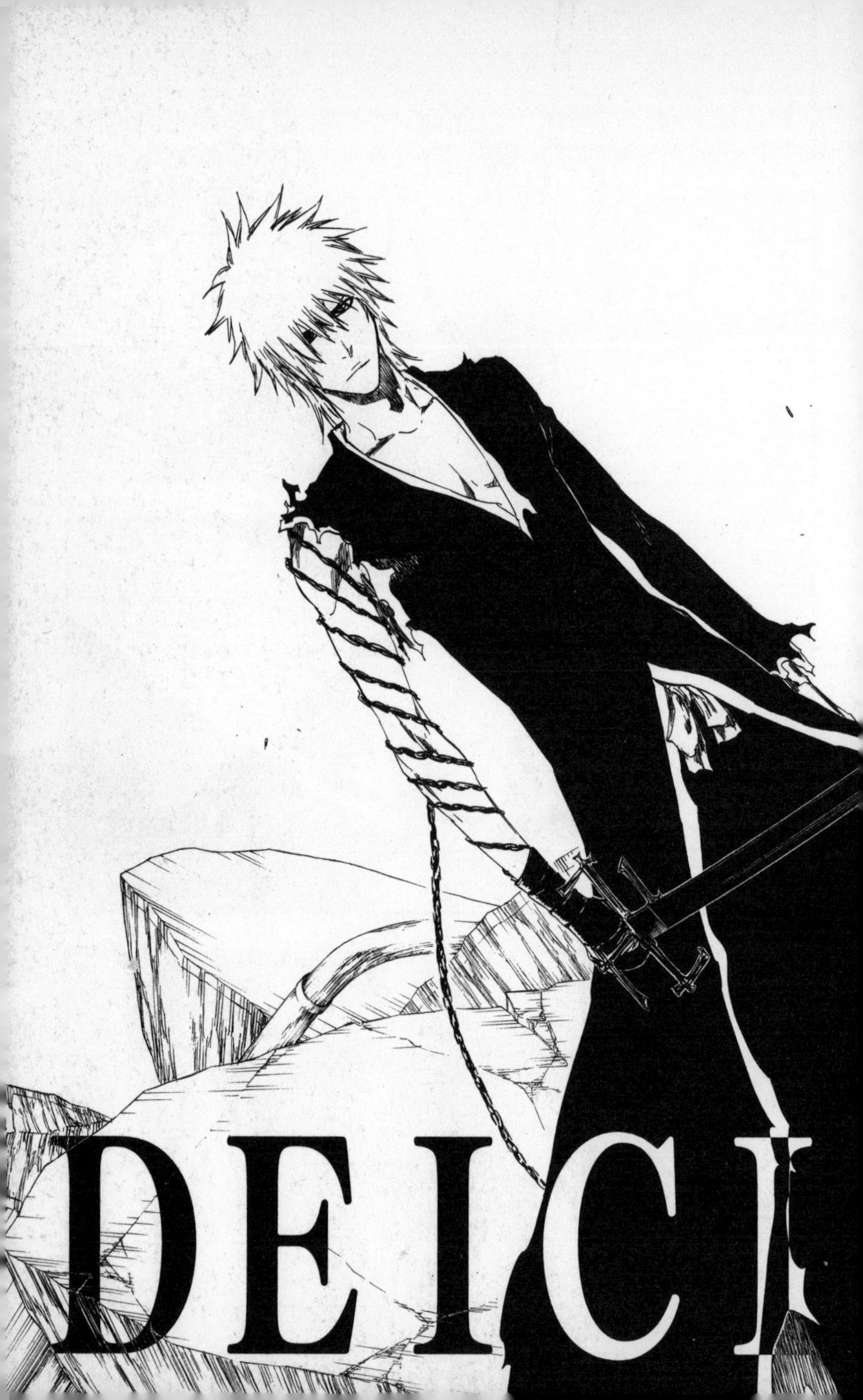
DEIC

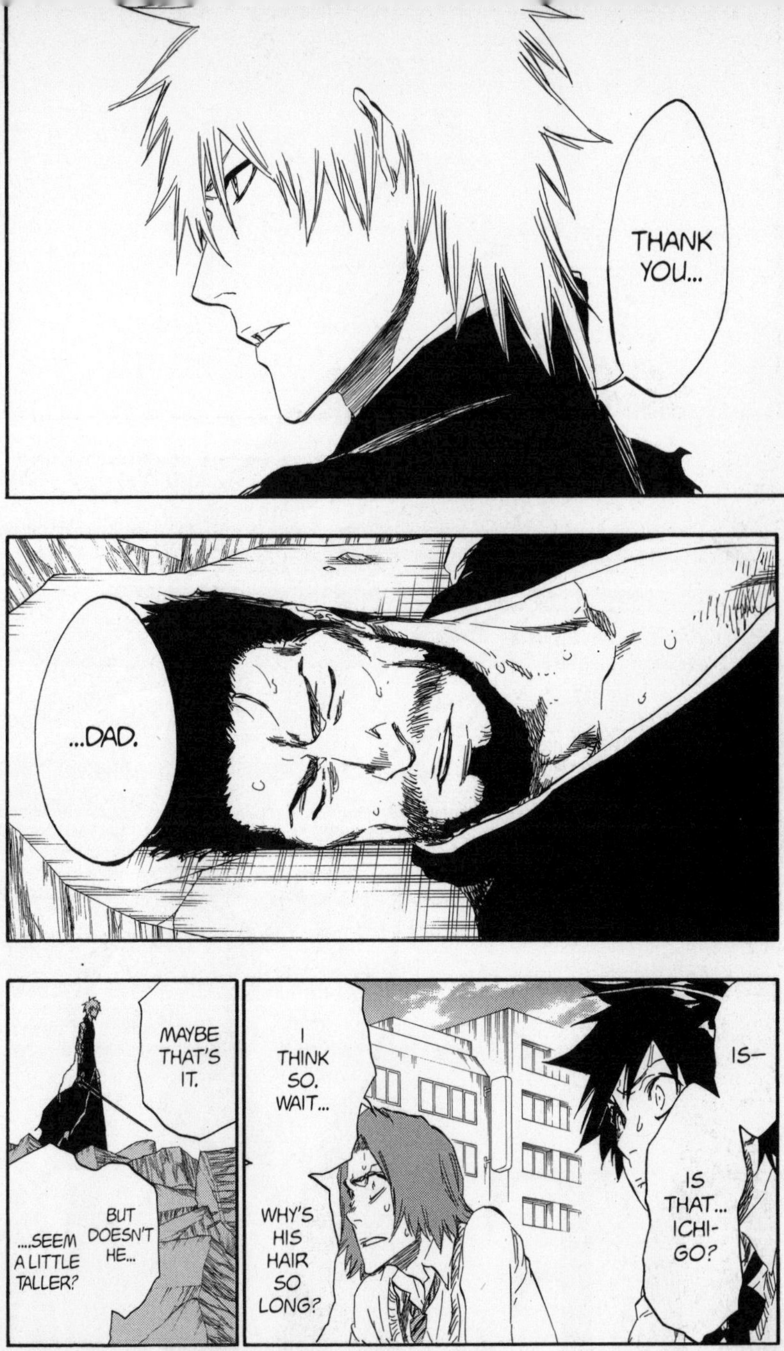
THANK YOU...
...DAD.
IS—
IS THAT... ICHI-GO?
I THINK SO. WAIT...
WHY'S HIS HAIR SO LONG?
MAYBE THAT'S IT.
BUT DOESN'T HE...
....SEEM A LITTLE TALLER?

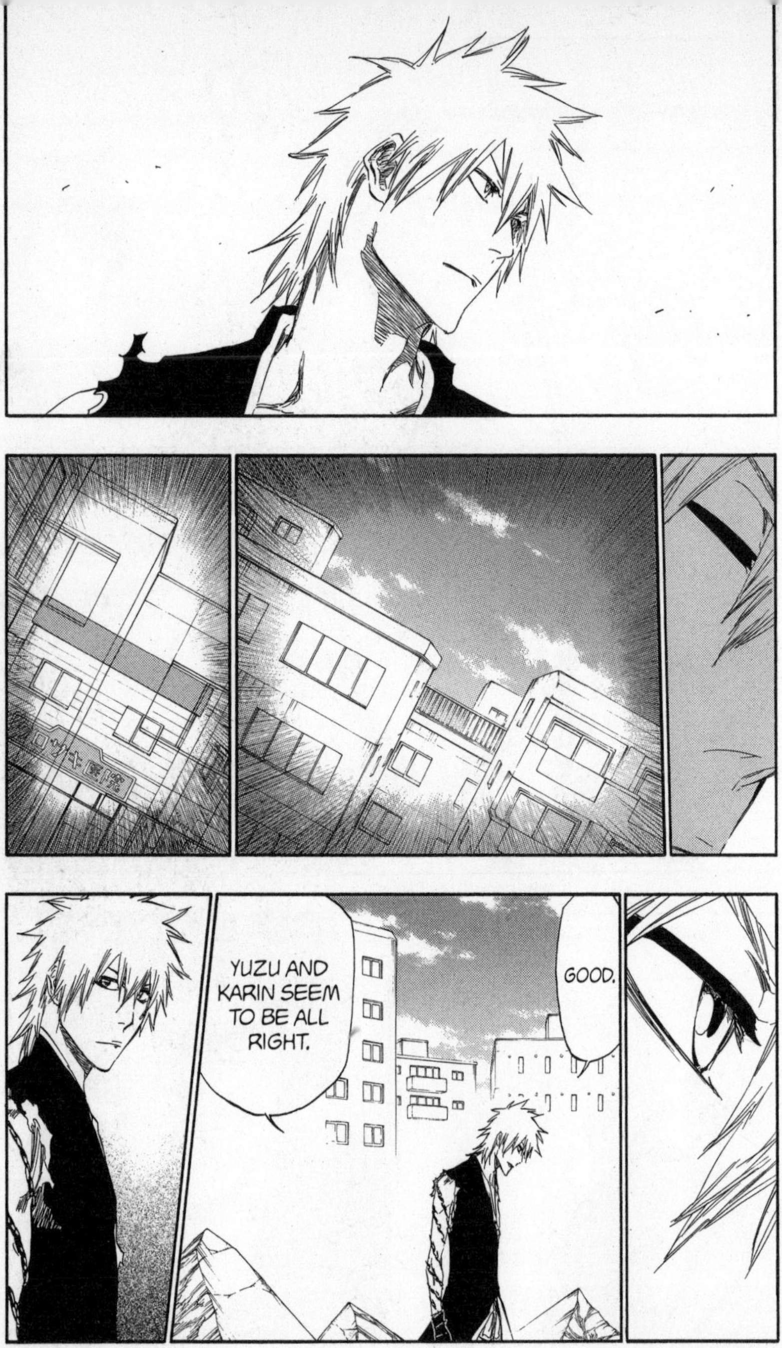
GOOD.
YUZU AND KARIN SEEM TO BE ALL RIGHT.

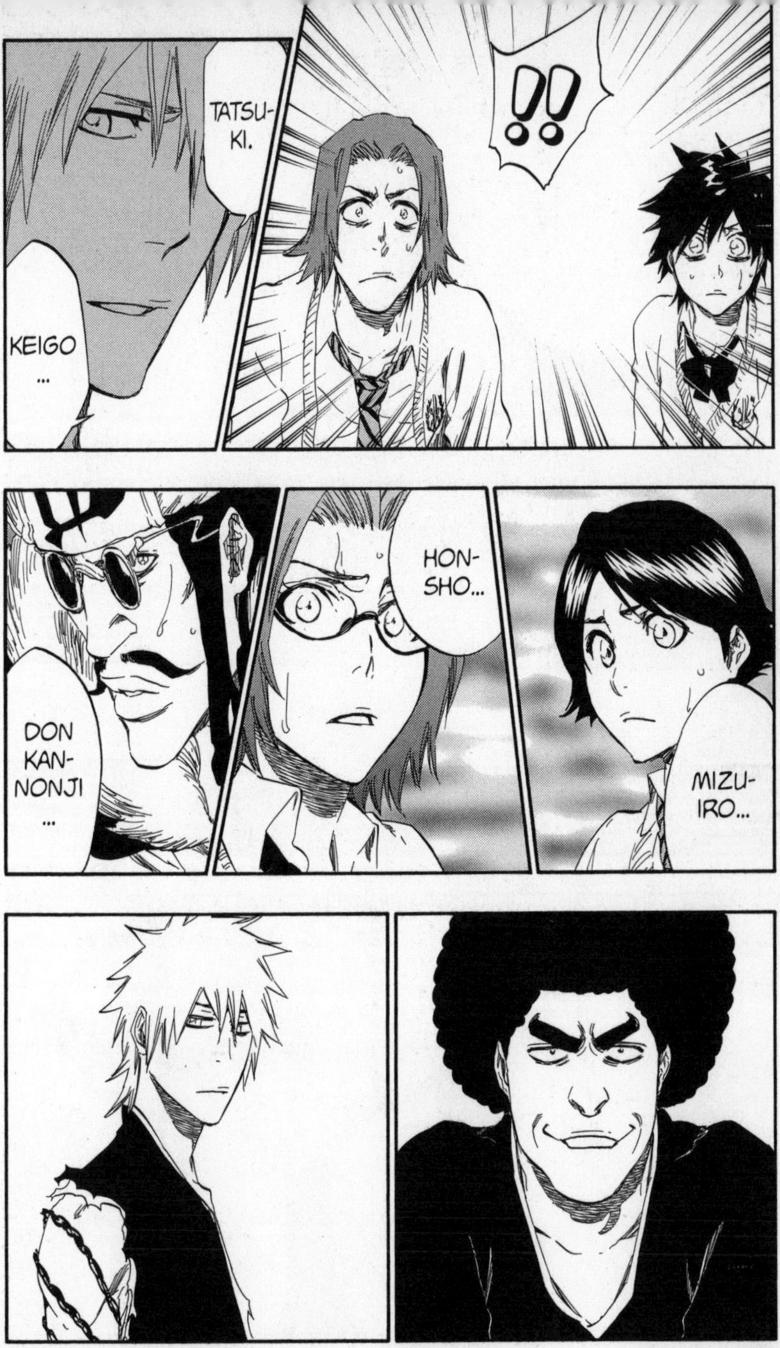
!!
TATSU-
KI.
KEIGO
...
MIZU-
IRO...
HON-
SHO...
DON
KAN-
NONJI
...

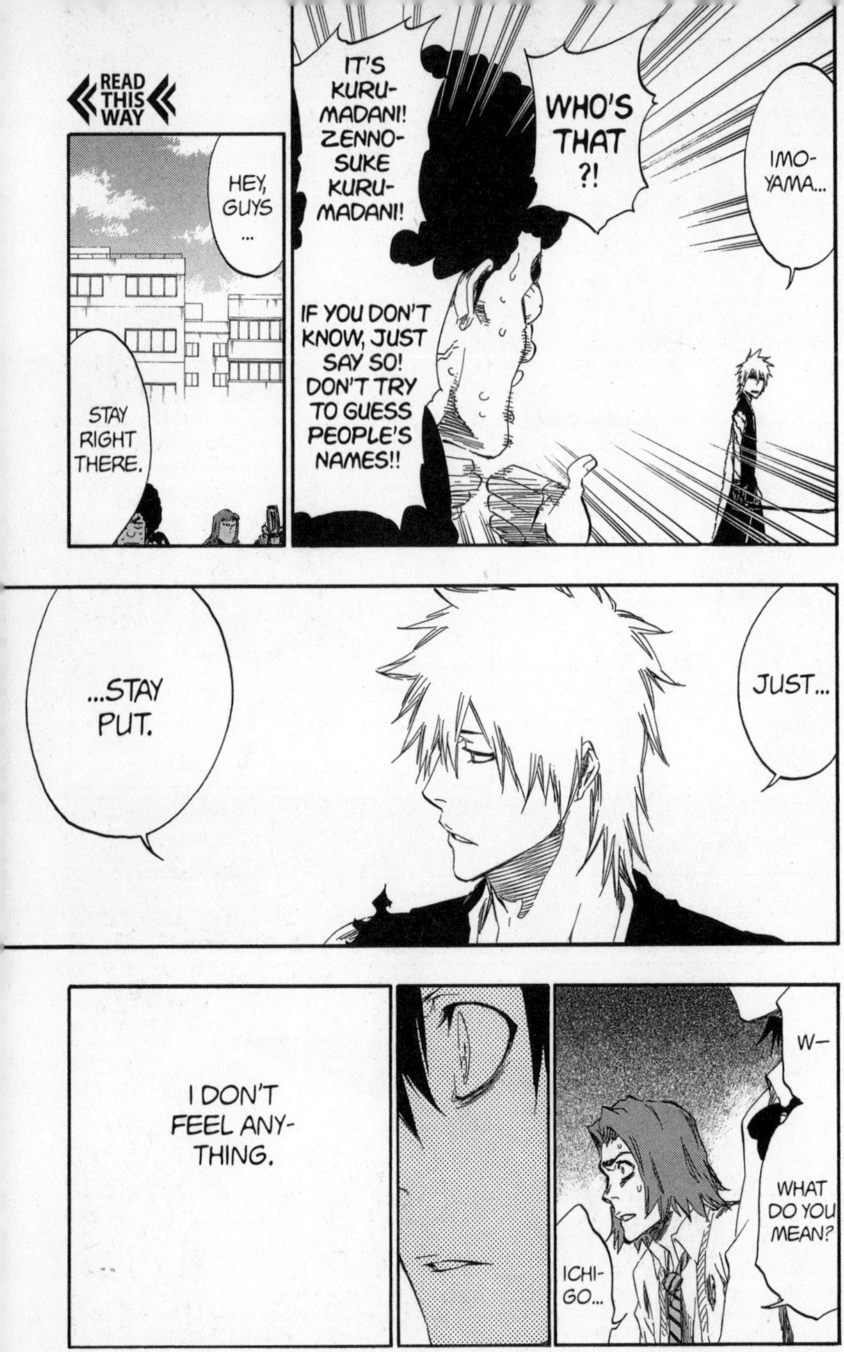
READ THIS WAY
IMO-YAMA...
WHO'S THAT ?!
IT'S KURU-MADANI! ZENNO-SUKE KURU-MADANI!
IF YOU DON'T KNOW, JUST SAY SO! DON'T TRY TO GUESS PEOPLE'S NAMES!!
HEY, GUYS ...
STAY RIGHT THERE.
JUST...
...STAY PUT.
W—
WHAT DO YOU MEAN?
ICHI-GO...
I DON'T FEEL ANY-THING.

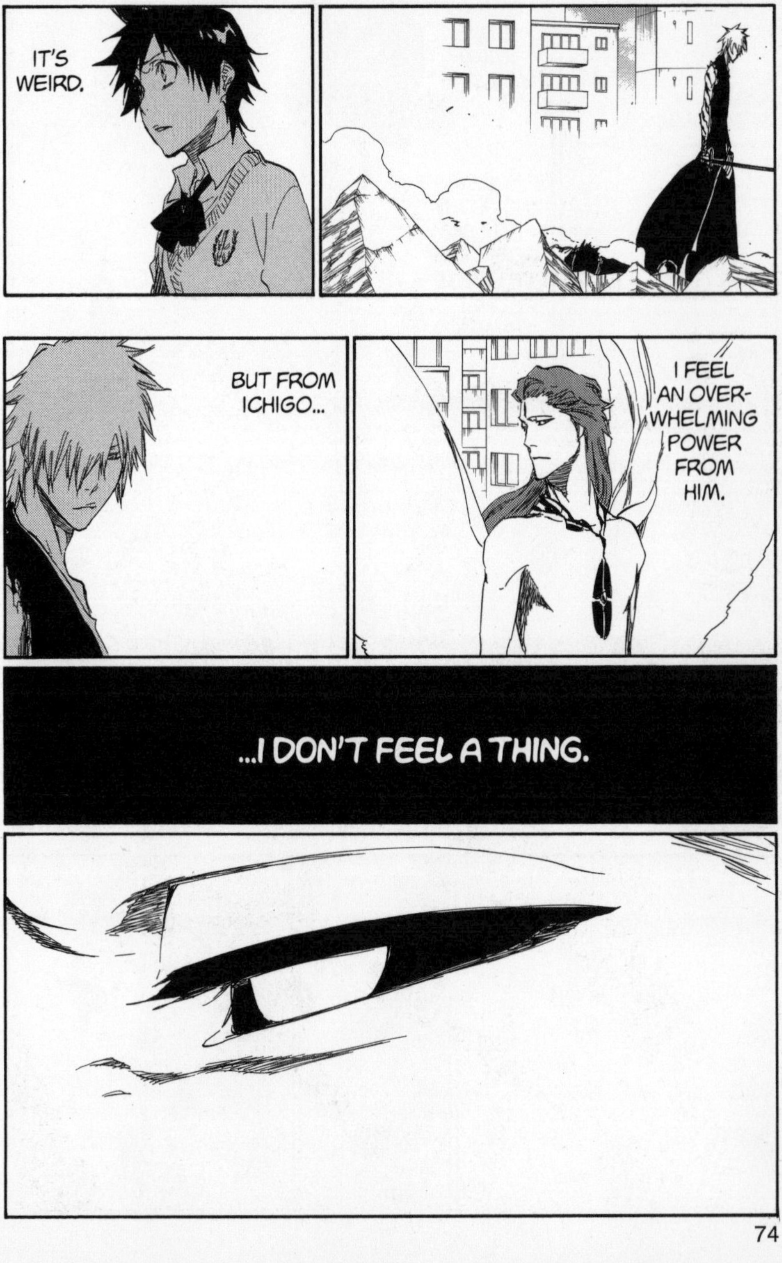
IT'S WEIRD.
BUT FROM ICHIGO...
I FEEL AN OVER-WHELMING POWER FROM HIM.
...I DON'T FEEL A THING.

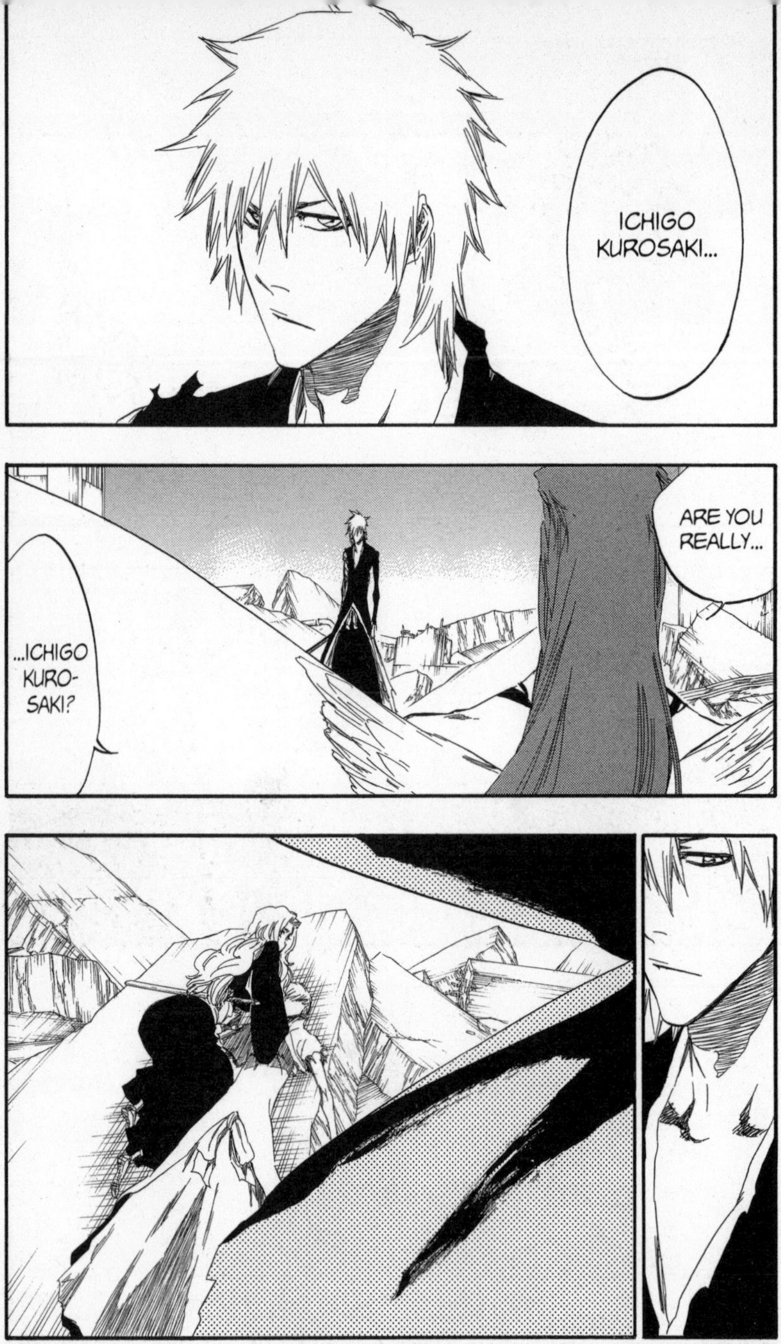
ICHIGO KUROSAKI...
ARE YOU REALLY...
...ICHIGO KURO-SAKI?

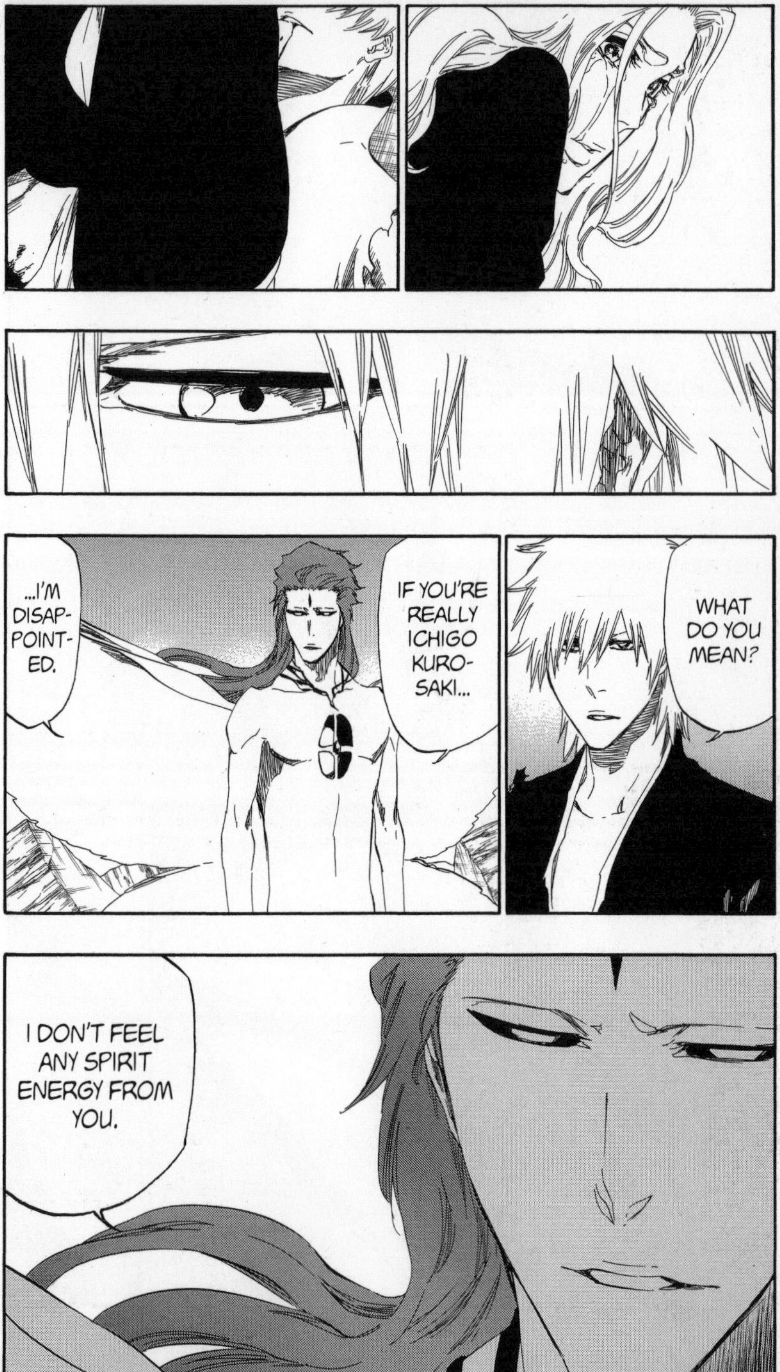
WHAT DO YOU MEAN?
IF YOU'RE REALLY ICHIGO KUROSAKI...
...I'M DISAPPOINTED.
I DON'T FEEL ANY SPIRIT ENERGY FROM YOU.

READ THIS WAY

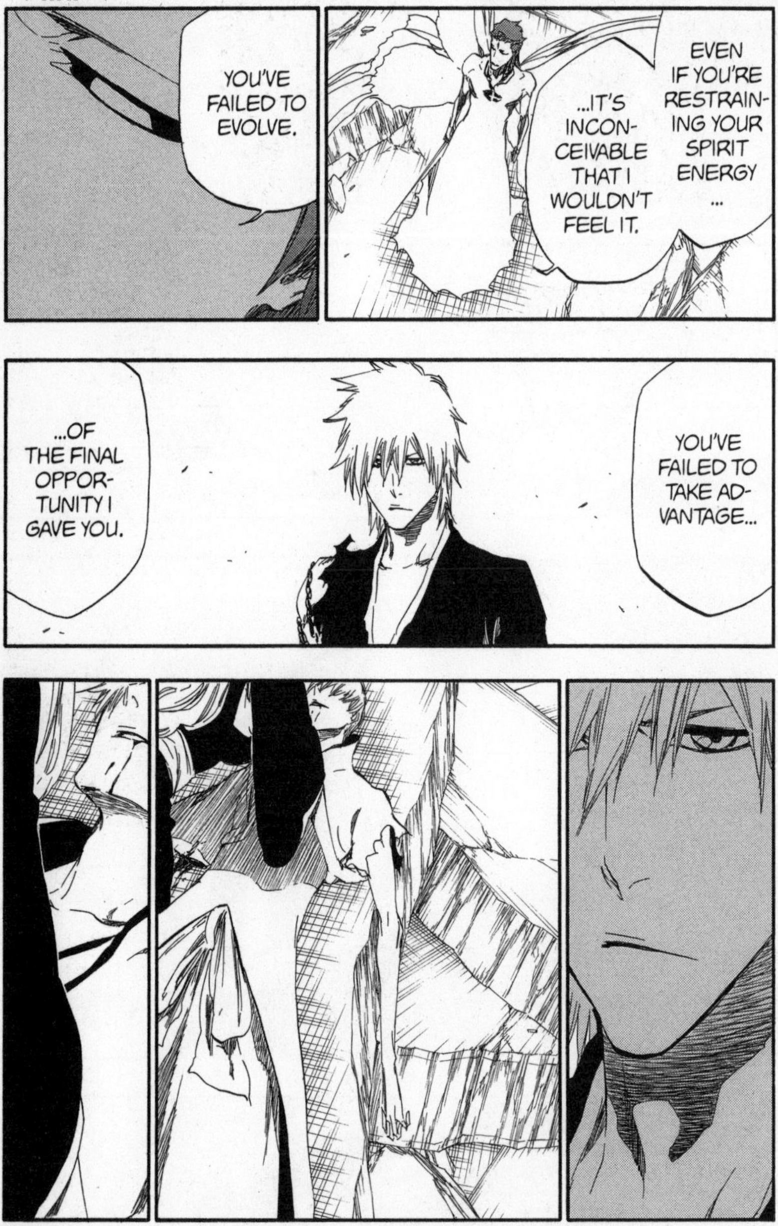
EVEN IF YOU'RE RESTRAINING YOUR SPIRIT ENERGY ...
...IT'S INCONCEIVABLE THAT I WOULDN'T FEEL IT.
YOU'VE FAILED TO EVOLVE.
YOU'VE FAILED TO TAKE ADVANTAGE...
...OF THE FINAL OPPORTUNITY I GAVE YOU.

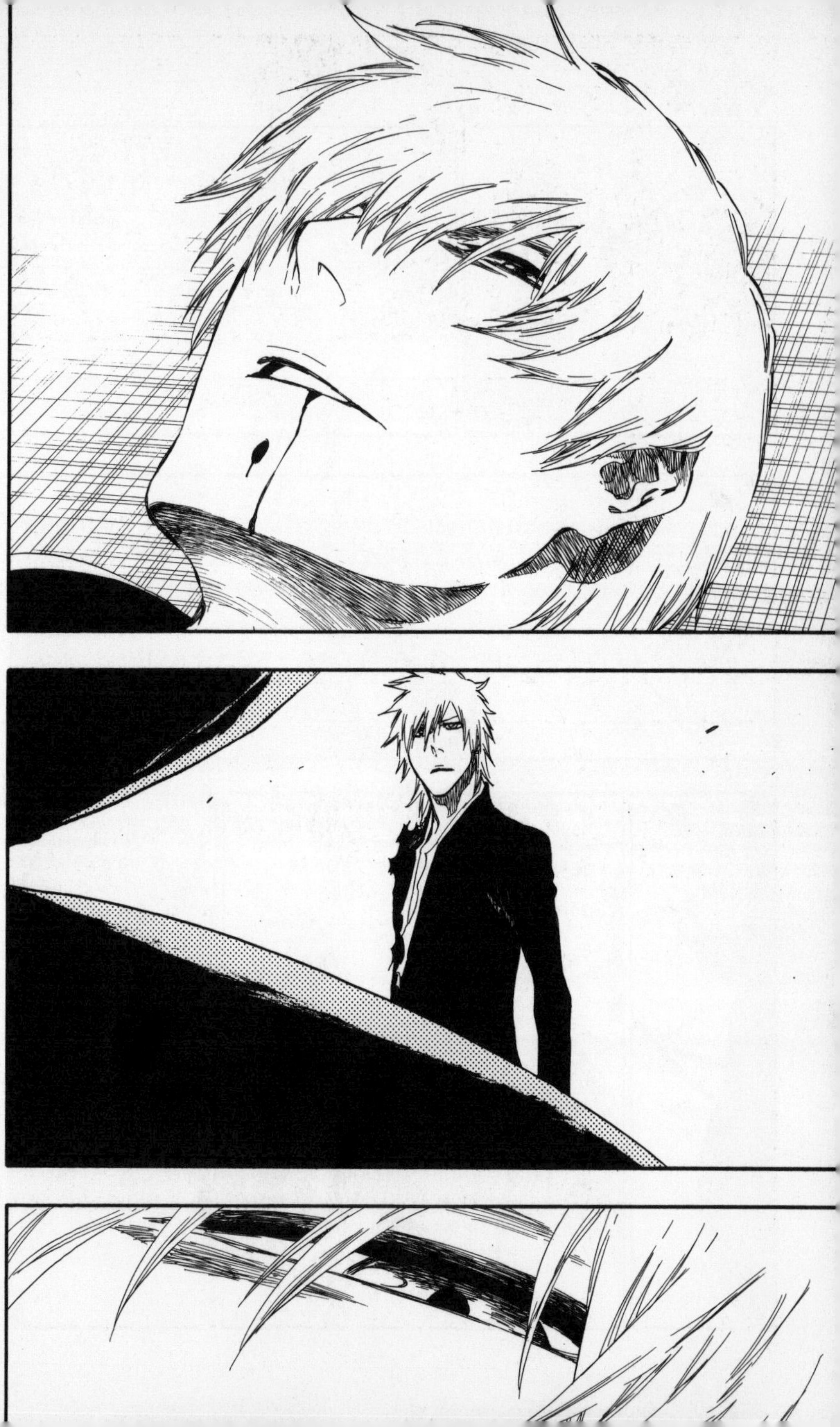

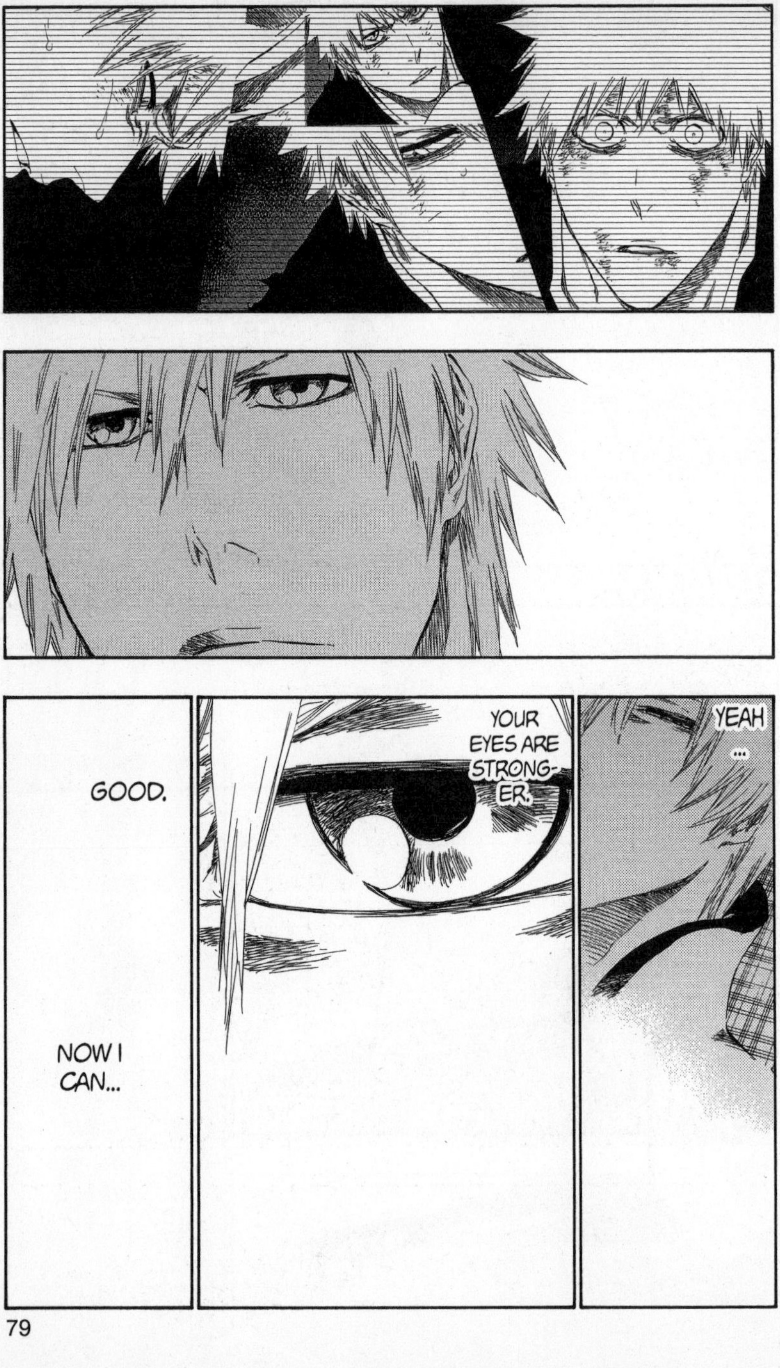
YEAH...
YOUR EYES ARE STRONGER.
GOOD.
NOW I CAN...

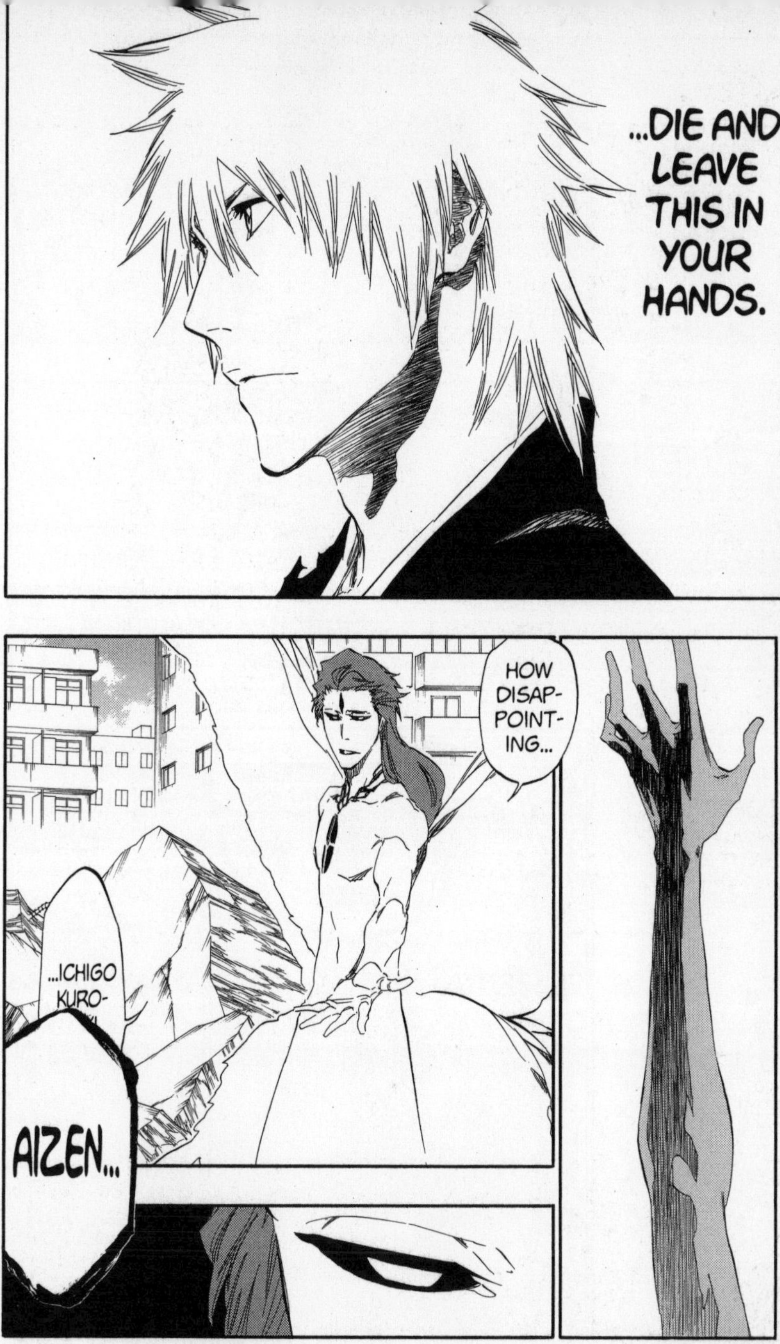
...DIE AND LEAVE THIS IN YOUR HANDS.
HOW DISAP-POINT-ING...
...ICHIGO KURO-
AIZEN...

READ THIS WAY

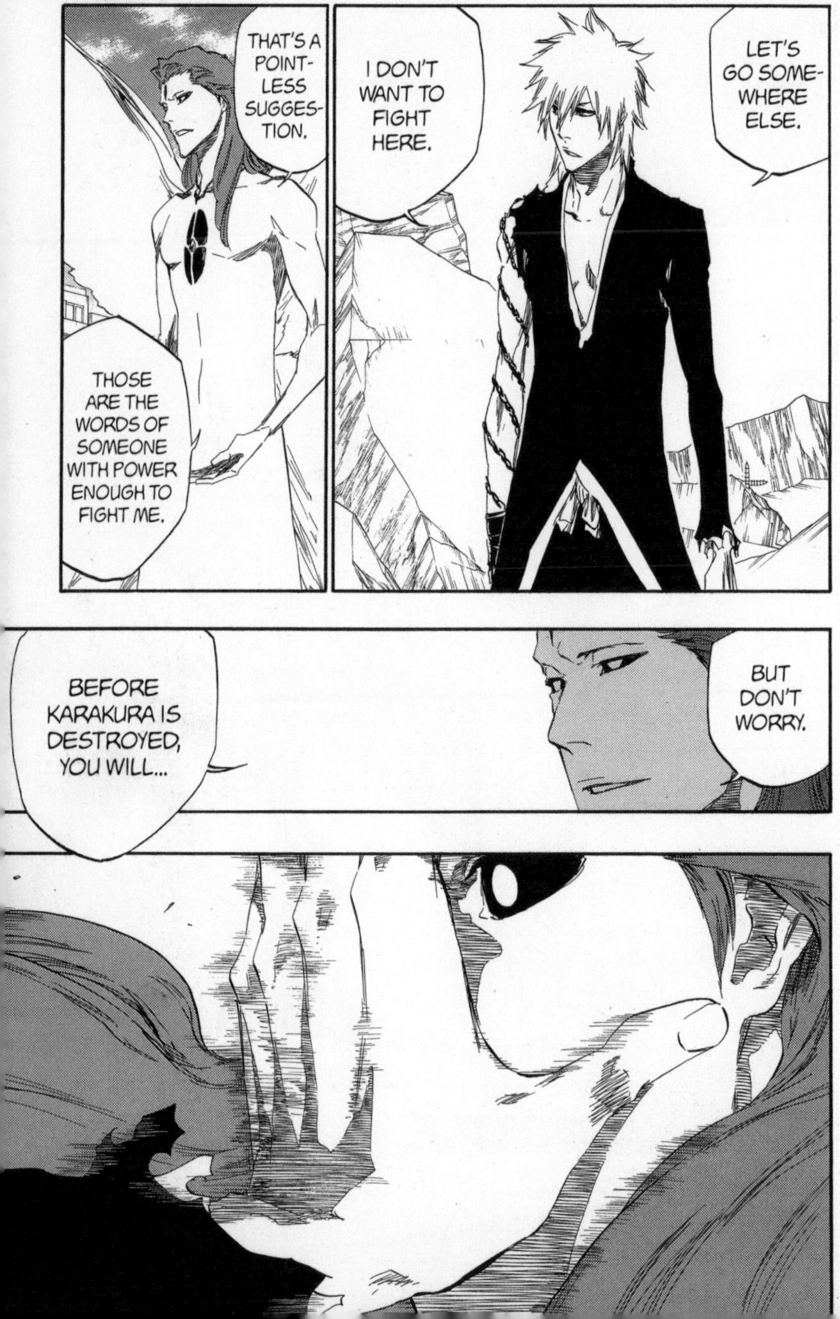
LET'S GO SOME-WHERE ELSE.
I DON'T WANT TO FIGHT HERE.
THAT'S A POINT-LESS SUGGES-TION.
THOSE ARE THE WORDS OF SOMEONE WITH POWER ENOUGH TO FIGHT ME.
BUT DON'T WORRY.
BEFORE KARAKURA IS DESTROYED, YOU WILL...

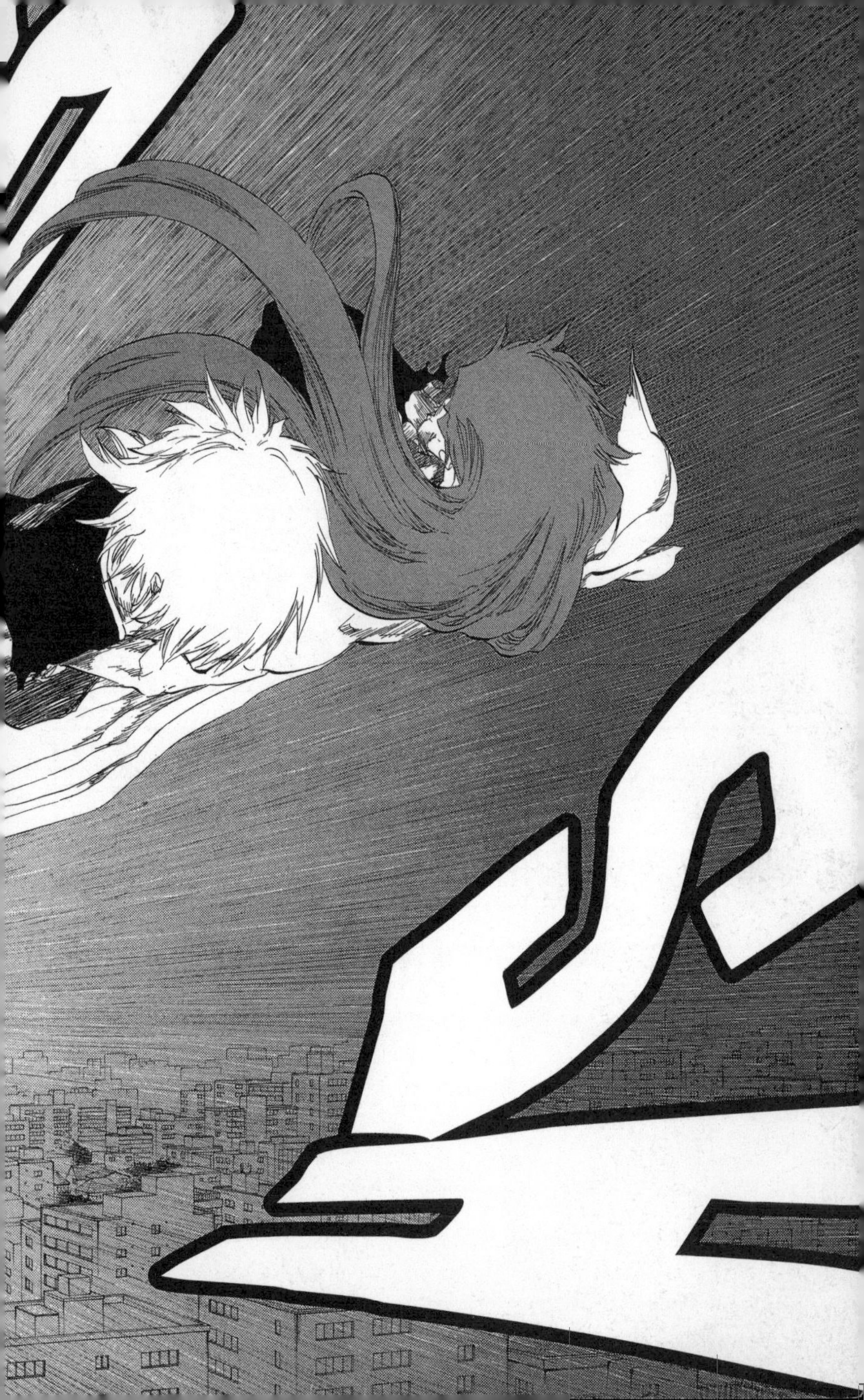

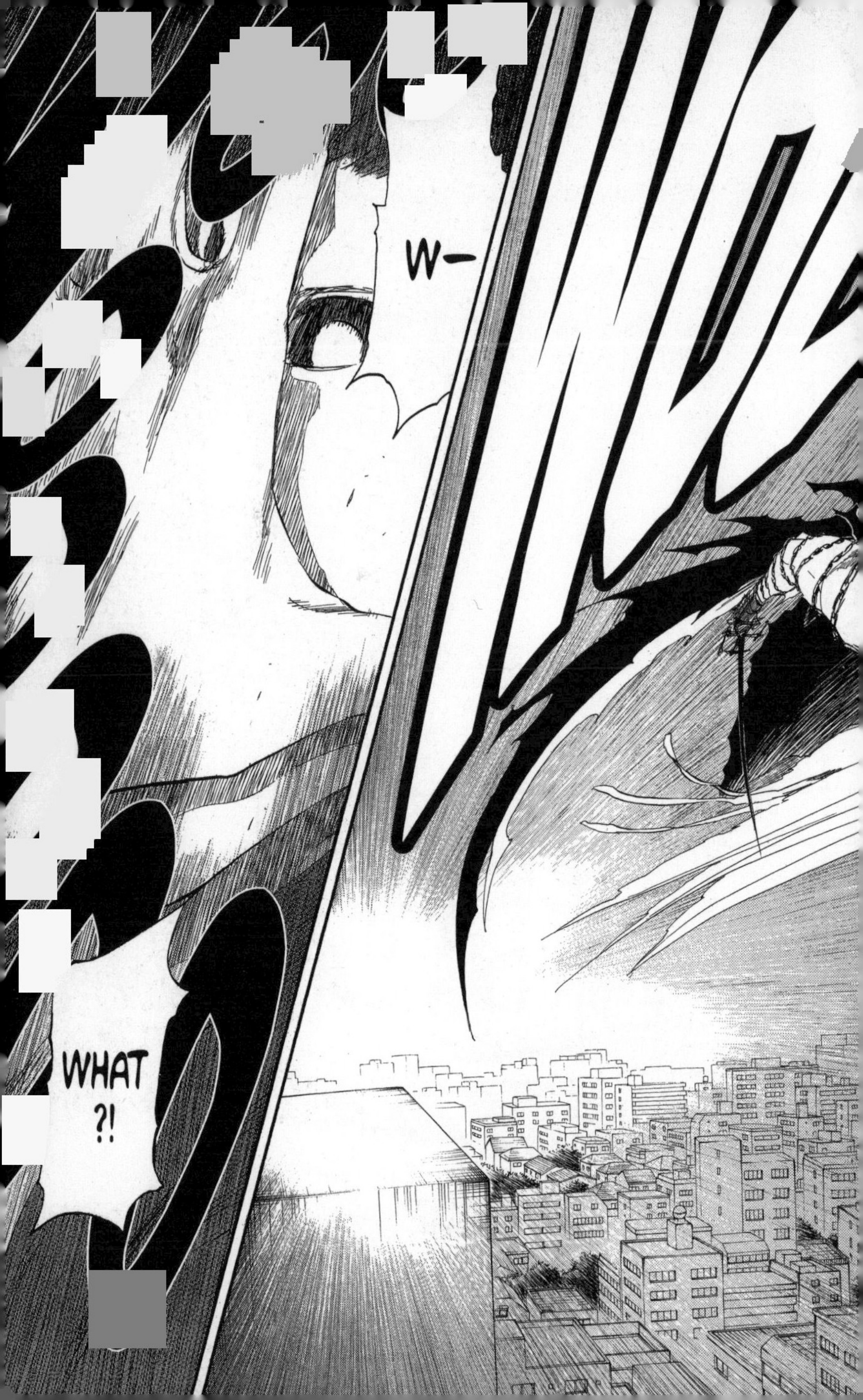
W–
WHAT ?!

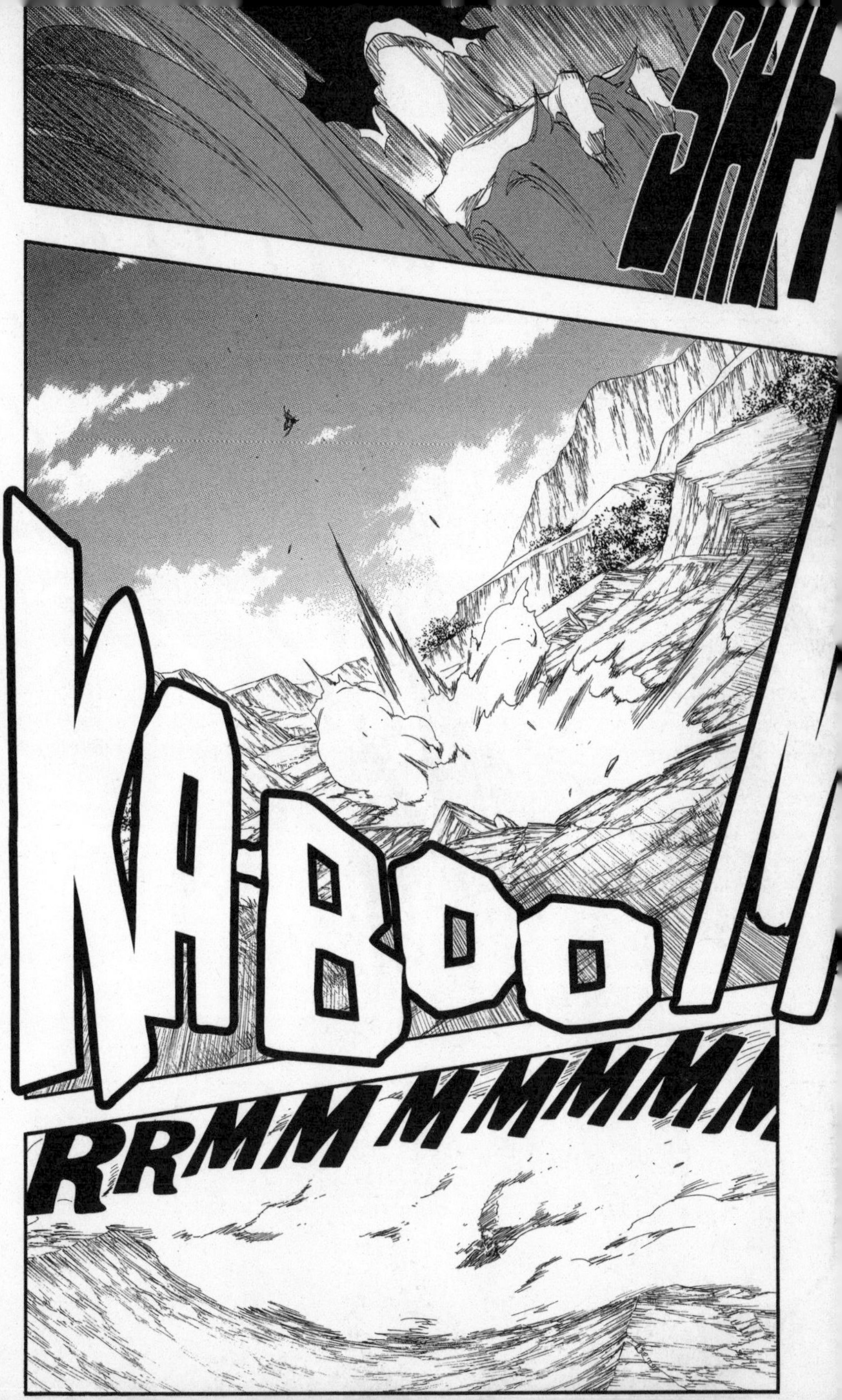
KA-BOO
RRMMMMMMMM

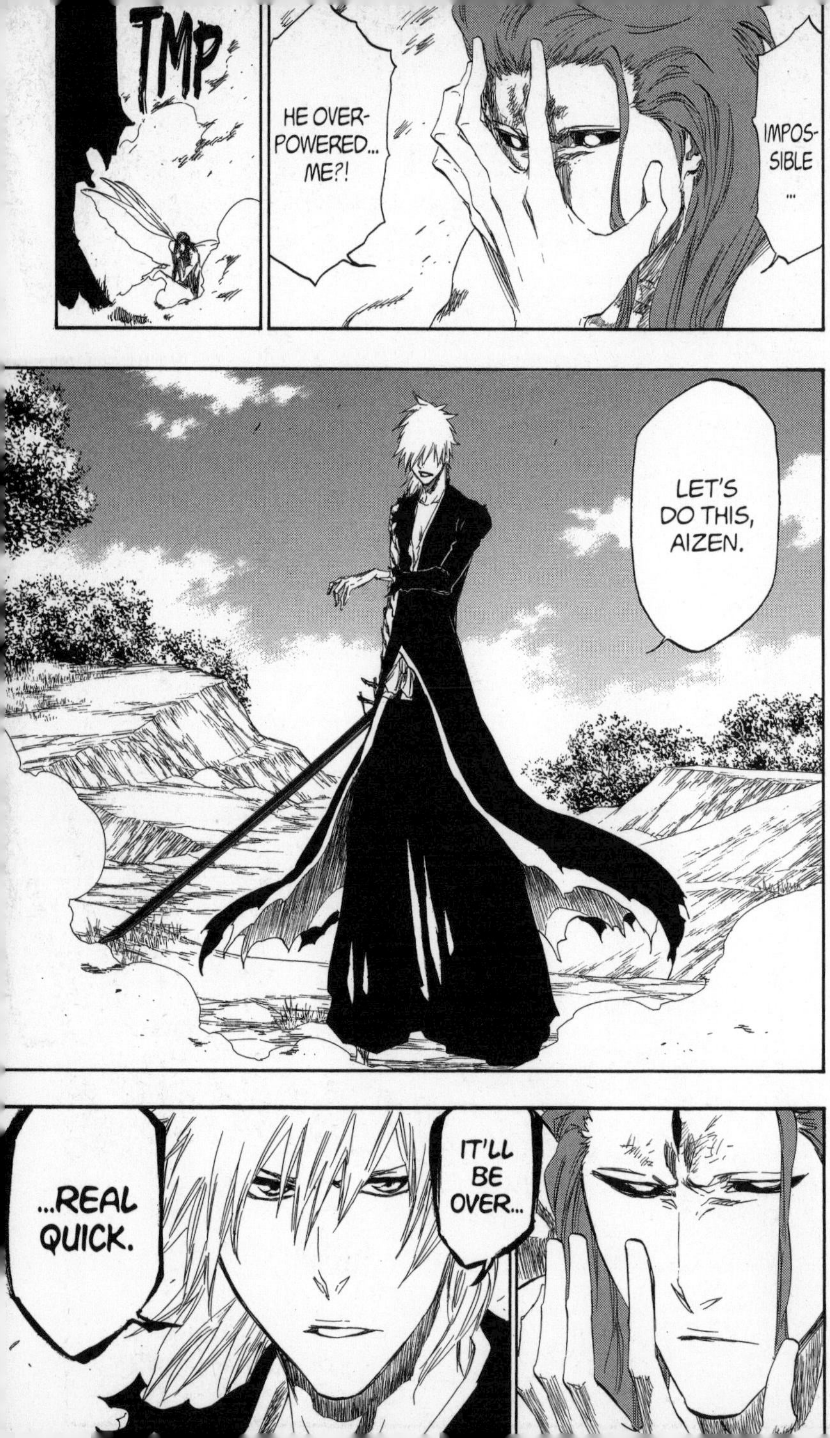
IMPOSSIBLE...
HE OVERPOWERED... ME?!
TMP
LET'S DO THIS, AIZEN.
IT'LL BE OVER...
...REAL QUICK.

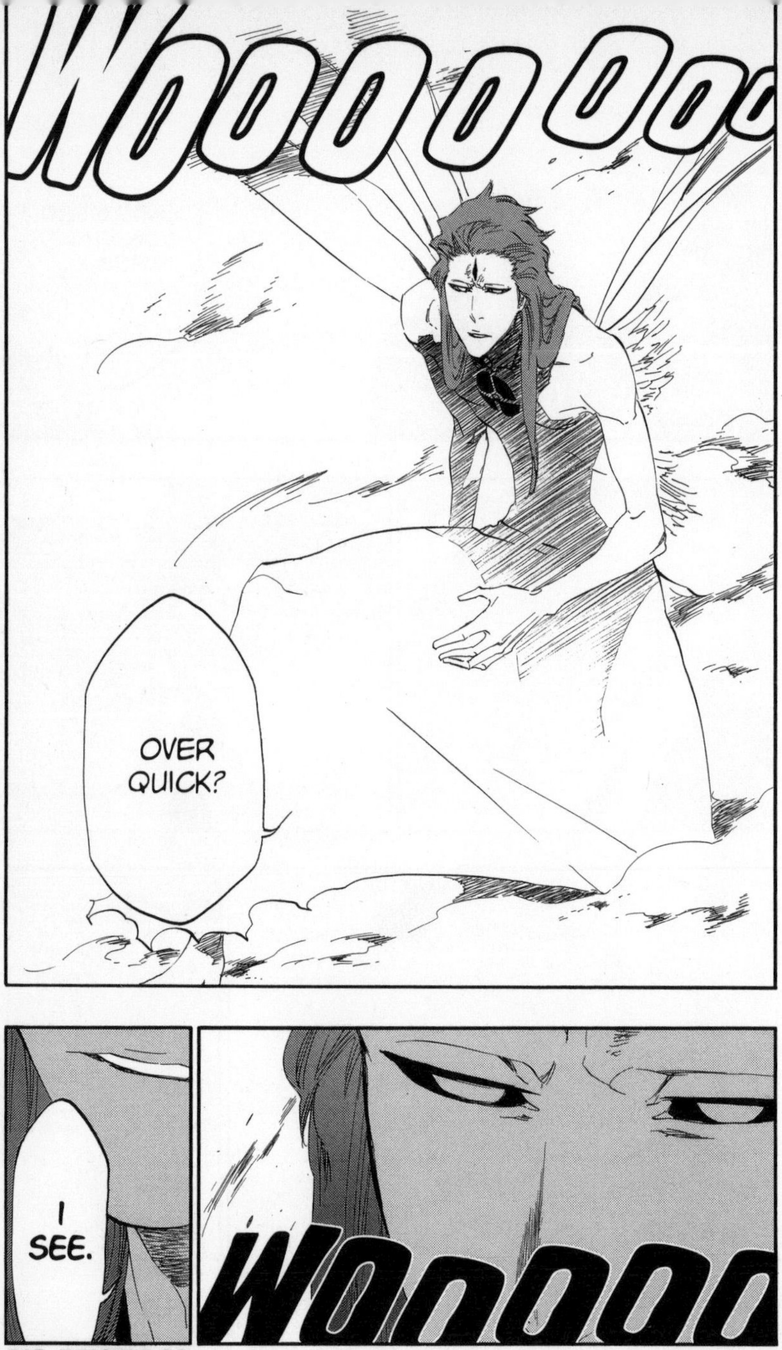
WOOOOOOO
OVER QUICK?
WOOOOOO
I SEE.

418. DEICIDE 20

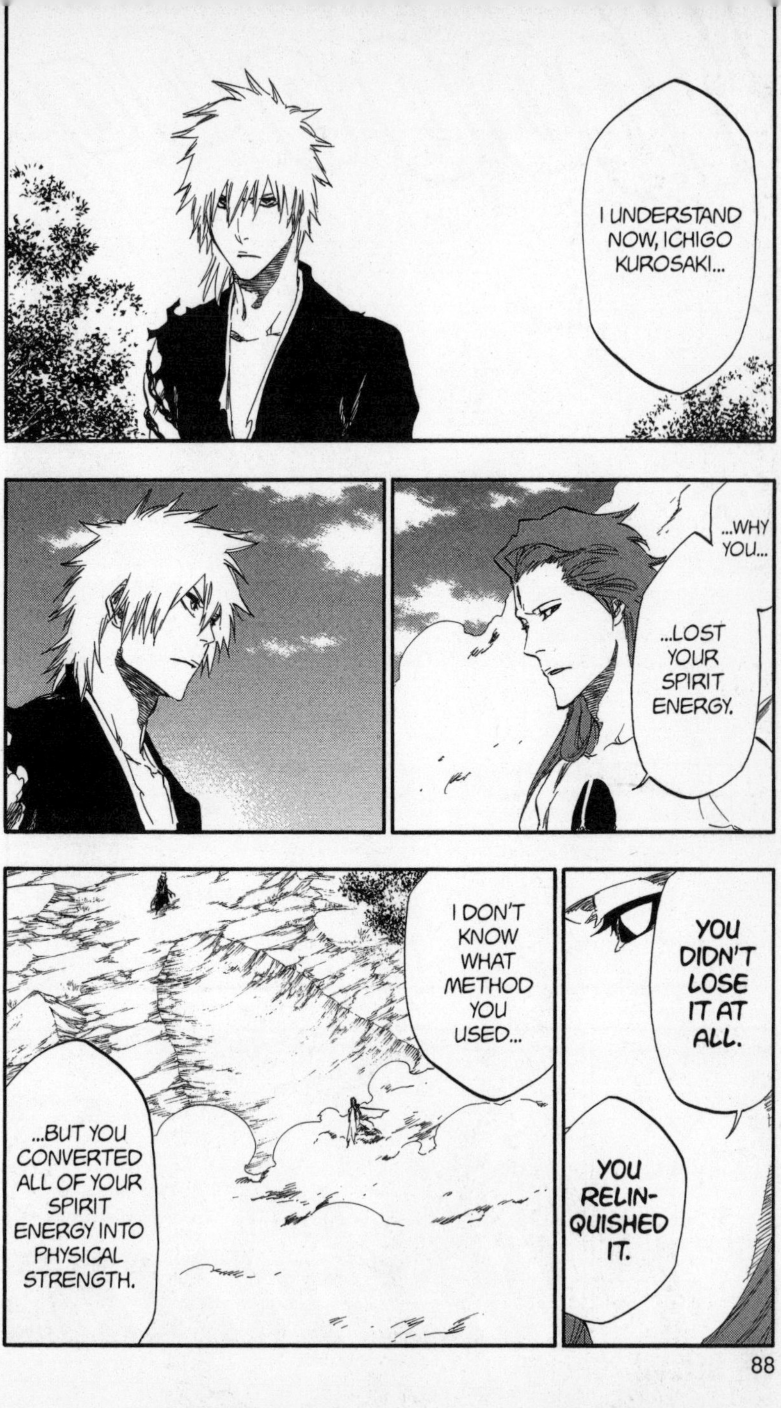
I UNDERSTAND NOW, ICHIGO KUROSAKI...
...WHY YOU...
...LOST YOUR SPIRIT ENERGY.
YOU DIDN'T LOSE IT AT ALL.
YOU RELINQUISHED IT.
I DON'T KNOW WHAT METHOD YOU USED...
...BUT YOU CONVERTED ALL OF YOUR SPIRIT ENERGY INTO PHYSICAL STRENGTH.

READ THIS WAY

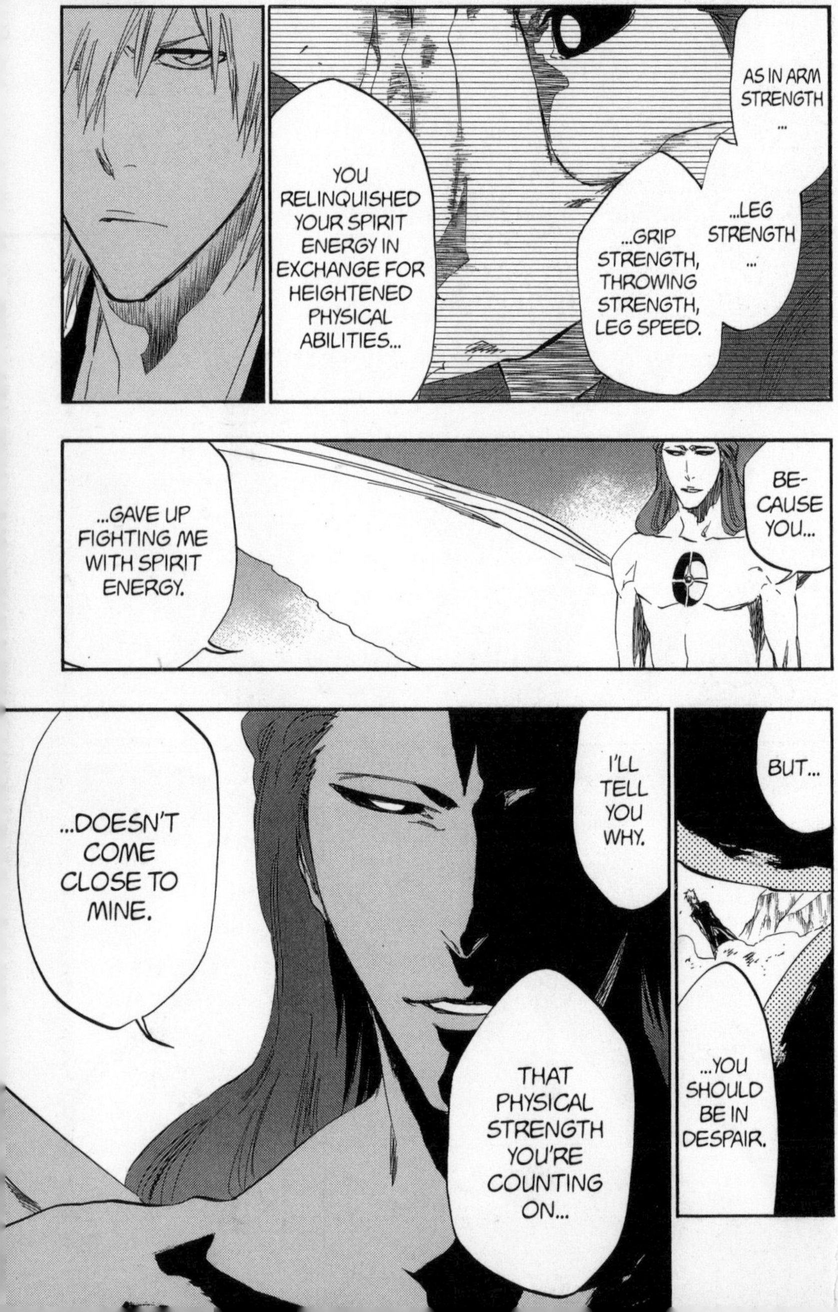
AS IN ARM STRENGTH ...
...LEG STRENGTH ...
...GRIP STRENGTH, THROWING STRENGTH, LEG SPEED.
YOU RELINQUISHED YOUR SPIRIT ENERGY IN EXCHANGE FOR HEIGHTENED PHYSICAL ABILITIES...
BE-CAUSE YOU...
...GAVE UP FIGHTING ME WITH SPIRIT ENERGY.
BUT...
...YOU SHOULD BE IN DESPAIR.
I'LL TELL YOU WHY.
THAT PHYSICAL STRENGTH YOU'RE COUNTING ON...
...DOESN'T COME CLOSE TO MINE.

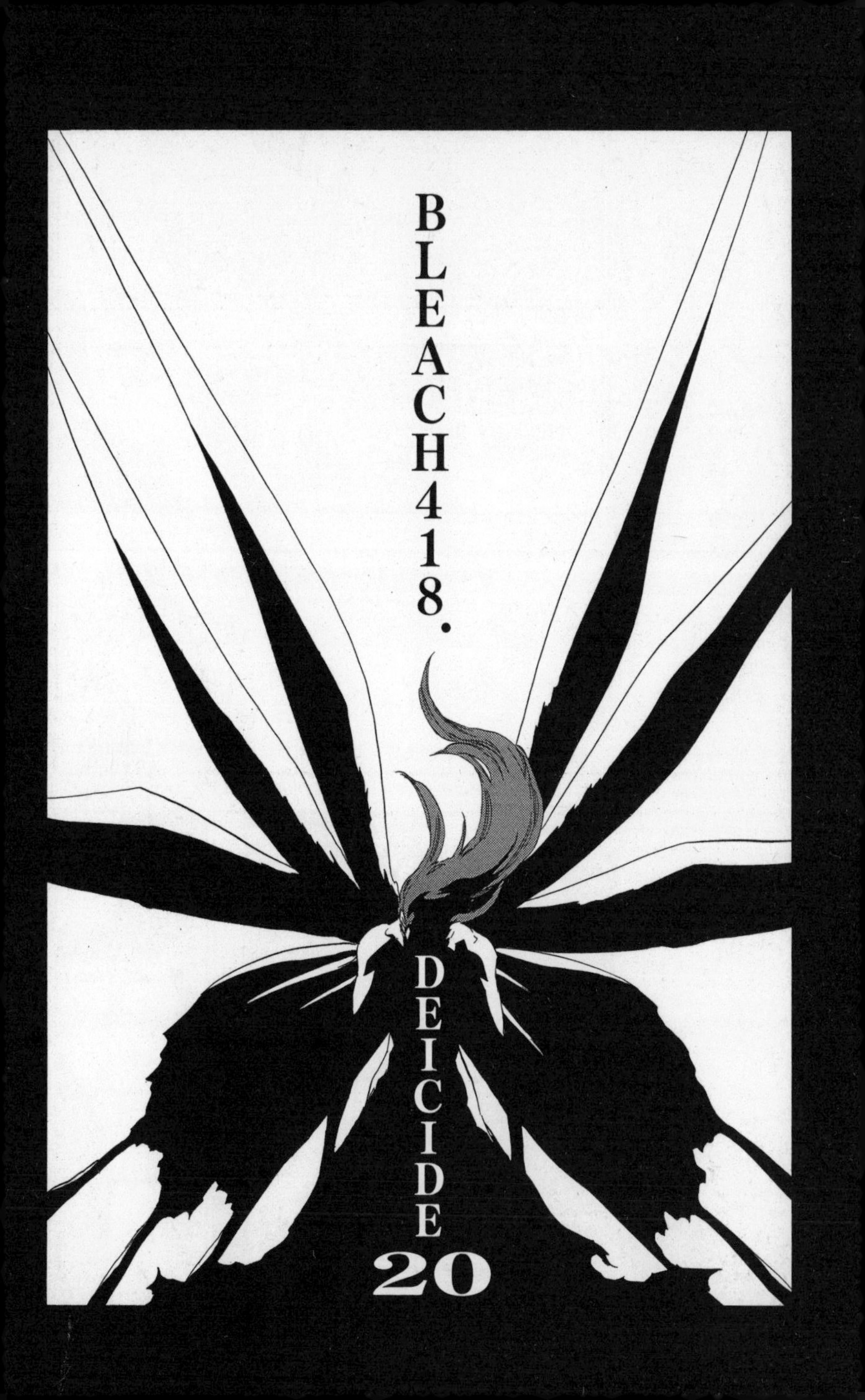
BLEACH418.
DEICIDE20

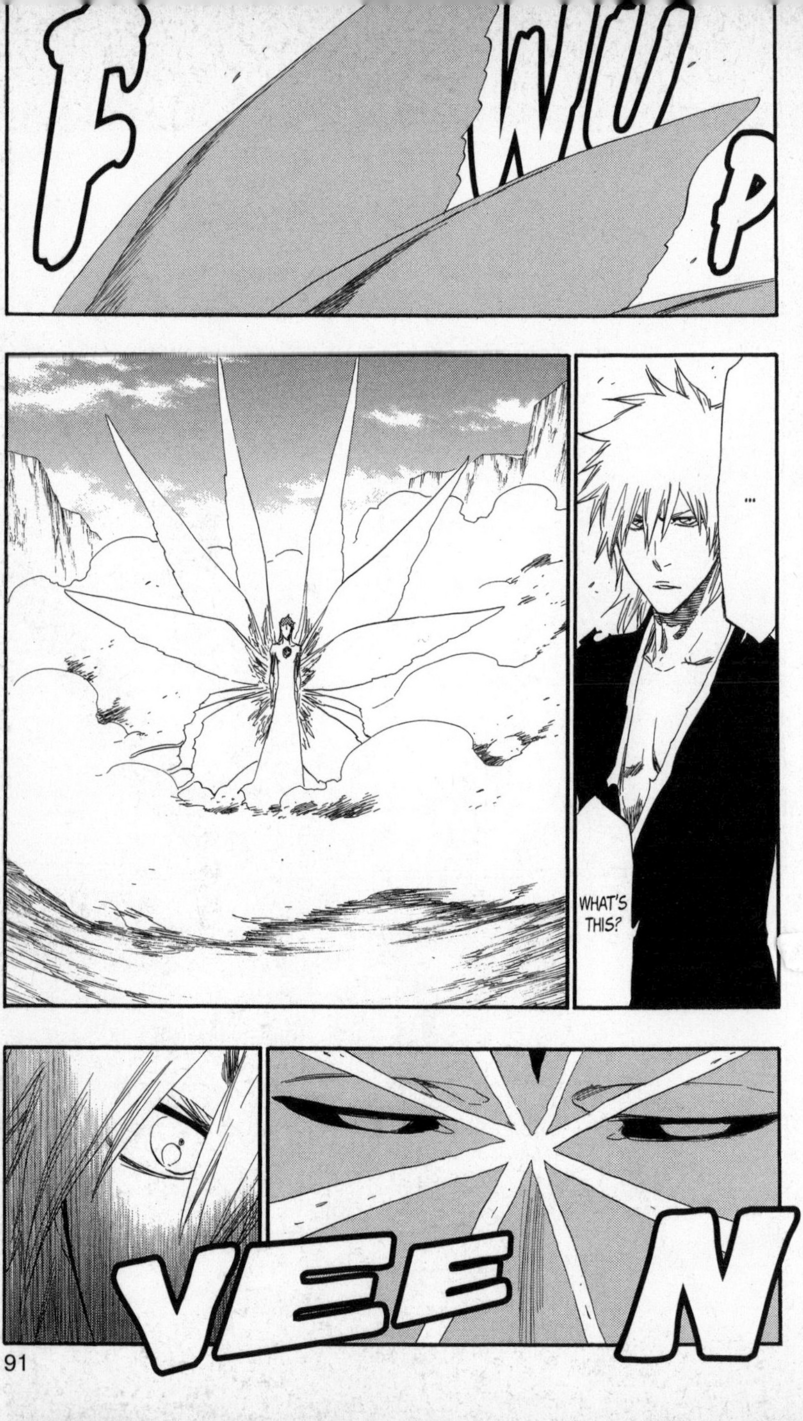
FWOP
...
WHAT'S THIS?
VEEN

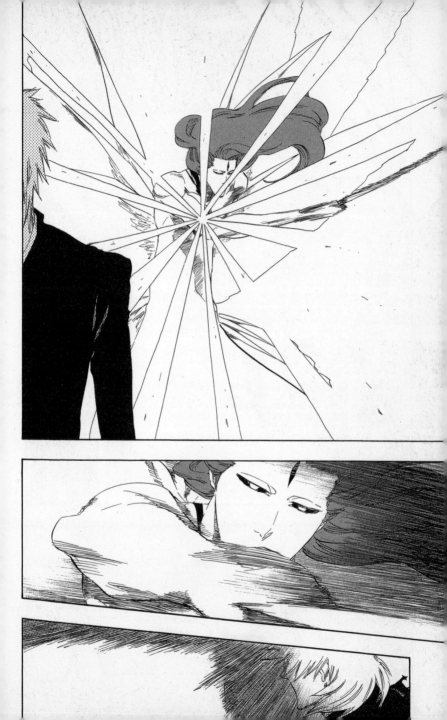

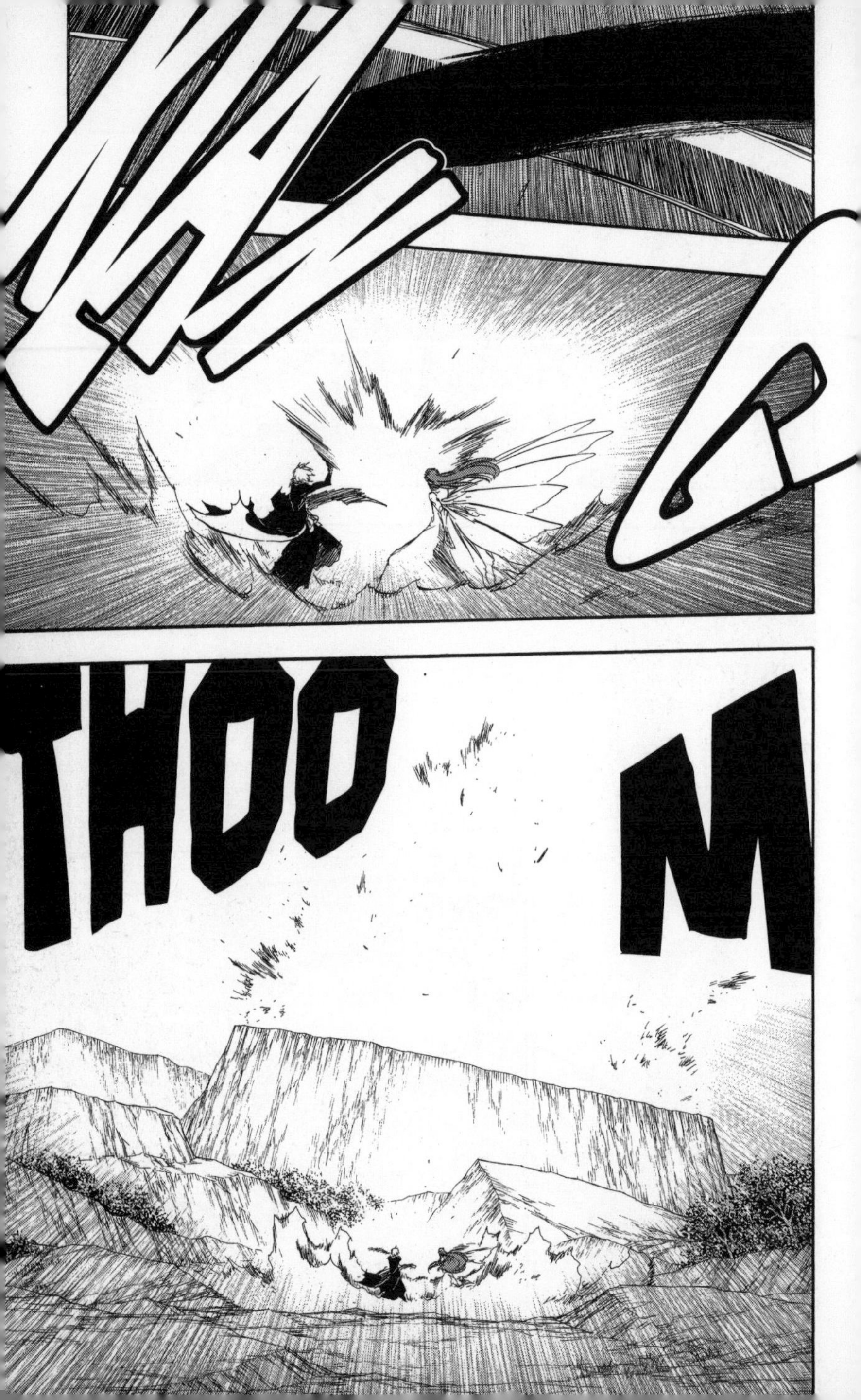
THOOM

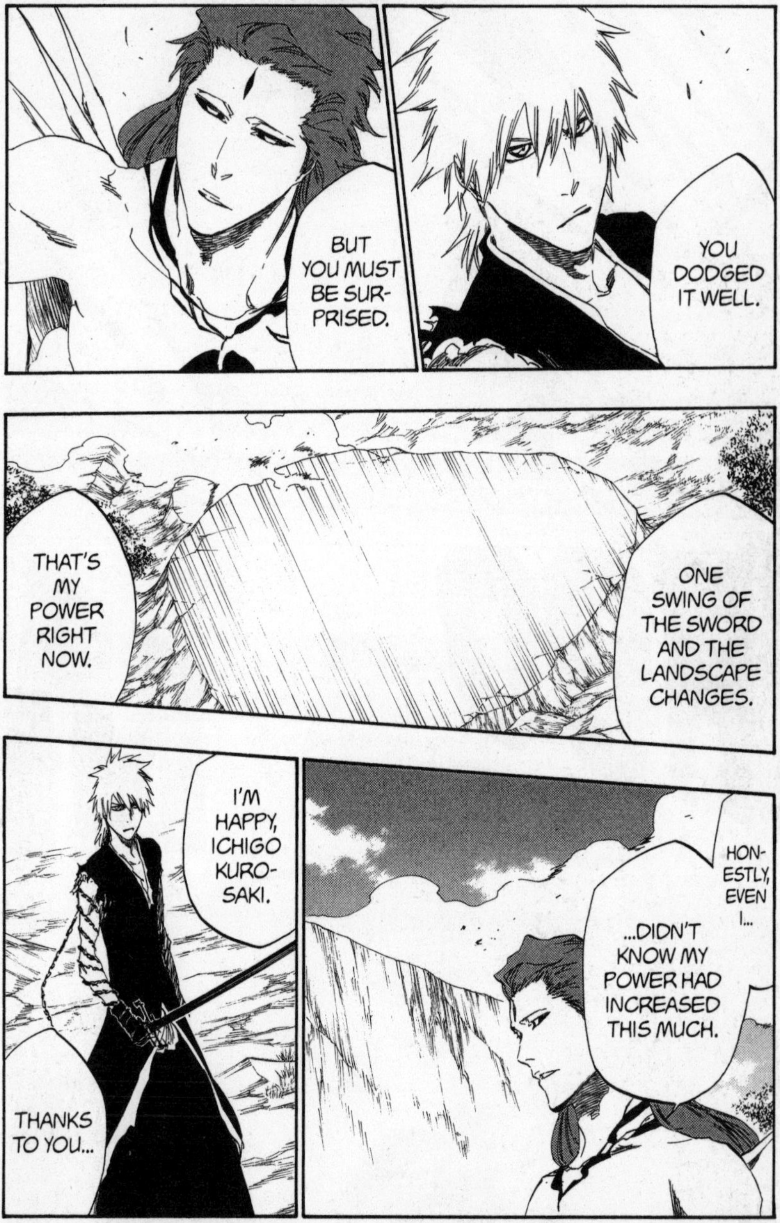
YOU DODGED IT WELL.
BUT YOU MUST BE SURPRISED.
ONE SWING OF THE SWORD AND THE LANDSCAPE CHANGES.
THAT'S MY POWER RIGHT NOW.
HONESTLY, EVEN I...
...DIDN'T KNOW MY POWER HAD INCREASED THIS MUCH.
I'M HAPPY, ICHIGO KUROSAKI.
THANKS TO YOU...

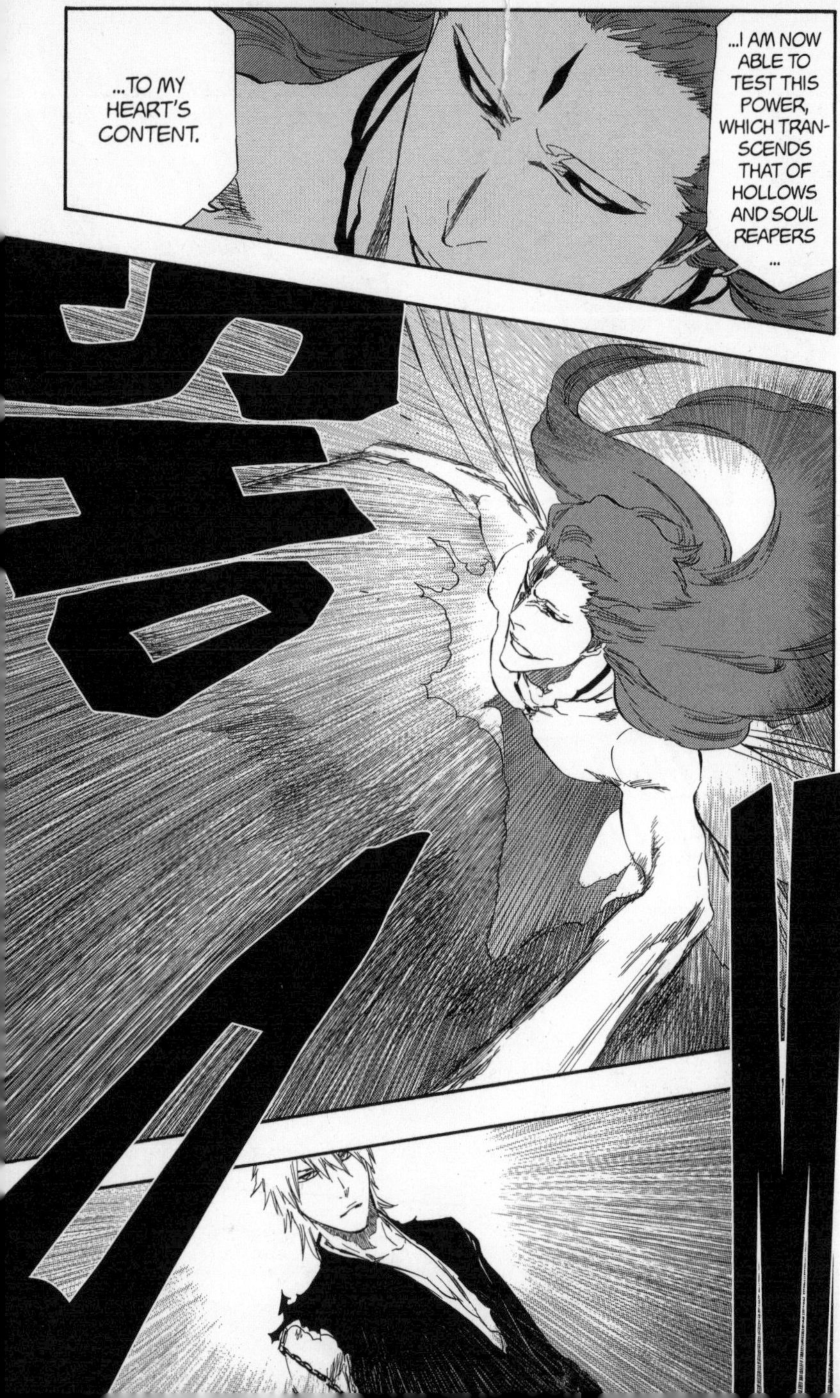
...I AM NOW ABLE TO TEST THIS POWER, WHICH TRAN-SCENDS THAT OF HOLLOWS AND SOUL REAPERS ...
...TO MY HEART'S CONTENT.

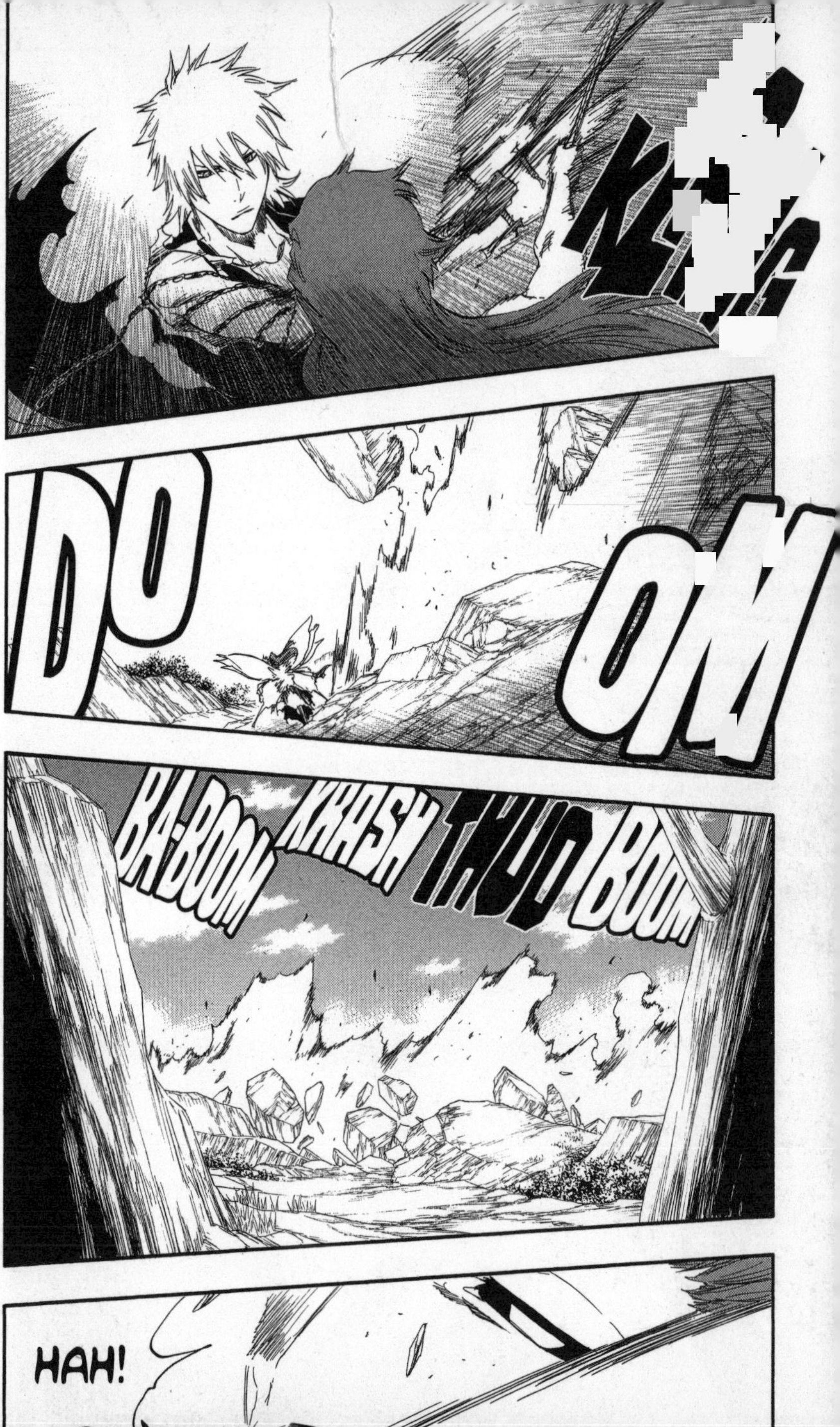
DO
OM
BOOM
THUD
KRASH
BA-BOOM
HAH!

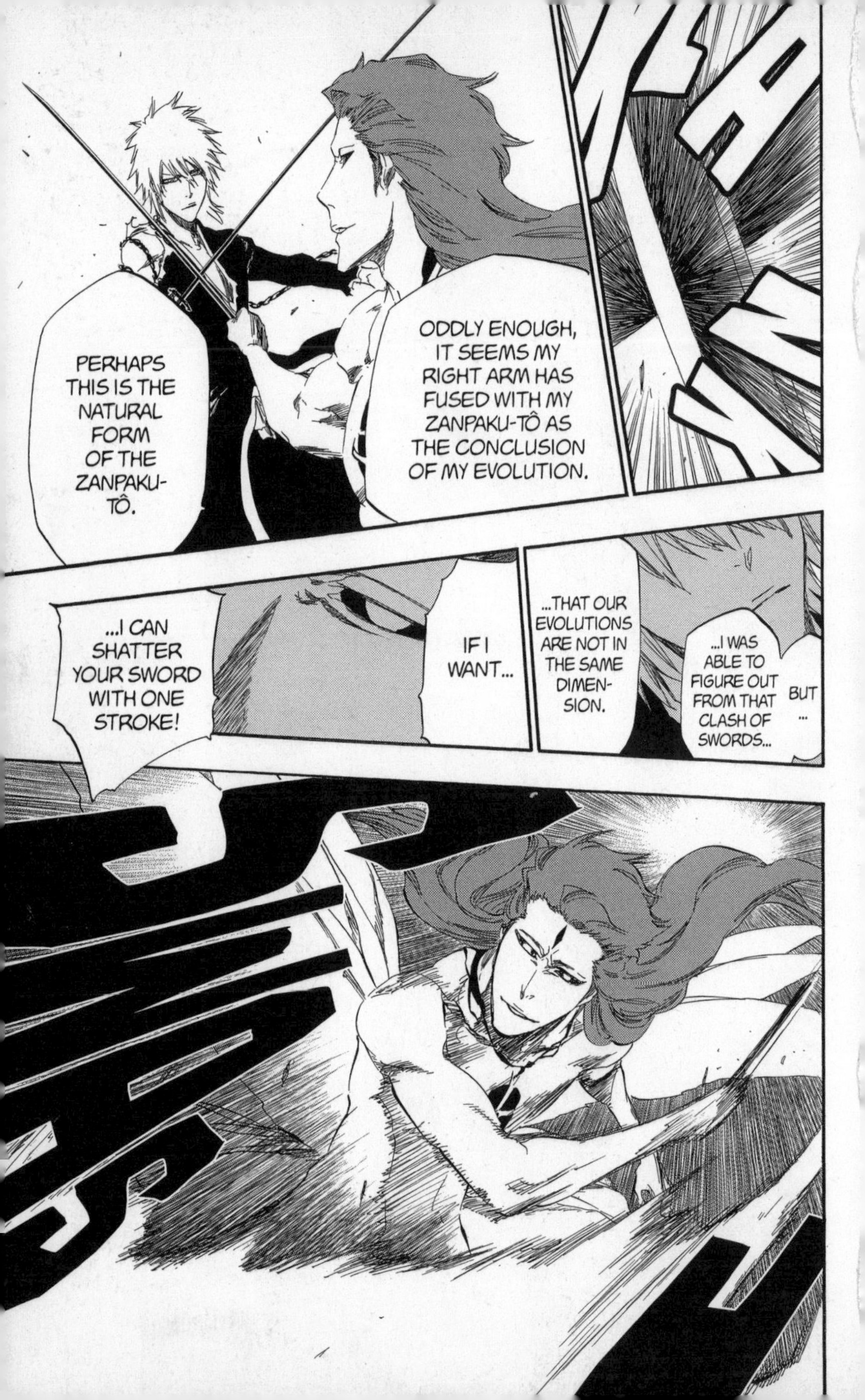
ODDLY ENOUGH, IT SEEMS MY RIGHT ARM HAS FUSED WITH MY ZANPAKU-TÔ AS THE CONCLUSION OF MY EVOLUTION.
PERHAPS THIS IS THE NATURAL FORM OF THE ZANPAKU-TÔ.
BUT ...
...I WAS ABLE TO FIGURE OUT FROM THAT CLASH OF SWORDS...
...THAT OUR EVOLUTIONS ARE NOT IN THE SAME DIMENSION.
IF I WANT...
...I CAN SHATTER YOUR SWORD WITH ONE STROKE!

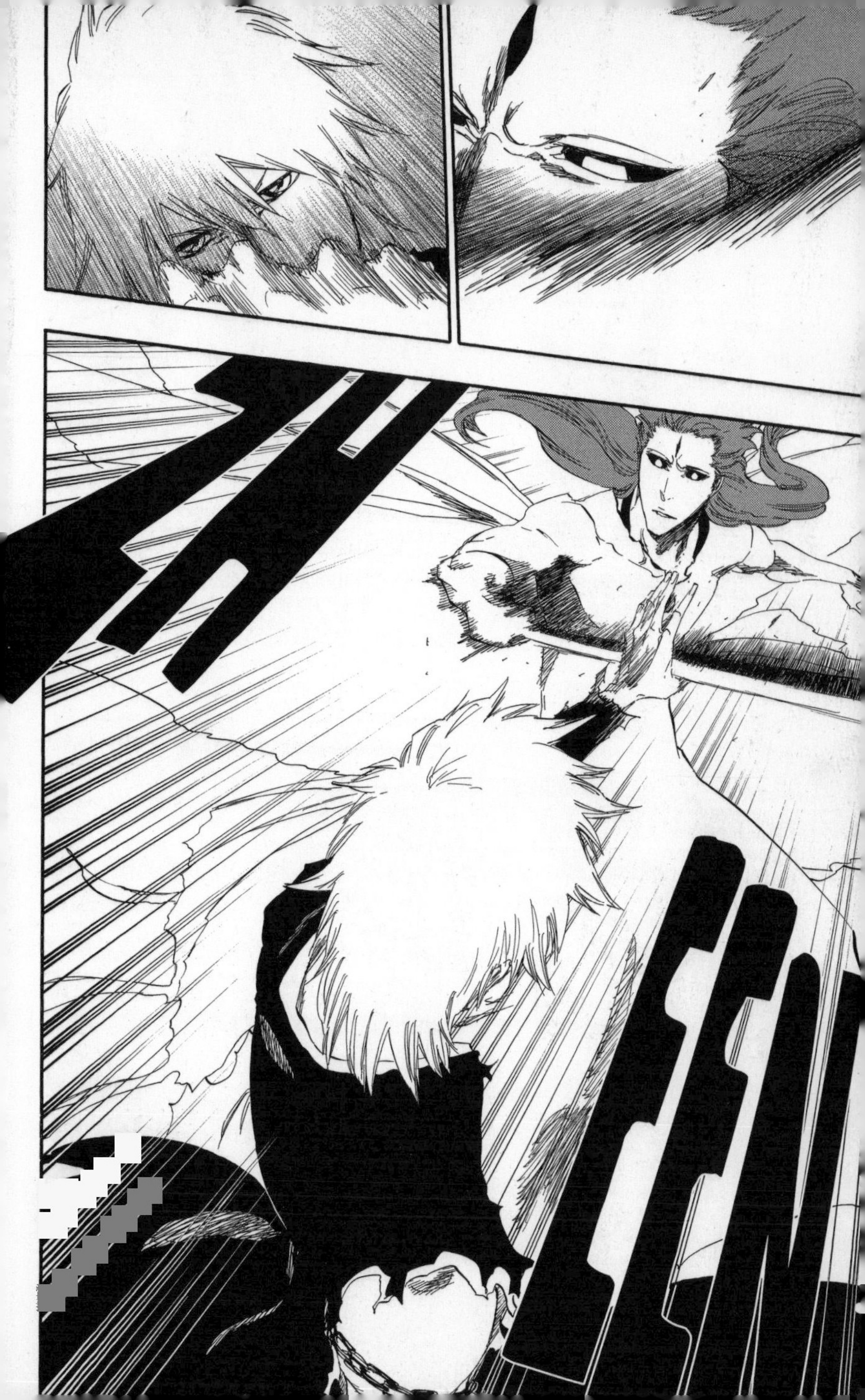

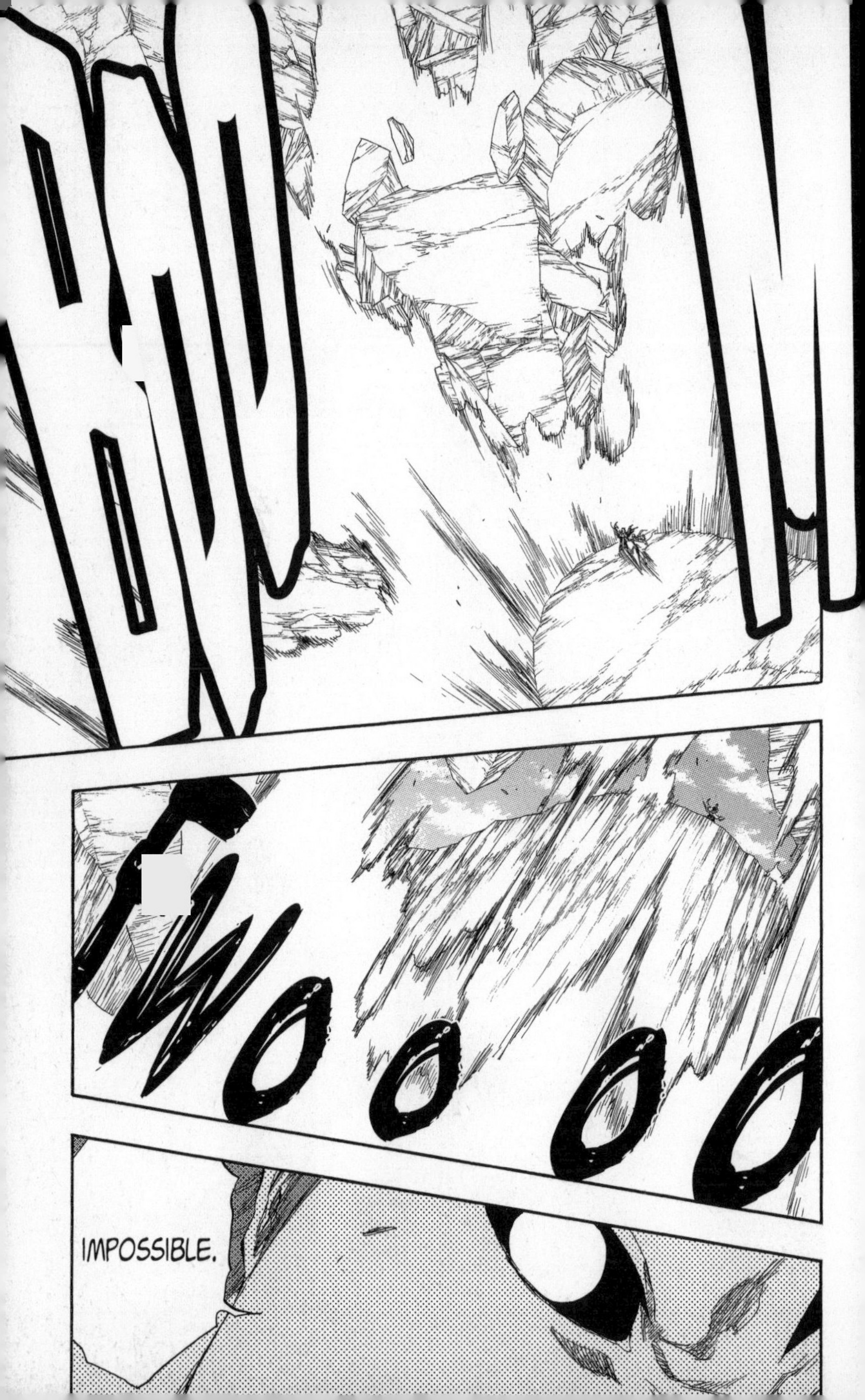
IMPOSSIBLE.

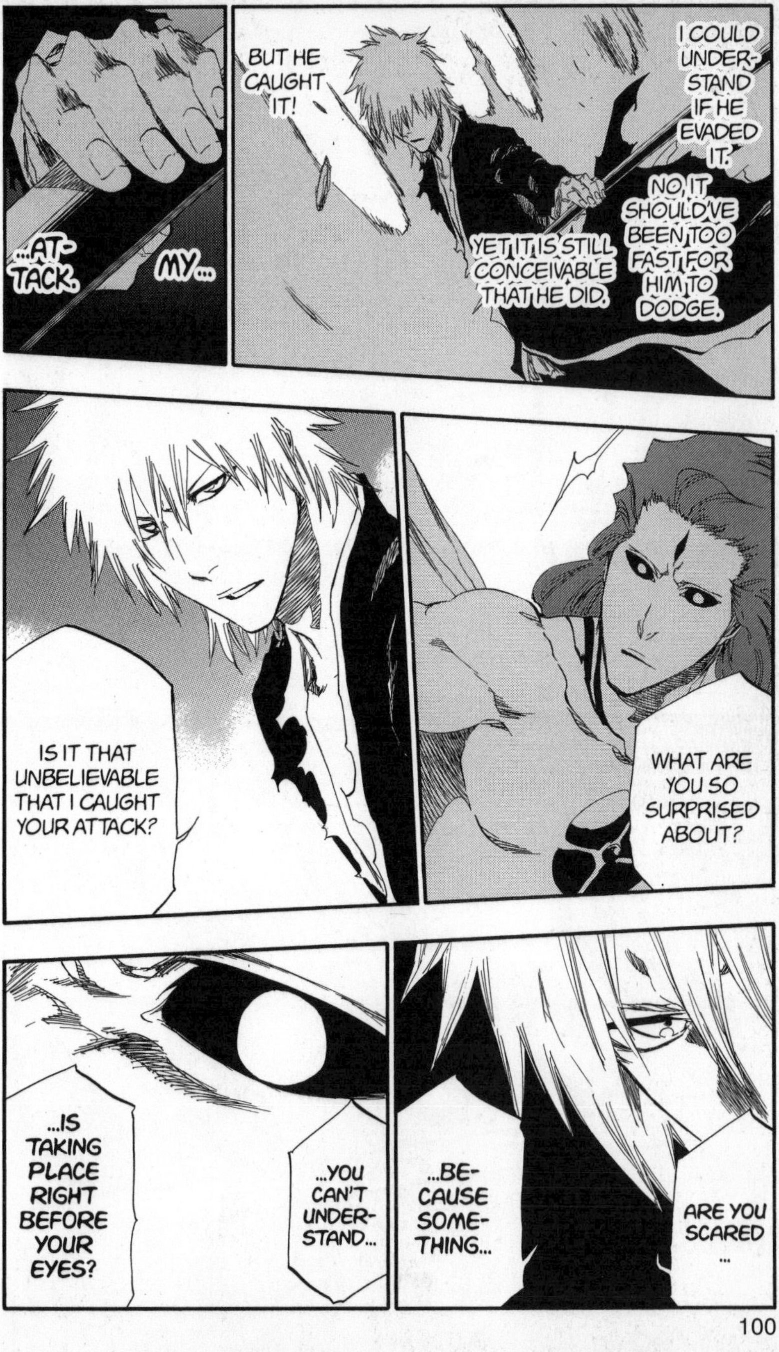

I COULD UNDERSTAND IF HE EVADED IT.
NO, IT SHOULD'VE BEEN TOO FAST FOR HIM TO DODGE.
YET IT IS STILL CONCEIVABLE THAT HE DID.
BUT HE CAUGHT IT!
MY...
...ATTACK.
WHAT ARE YOU SO SURPRISED ABOUT?
IS IT THAT UNBELIEVABLE THAT I CAUGHT YOUR ATTACK?
ARE YOU SCARED...
...BECAUSE SOMETHING...
...YOU CAN'T UNDERSTAND...
...IS TAKING PLACE RIGHT BEFORE YOUR EYES?

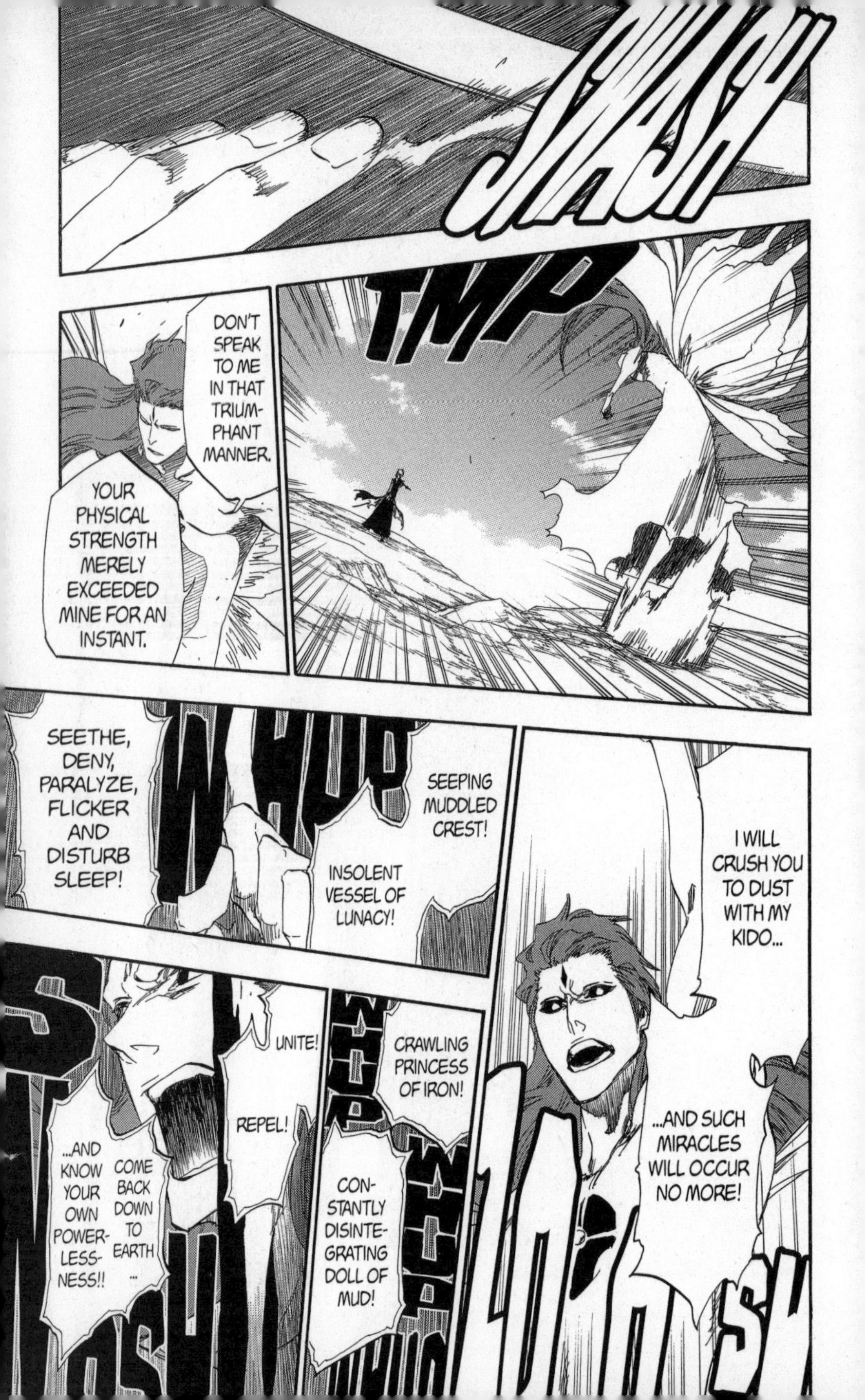
SWASH
TMP
DON'T SPEAK TO ME IN THAT TRIUM-PHANT MANNER.
YOUR PHYSICAL STRENGTH MERELY EXCEEDED MINE FOR AN INSTANT.
I WILL CRUSH YOU TO DUST WITH MY KIDO...
SEEPING MUDDLED CREST!
INSOLENT VESSEL OF LUNACY!
SEETHE, DENY, PARALYZE, FLICKER AND DISTURB SLEEP!
...AND SUCH MIRACLES WILL OCCUR NO MORE!
CRAWLING PRINCESS OF IRON!
CON-STANTLY DISINTE-GRATING DOLL OF MUD!
UNITE!
REPEL!
COME BACK DOWN TO EARTH...
...AND KNOW YOUR OWN POWER-LESS-NESS!!

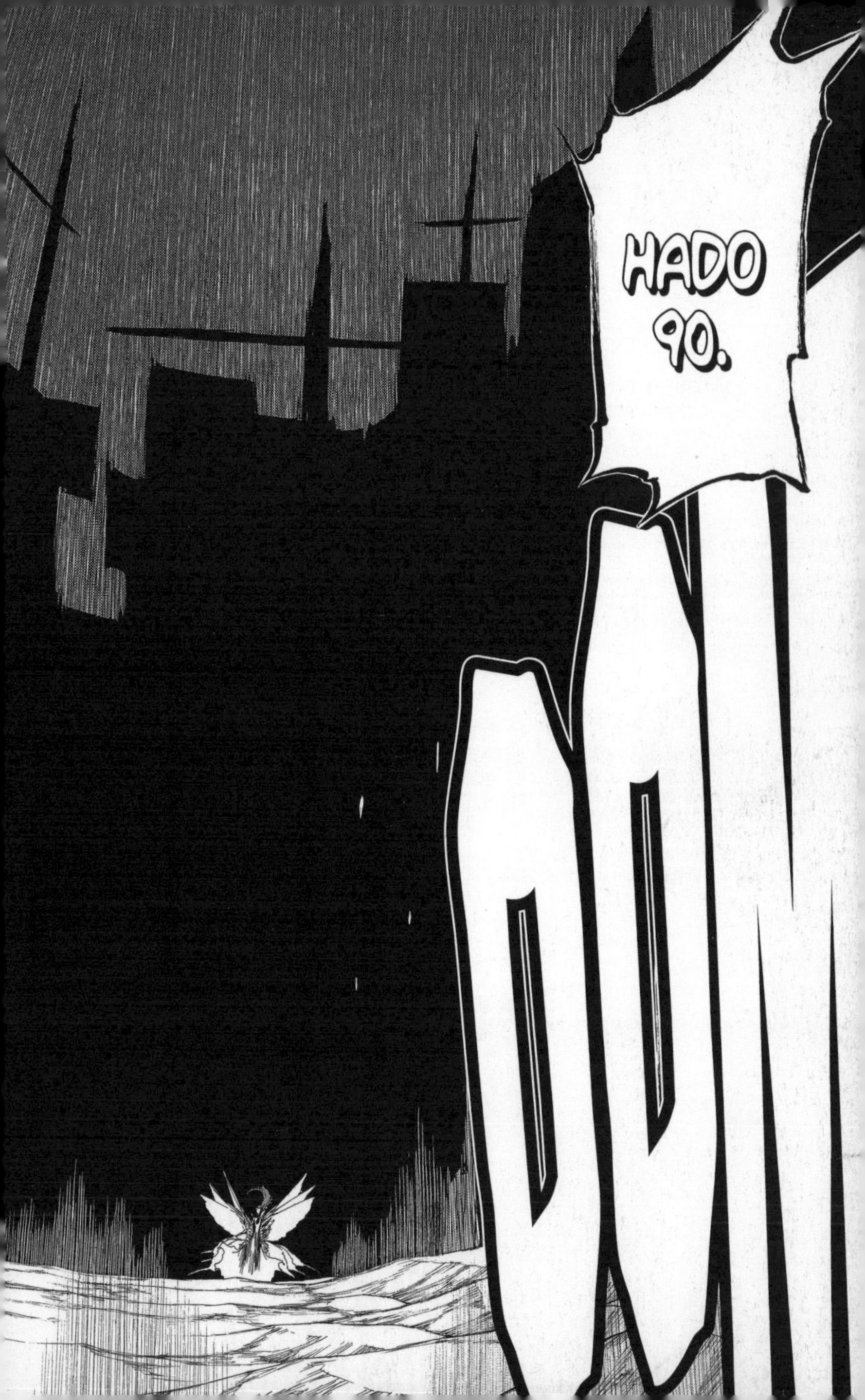
HADO 90.

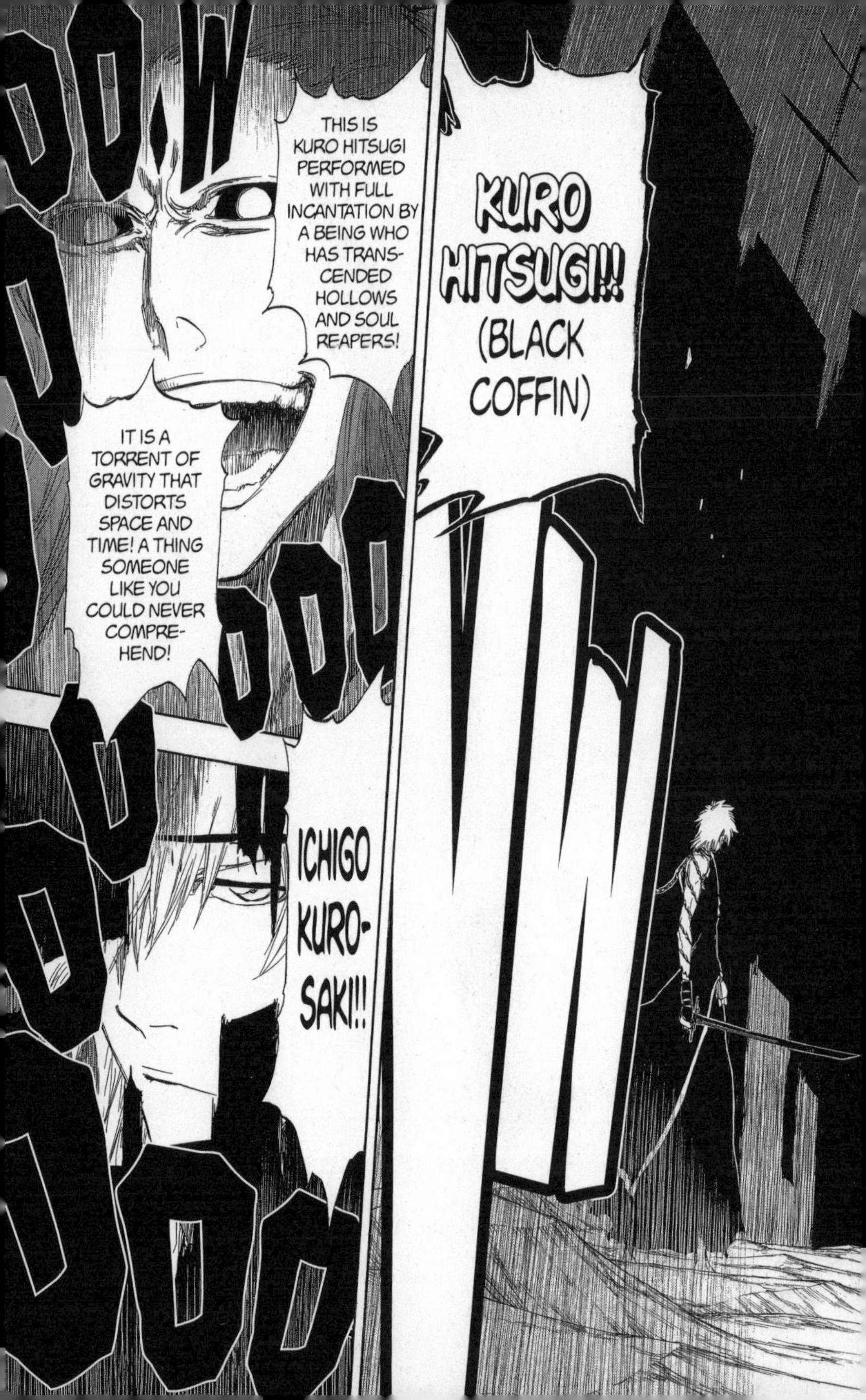
KURO HITSUGI!! (BLACK COFFIN)
THIS IS KURO HITSUGI PERFORMED WITH FULL INCANTATION BY A BEING WHO HAS TRANSCENDED HOLLOWS AND SOUL REAPERS!
IT IS A TORRENT OF GRAVITY THAT DISTORTS SPACE AND TIME! A THING SOMEONE LIKE YOU COULD NEVER COMPREHEND!
ICHIGO KUROSAKI!!

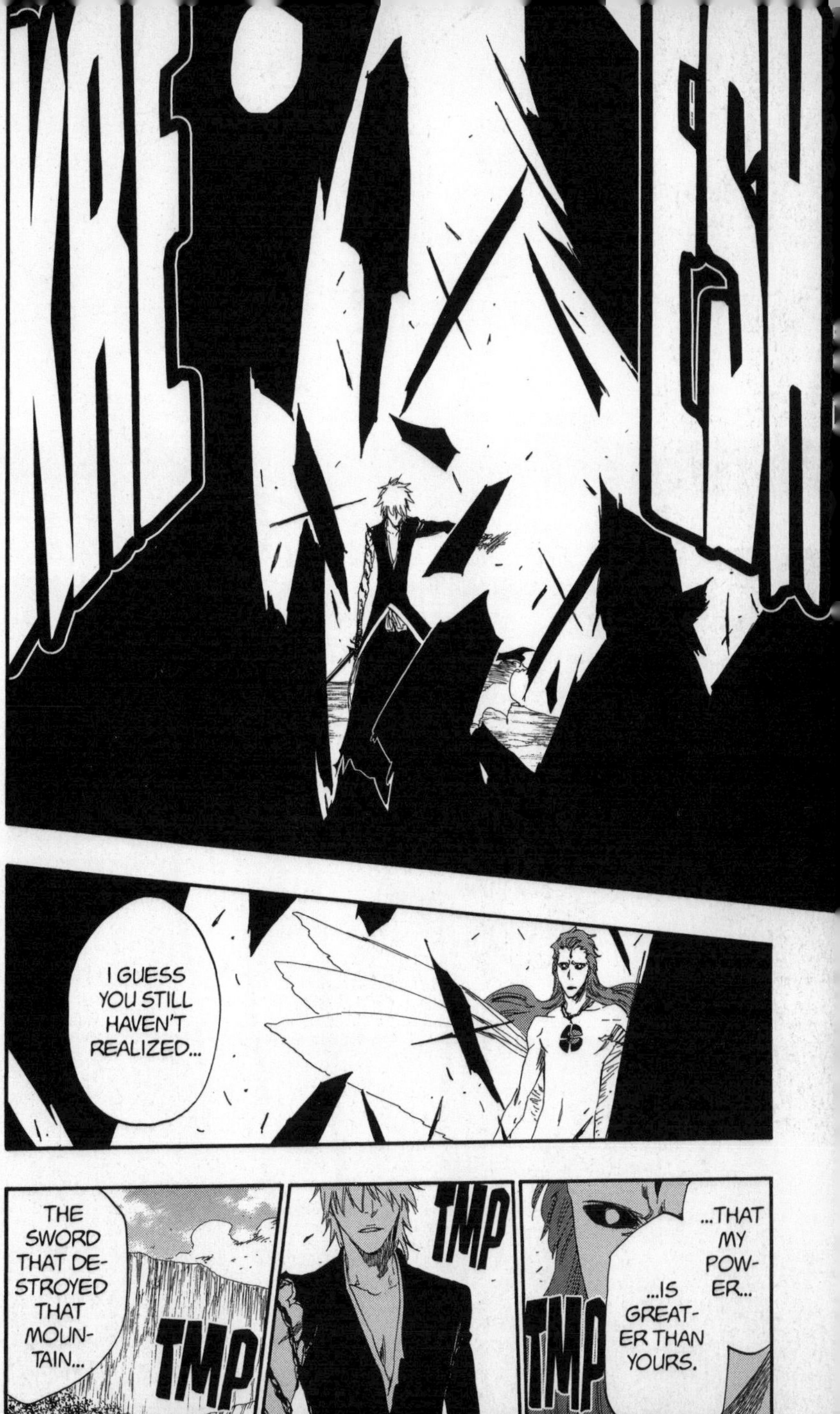
I GUESS YOU STILL HAVEN'T REALIZED...
...THAT MY POWER...
...IS GREATER THAN YOURS.
TMP
TMP
THE SWORD THAT DESTROYED THAT MOUNTAIN...
TMP

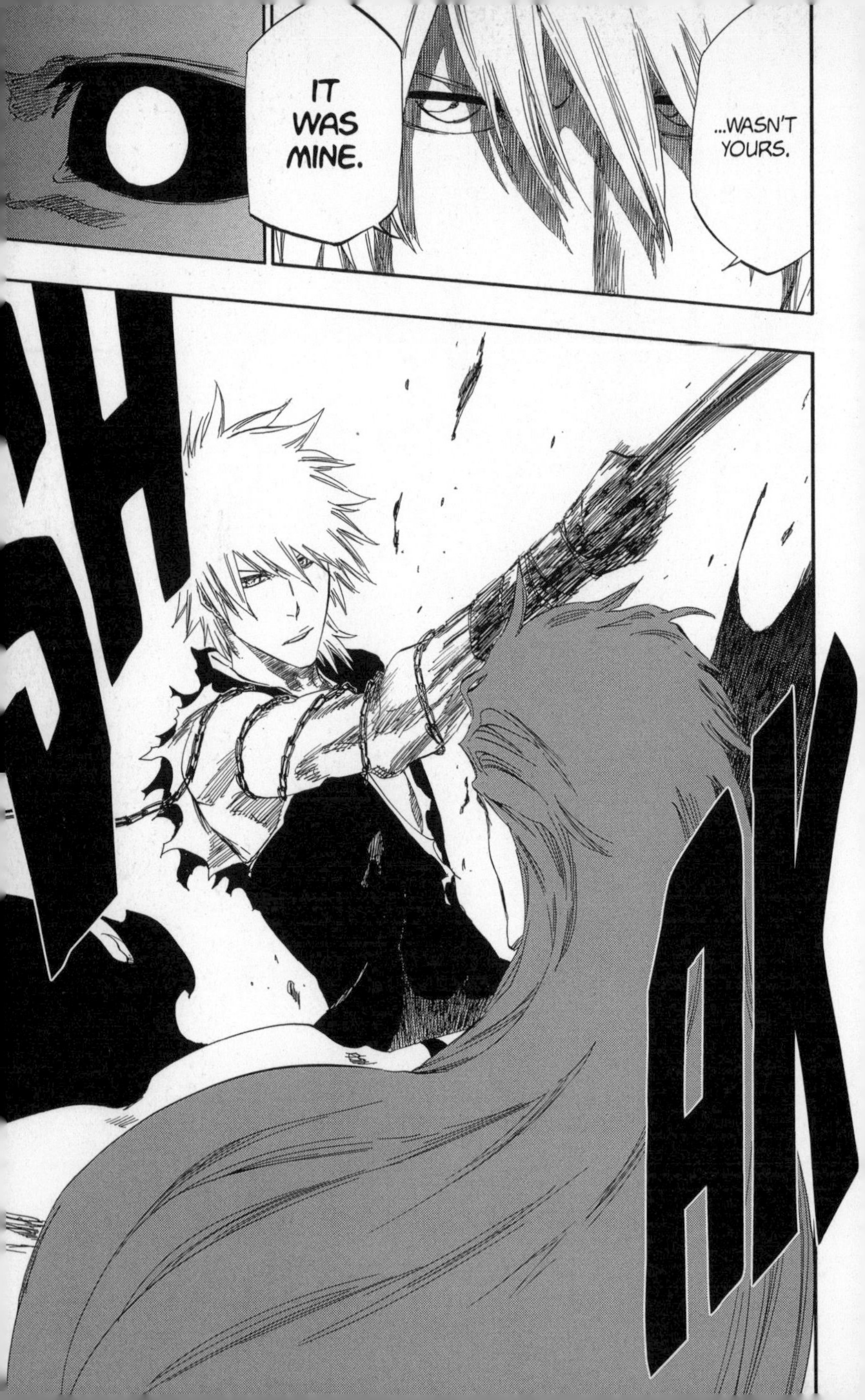
IT WAS MINE.
...WASN'T YOURS.

419. DEICIDE 21 (Transcendent God Rock)

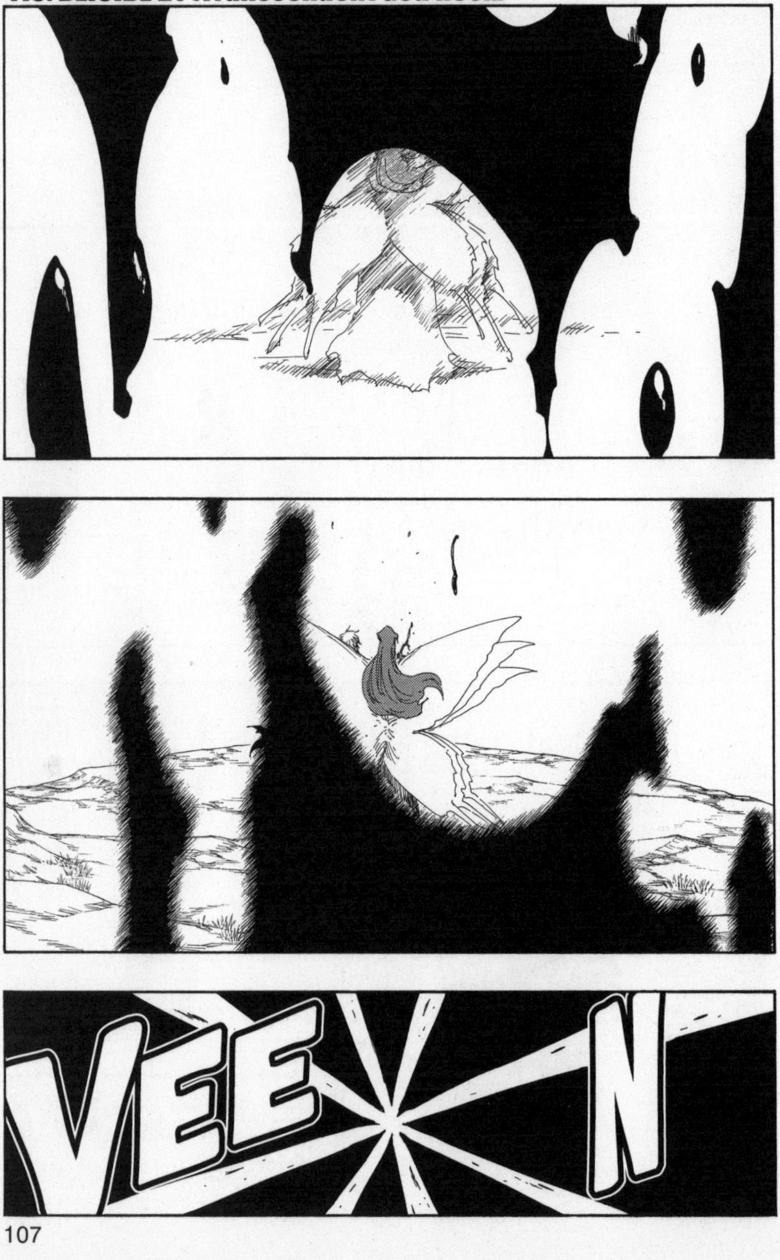
VEE N

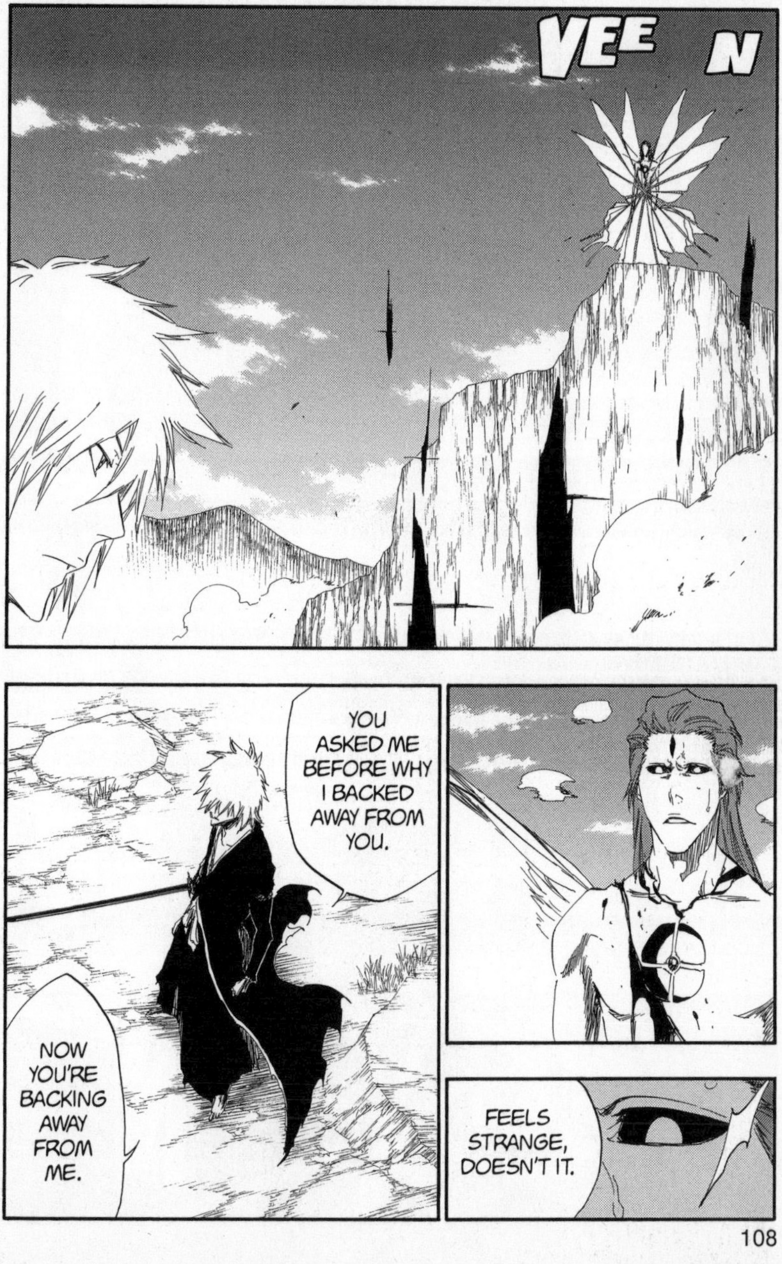
VEEN
FEELS STRANGE, DOESN'T IT.
YOU ASKED ME BEFORE WHY I BACKED AWAY FROM YOU.
NOW YOU'RE BACKING AWAY FROM ME.

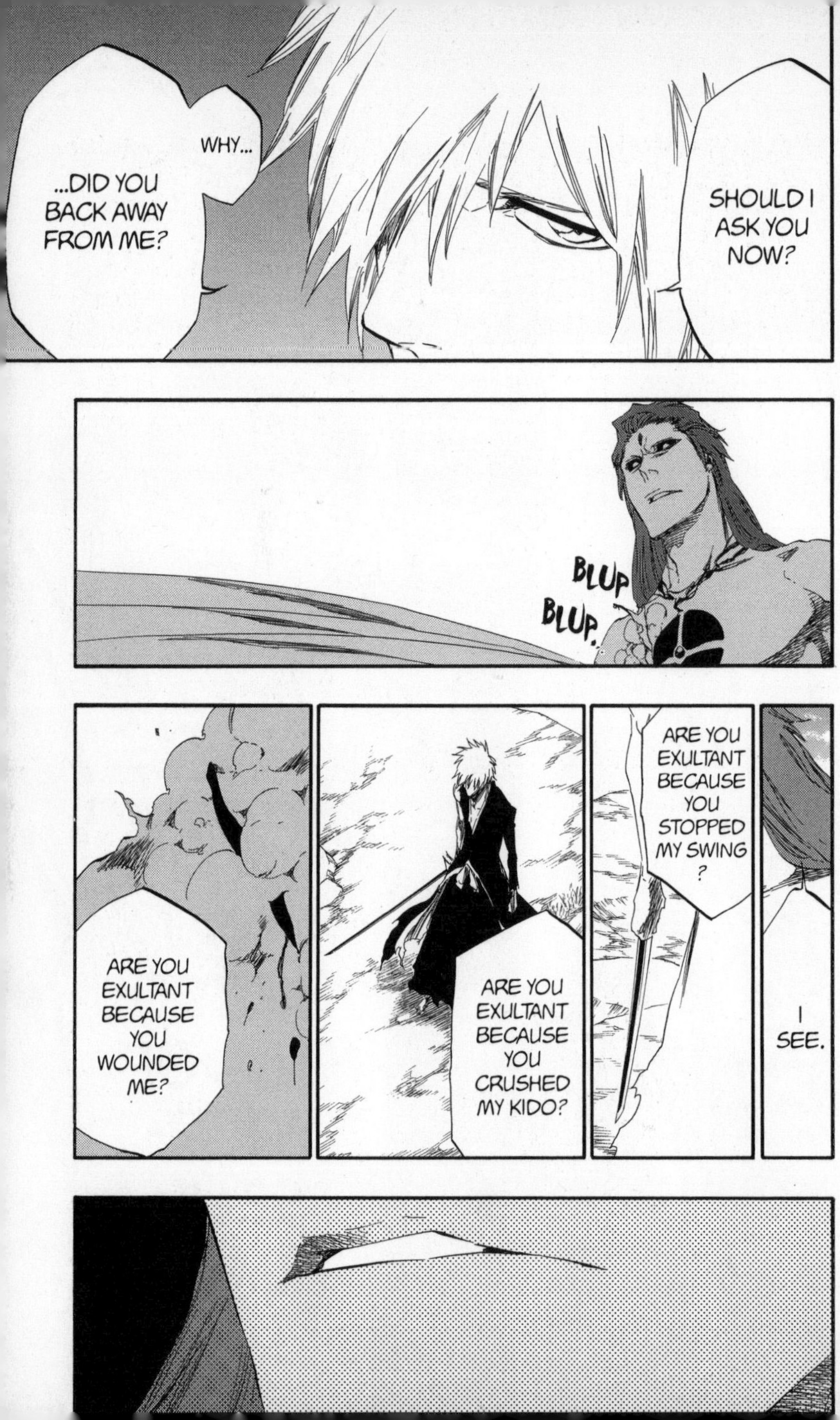
SHOULD I ASK YOU NOW?
WHY...
...DID YOU BACK AWAY FROM ME?
BLUP
BLUP.
I SEE.
ARE YOU EXULTANT BECAUSE YOU STOPPED MY SWING?
ARE YOU EXULTANT BECAUSE YOU CRUSHED MY KIDO?
ARE YOU EXULTANT BECAUSE YOU WOUNDED ME?

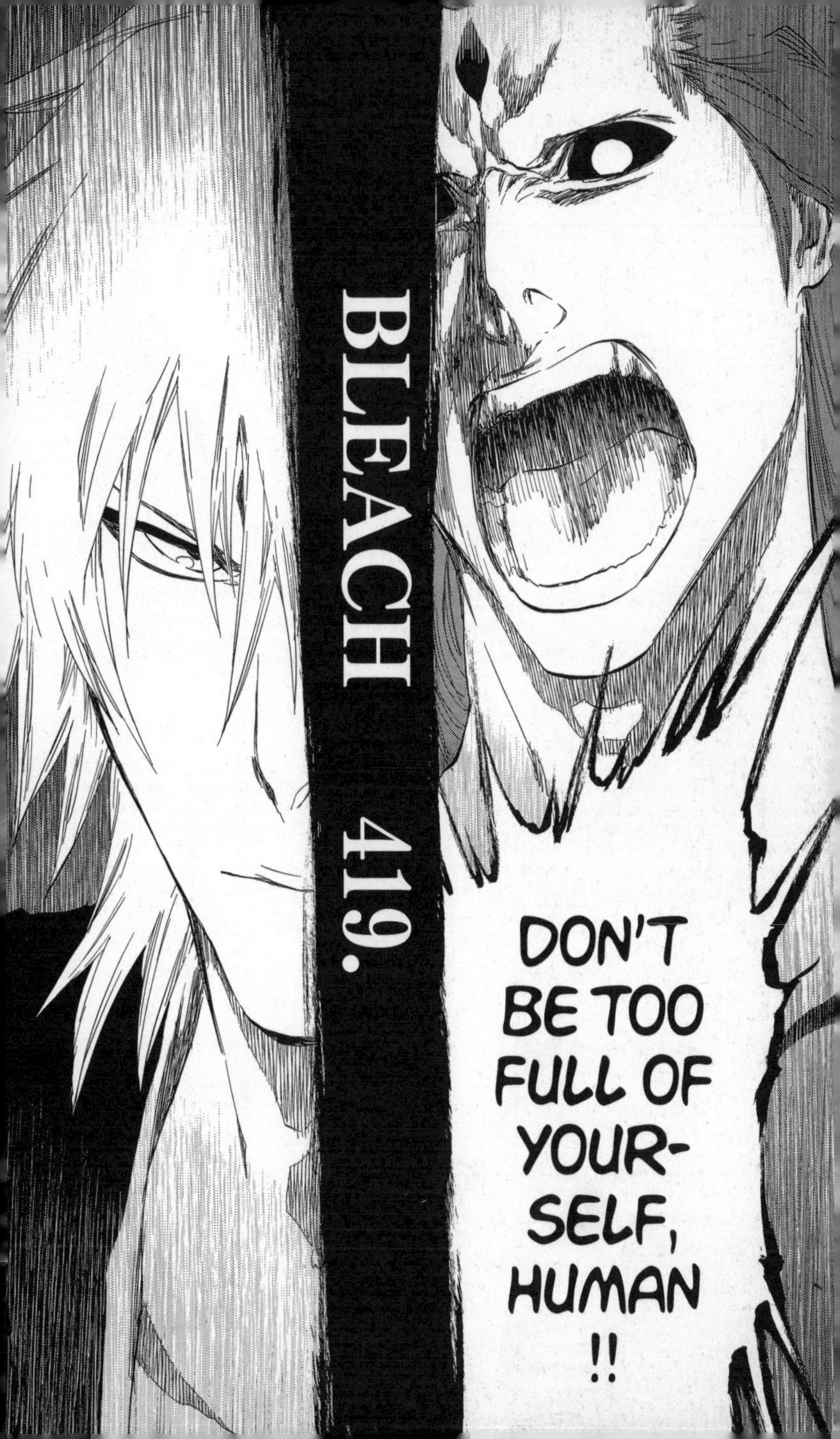
BLEACH 419.
DON'T BE TOO FULL OF YOURSELF, HUMAN!!

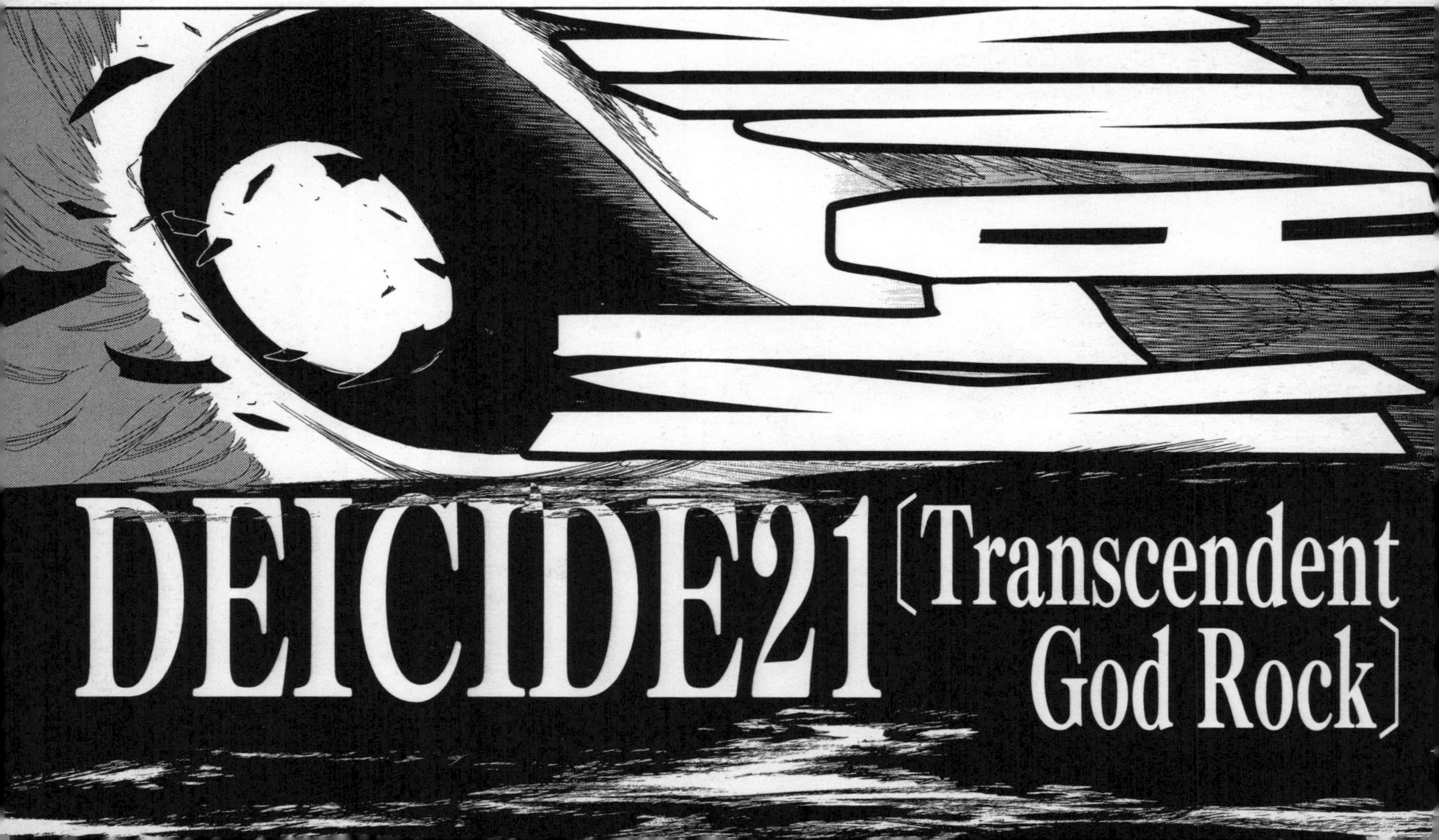
DEICIDE21
〔Transcendent God Rock〕

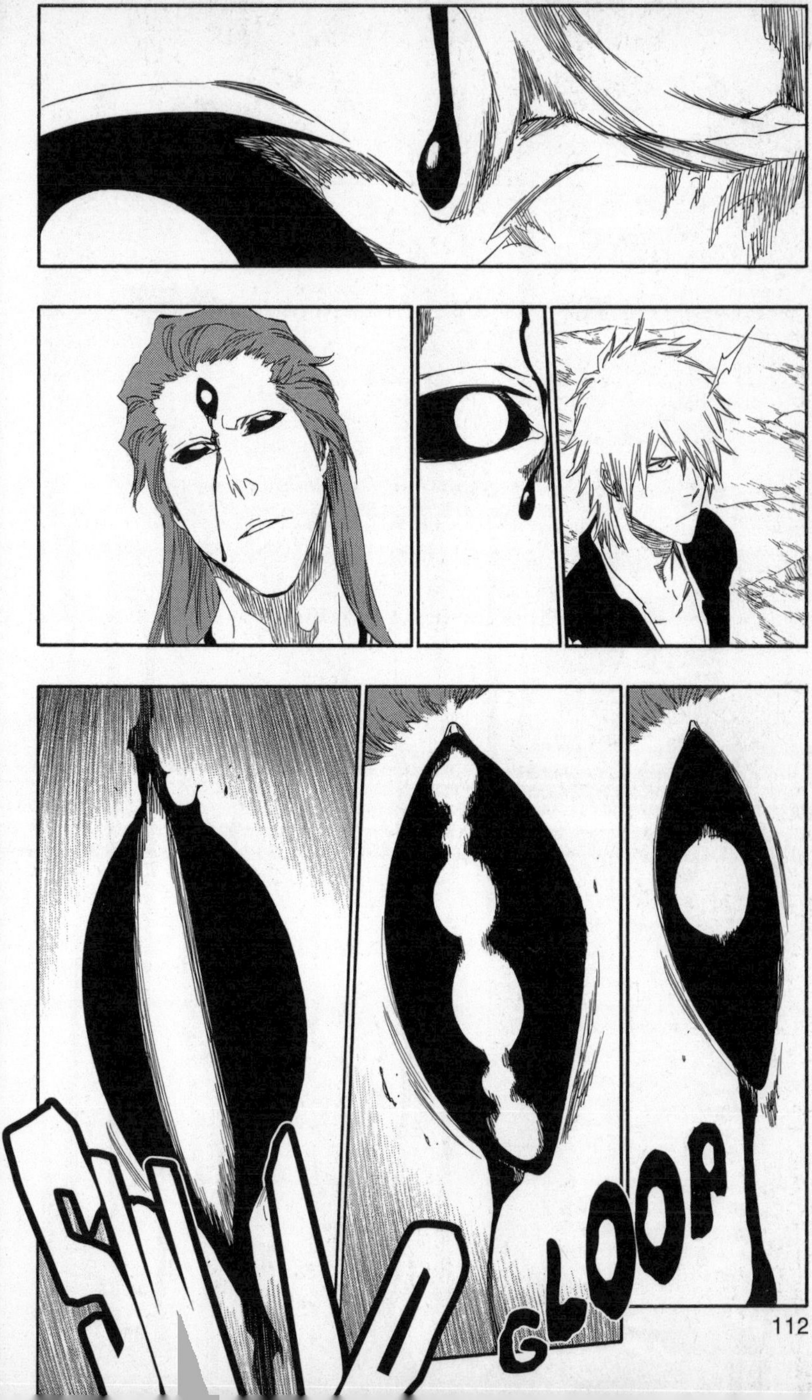
GLOOP

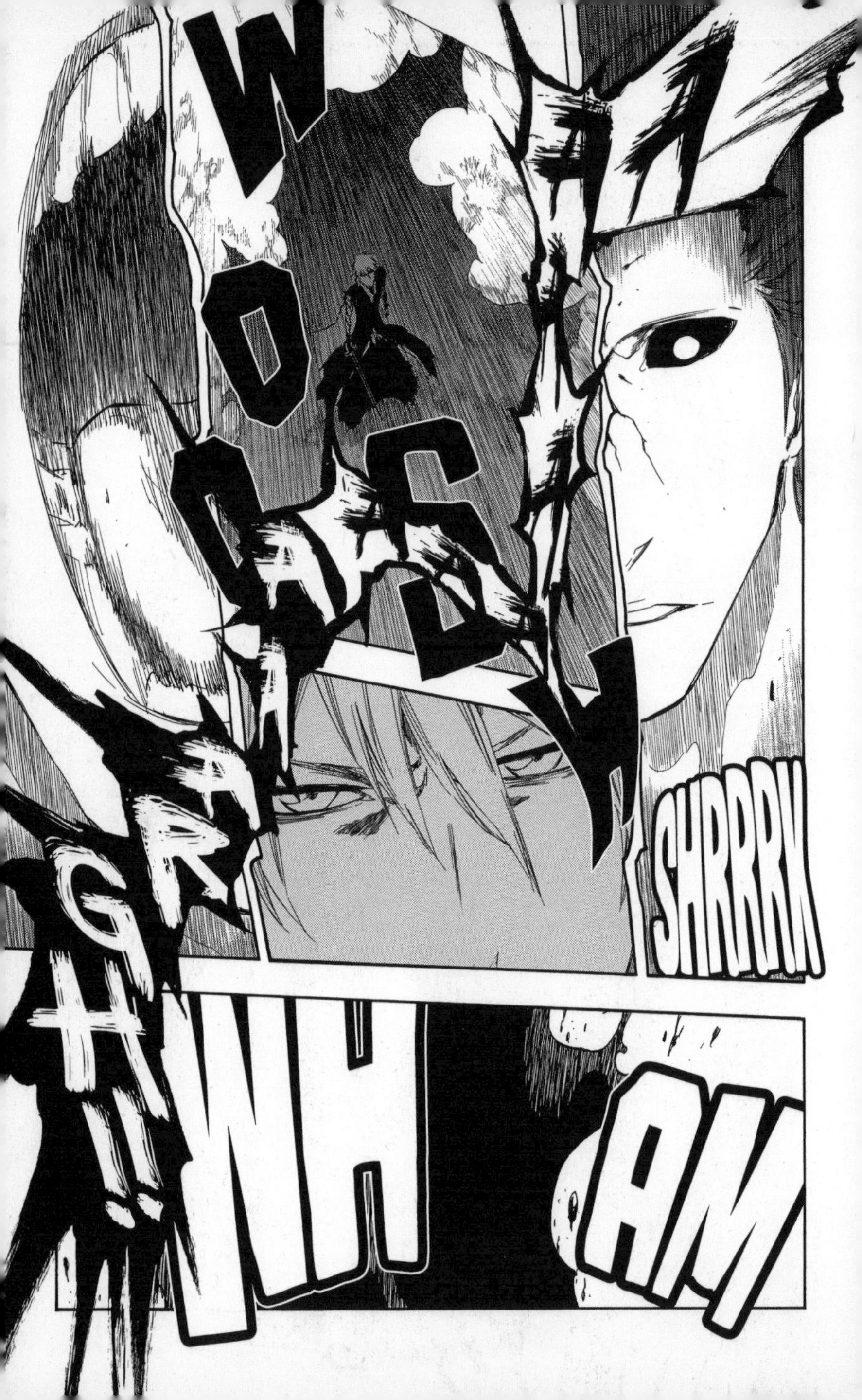
SHRRRK
WHAM

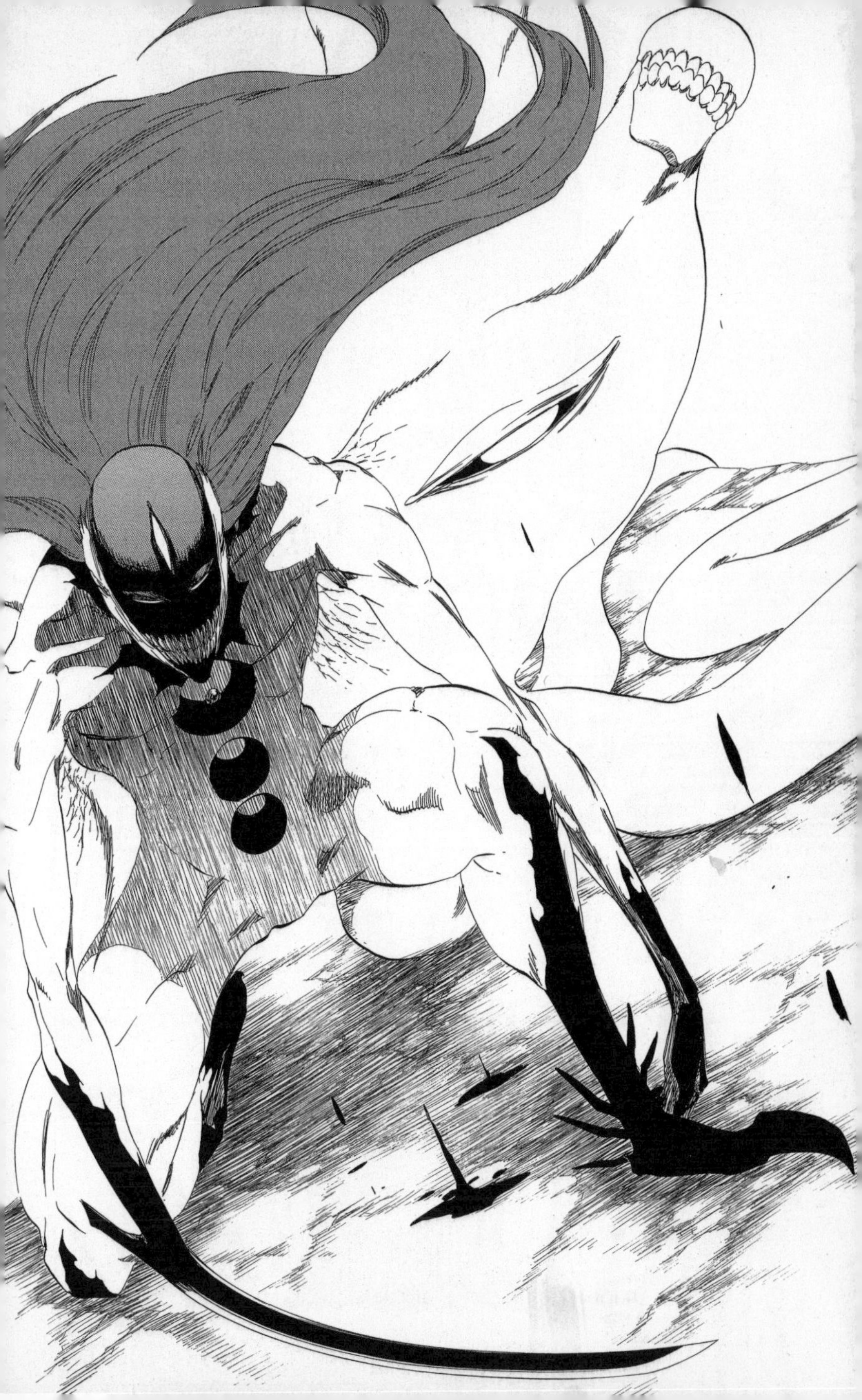

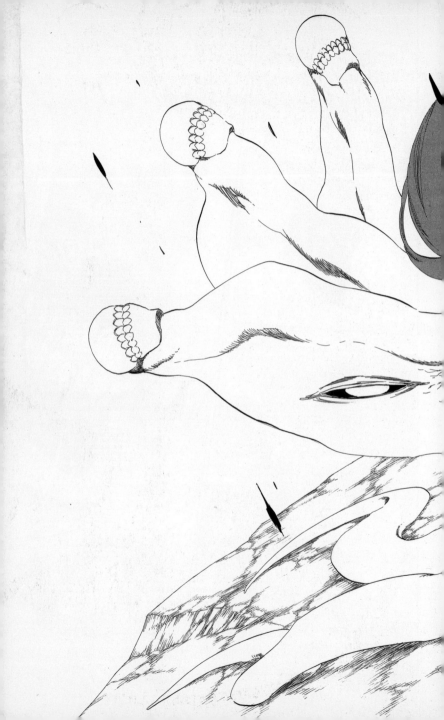

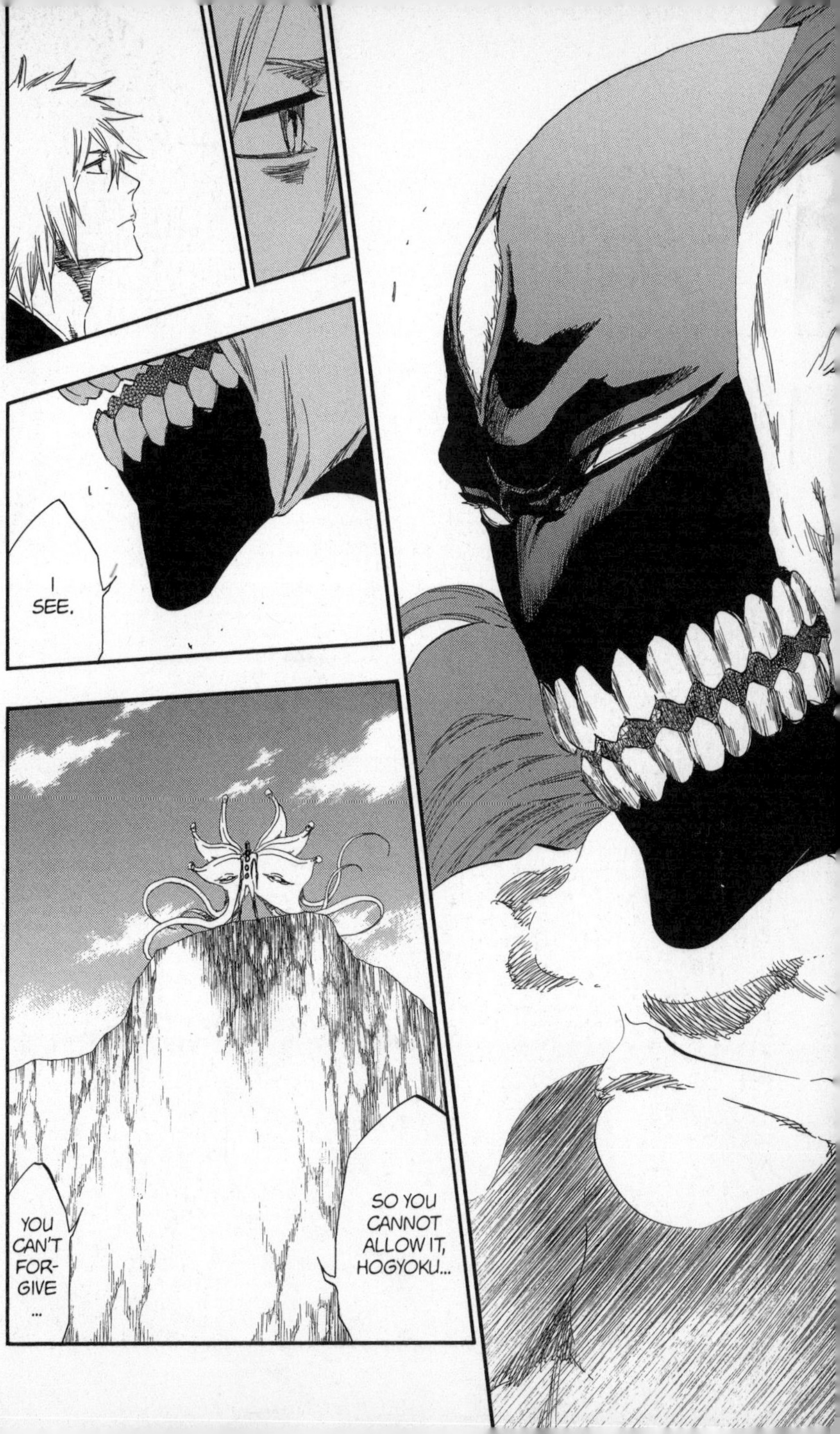
I SEE.
SO YOU CANNOT ALLOW IT, HOGYOKU...
YOU CAN'T FOR-GIVE ...

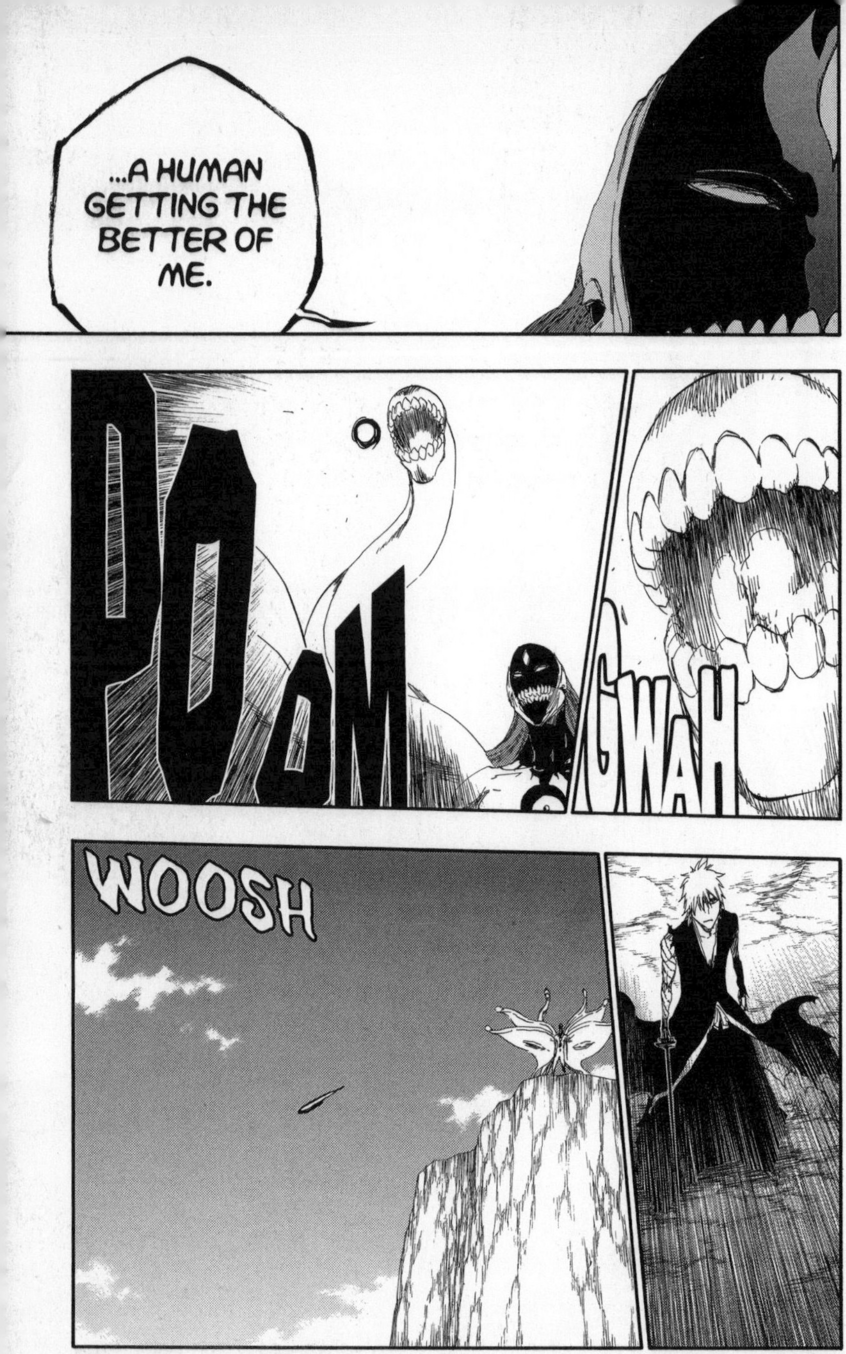
...A HUMAN GETTING THE BETTER OF ME.
GWAH
DOOM
WOOSH

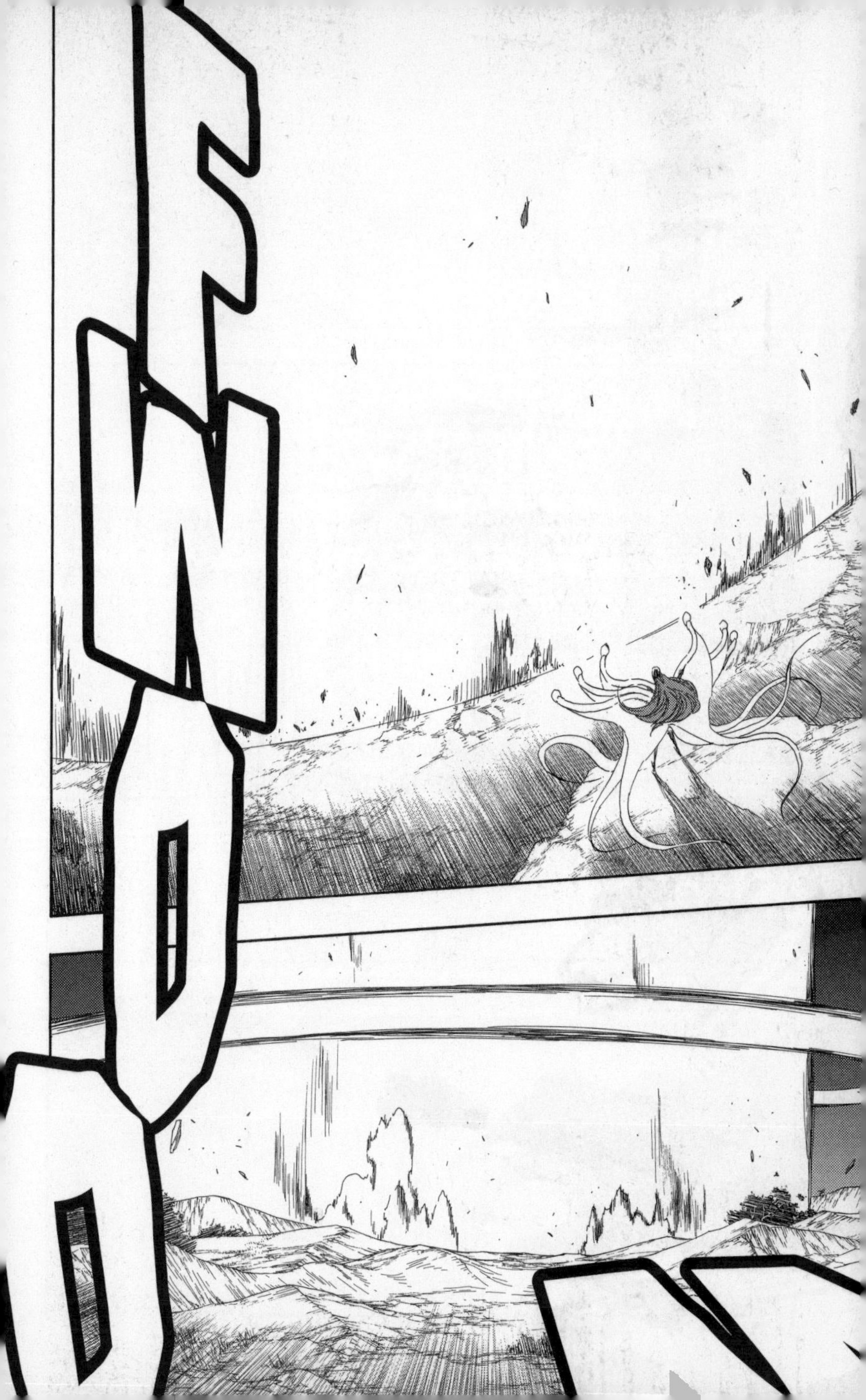

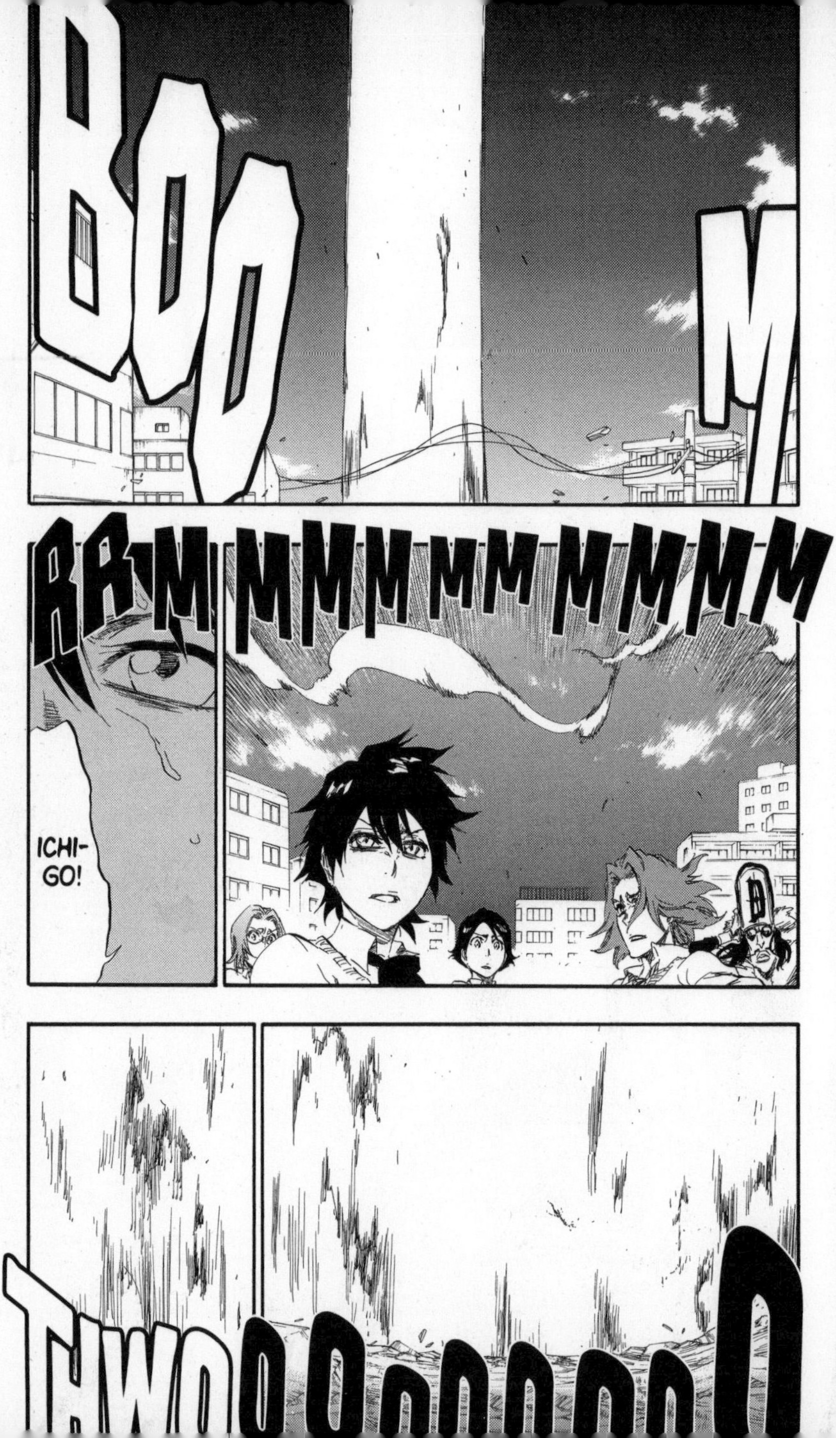
BOOM
RRMMMMMMMMMMMMM
ICHI-GO!
THWOOOOOOOOOO

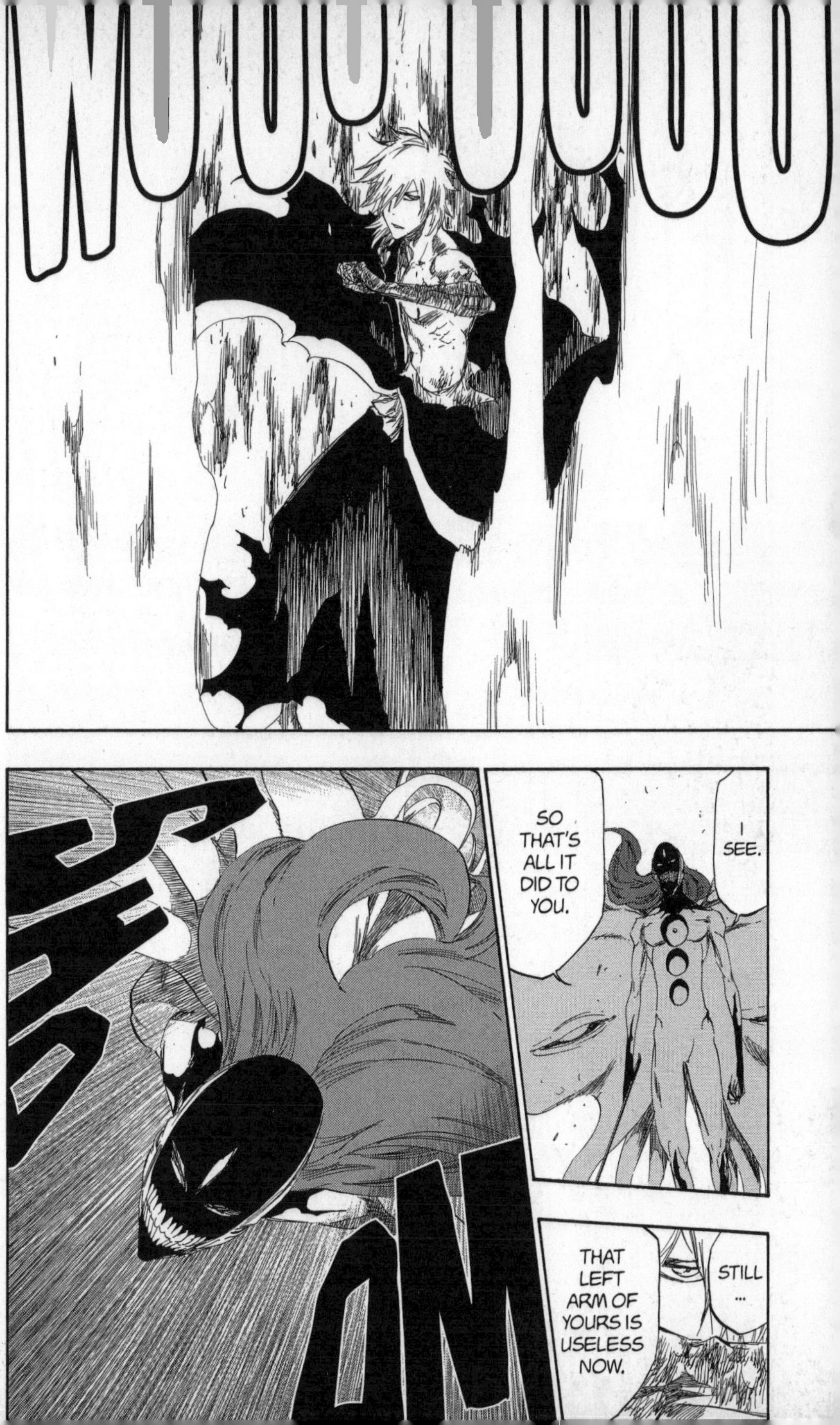
I SEE.
SO THAT'S ALL IT DID TO YOU.
STILL...
THAT LEFT ARM OF YOURS IS USELESS NOW.

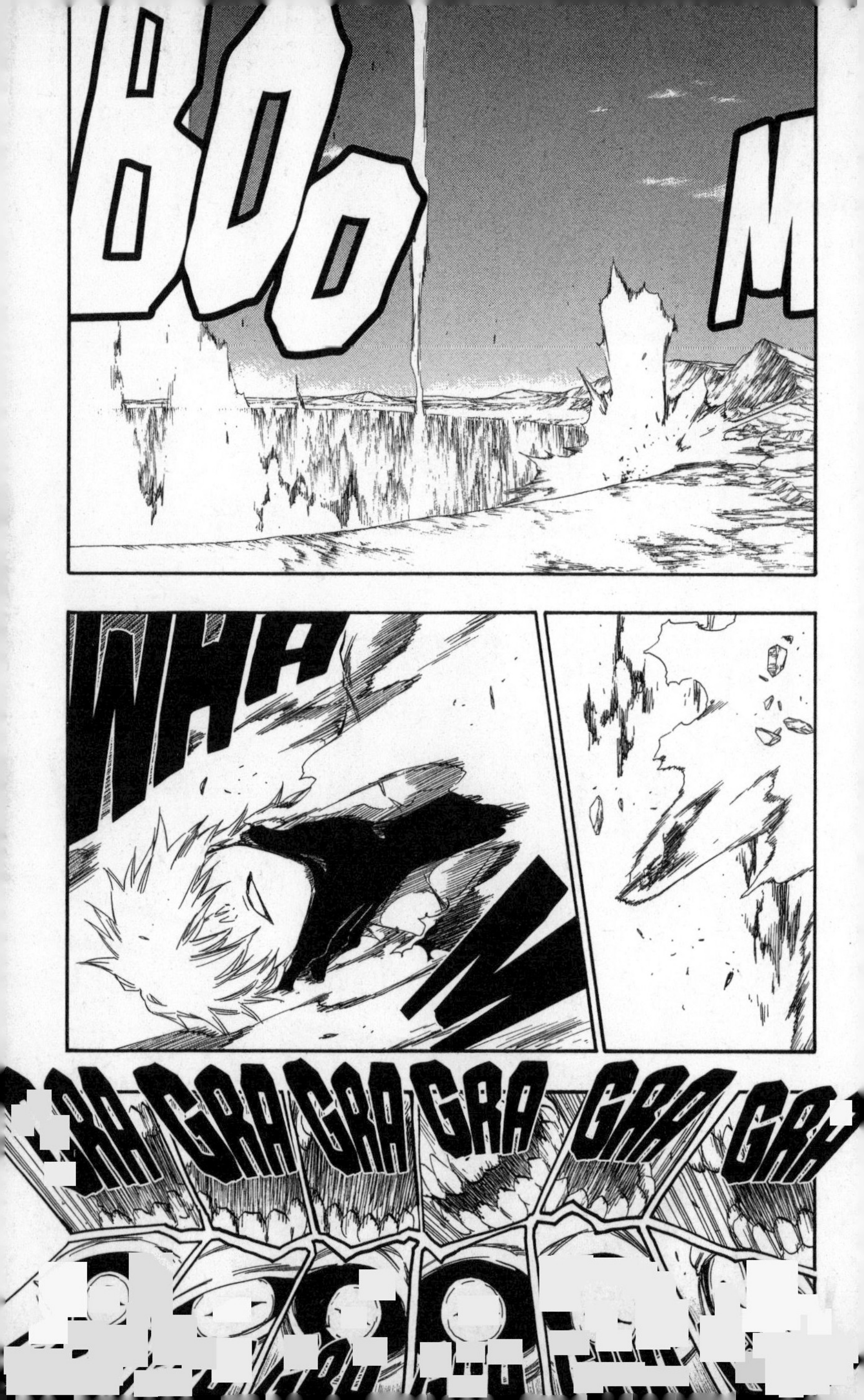
BOO
M
WHA
M
GRA GRA GRA GRA GRA

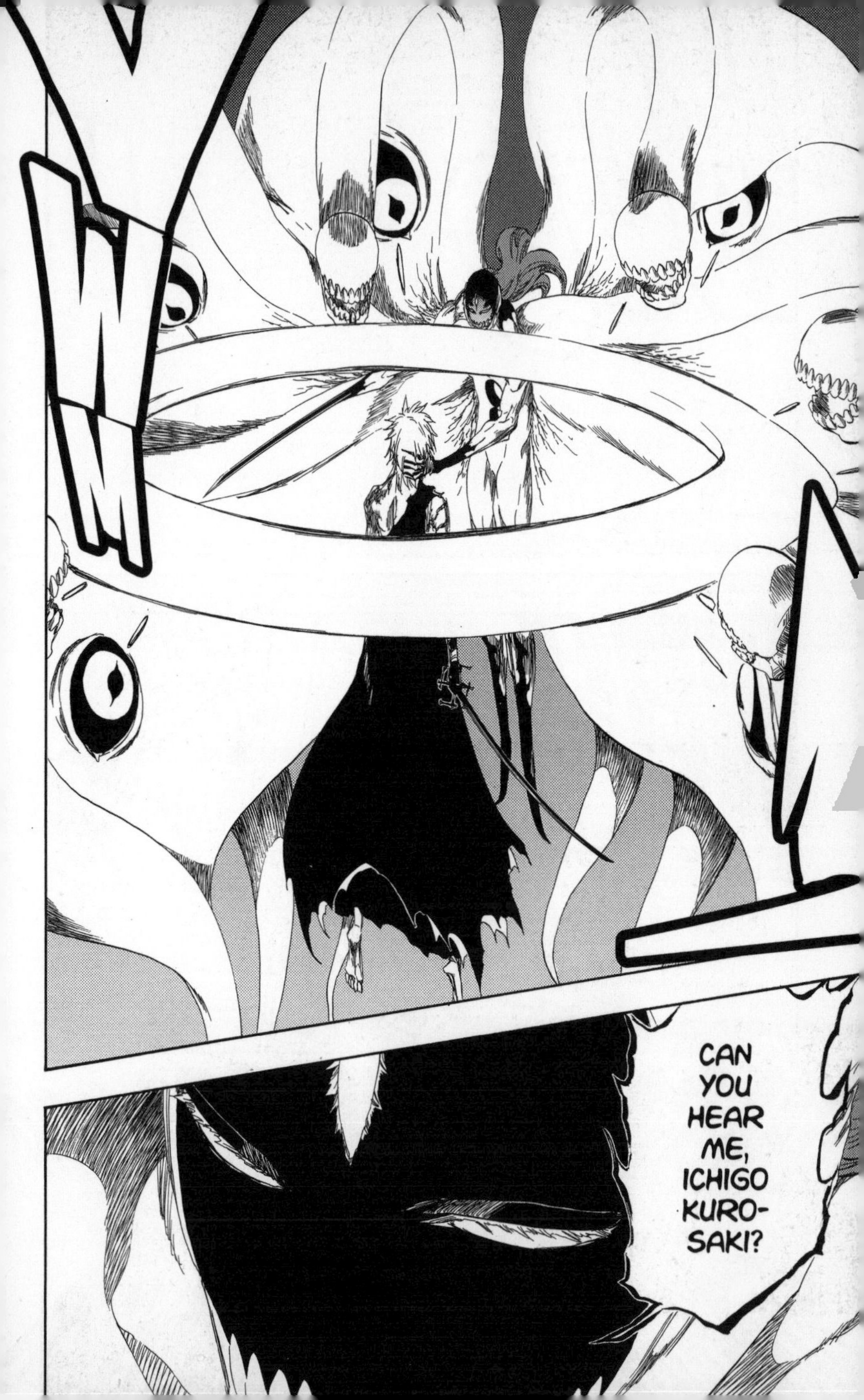
VWM
CAN YOU HEAR ME, ICHIGO KURO-SAKI?

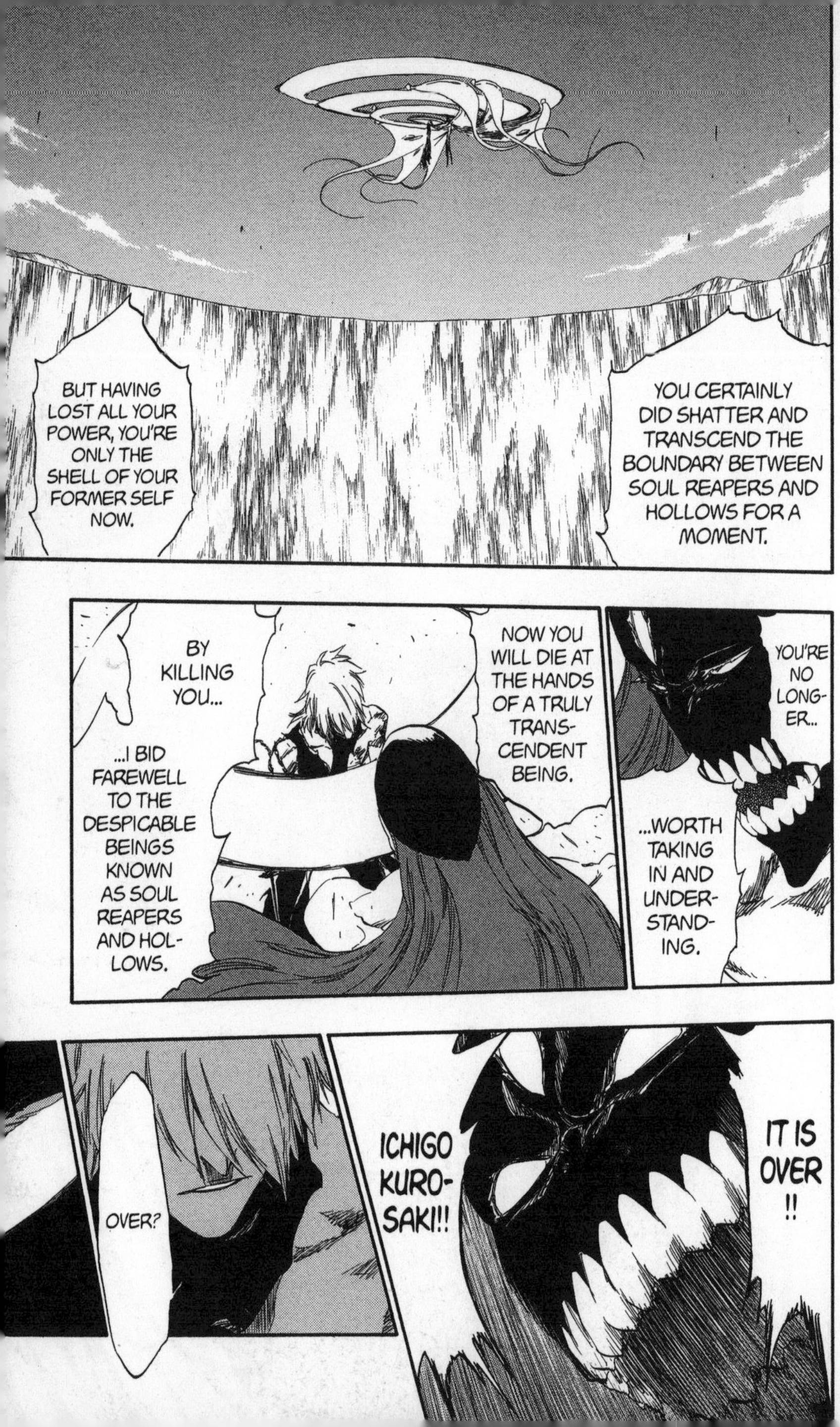
YOU CERTAINLY DID SHATTER AND TRANSCEND THE BOUNDARY BETWEEN SOUL REAPERS AND HOLLOWS FOR A MOMENT.
BUT HAVING LOST ALL YOUR POWER, YOU'RE ONLY THE SHELL OF YOUR FORMER SELF NOW.
YOU'RE NO LONG-ER...
...WORTH TAKING IN AND UNDER-STAND-ING.
NOW YOU WILL DIE AT THE HANDS OF A TRULY TRANS-CENDENT BEING.
BY KILLING YOU...
...I BID FAREWELL TO THE DESPICABLE BEINGS KNOWN AS SOUL REAPERS AND HOL-LOWS.
IT IS OVER!!
ICHIGO KURO-SAKI!!!
OVER?

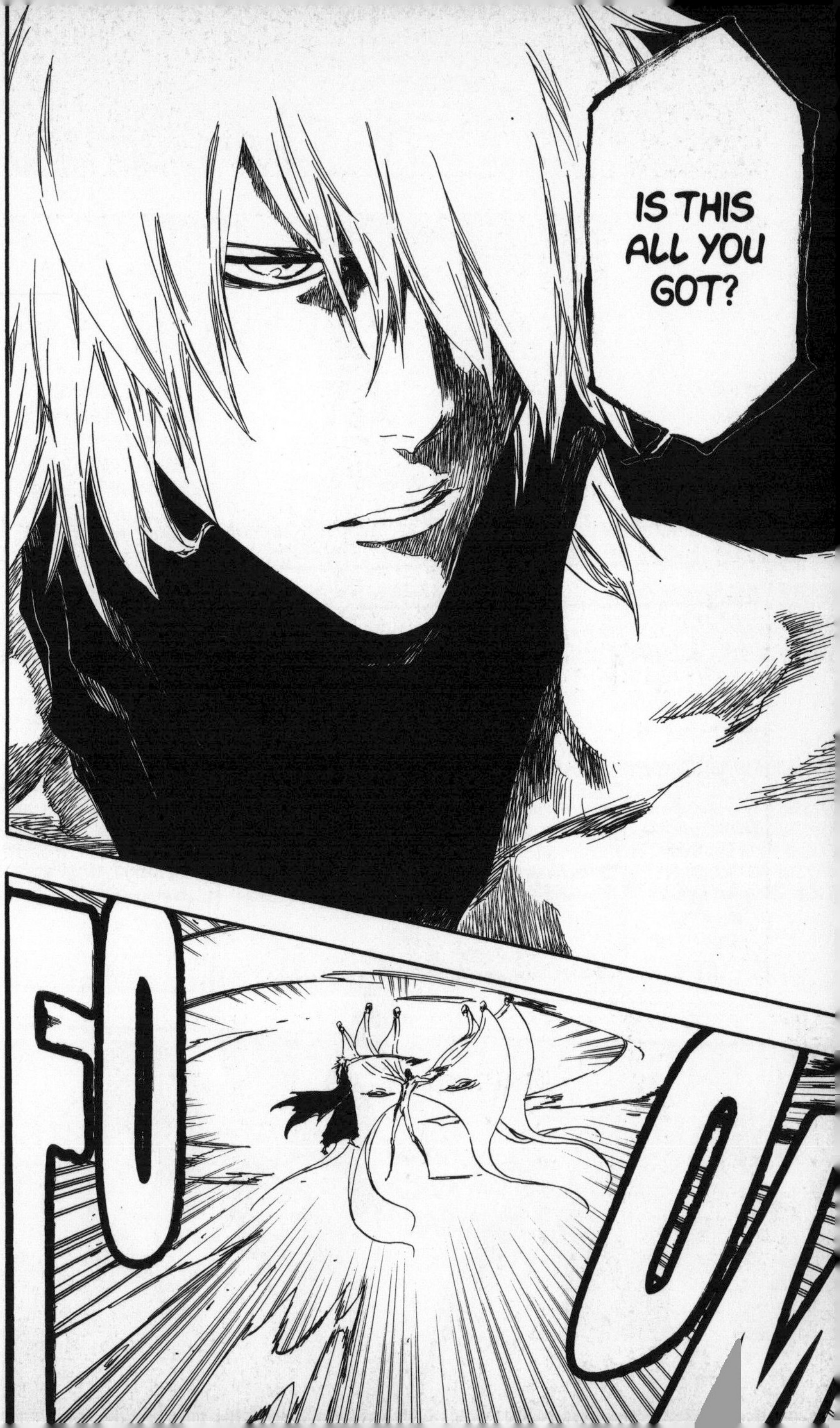
IS THIS ALL YOU GOT?

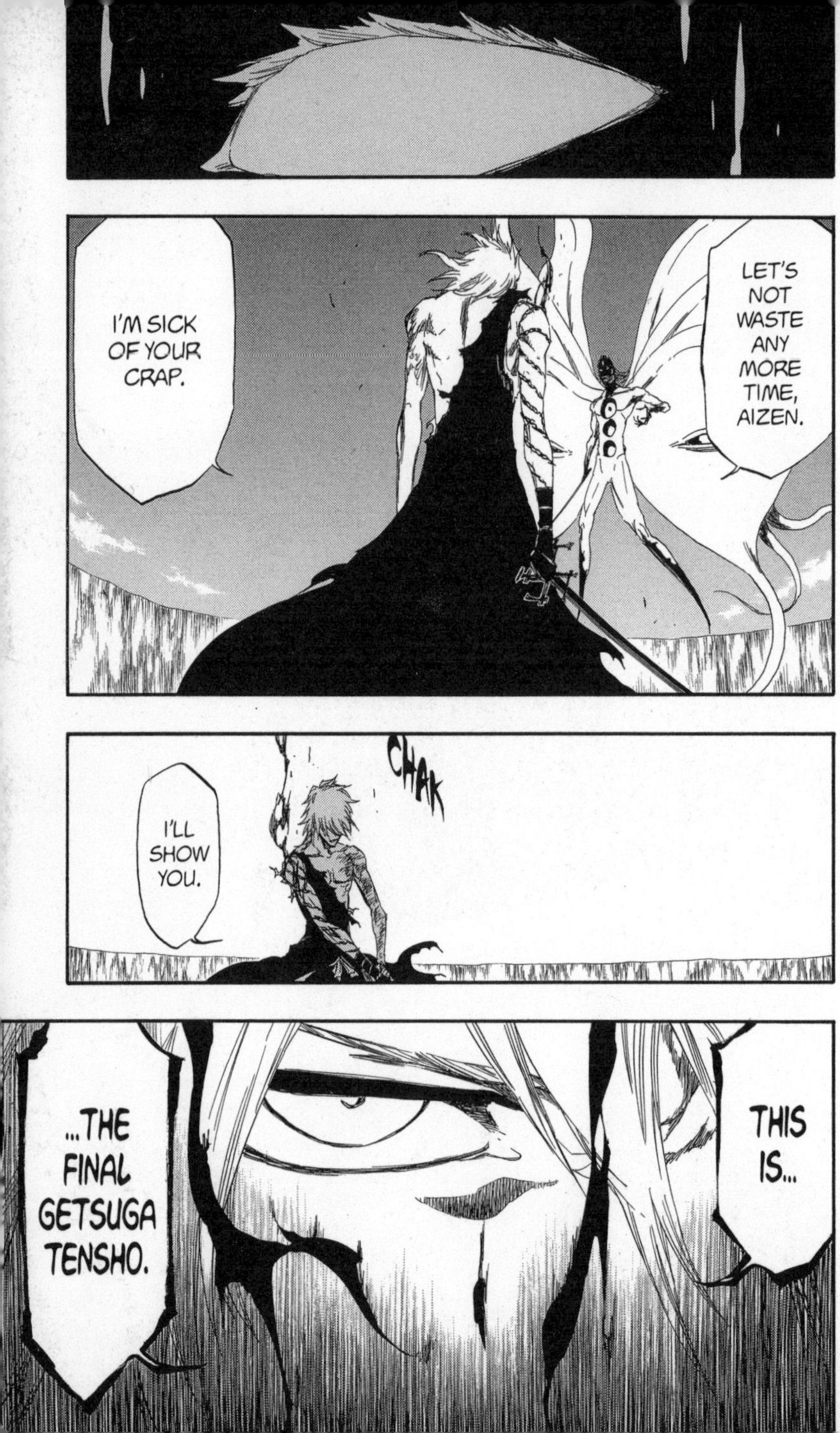
LET'S NOT WASTE ANY MORE TIME, AIZEN.
I'M SICK OF YOUR CRAP.
CHAK
I'LL SHOW YOU.
THIS IS...
...THE FINAL GETSUGA TENSHO.

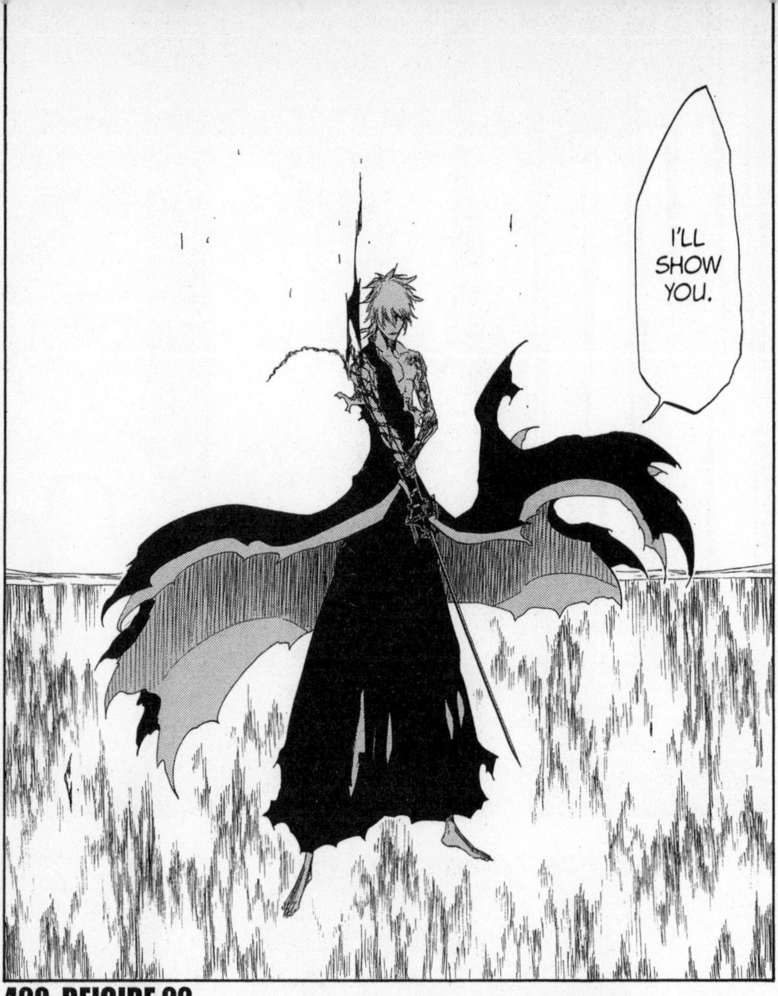
I'LL SHOW YOU.

420. DEICIDE 22

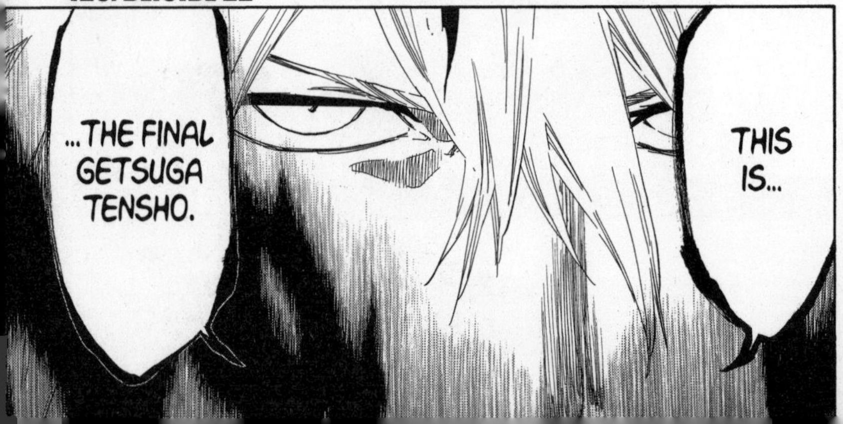
THIS IS...
...THE FINAL GETSUGA TENSHO.

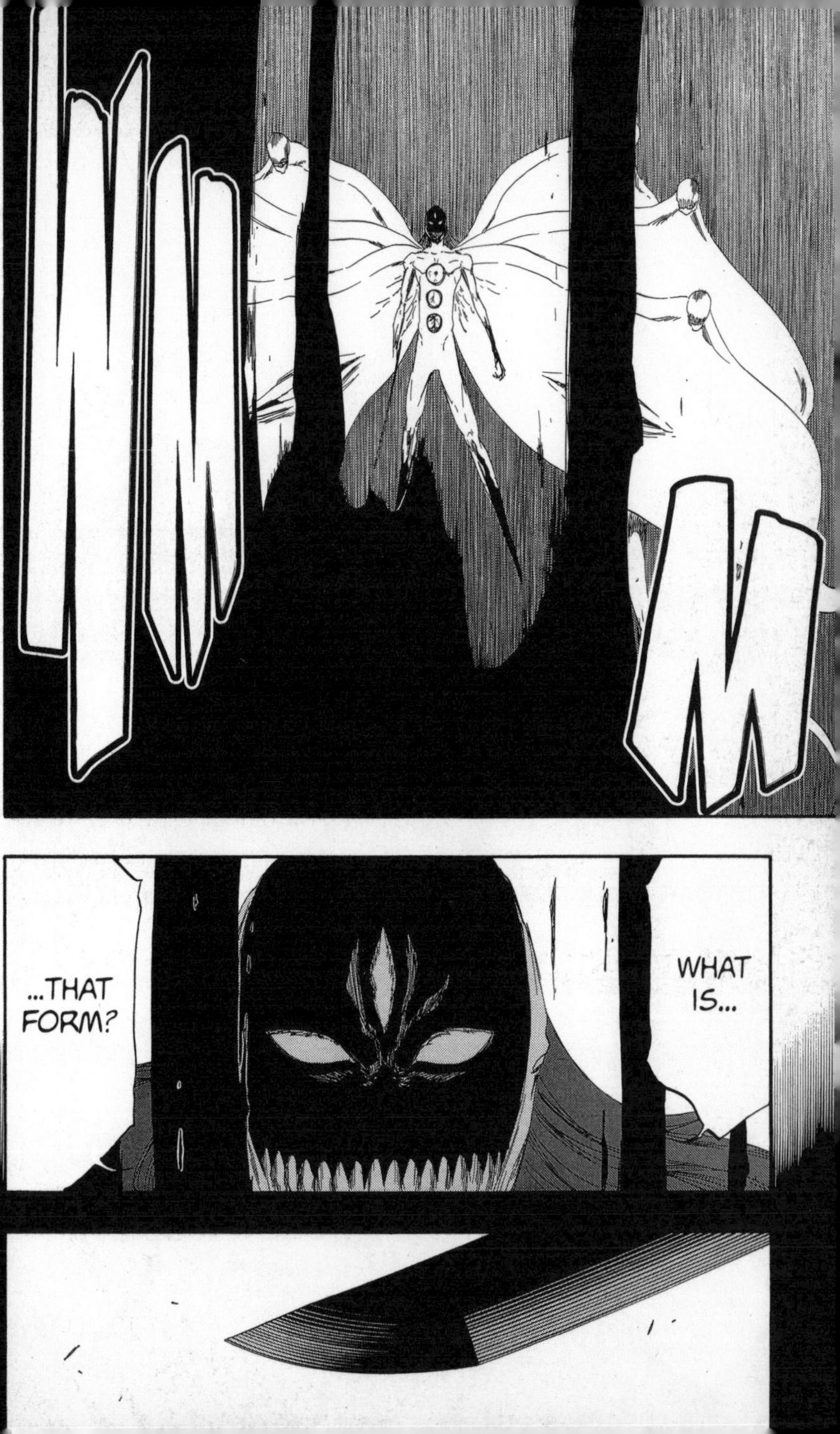
WHAT IS...
...THAT FORM?

BLEACH 420.

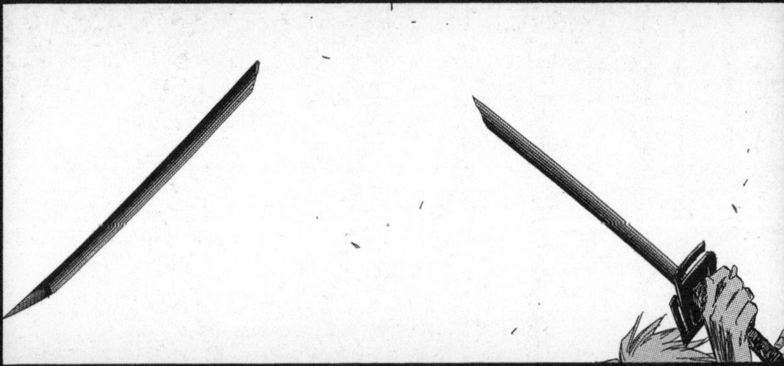

DEICIDE22

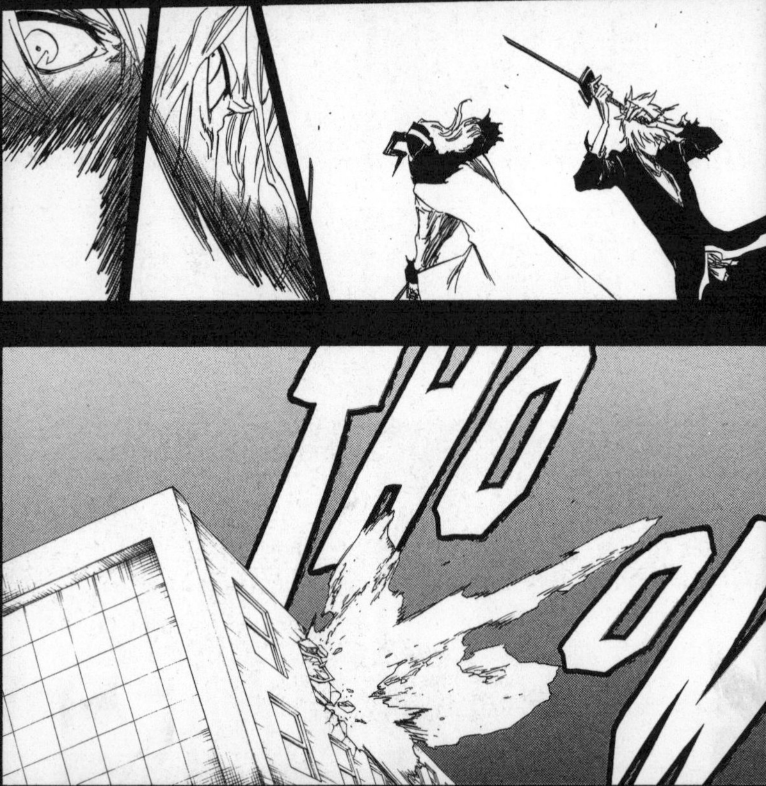

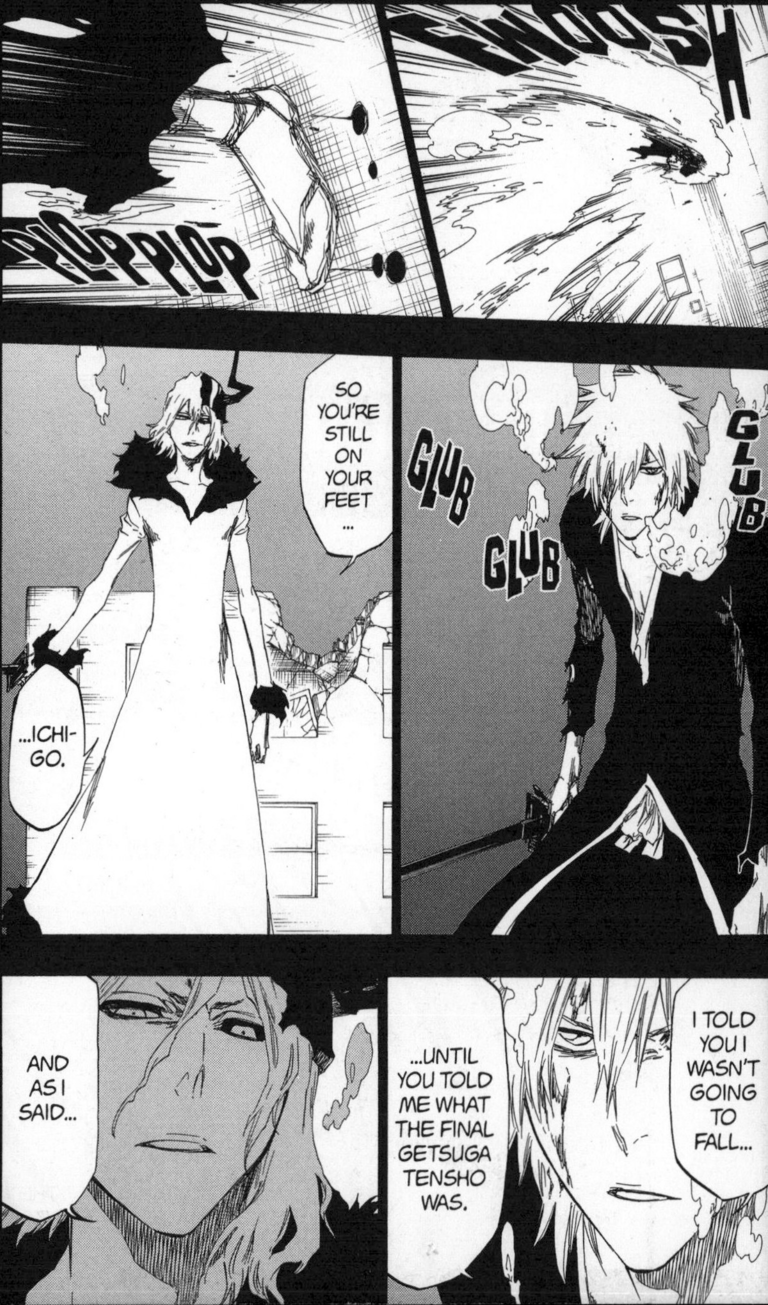
WHOOSH
PLOPPLOP
GLUB
GLUB
GLUB
SO YOU'RE STILL ON YOUR FEET ...
...ICHIGO.
I TOLD YOU I WASN'T GOING TO FALL...
...UNTIL YOU TOLD ME WHAT THE FINAL GETSUGA TENSHO WAS.
AND AS I SAID...

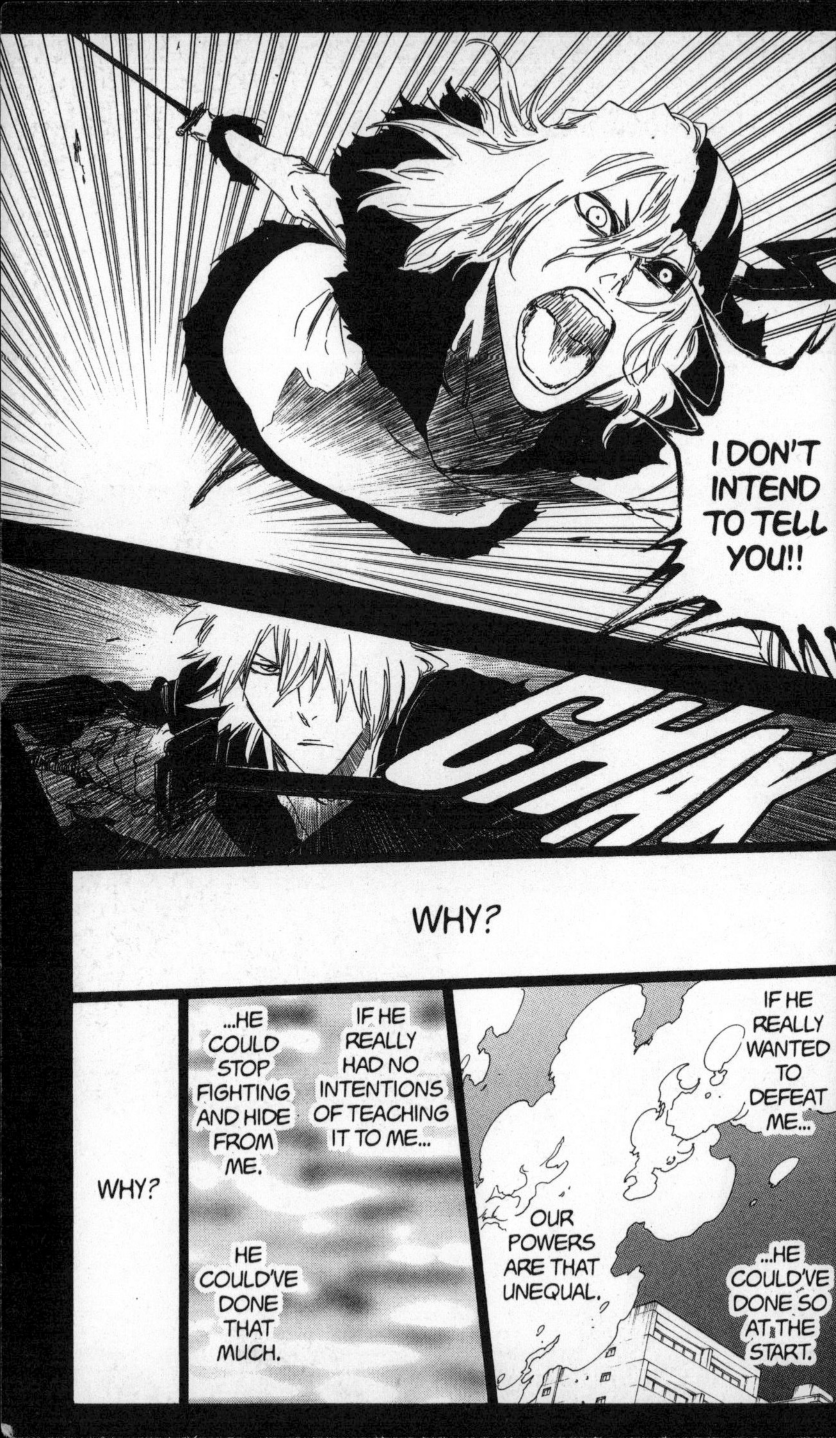
I DON'T INTEND TO TELL YOU!!
WHY?
IF HE REALLY WANTED TO DEFEAT ME...
...HE COULD'VE DONE SO AT THE START.
OUR POWERS ARE THAT UNEQUAL.
IF HE REALLY HAD NO INTENTIONS OF TEACHING IT TO ME...
...HE COULD STOP FIGHTING AND HIDE FROM ME.
HE COULD'VE DONE THAT MUCH.
WHY?

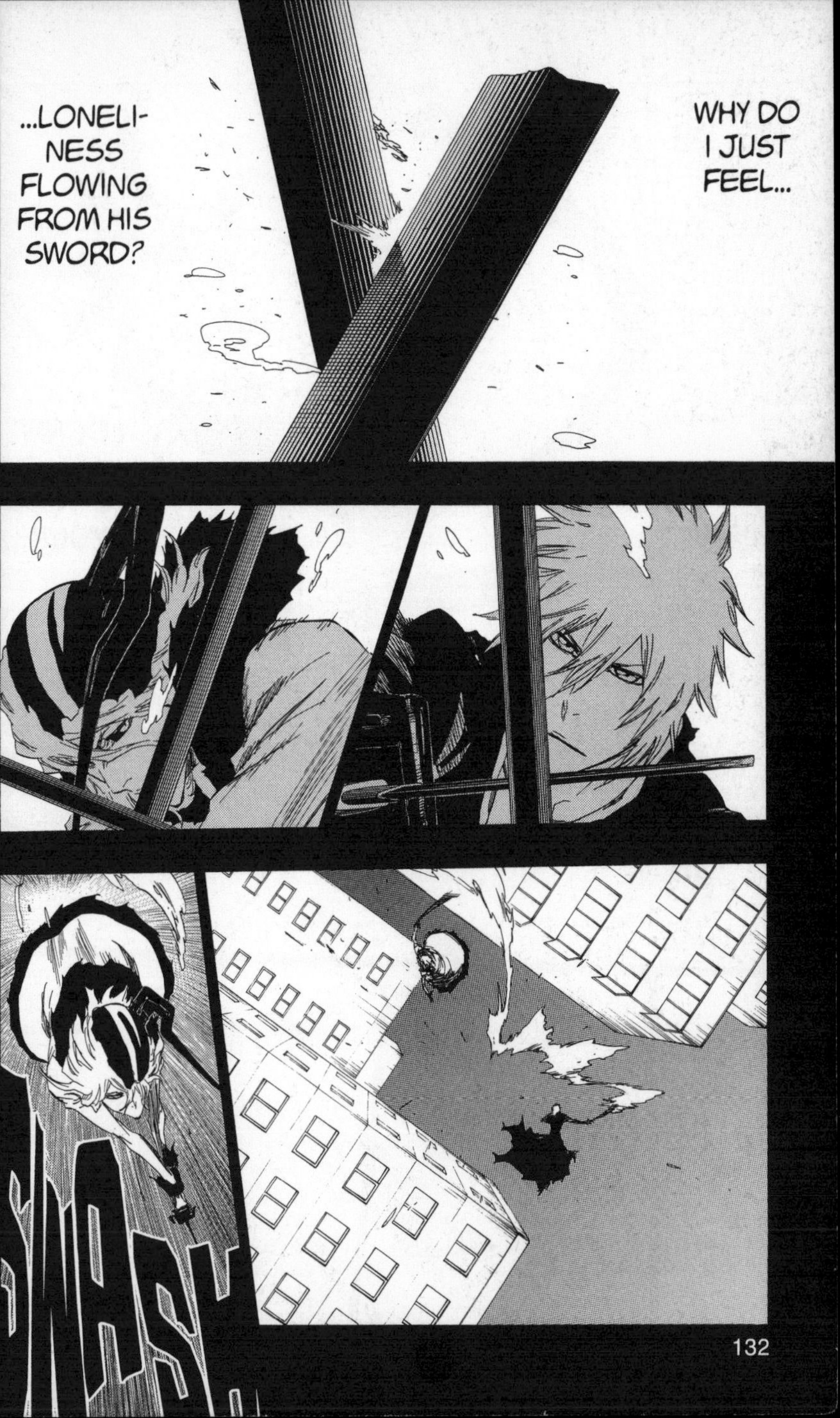
WHY DO I JUST FEEL...
...LONELINESS FLOWING FROM HIS SWORD?

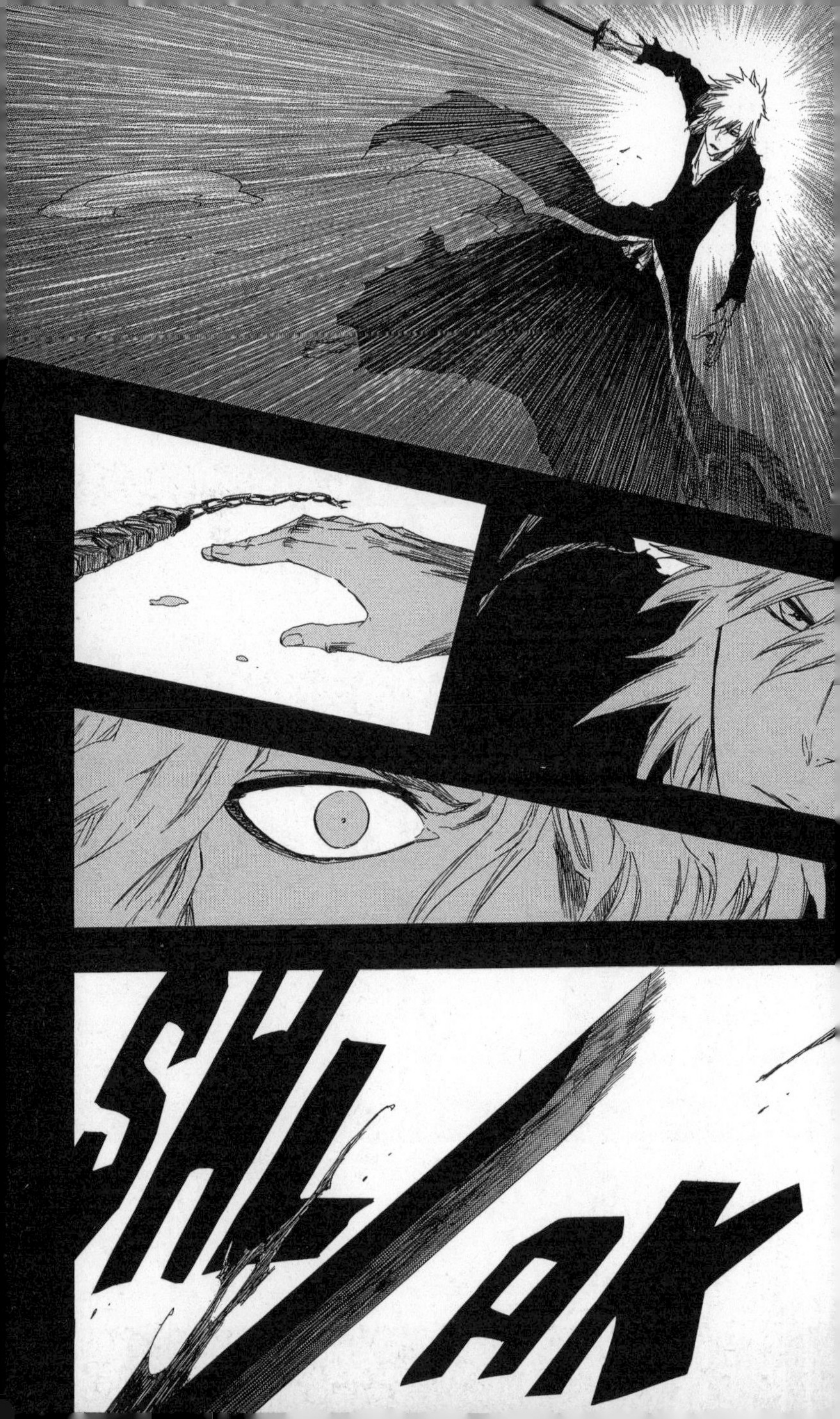
SHLAK

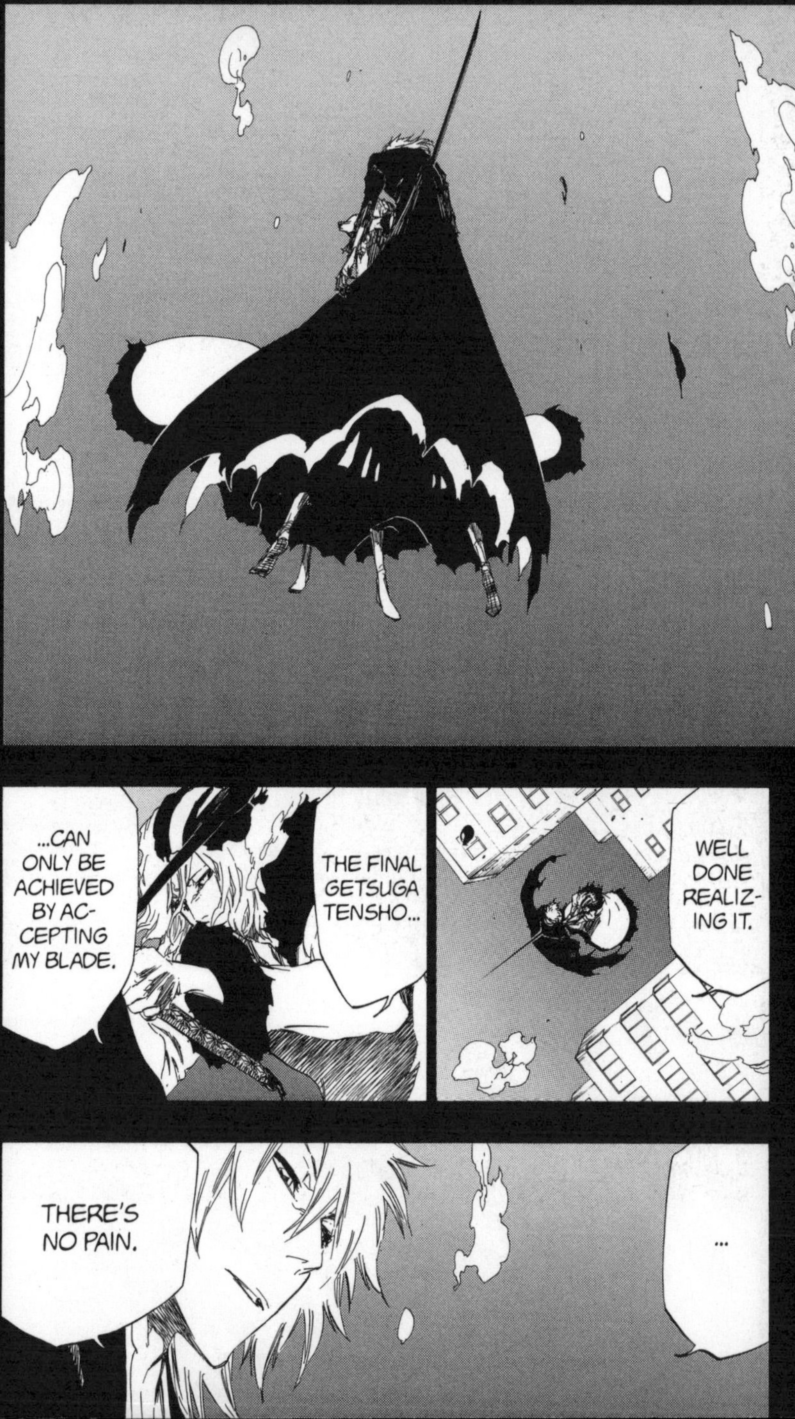
WELL DONE REALIZING IT.
THE FINAL GETSUGA TENSHO...
...CAN ONLY BE ACHIEVED BY ACCEPTING MY BLADE.
...
THERE'S NO PAIN.

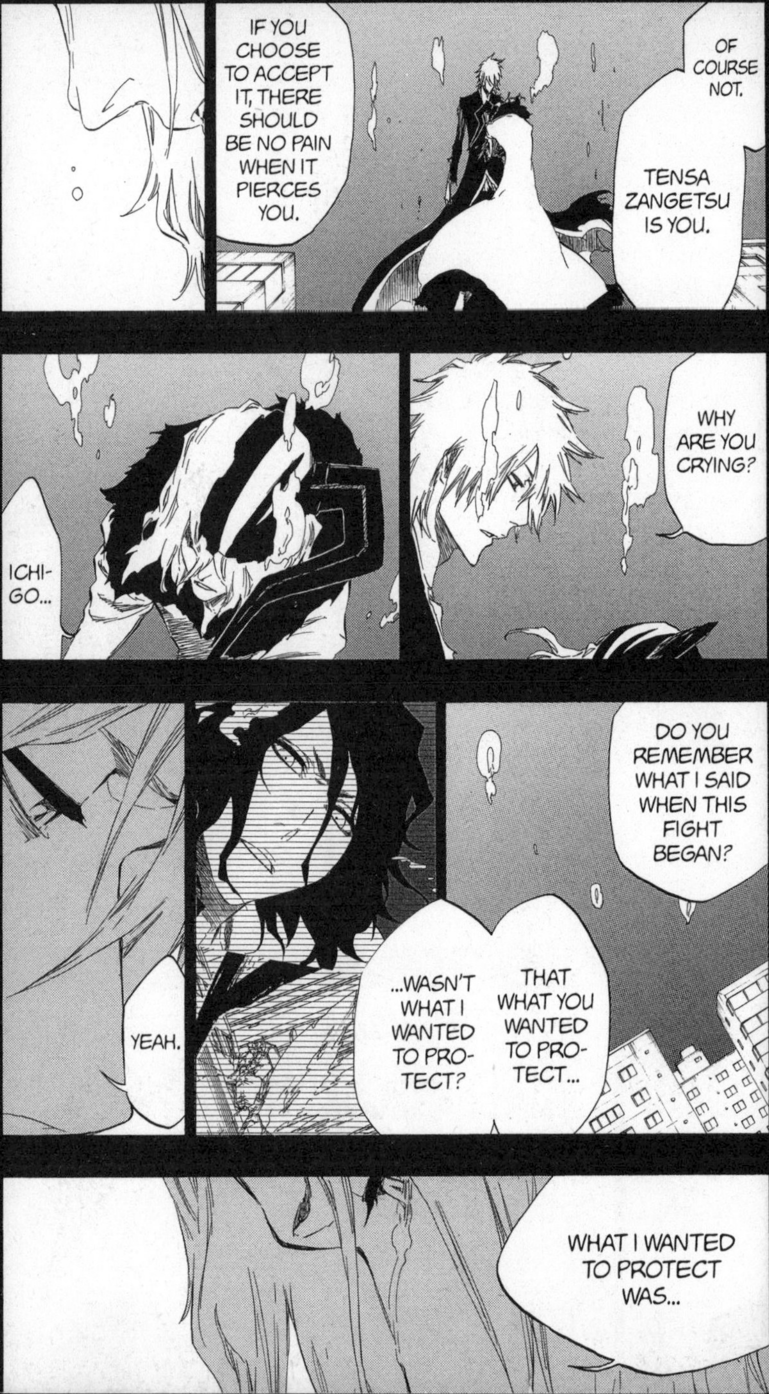
OF COURSE NOT.
TENSA ZANGETSU IS YOU.
IF YOU CHOOSE TO ACCEPT IT, THERE SHOULD BE NO PAIN WHEN IT PIERCES YOU.
WHY ARE YOU CRYING?
ICHI-GO...
DO YOU REMEMBER WHAT I SAID WHEN THIS FIGHT BEGAN?
THAT WHAT YOU WANTED TO PRO-TECT...
...WASN'T WHAT I WANTED TO PRO-TECT?
YEAH.
WHAT I WANTED TO PROTECT WAS...

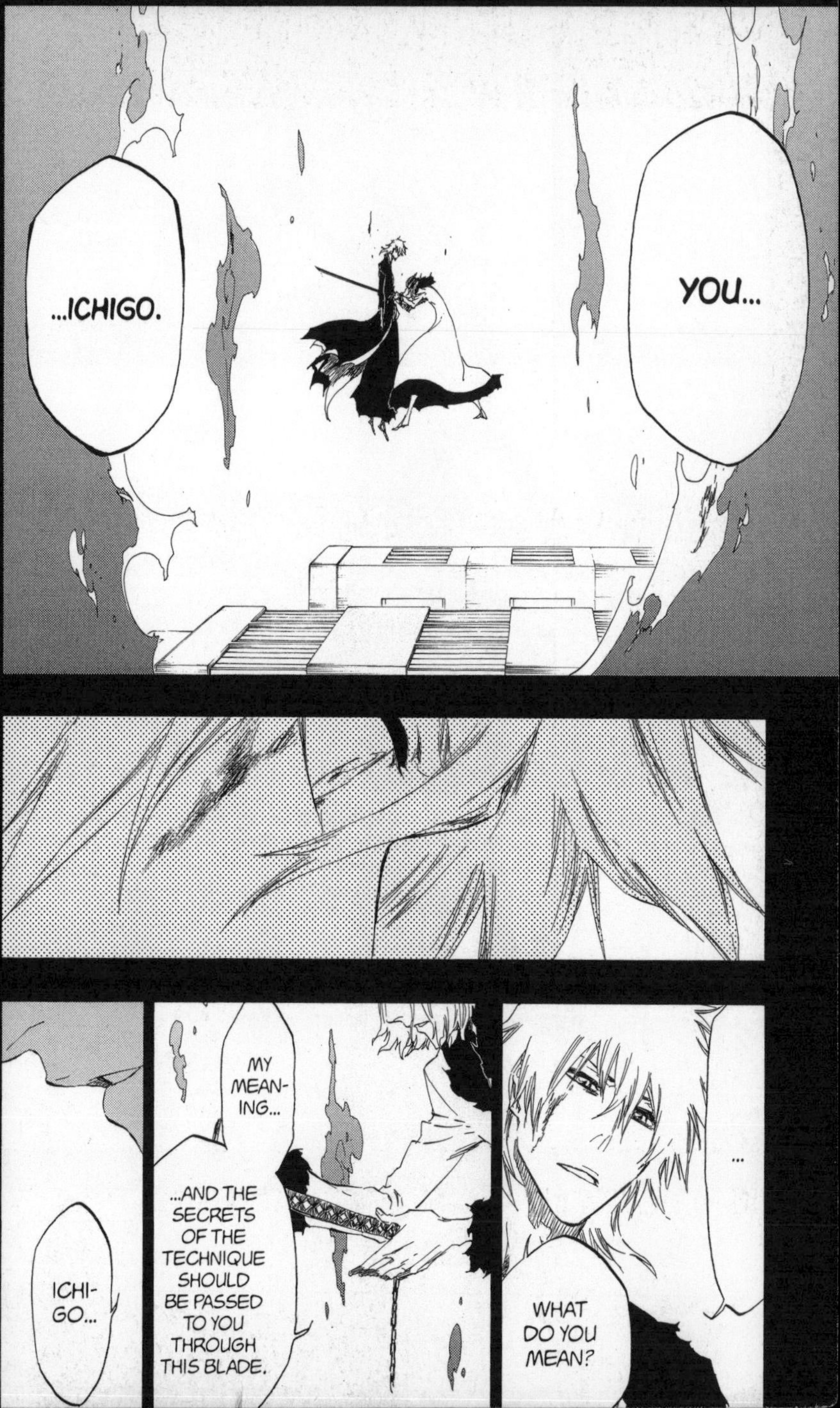
YOU...
...ICHIGO.
...
WHAT DO YOU MEAN?
MY MEANING...
...AND THE SECRETS OF THE TECHNIQUE SHOULD BE PASSED TO YOU THROUGH THIS BLADE.
ICHIGO...

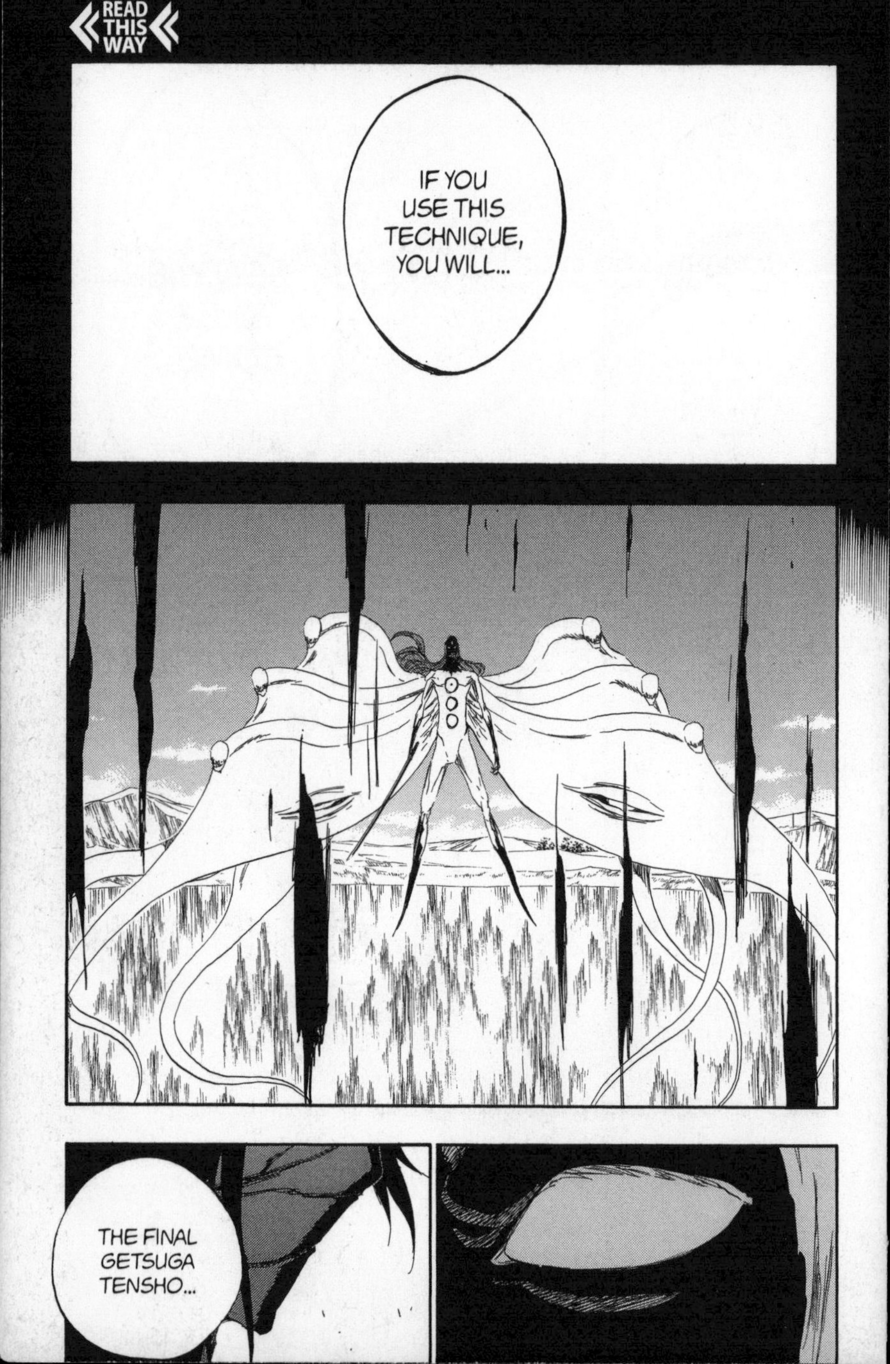
READ THIS WAY
IF YOU USE THIS TECHNIQUE, YOU WILL...
THE FINAL GETSUGA TENSHO...

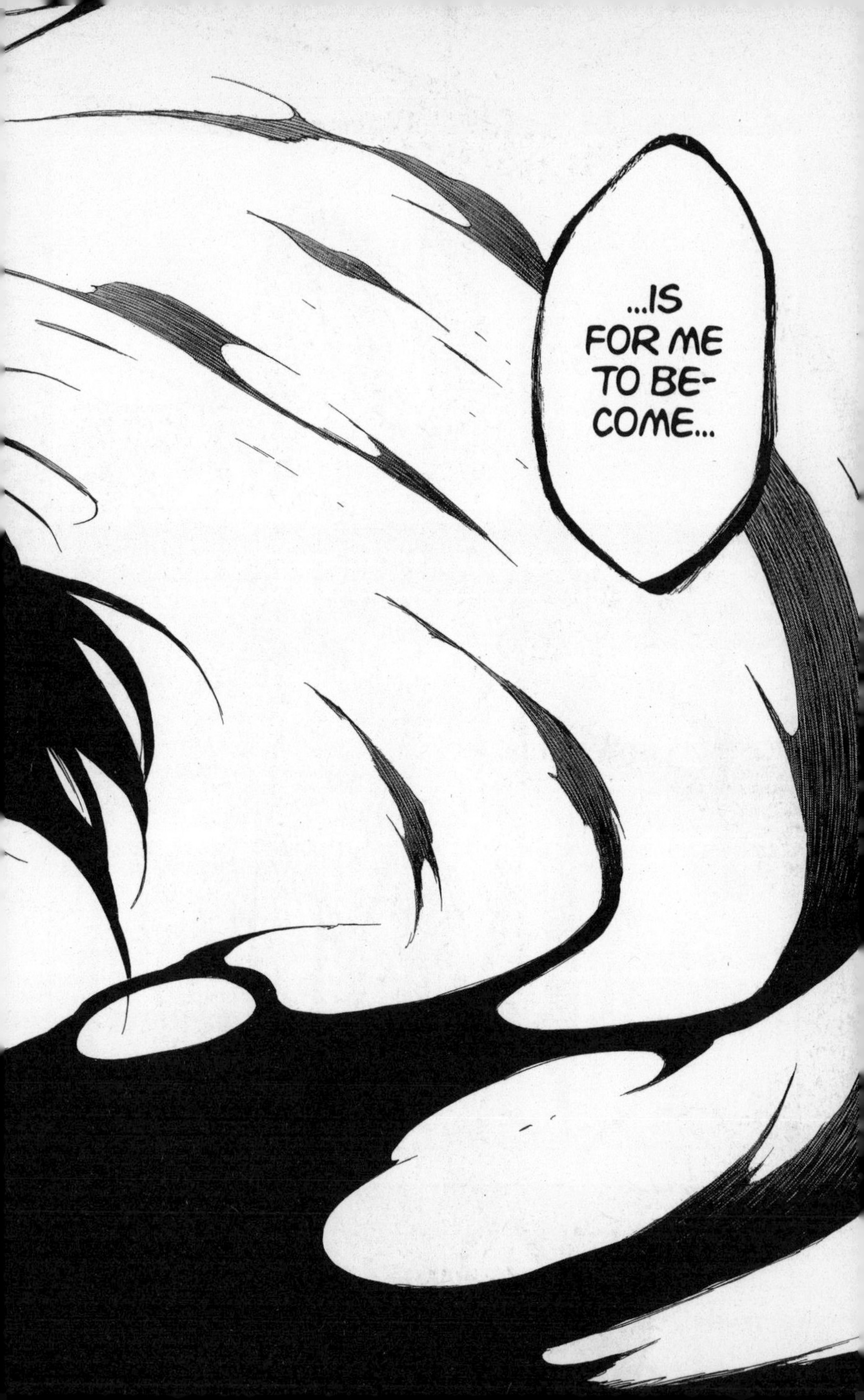
...IS FOR ME TO BE-COME...

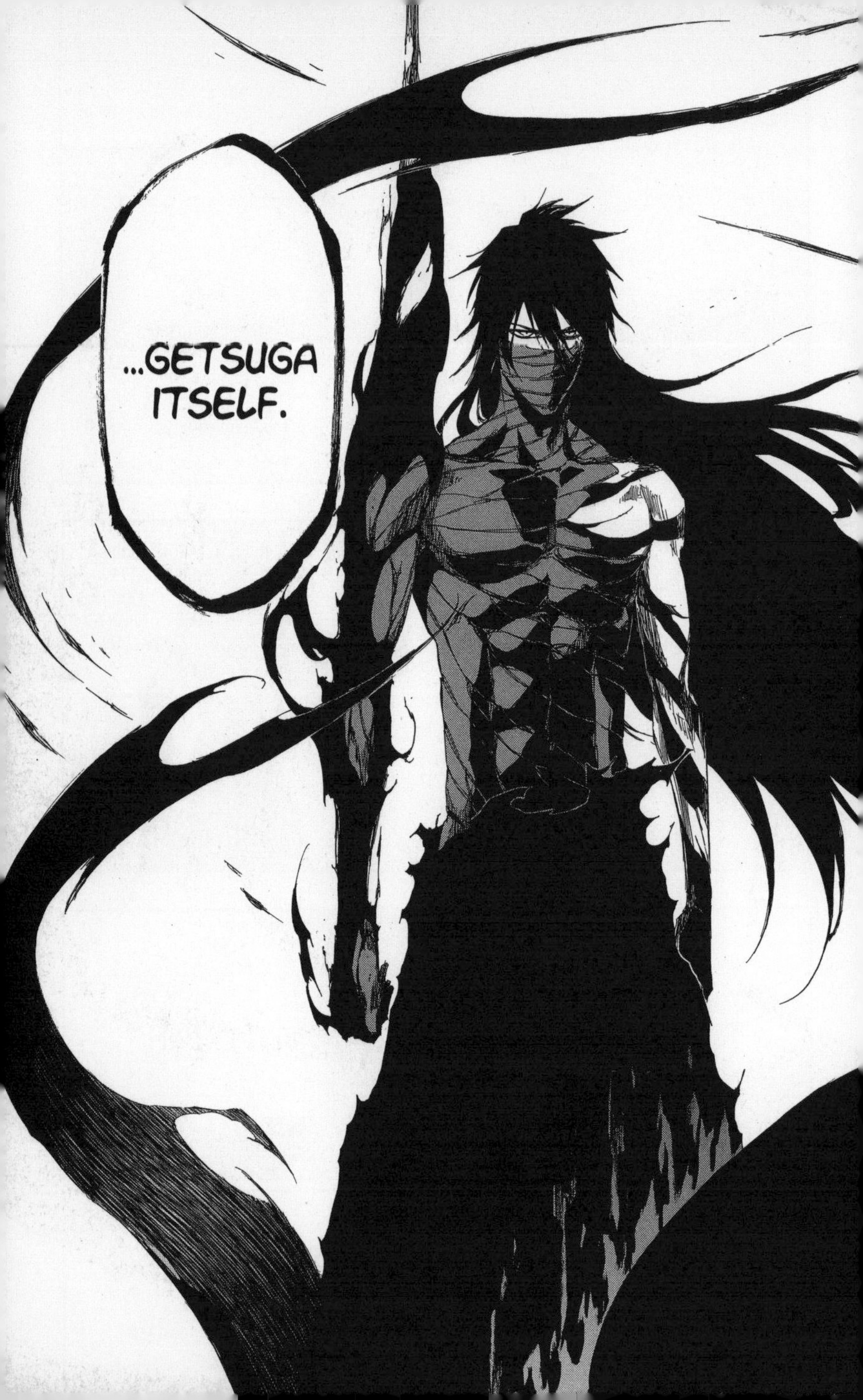
...GETSUGA ITSELF.

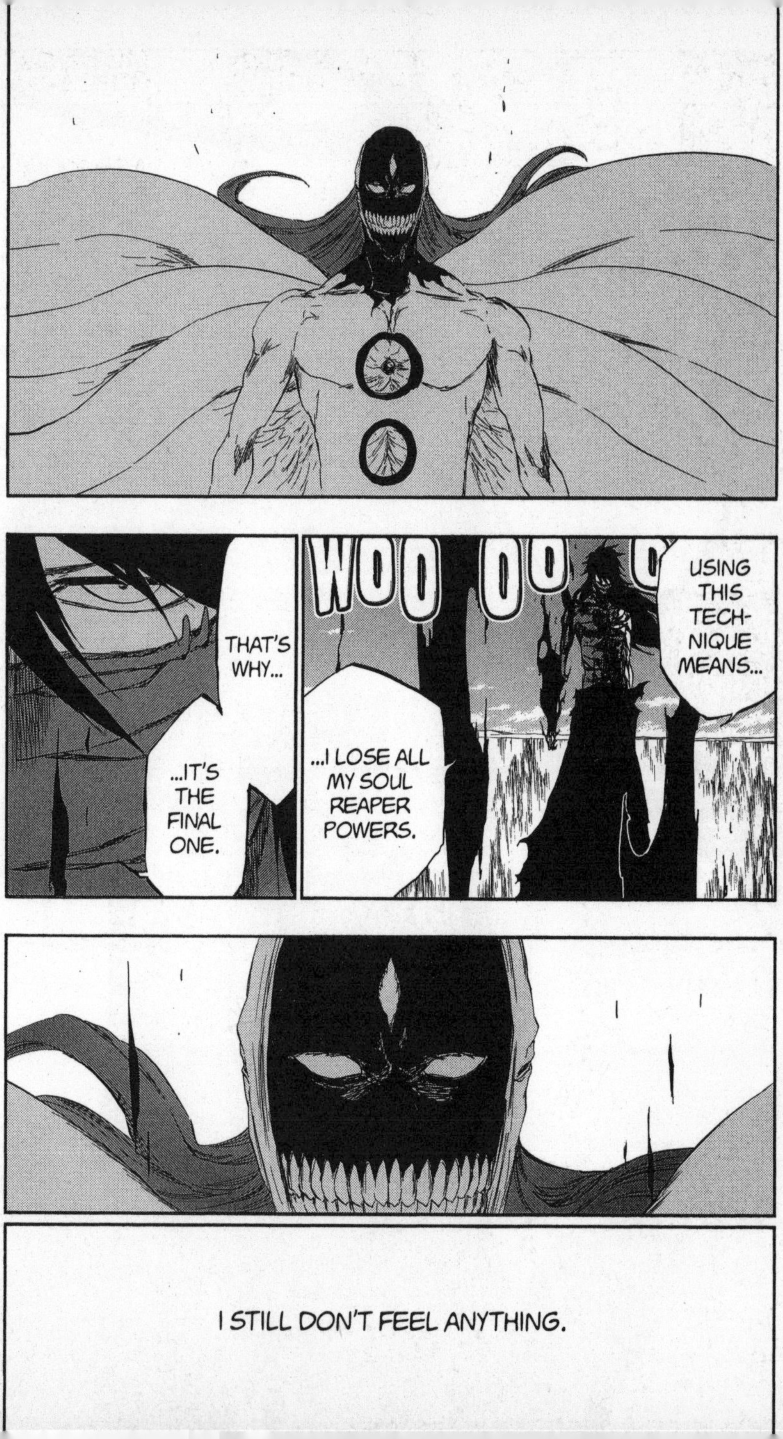
WOO OO
USING THIS TECH-NIQUE MEANS...
...I LOSE ALL MY SOUL REAPER POWERS.
THAT'S WHY...
...IT'S THE FINAL ONE.
I STILL DON'T FEEL ANYTHING.

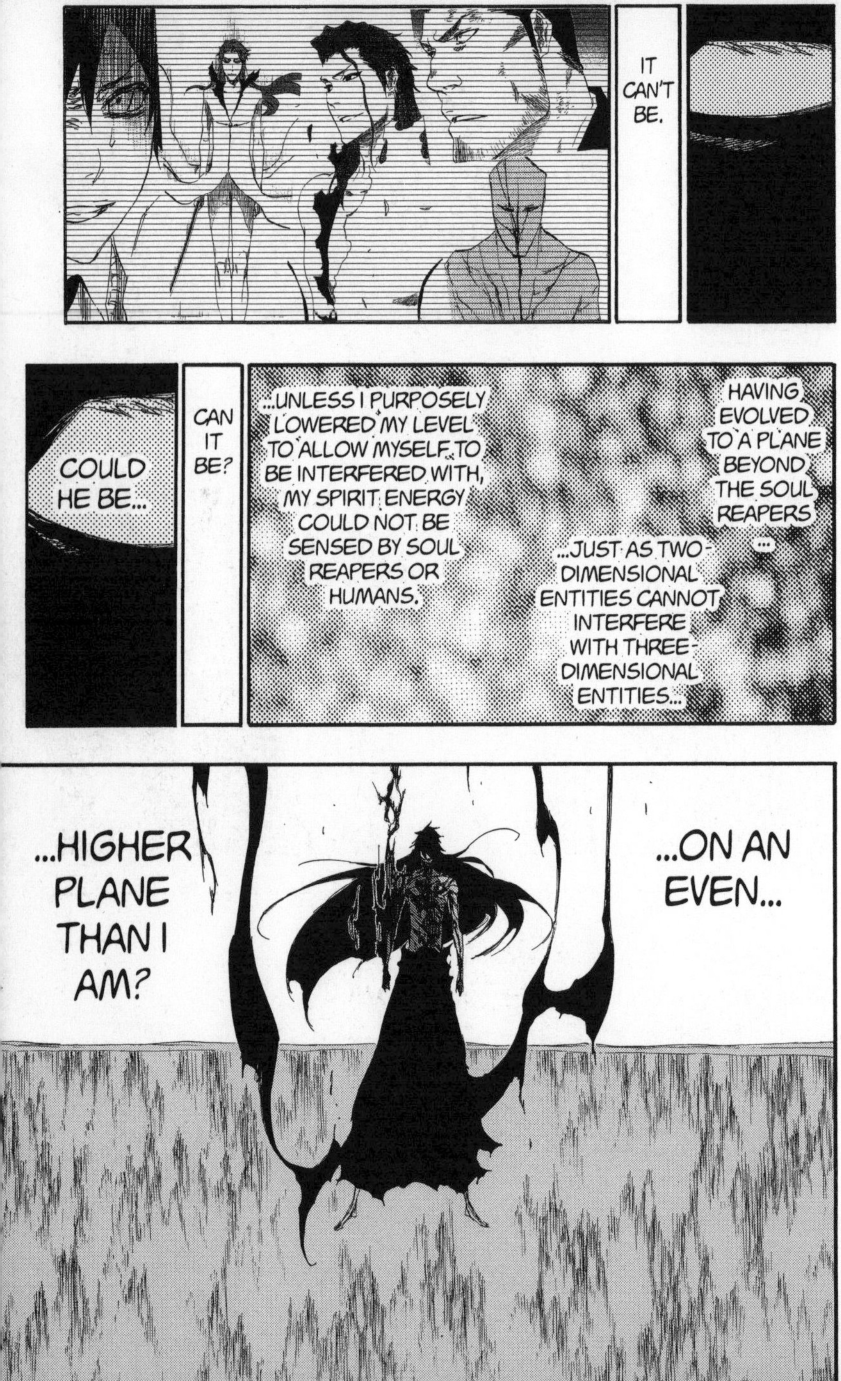
IT CAN'T BE.
HAVING EVOLVED TO A PLANE BEYOND THE SOUL REAPERS...
...JUST AS TWO-DIMENSIONAL ENTITIES CANNOT INTERFERE WITH THREE-DIMENSIONAL ENTITIES...
...UNLESS I PURPOSELY LOWERED MY LEVEL TO ALLOW MYSELF TO BE INTERFERED WITH, MY SPIRIT ENERGY COULD NOT BE SENSED BY SOUL REAPERS OR HUMANS.
CAN IT BE?
COULD HE BE...
...ON AN EVEN...
...HIGHER PLANE THAN I AM?

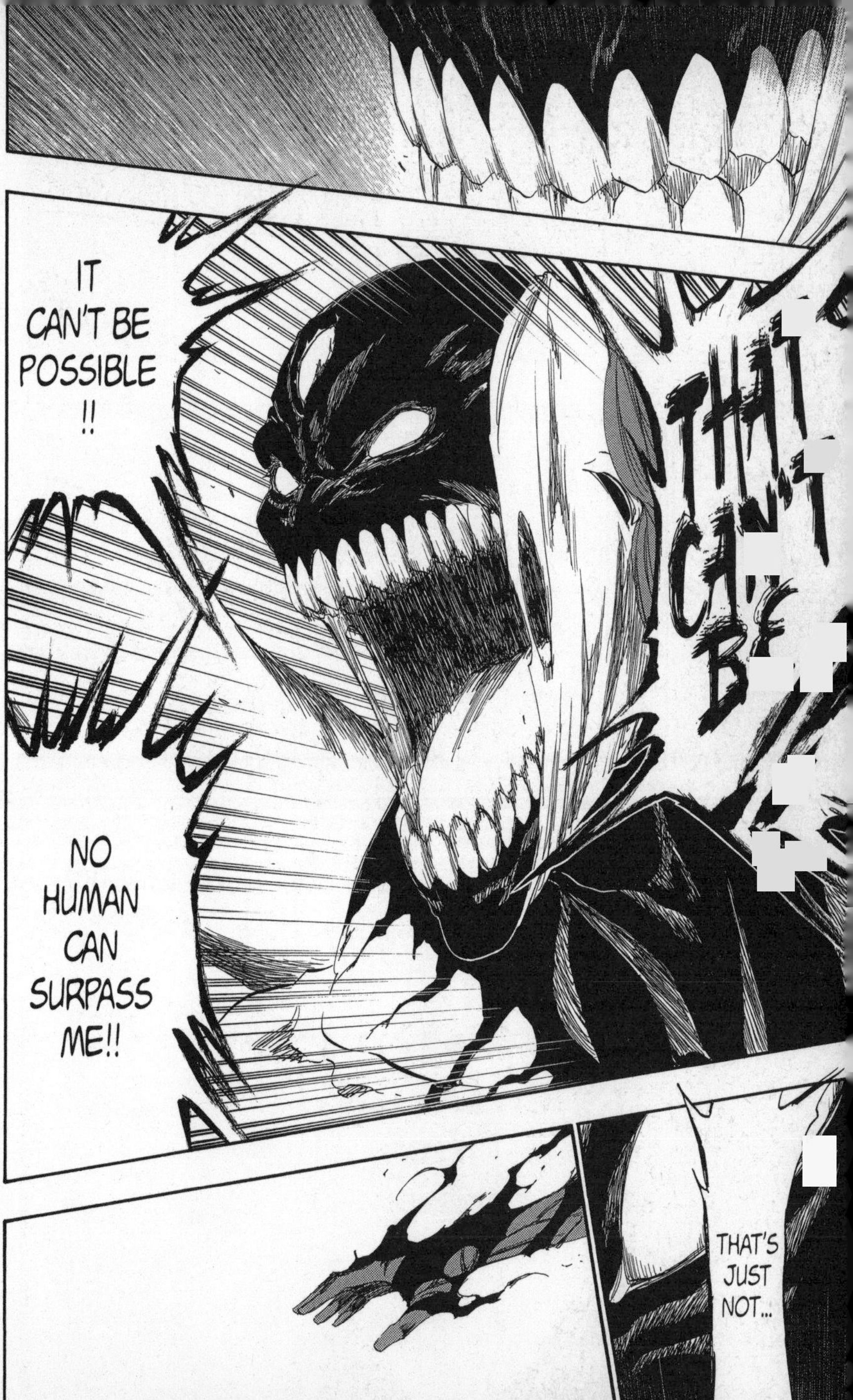
THAT CAN'T BE
IT CAN'T BE POSSIBLE!!
NO HUMAN CAN SURPASS ME!!
THAT'S JUST NOT...

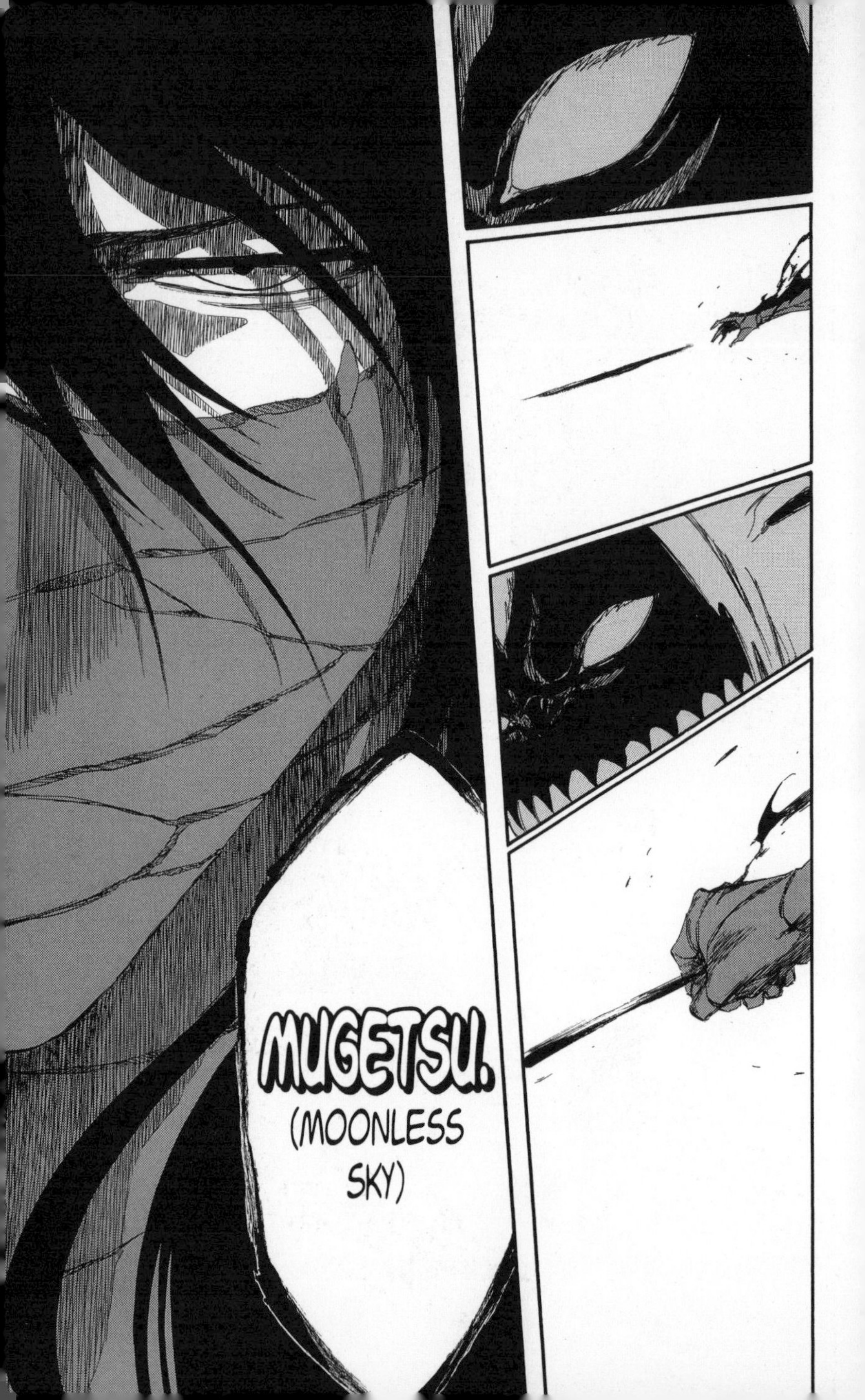
MUGETSU.
(MOONLESS SKY)

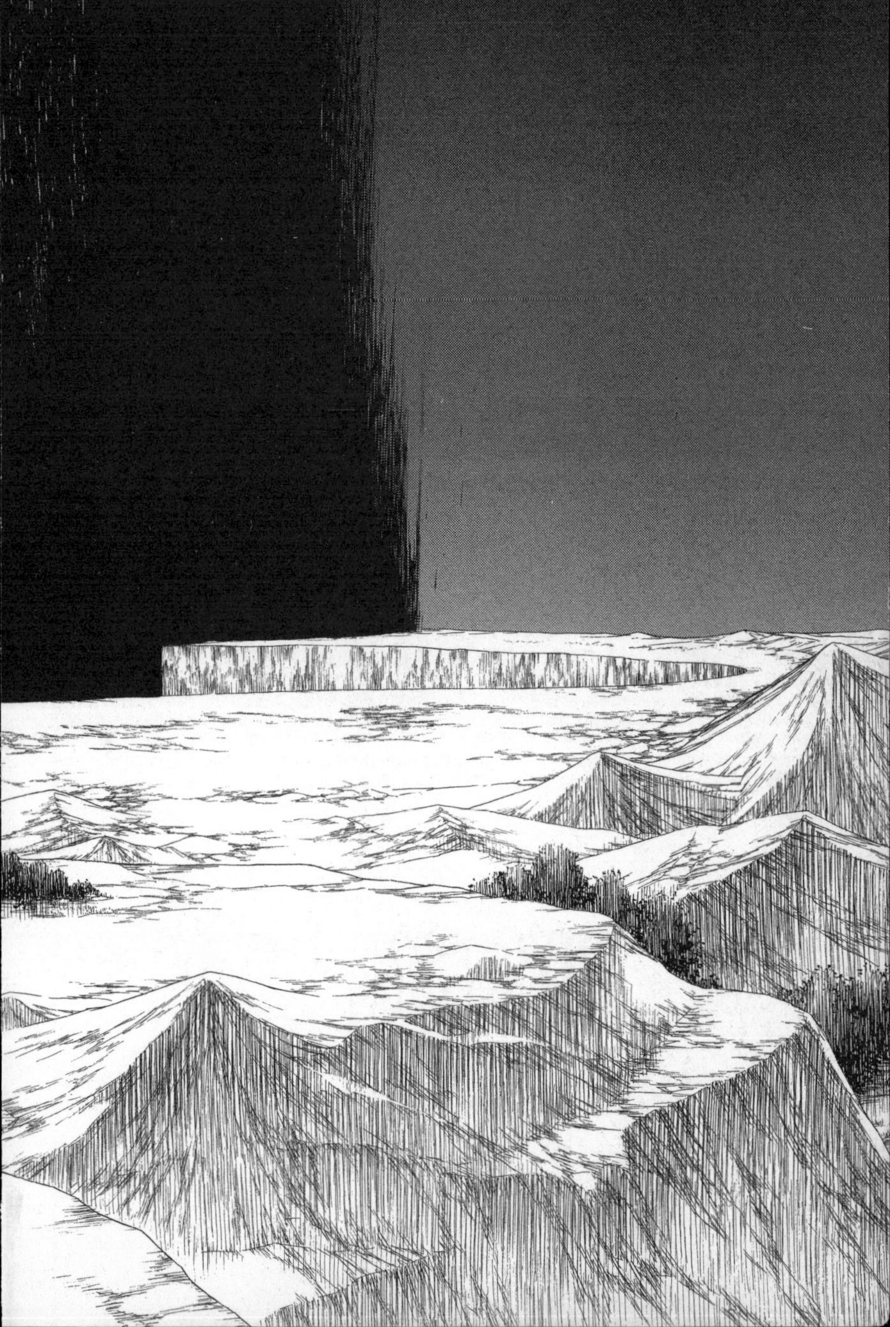

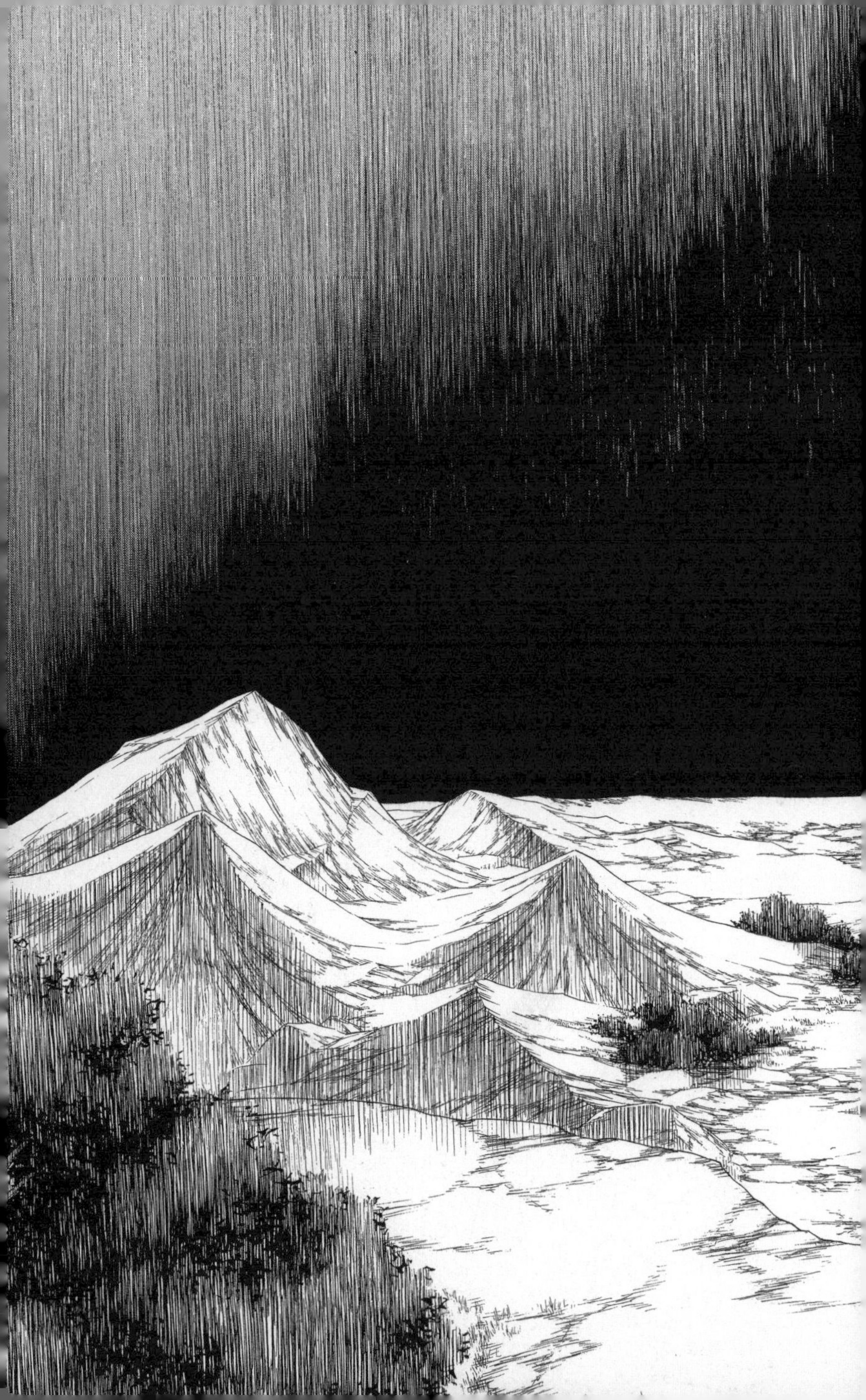

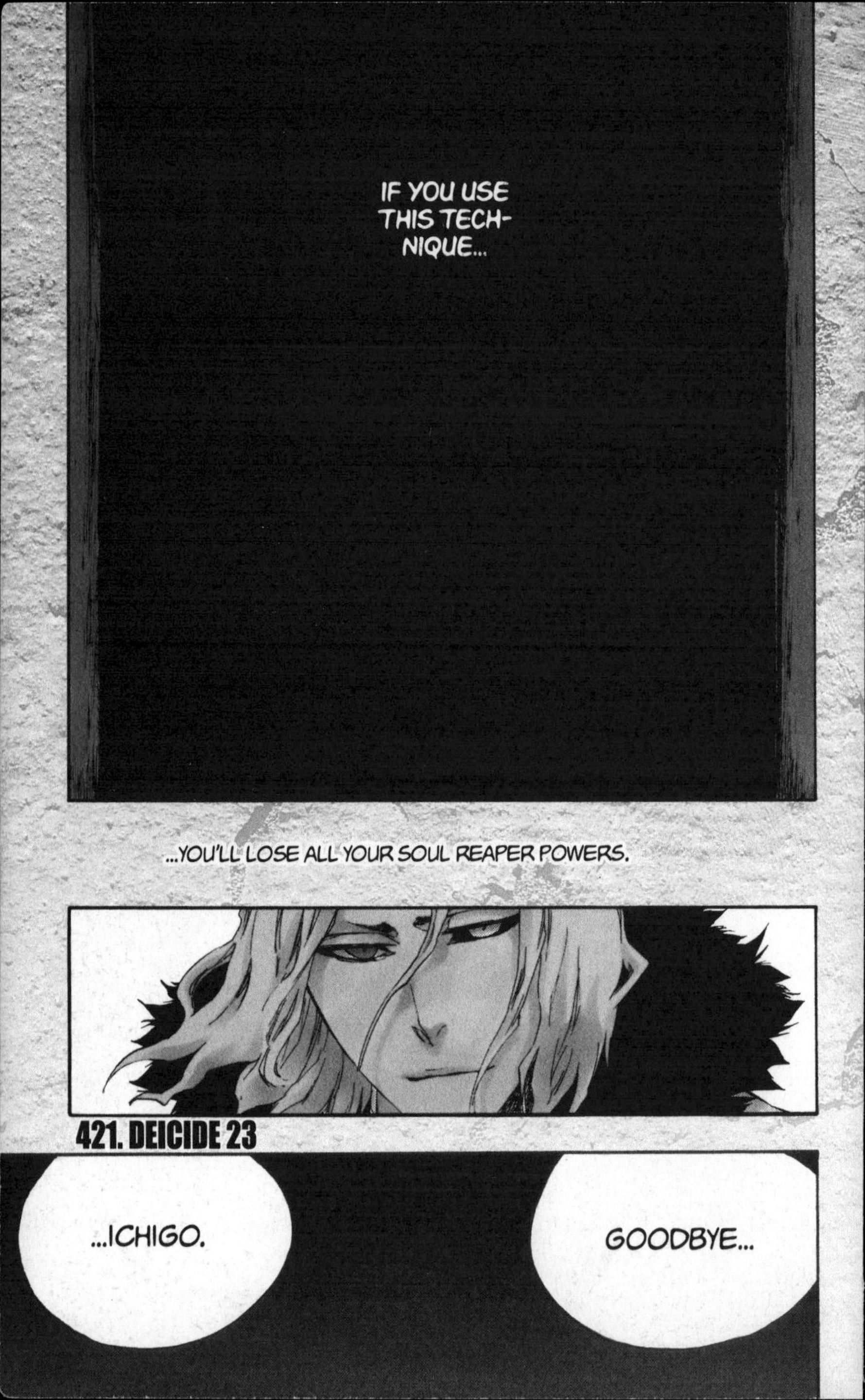
IF YOU USE THIS TECH-NIQUE...
...YOU'LL LOSE ALL YOUR SOUL REAPER POWERS.
421. DEICIDE 23
GOODBYE...
...ICHIGO.

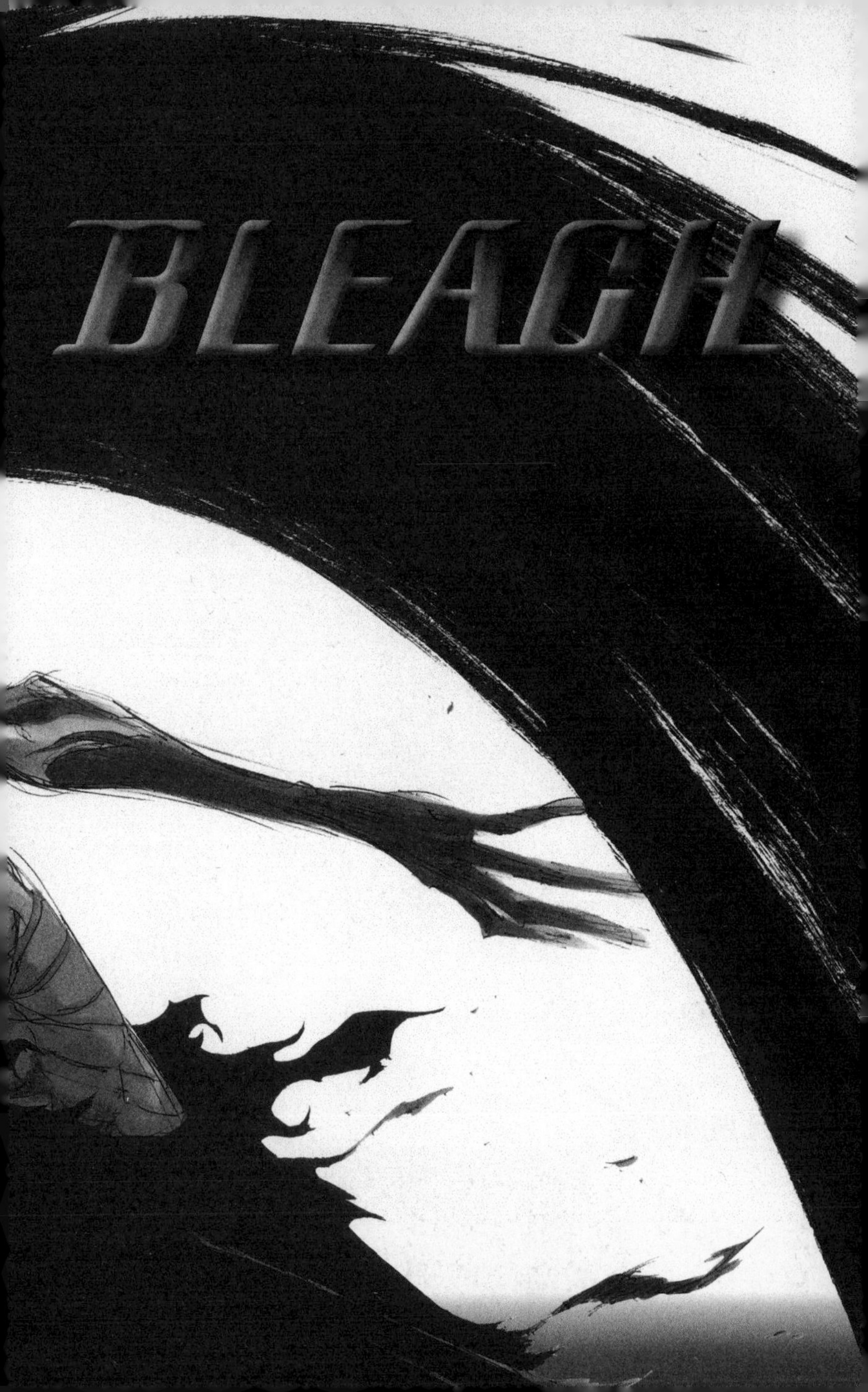
BLEACH

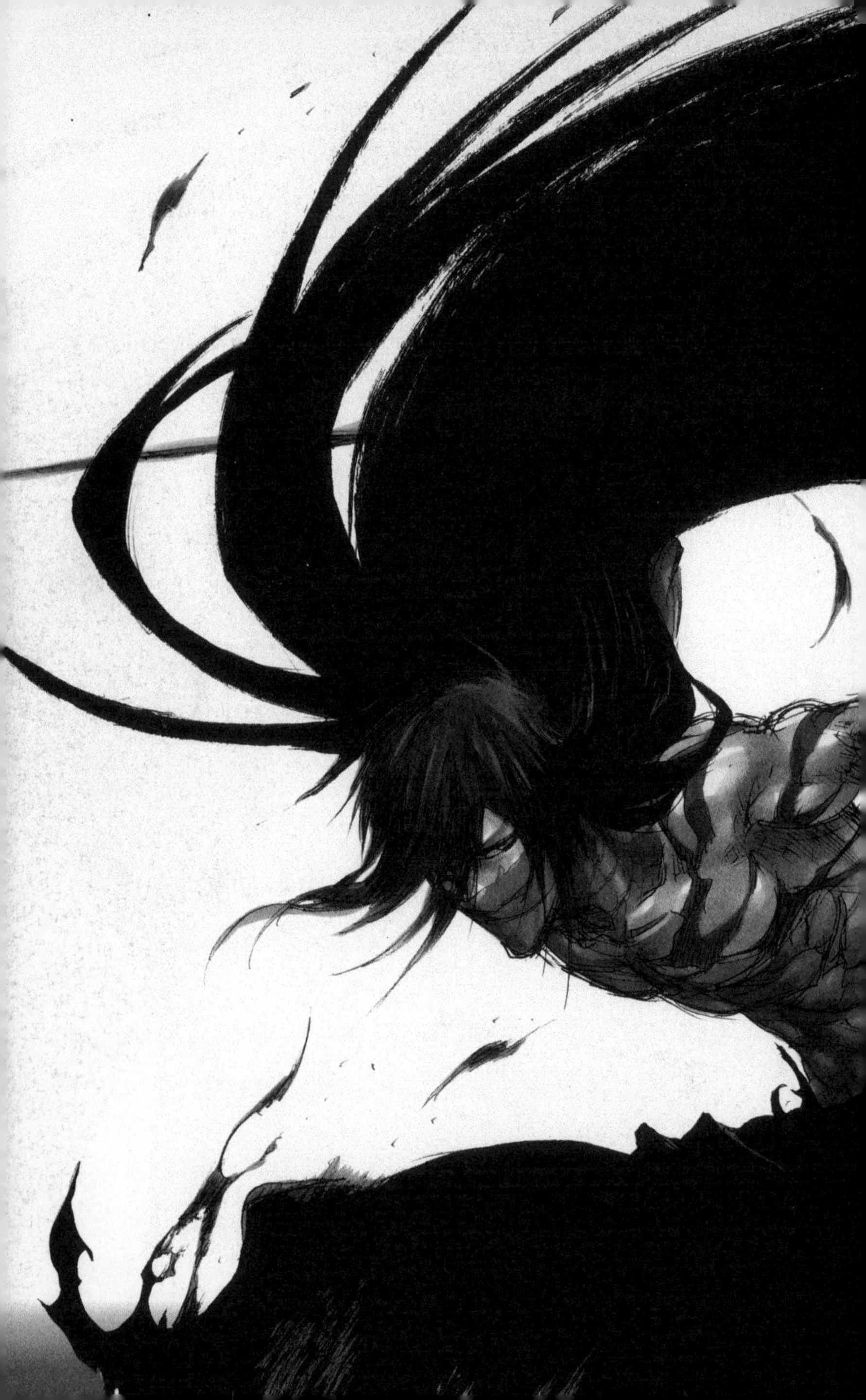

BLEACH
ブリーチ

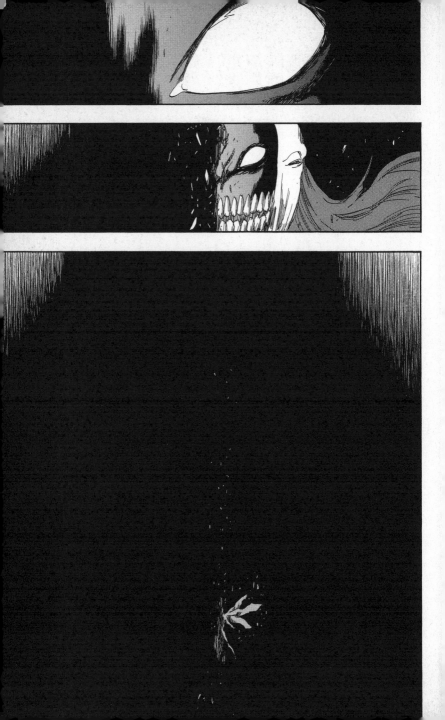

BLEACH
421.

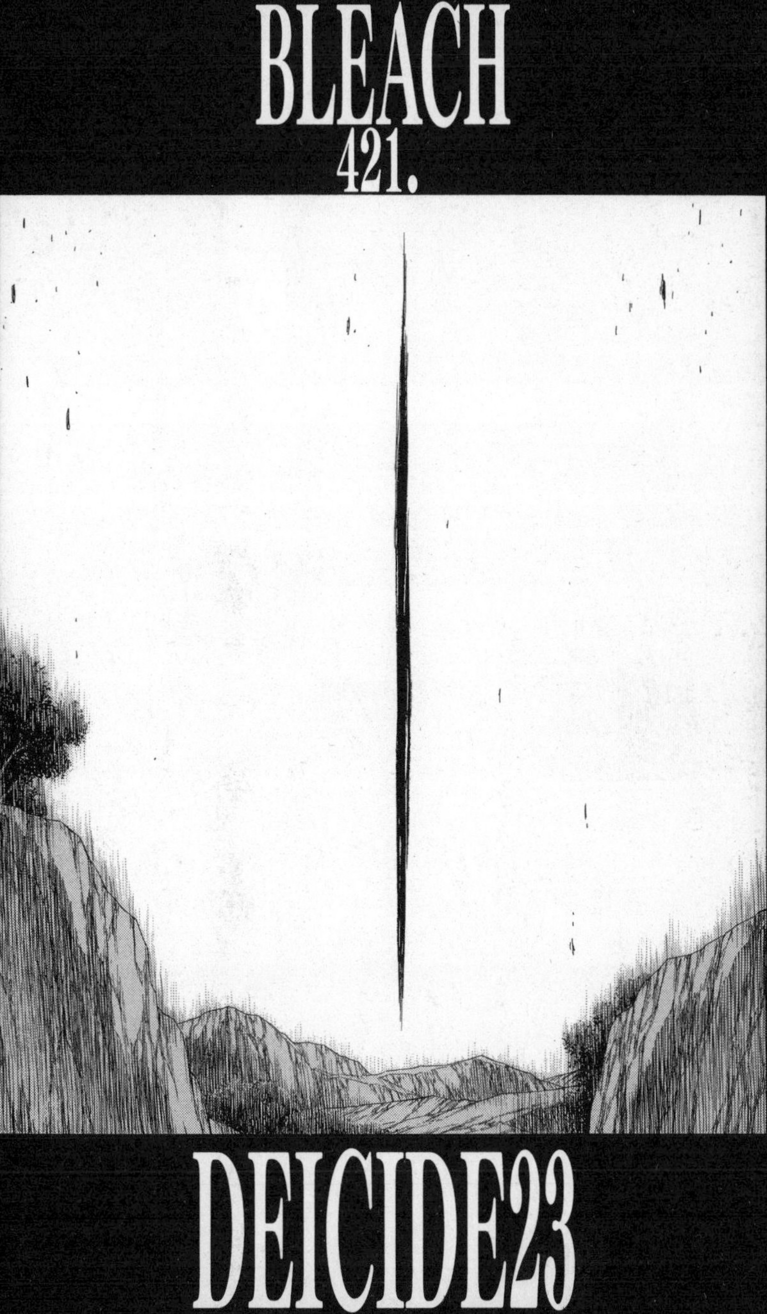

DEICIDE23

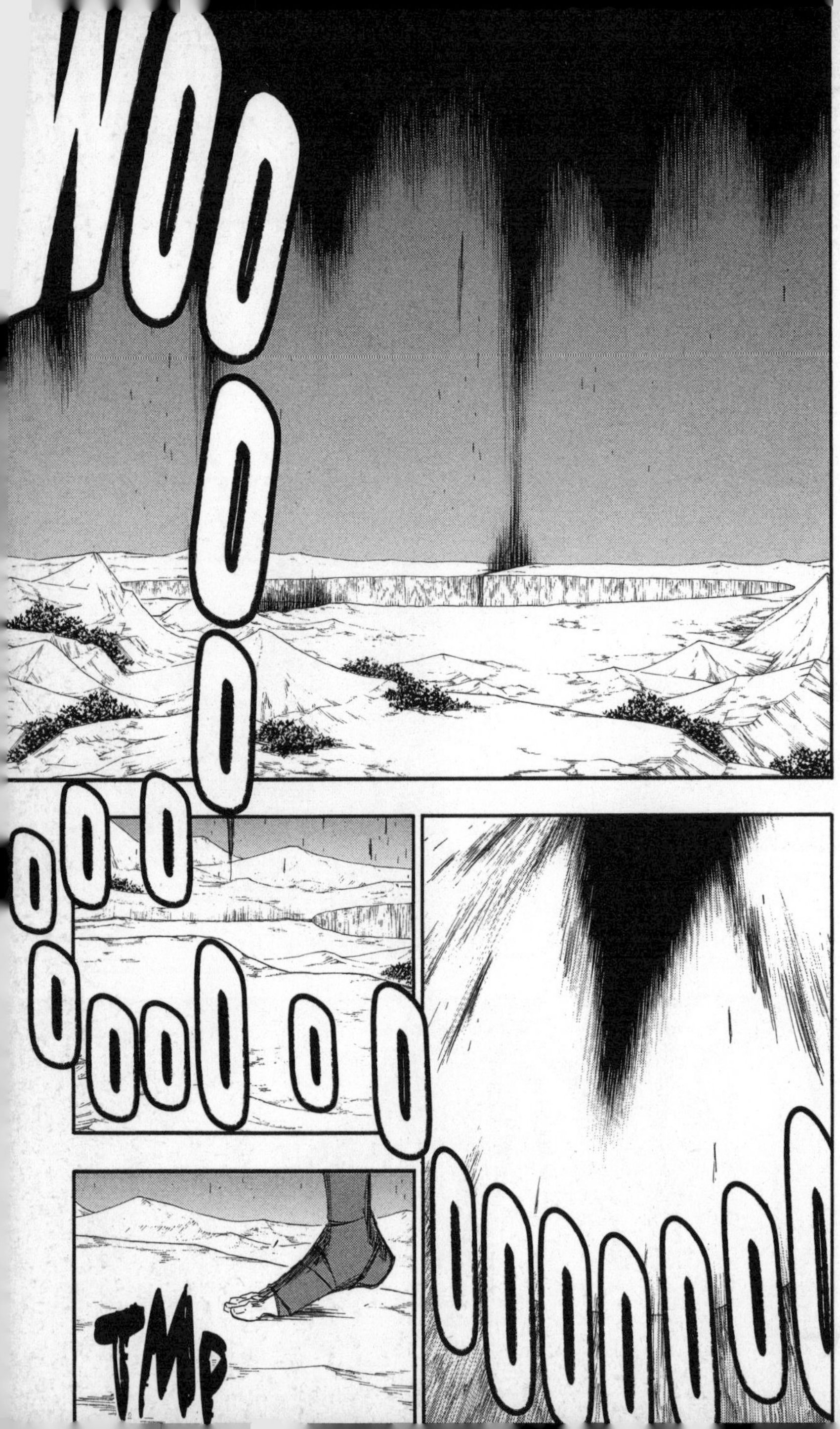
WOOOOOOOOOOOOO
OOOOOOOOO
TMP

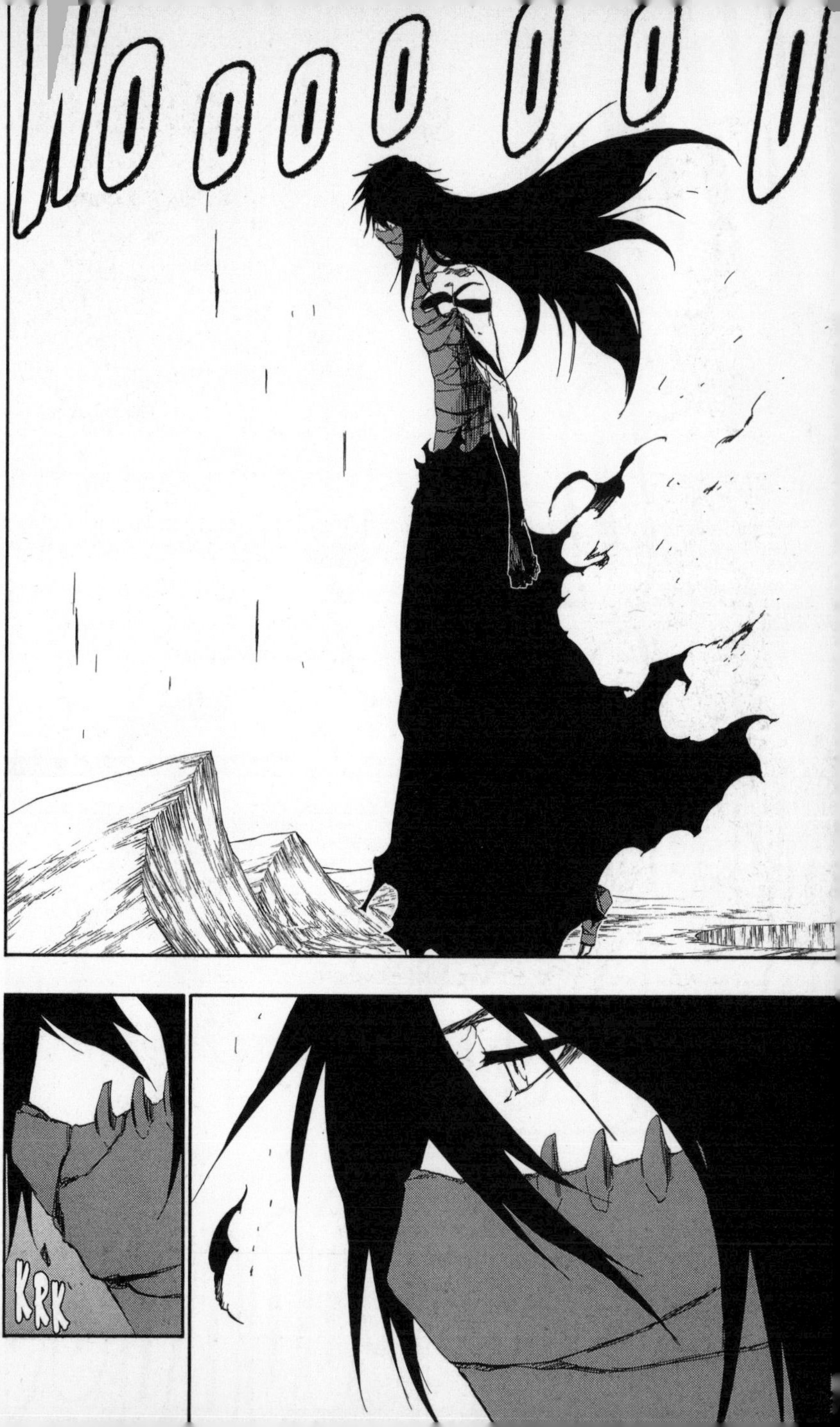
WOOOOOOO
KRK

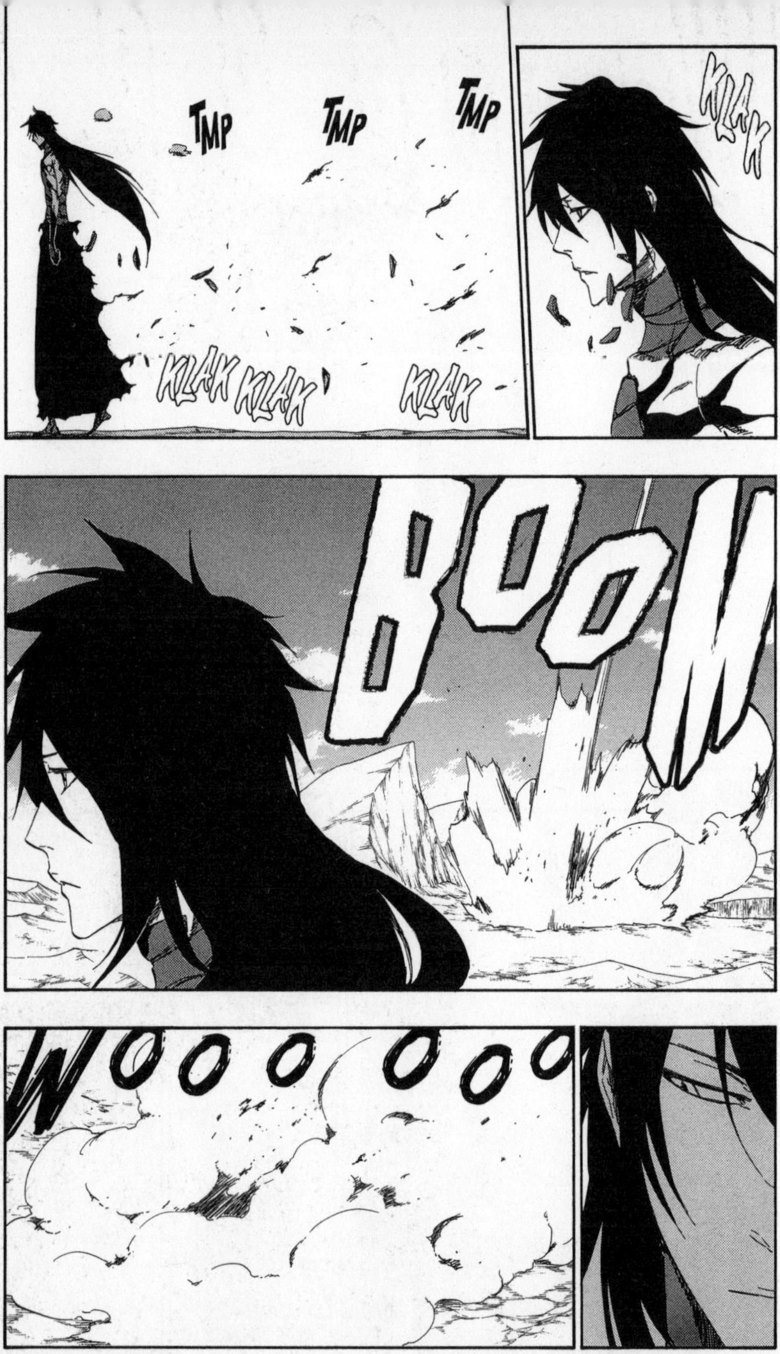
KLAK
TMP
TMP
TMP
KLAK KLAK
KLAK
BOOM
WOOO OOO

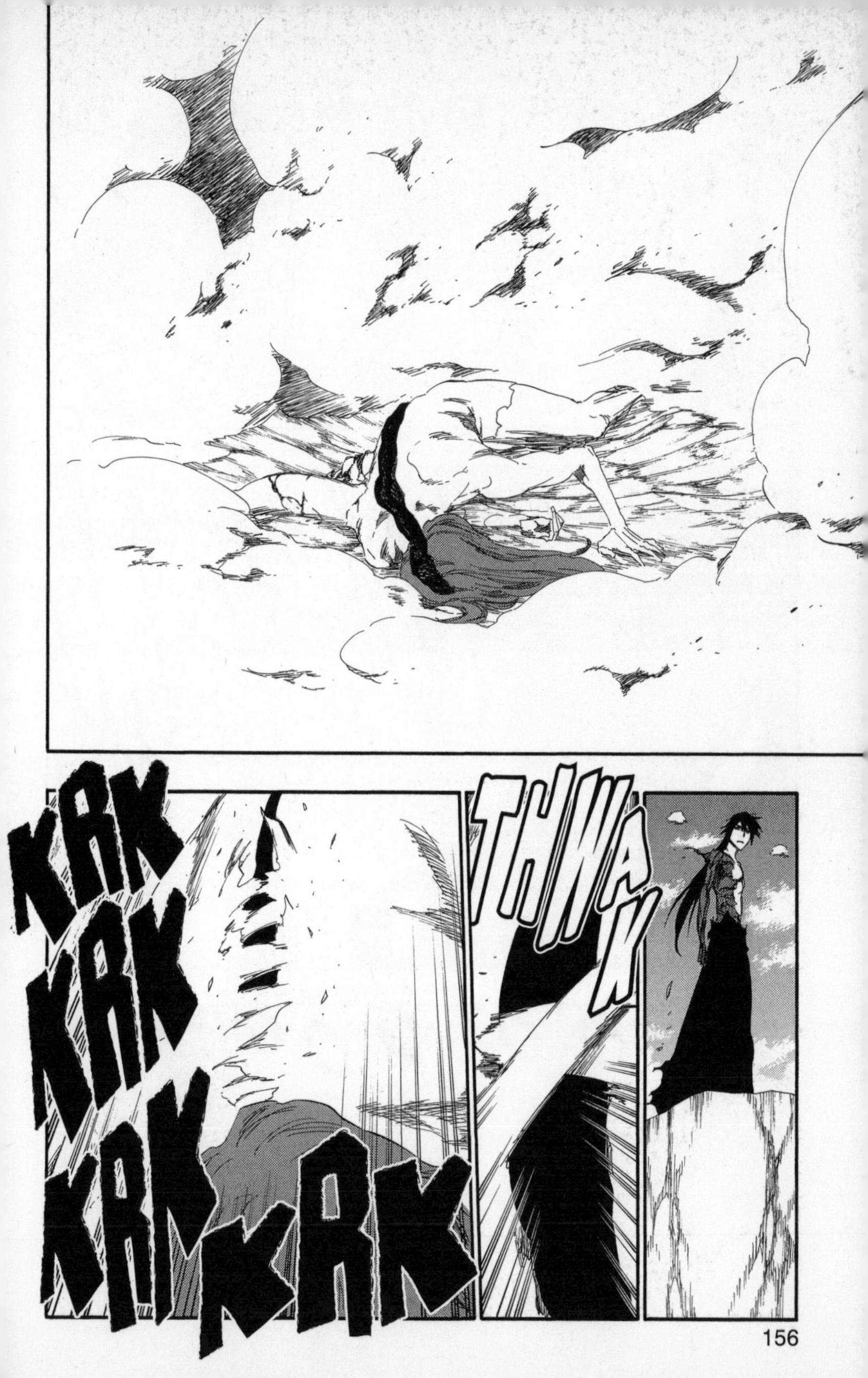
KRK KRK KRK KRK KRK
THWAK

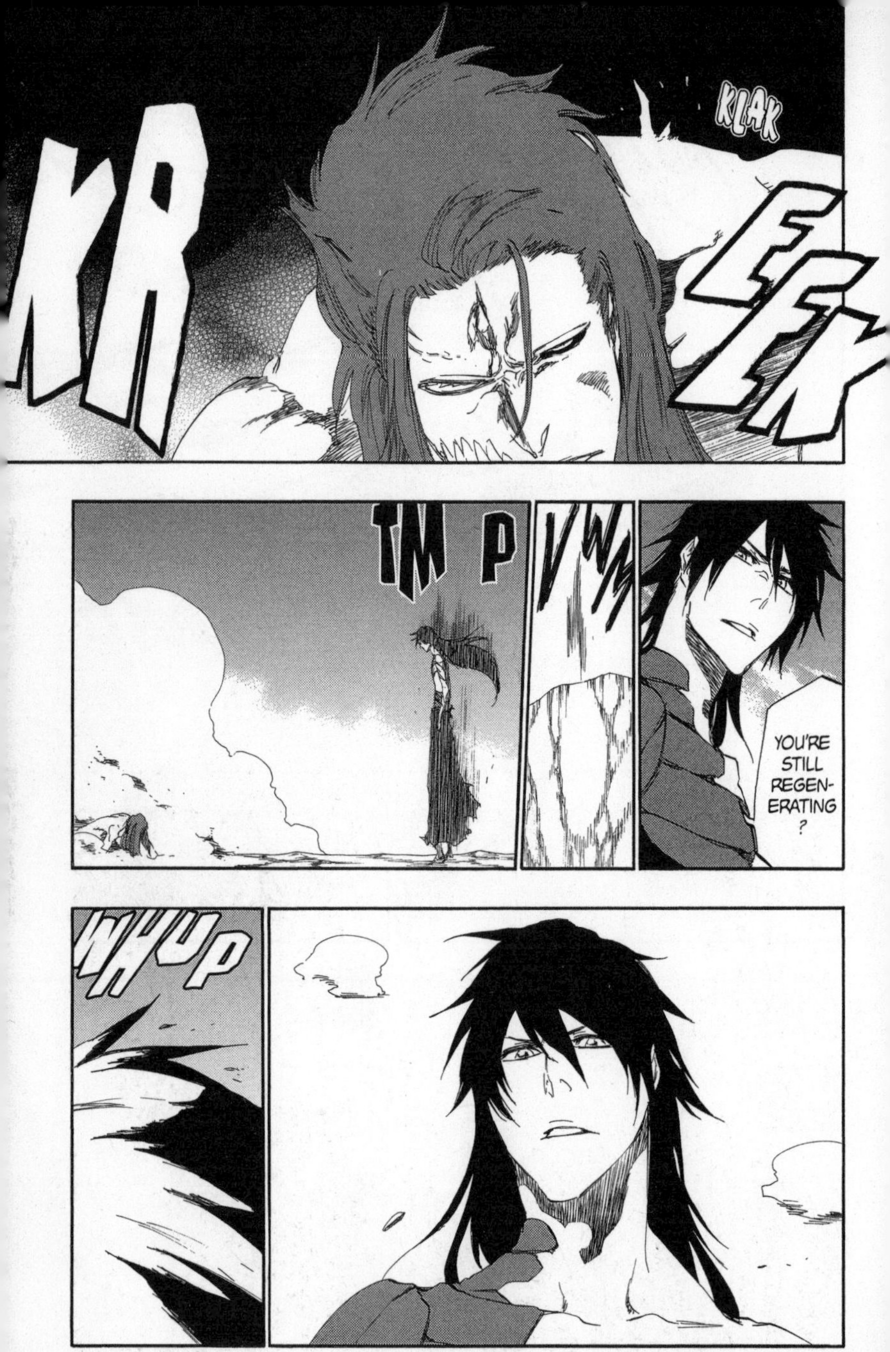
KLAK
KR
EEEK
TMP
PWW
YOU'RE STILL REGEN-ERATING?
WHUP

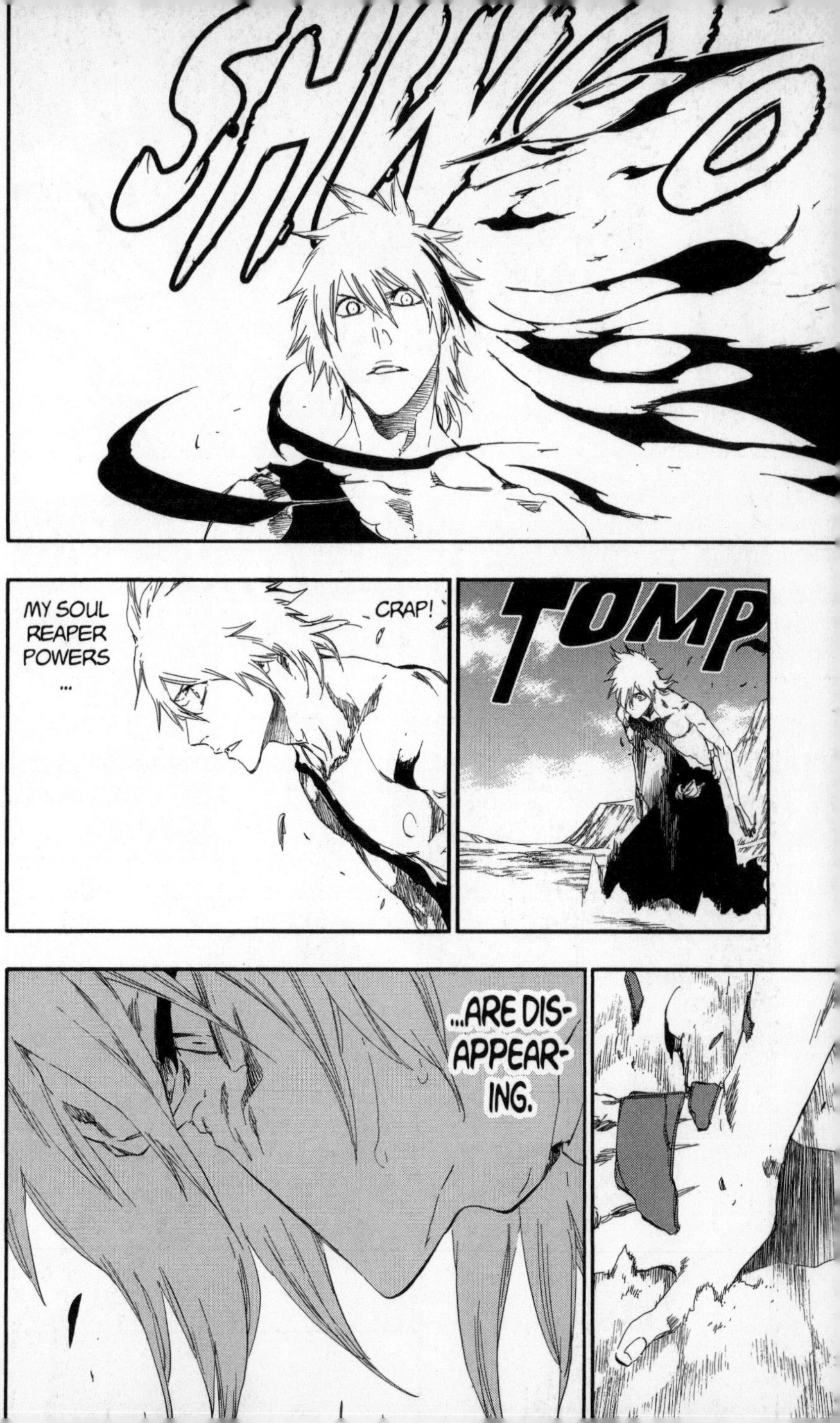
TOMP
CRAP!
MY SOUL REAPER POWERS ...
...ARE DIS-APPEAR-ING.

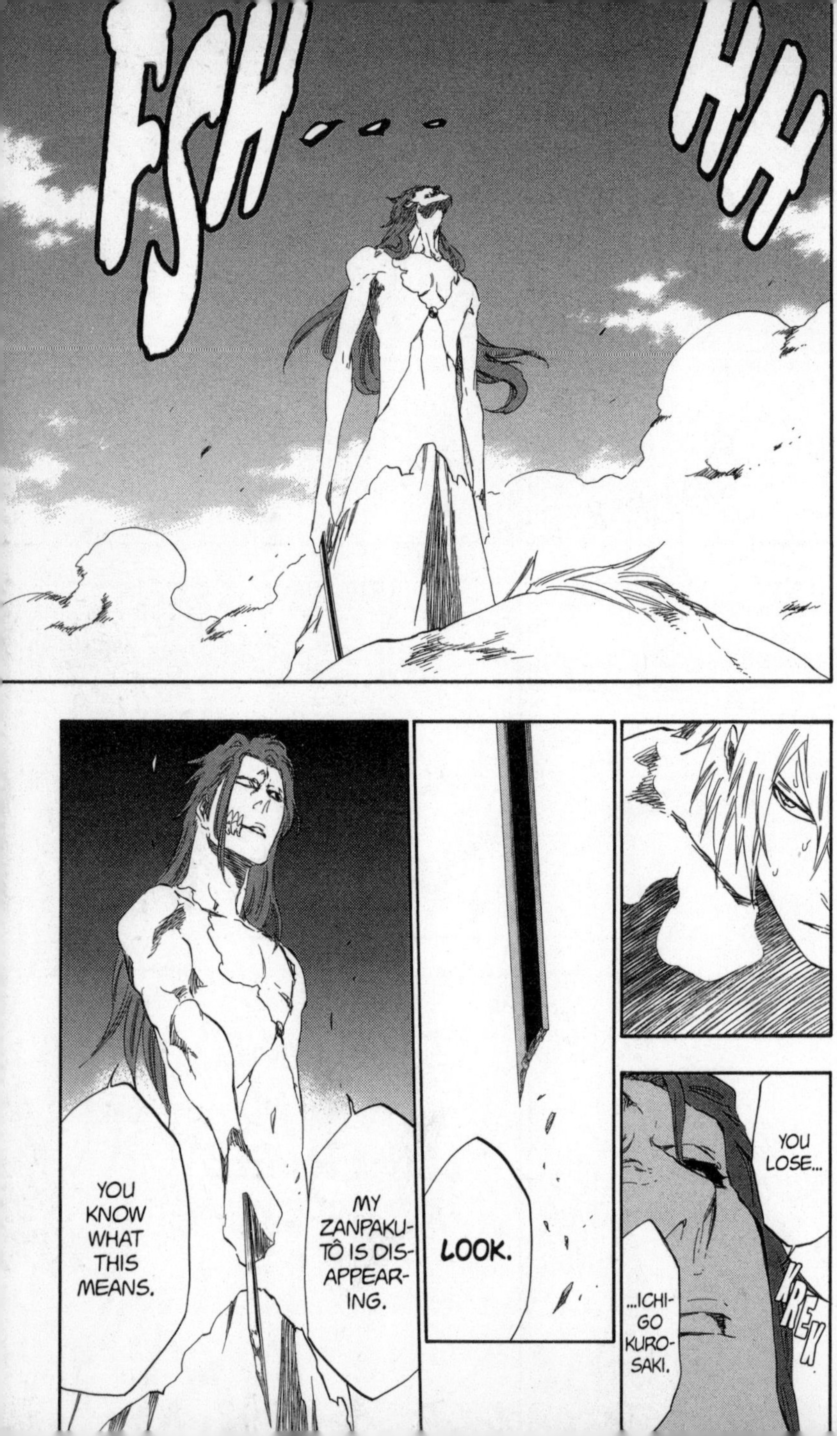
FSH...
HH
YOU LOSE...
...ICHI-GO KURO-SAKI.
KREK
LOOK.
MY ZANPAKU-TÔ IS DIS-APPEAR-ING.
YOU KNOW WHAT THIS MEANS.

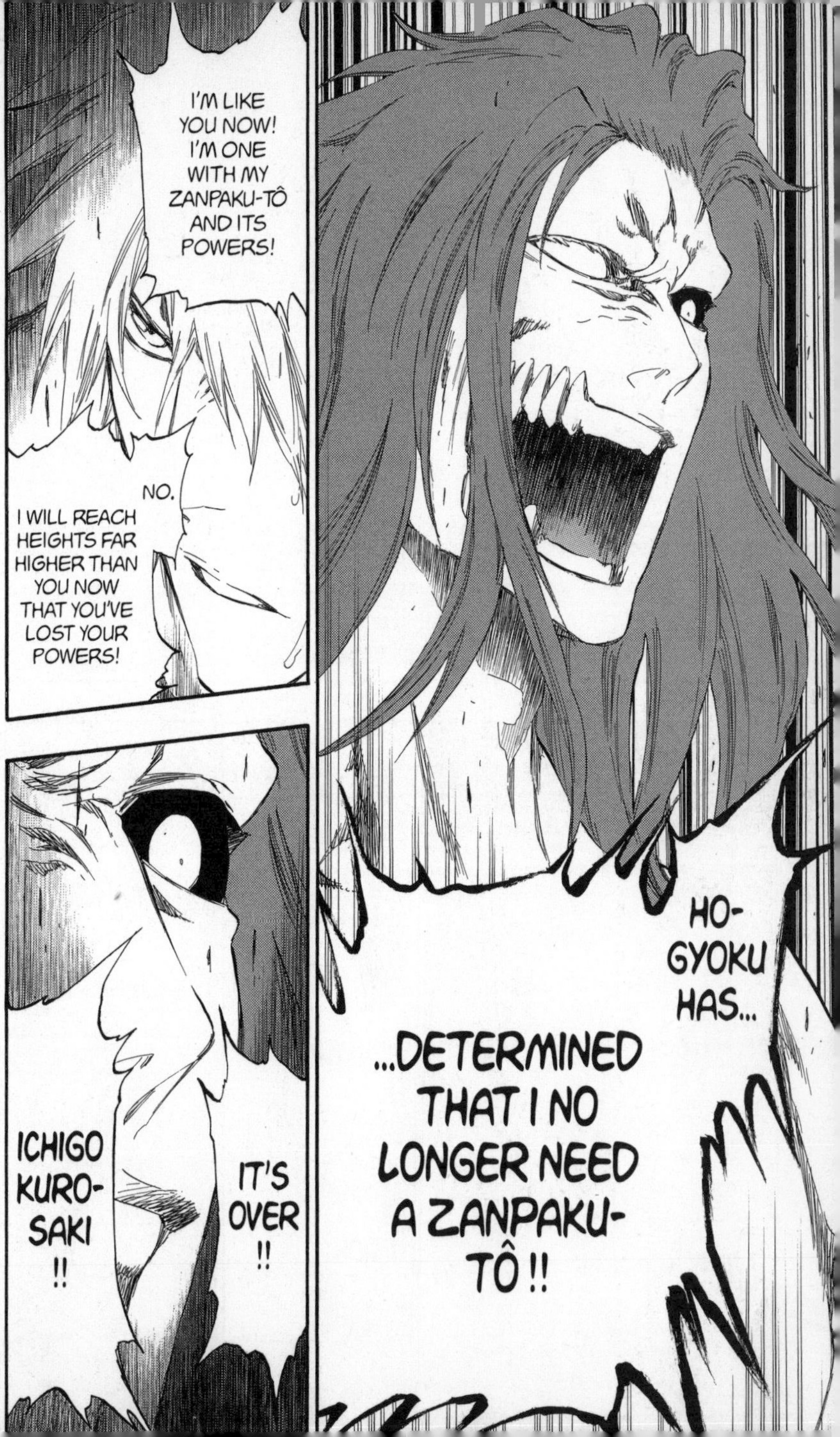
I'M LIKE YOU NOW! I'M ONE WITH MY ZANPAKU-TÔ AND ITS POWERS!
NO.
I WILL REACH HEIGHTS FAR HIGHER THAN YOU NOW THAT YOU'VE LOST YOUR POWERS!
HO-GYOKU HAS...
...DETERMINED THAT I NO LONGER NEED A ZANPAKU-TÔ!!
IT'S OVER!!
ICHIGO KUROSAKI!!

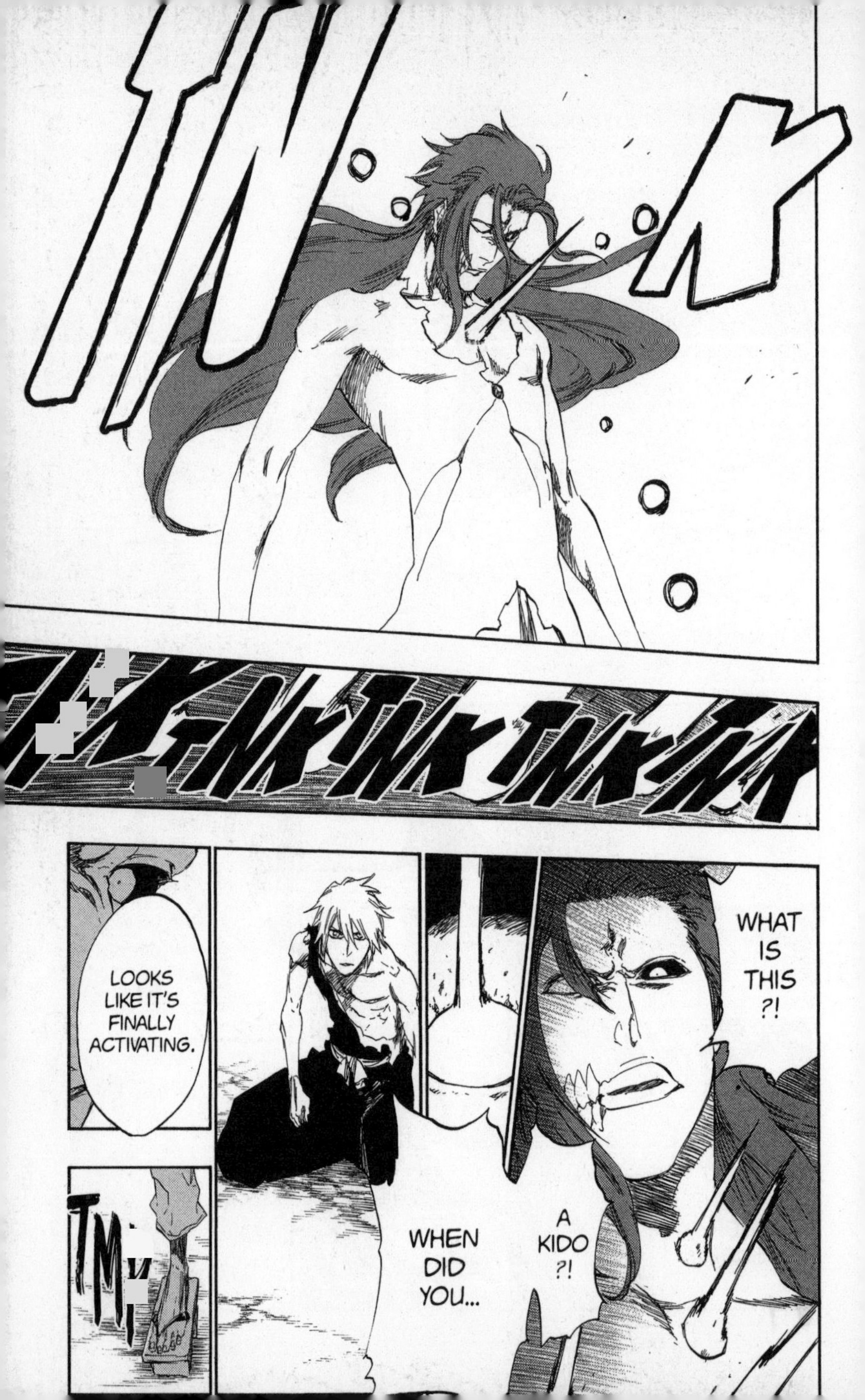
WHAT IS THIS ?!
A KIDO ?!
WHEN DID YOU...
LOOKS LIKE IT'S FINALLY ACTIVATING.

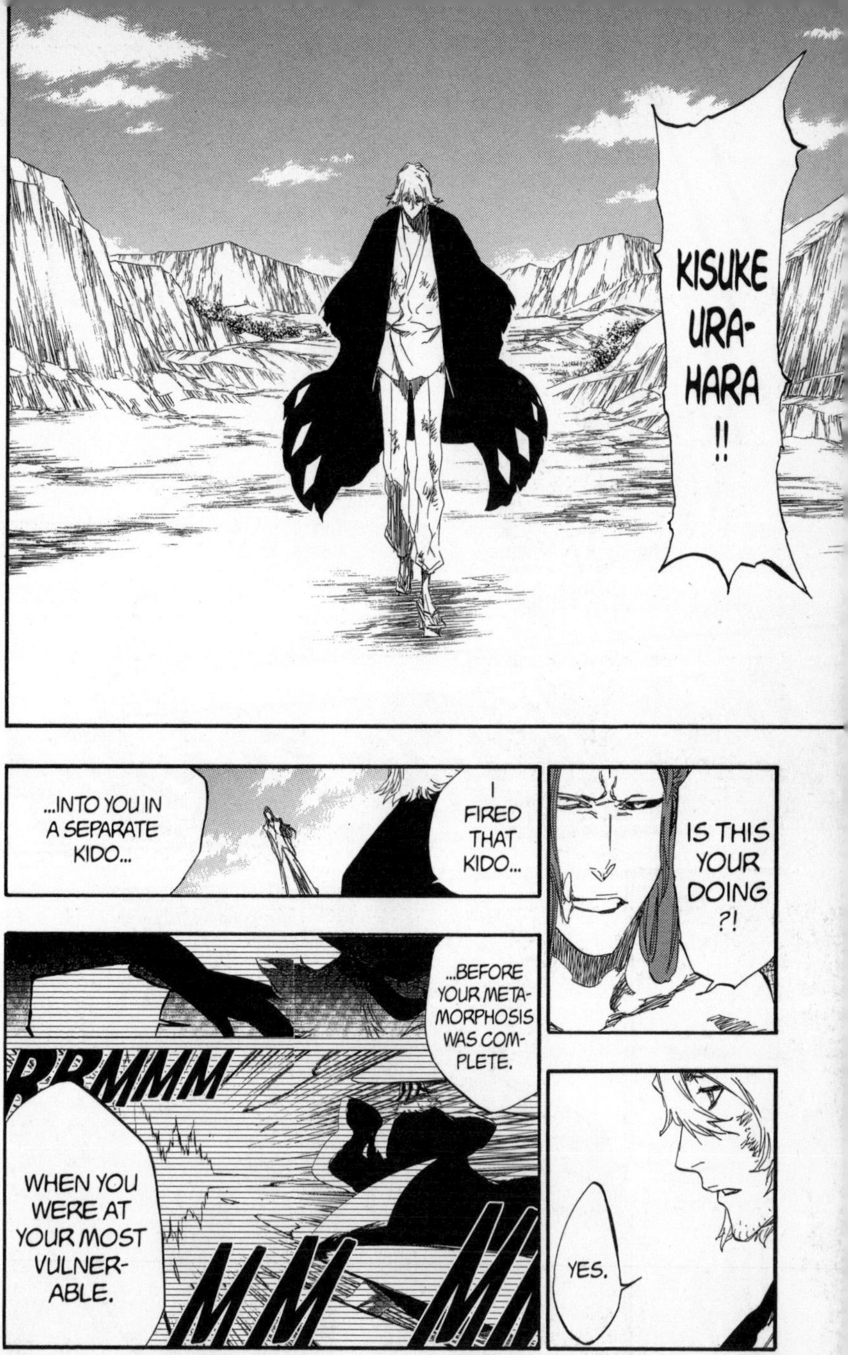
KISUKE URA-HARA!!
IS THIS YOUR DOING?!
YES.
I FIRED THAT KIDO...
...INTO YOU IN A SEPARATE KIDO...
...BEFORE YOUR META-MORPHOSIS WAS COM-PLETE.
BRMMMM
MM MM
WHEN YOU WERE AT YOUR MOST VULNER-ABLE.

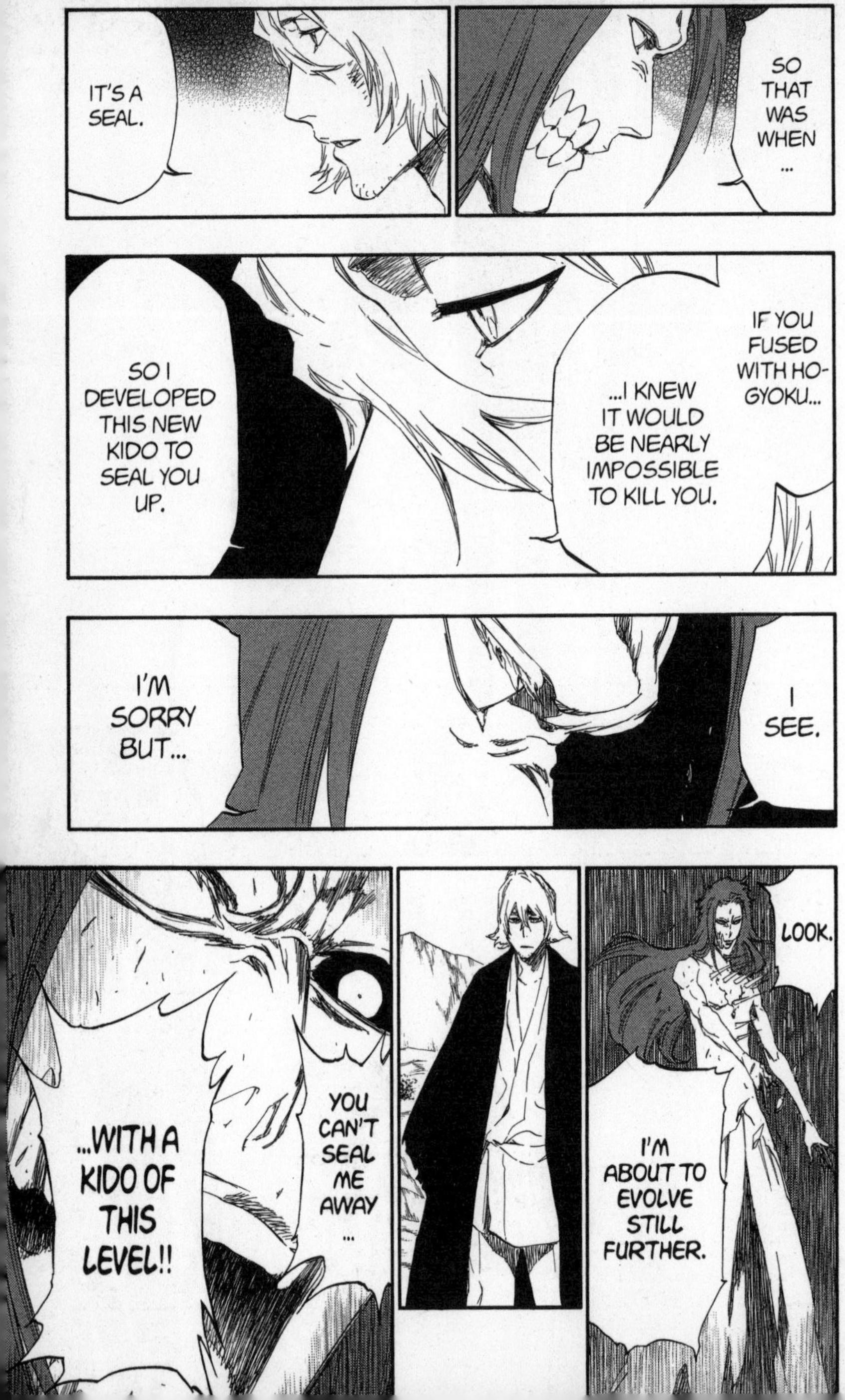
SO THAT WAS WHEN ...
IT'S A SEAL.
IF YOU FUSED WITH HO-GYOKU...
...I KNEW IT WOULD BE NEARLY IMPOSSIBLE TO KILL YOU.
SO I DEVELOPED THIS NEW KIDO TO SEAL YOU UP.
I SEE.
I'M SORRY BUT...
LOOK.
I'M ABOUT TO EVOLVE STILL FURTHER.
YOU CAN'T SEAL ME AWAY ...
...WITH A KIDO OF THIS LEVEL!!

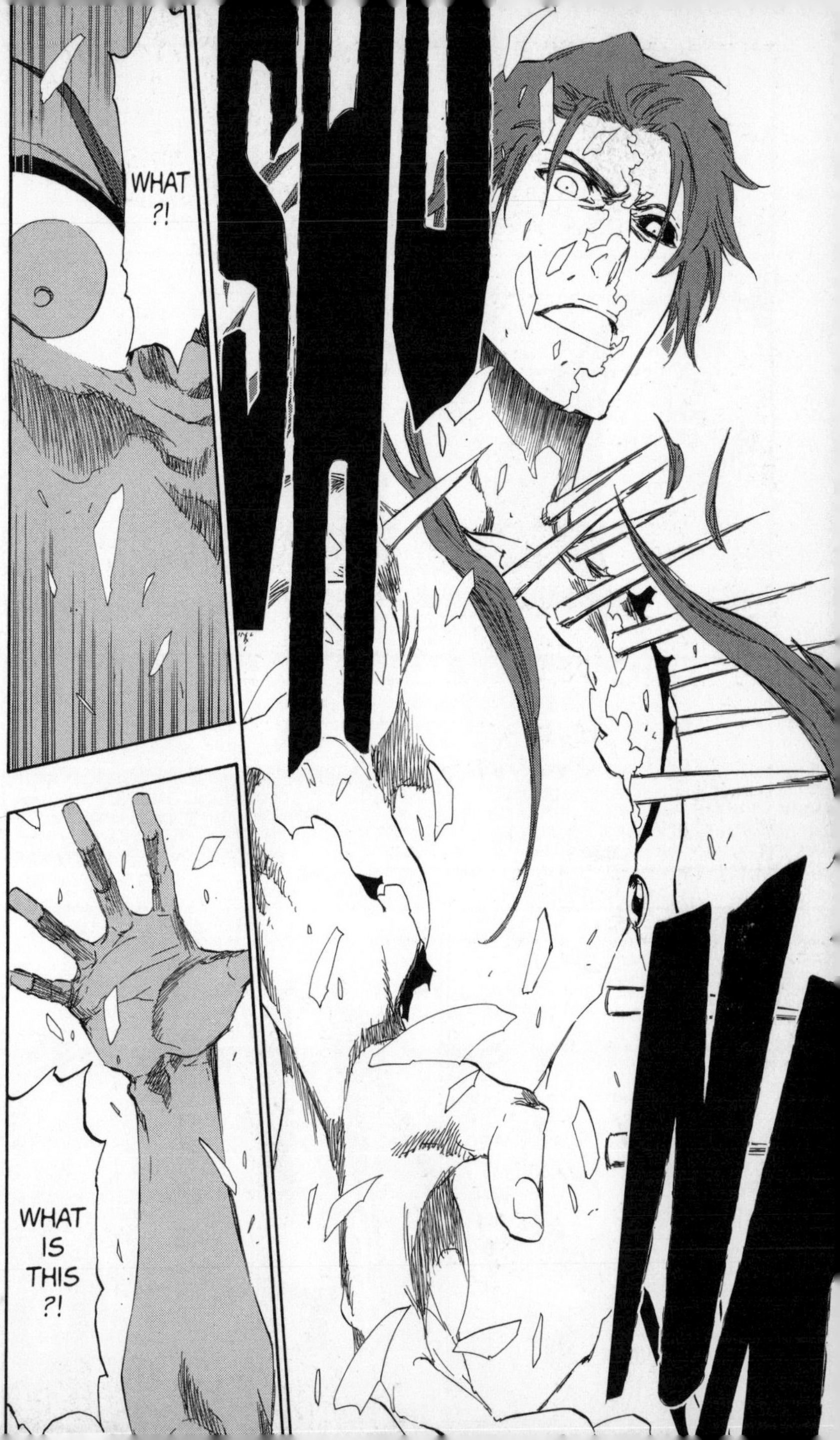
WHAT ?!
WHAT IS THIS ?!

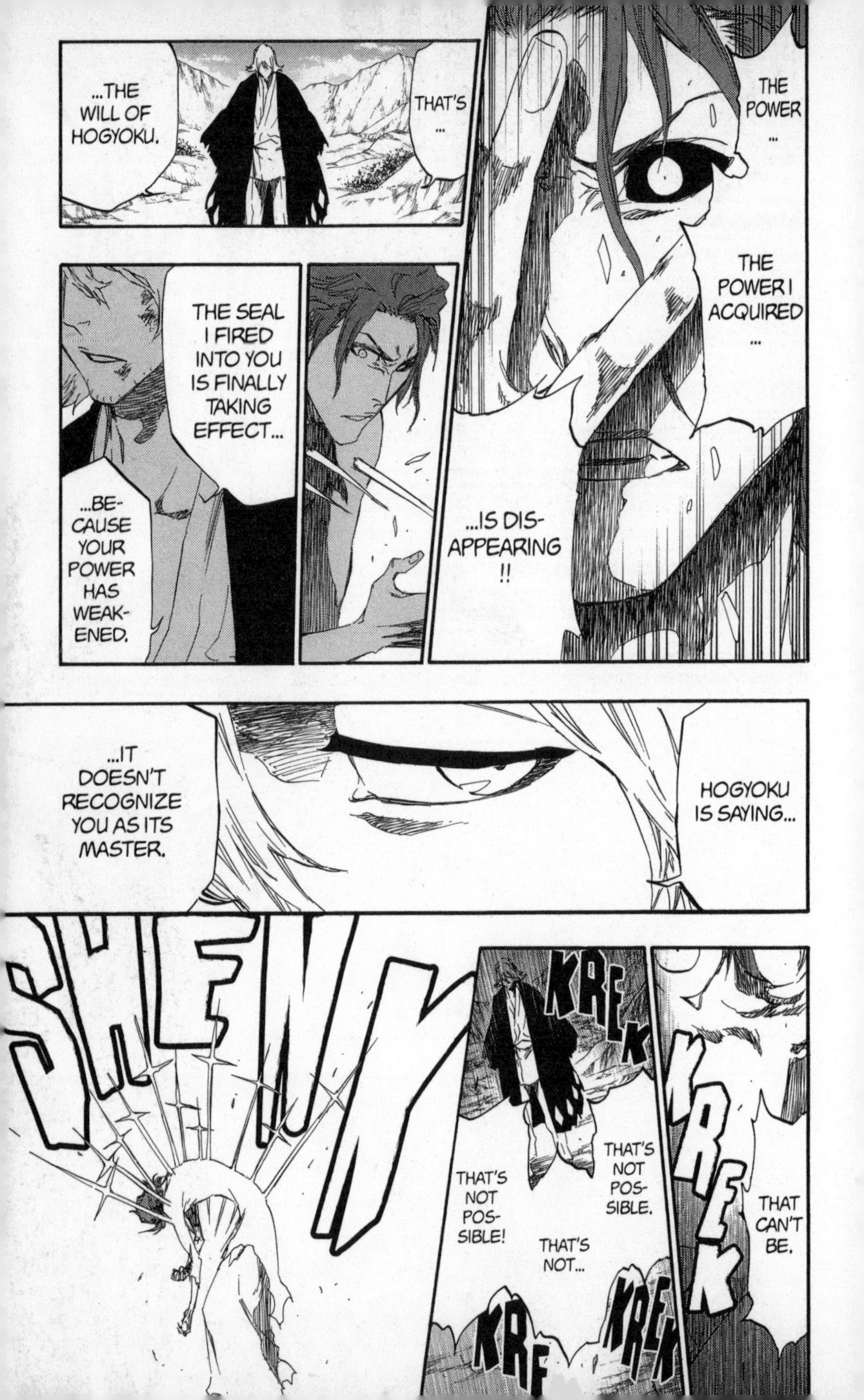
THE POWER ...
THE POWER I ACQUIRED ...
...IS DIS-APPEARING !!
THAT'S ...
...THE WILL OF HOGYOKU.
THE SEAL I FIRED INTO YOU IS FINALLY TAKING EFFECT...
...BE-CAUSE YOUR POWER HAS WEAK-ENED.
HOGYOKU IS SAYING...
...IT DOESN'T RECOGNIZE YOU AS ITS MASTER.
KREK
THAT CAN'T BE.
KREK
THAT'S NOT POS-SIBLE.
THAT'S NOT POS-SIBLE!
THAT'S NOT...
KREK
KRF

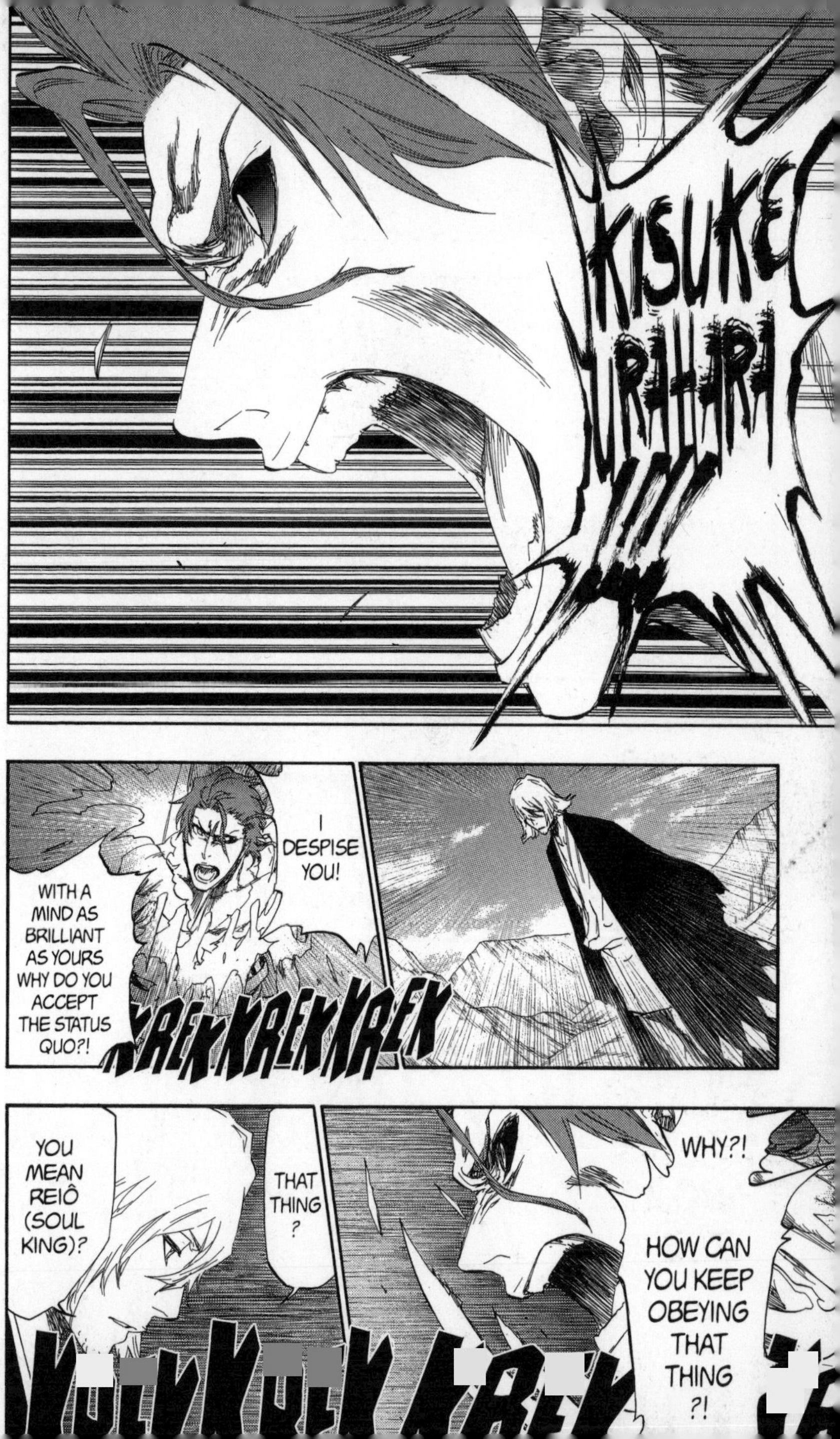
KISUKE URAHARA!!
I DESPISE YOU!
WITH A MIND AS BRILLIANT AS YOURS WHY DO YOU ACCEPT THE STATUS QUO?!
KREK KREK KREK
WHY?!
HOW CAN YOU KEEP OBEYING THAT THING?!
THAT THING?
YOU MEAN REIÔ (SOUL KING)?

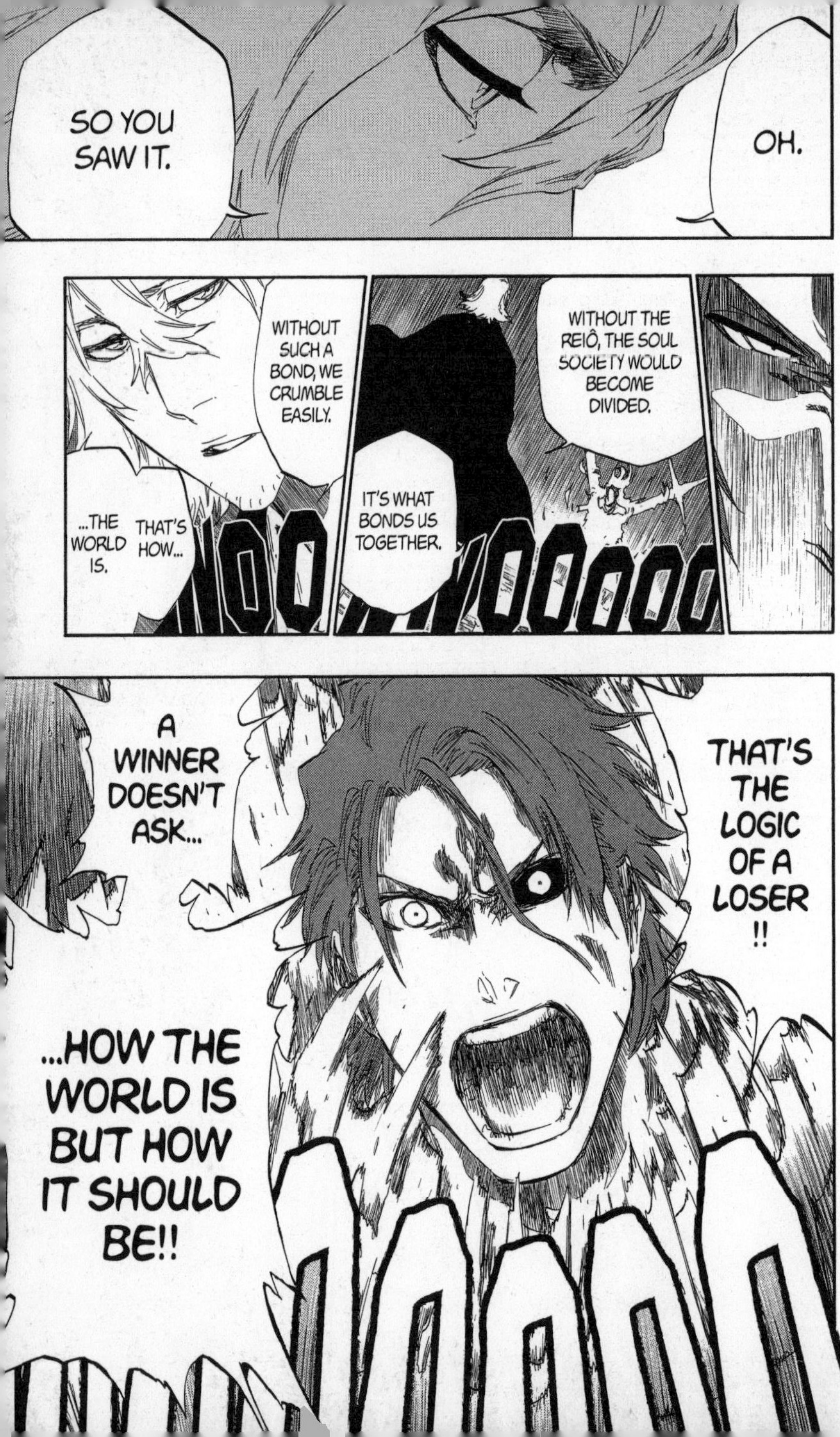
OH.
SO YOU SAW IT.
WITHOUT THE REIÔ, THE SOUL SOCIETY WOULD BECOME DIVIDED.
IT'S WHAT BONDS US TOGETHER.
WITHOUT SUCH A BOND, WE CRUMBLE EASILY.
THAT'S HOW...
...THE WORLD IS.
THAT'S THE LOGIC OF A LOSER!!
A WINNER DOESN'T ASK...
...HOW THE WORLD IS BUT HOW IT SHOULD BE!!

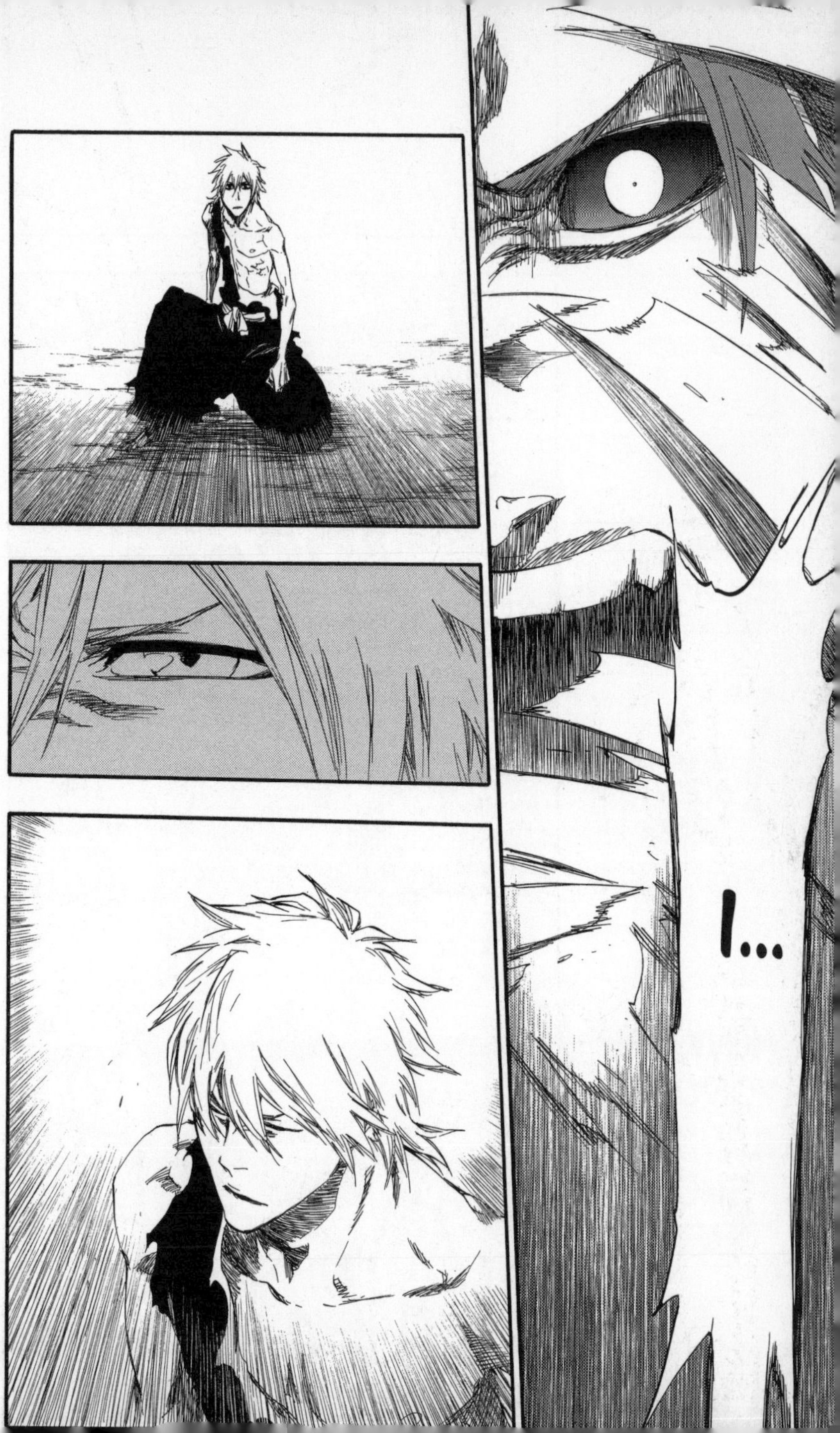

I...

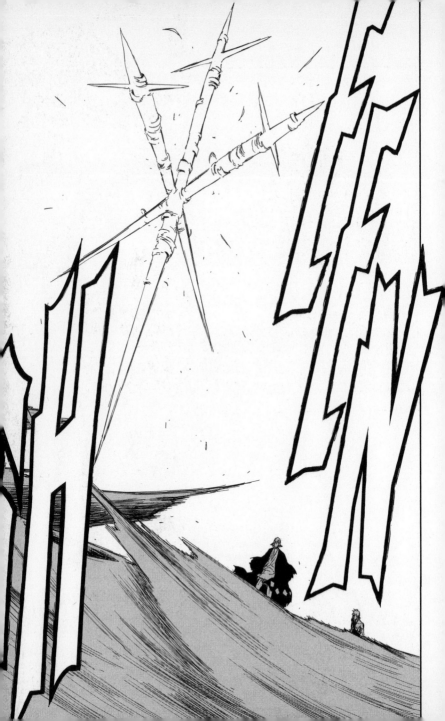

422. the silent victory

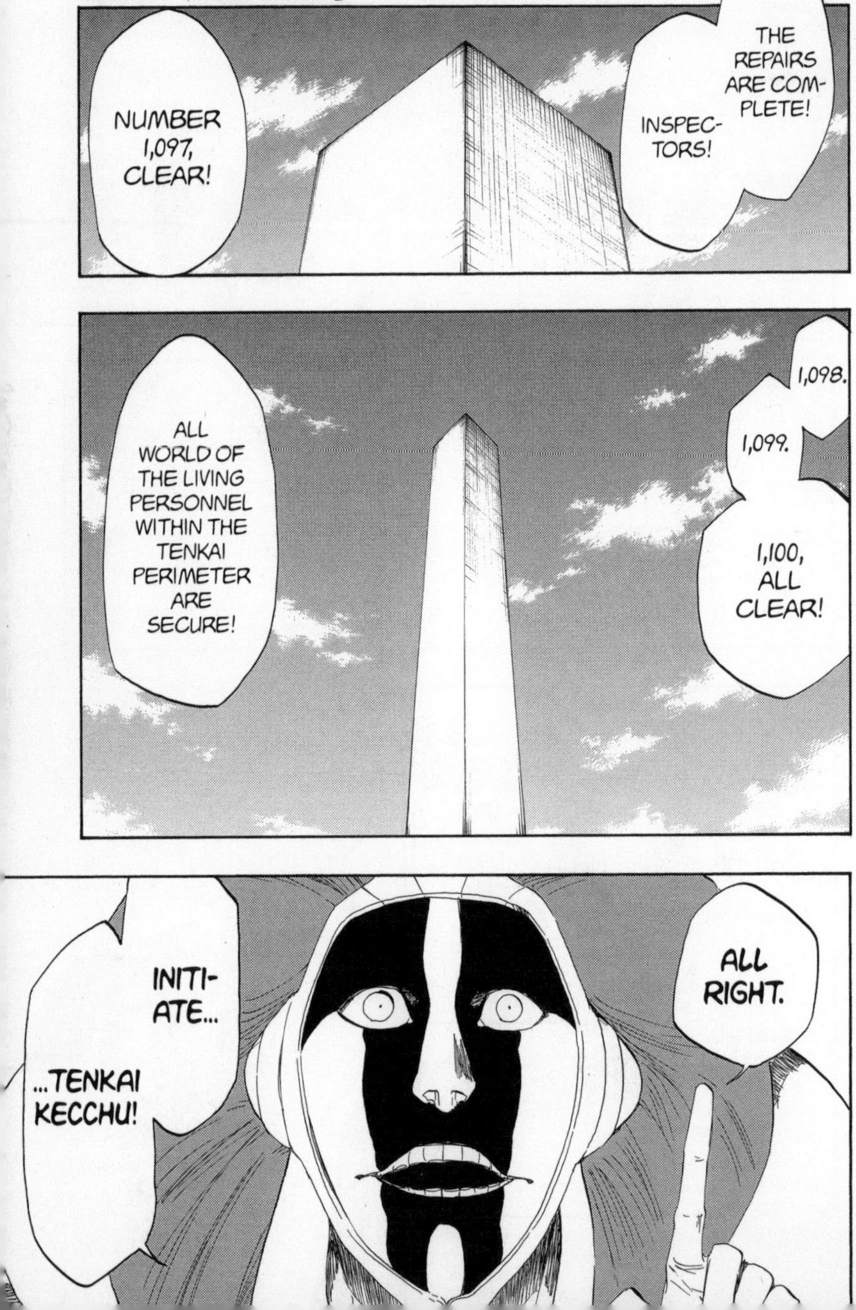
THE REPAIRS ARE COMPLETE!
INSPECTORS!
NUMBER 1,097, CLEAR!
1,098.
1,099.
1,100, ALL CLEAR!
ALL WORLD OF THE LIVING PERSONNEL WITHIN THE TENKAI PERIMETER ARE SECURE!
ALL RIGHT.
INITIATE...
...TENKAI KECCHU!

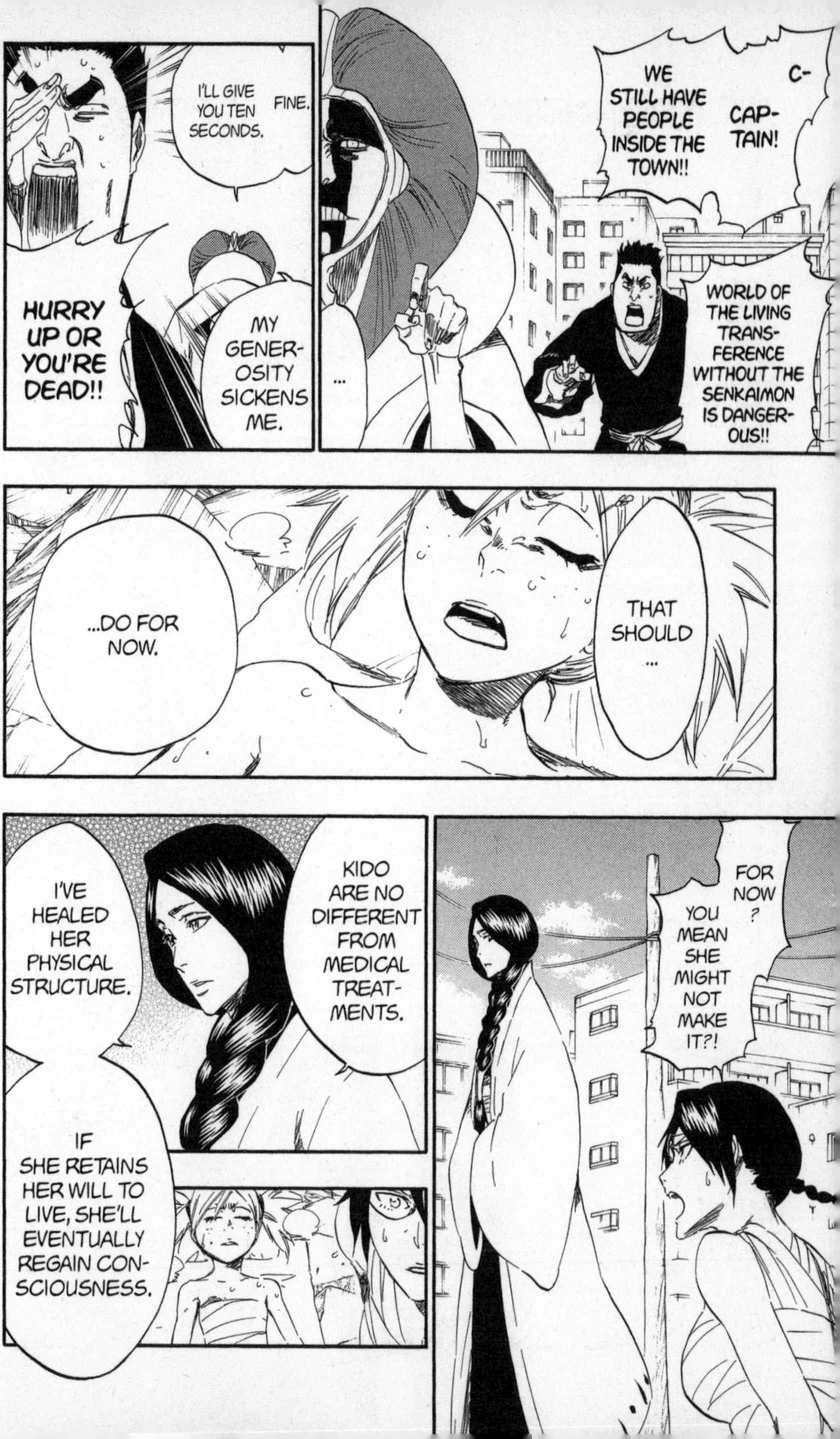
C- CAPTAIN!
WE STILL HAVE PEOPLE INSIDE THE TOWN!!
WORLD OF THE LIVING TRANSFERENCE WITHOUT THE SENKAIMON IS DANGEROUS!!
...
FINE.
I'LL GIVE YOU TEN SECONDS.
MY GENEROSITY SICKENS ME.
HURRY UP OR YOU'RE DEAD!!
THAT SHOULD...
...DO FOR NOW.
FOR NOW?
YOU MEAN SHE MIGHT NOT MAKE IT?!
KIDO ARE NO DIFFERENT FROM MEDICAL TREATMENTS.
I'VE HEALED HER PHYSICAL STRUCTURE.
IF SHE RETAINS HER WILL TO LIVE, SHE'LL EVENTUALLY REGAIN CONSCIOUSNESS.

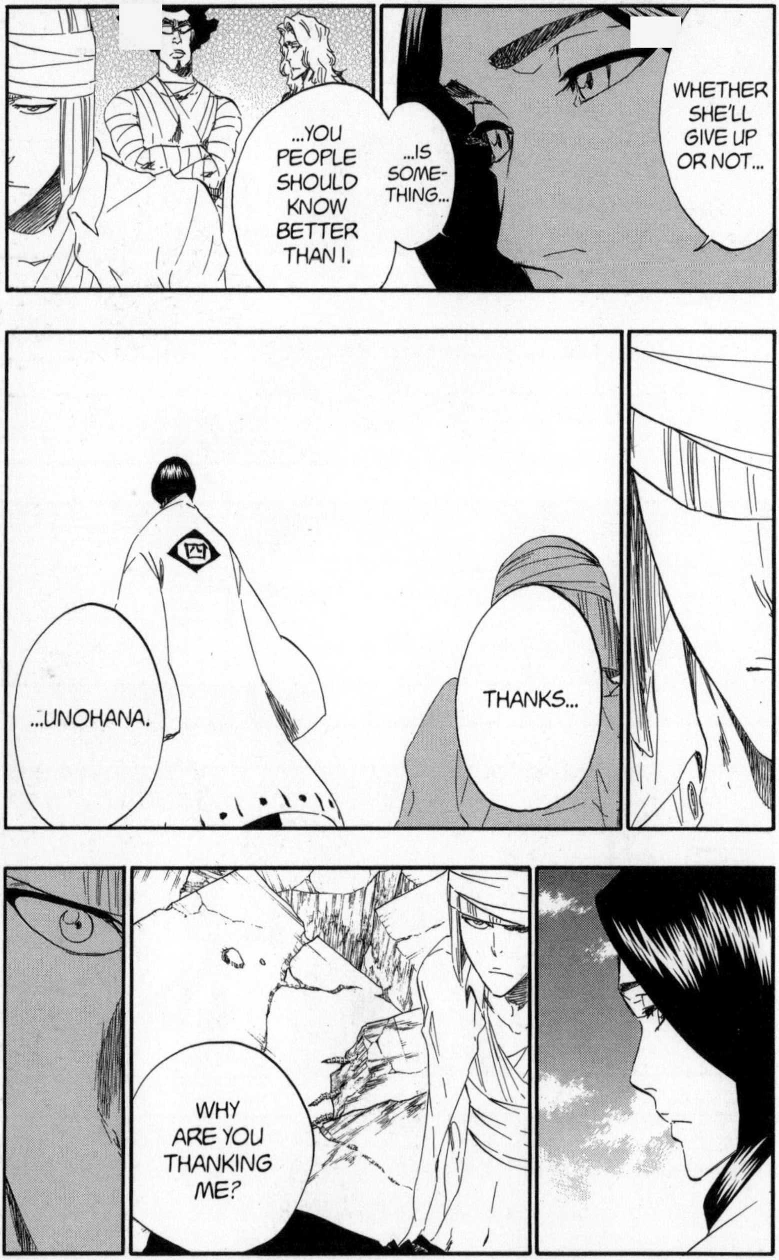
WHETHER SHE'LL GIVE UP OR NOT...
...IS SOMETHING...
...YOU PEOPLE SHOULD KNOW BETTER THAN I.
THANKS...
...UNOHANA.
WHY ARE YOU THANKING ME?

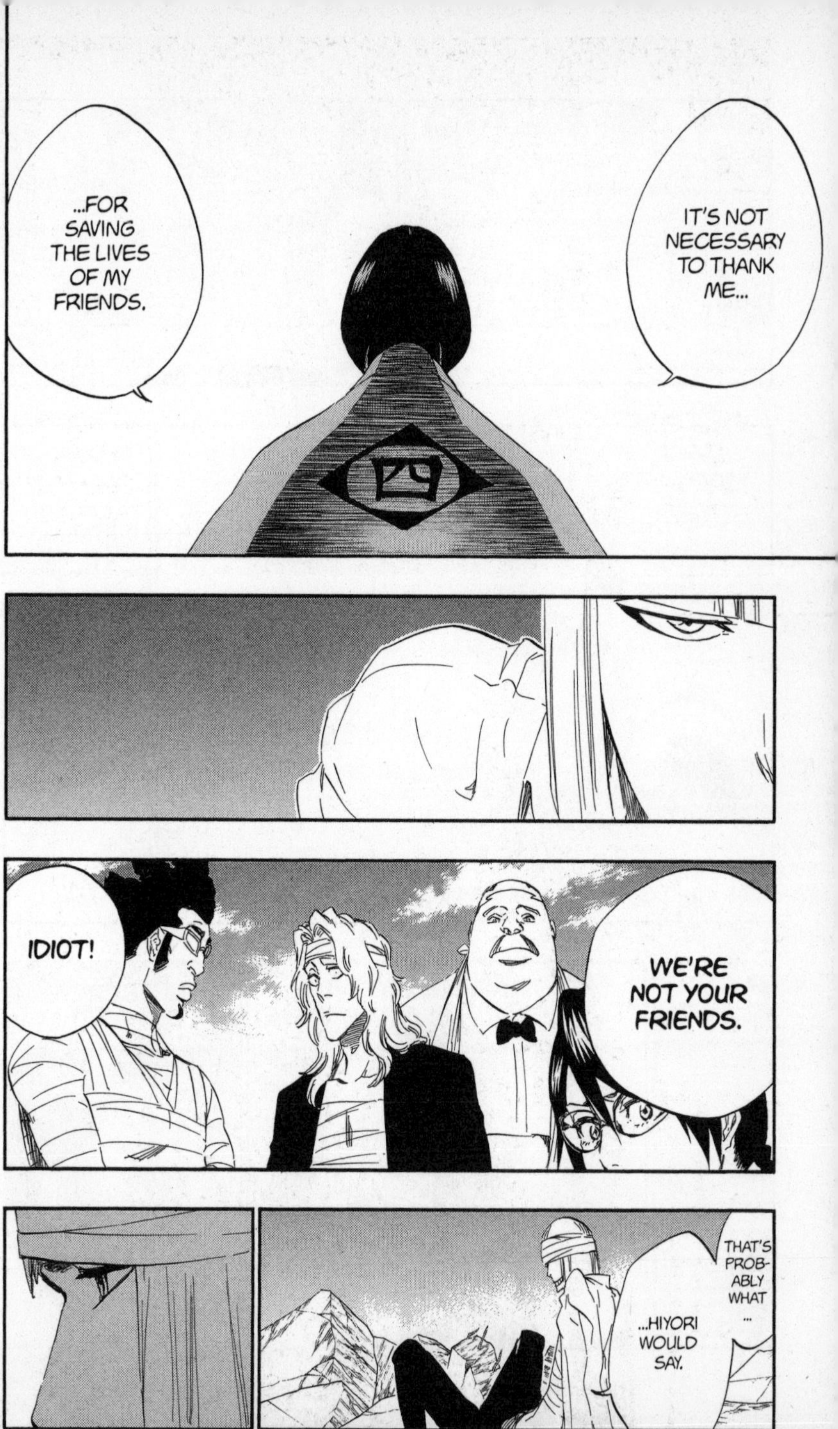
IT'S NOT NECESSARY TO THANK ME...
...FOR SAVING THE LIVES OF MY FRIENDS.
WE'RE NOT YOUR FRIENDS.
IDIOT!
THAT'S PROB-ABLY WHAT ...
...HIYORI WOULD SAY.

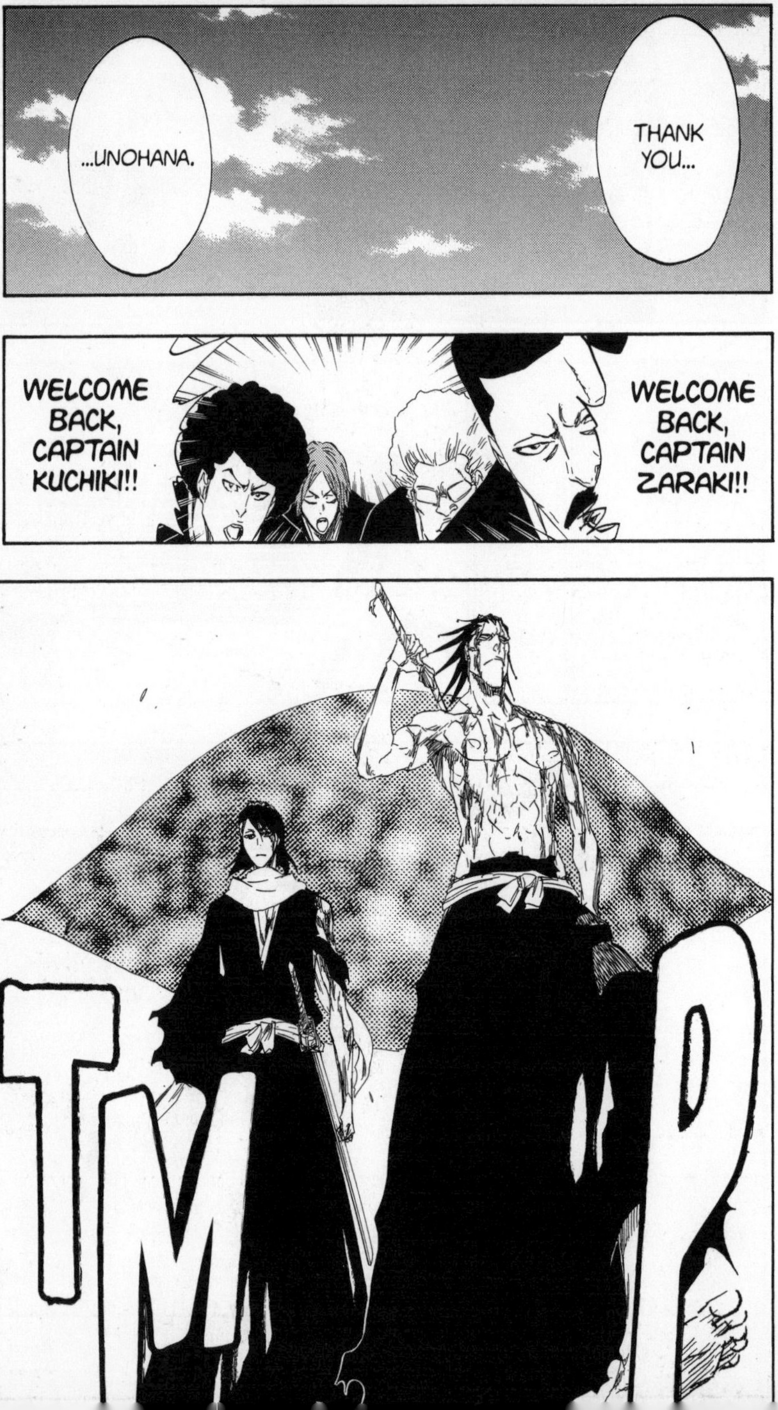
THANK YOU...
...UNOHANA.
WELCOME BACK, CAPTAIN ZARAKI!!
WELCOME BACK, CAPTAIN KUCHIKI!!

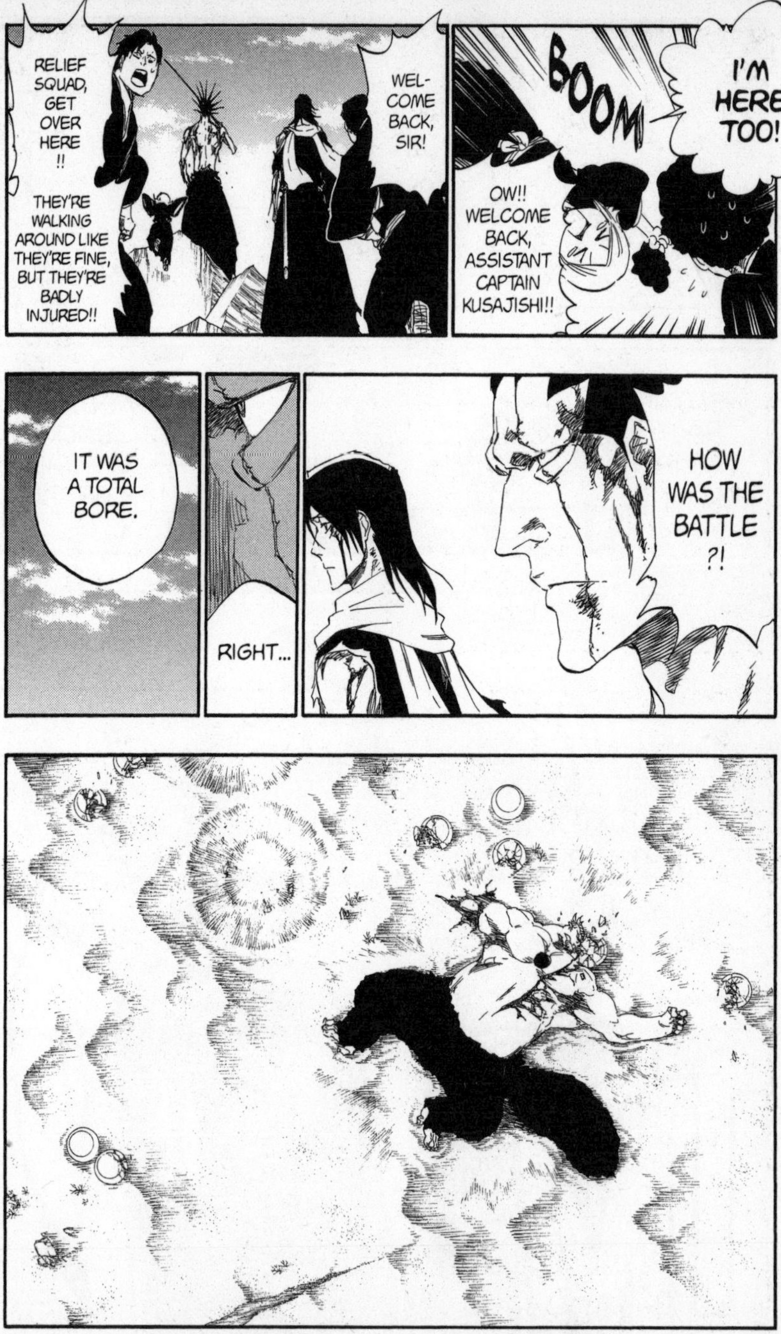
BOOM
I'M HERE TOO!
OW!! WELCOME BACK, ASSISTANT CAPTAIN KUSAJISHI!!
WEL-COME BACK, SIR!
RELIEF SQUAD, GET OVER HERE!!
THEY'RE WALKING AROUND LIKE THEY'RE FINE, BUT THEY'RE BADLY INJURED!!
HOW WAS THE BATTLE?!
RIGHT...
IT WAS A TOTAL BORE.

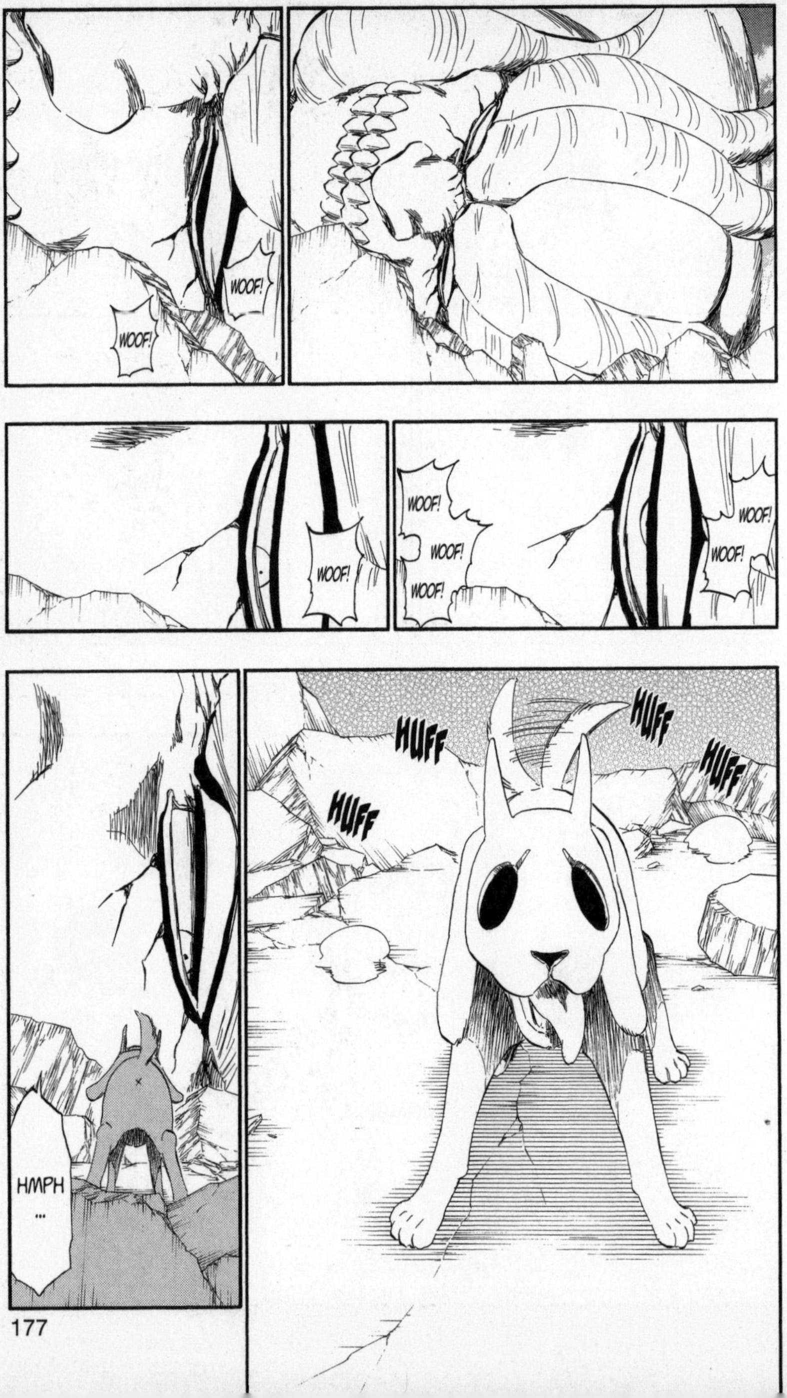
WOOF!
WOOF!
WOOF!
WOOF!
WOOF!
WOOF!
WOOF!
WOOF!
HUFF
HUFF
HUFF
HUFF
HMPH ...

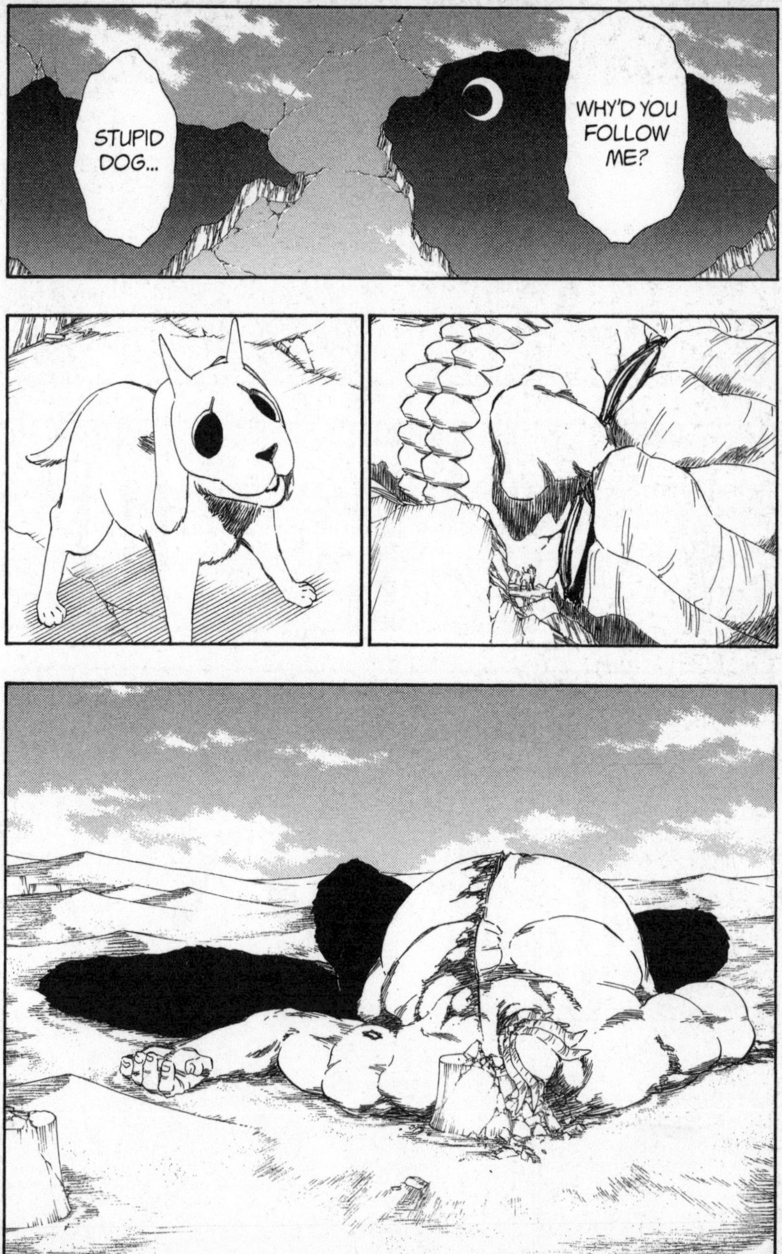
WHY'D YOU FOLLOW ME?
STUPID DOG...

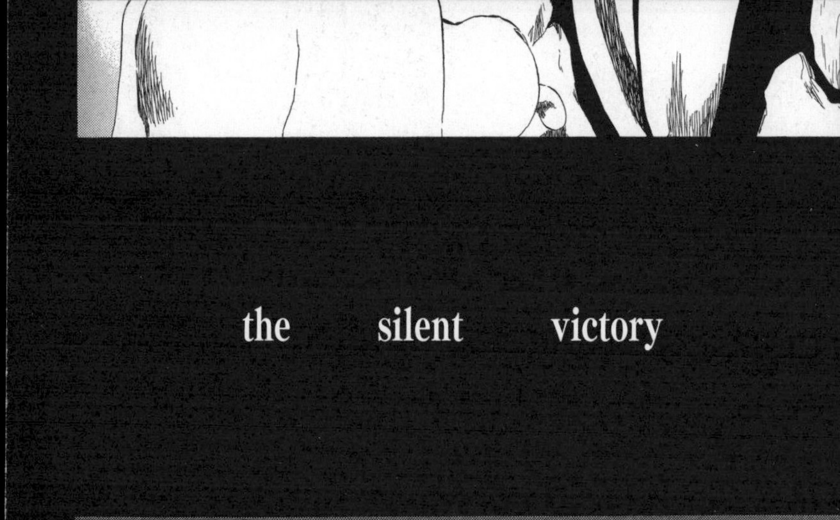

the silent victory

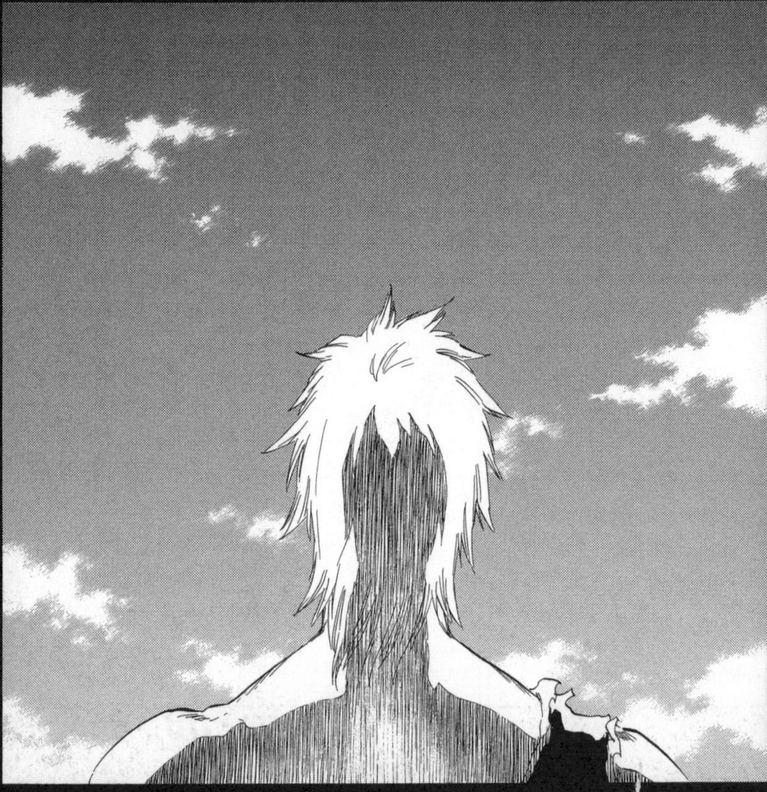

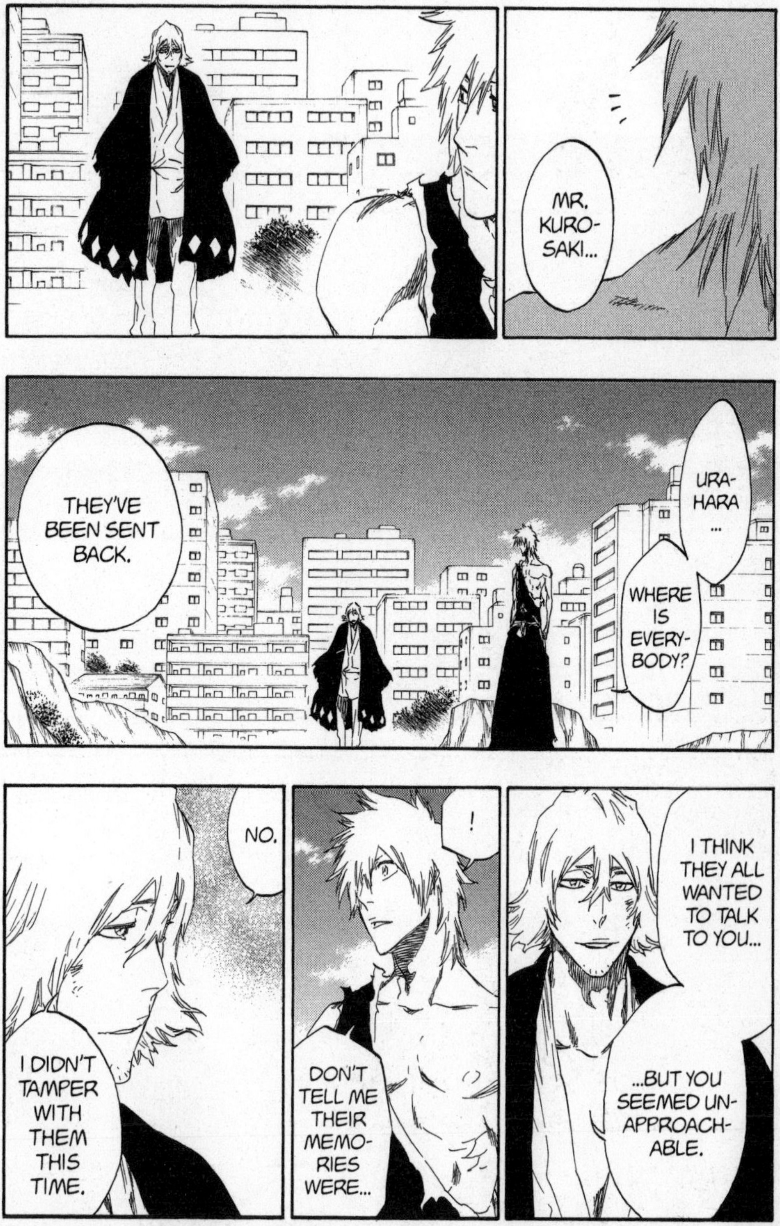
MR. KURO-SAKI...
URA-HARA ...
WHERE IS EVERY-BODY?
THEY'VE BEEN SENT BACK.
I THINK THEY ALL WANTED TO TALK TO YOU...
...BUT YOU SEEMED UN-APPROACH-ABLE.
!
DON'T TELL ME THEIR MEMO-RIES WERE...
NO.
I DIDN'T TAMPER WITH THEM THIS TIME.

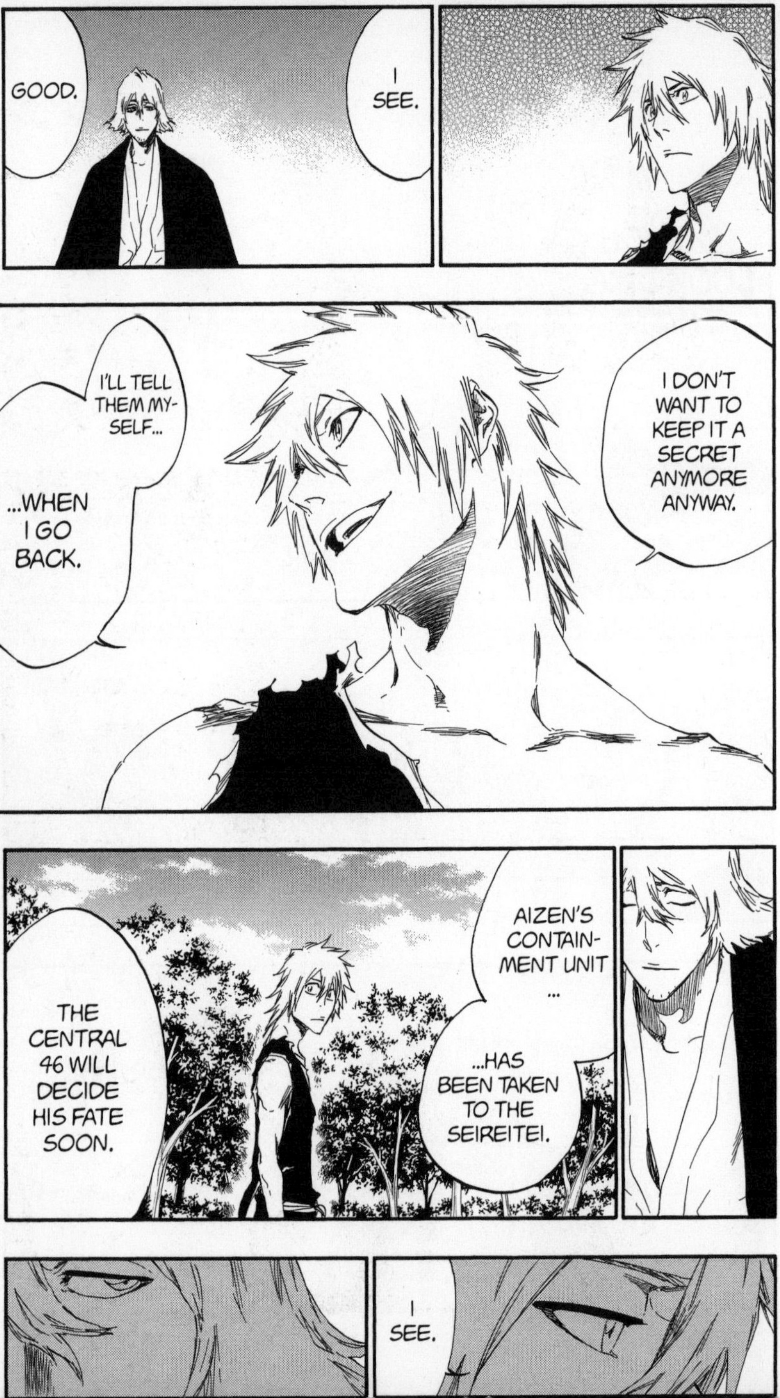
I SEE.
GOOD.
I DON'T WANT TO KEEP IT A SECRET ANYMORE ANYWAY.
I'LL TELL THEM MY-SELF...
...WHEN I GO BACK.
AIZEN'S CONTAIN-MENT UNIT ...
...HAS BEEN TAKEN TO THE SEIREITEI.
THE CENTRAL 46 WILL DECIDE HIS FATE SOON.
I SEE.

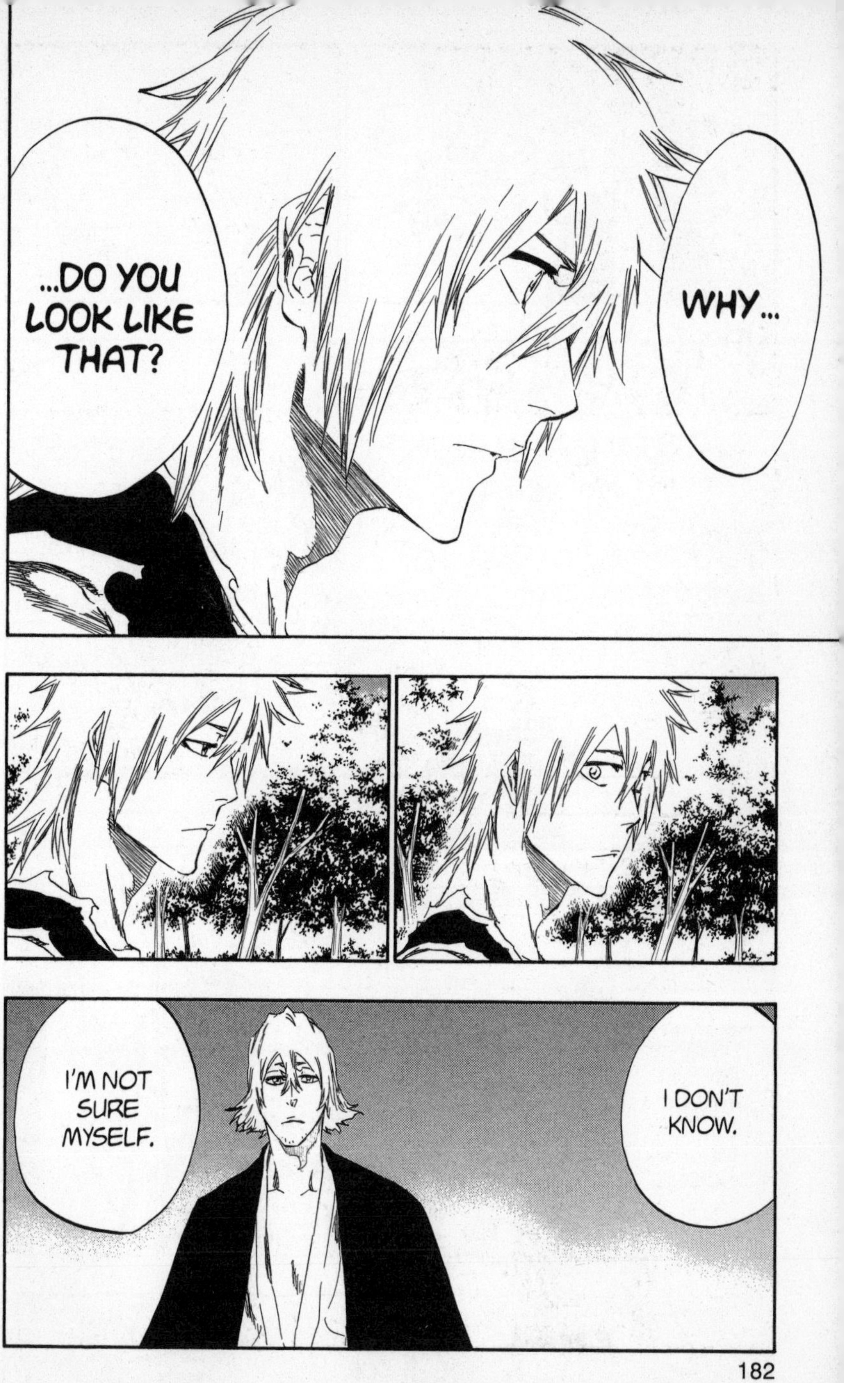
WHY...
...DO YOU LOOK LIKE THAT?
I DON'T KNOW.
I'M NOT SURE MYSELF.

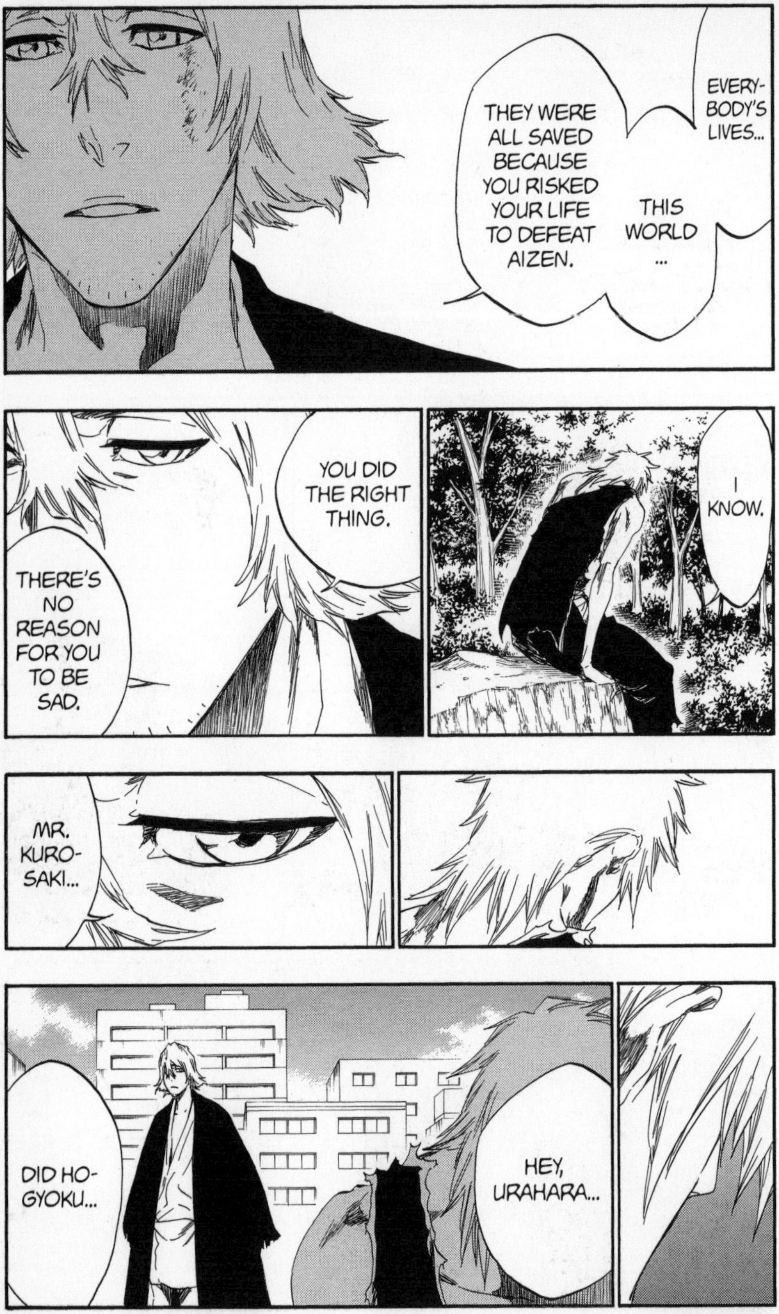
EVERY-BODY'S LIVES...
THIS WORLD ...
THEY WERE ALL SAVED BECAUSE YOU RISKED YOUR LIFE TO DEFEAT AIZEN.
I KNOW.
YOU DID THE RIGHT THING.
THERE'S NO REASON FOR YOU TO BE SAD.
MR. KURO-SAKI...
HEY, URAHARA...
DID HO-GYOKU...

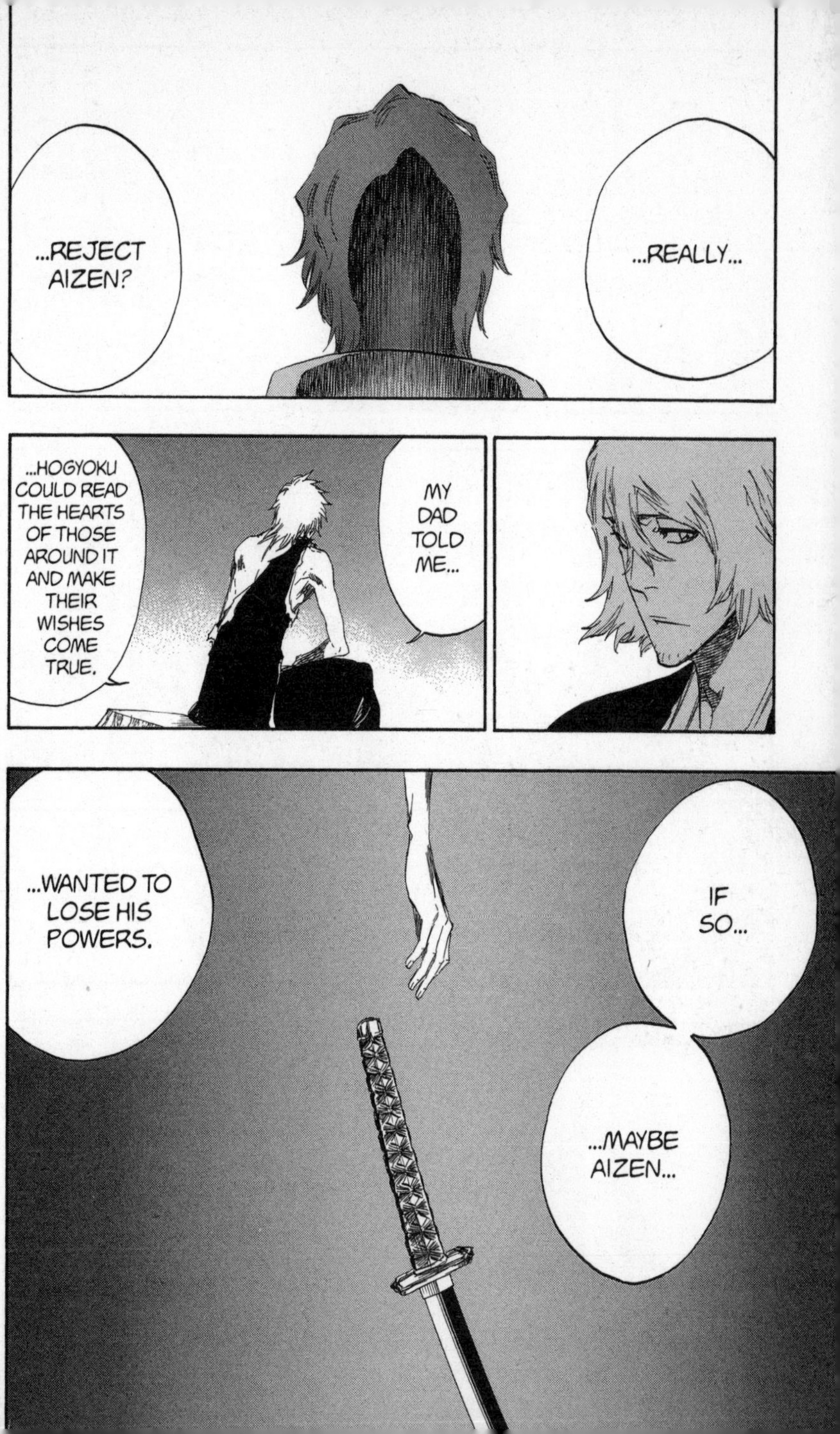
...REALLY...
...REJECT AIZEN?
MY DAD TOLD ME...
...HOGYOKU COULD READ THE HEARTS OF THOSE AROUND IT AND MAKE THEIR WISHES COME TRUE.
IF SO...
...MAYBE AIZEN...
...WANTED TO LOSE HIS POWERS.

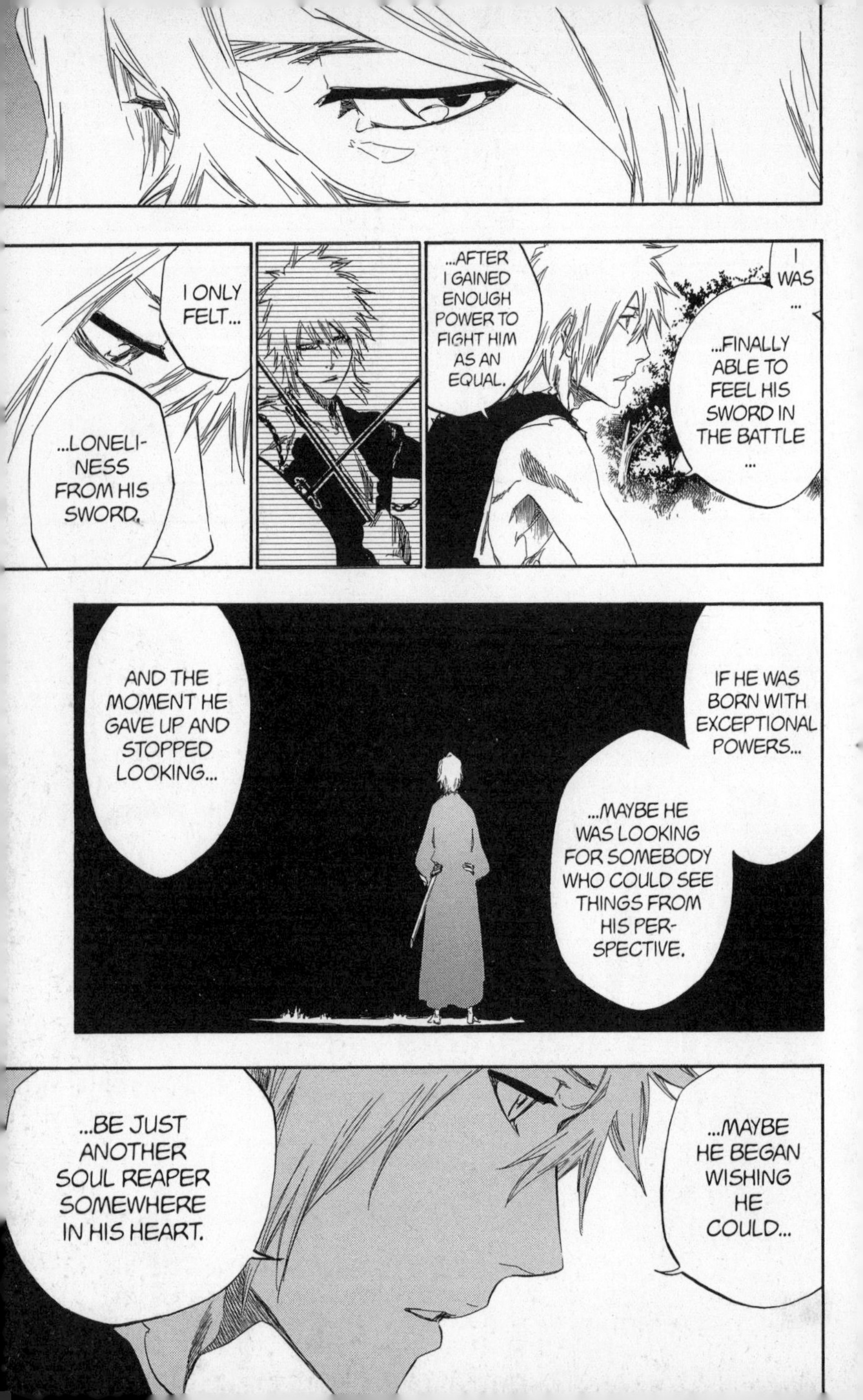
I WAS ...
...FINALLY ABLE TO FEEL HIS SWORD IN THE BATTLE ...
...AFTER I GAINED ENOUGH POWER TO FIGHT HIM AS AN EQUAL.
I ONLY FELT...
...LONELINESS FROM HIS SWORD.
IF HE WAS BORN WITH EXCEPTIONAL POWERS...
...MAYBE HE WAS LOOKING FOR SOMEBODY WHO COULD SEE THINGS FROM HIS PERSPECTIVE.
AND THE MOMENT HE GAVE UP AND STOPPED LOOKING...
...MAYBE HE BEGAN WISHING HE COULD...
...BE JUST ANOTHER SOUL REAPER SOMEWHERE IN HIS HEART.

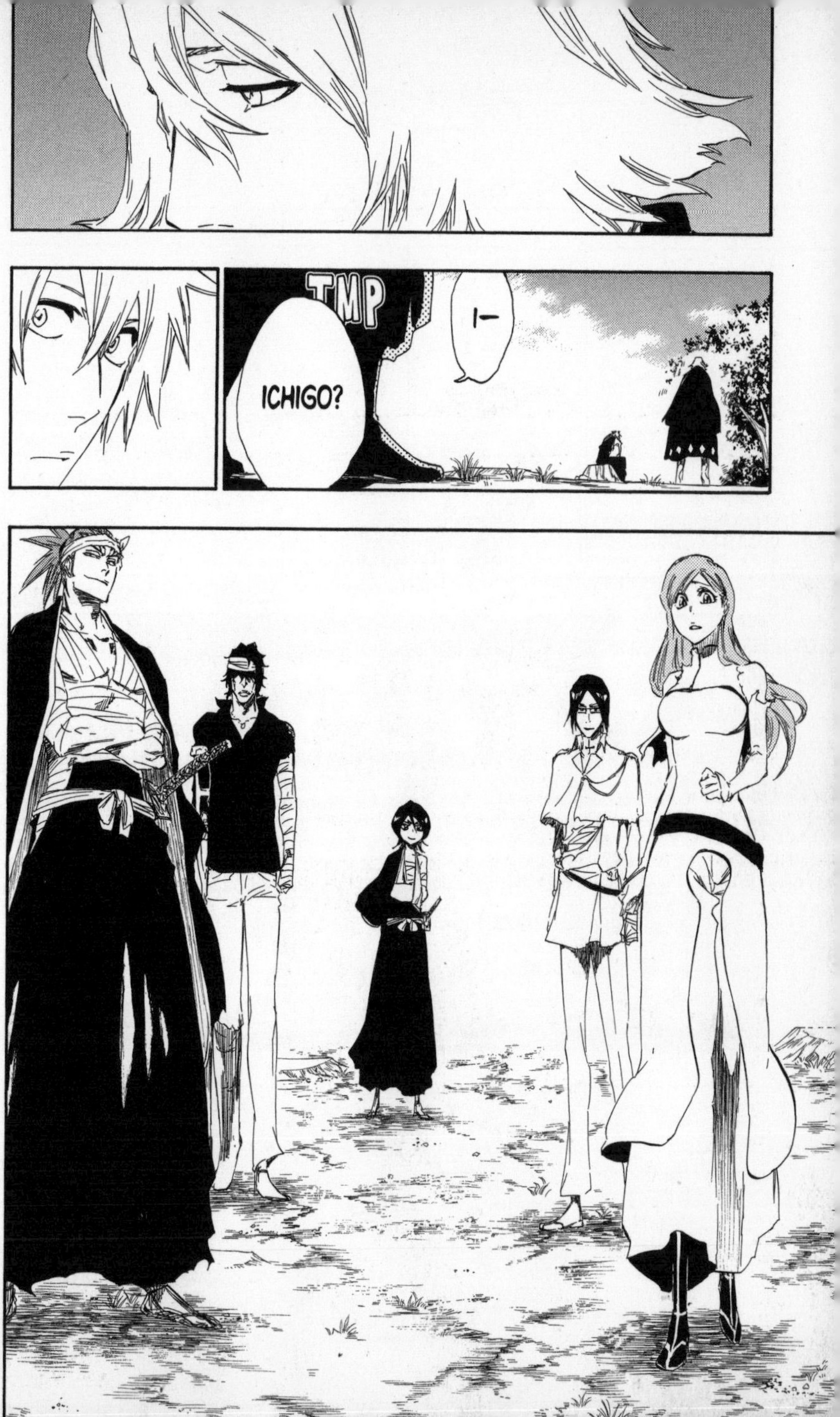
I—
TMP
ICHIGO?

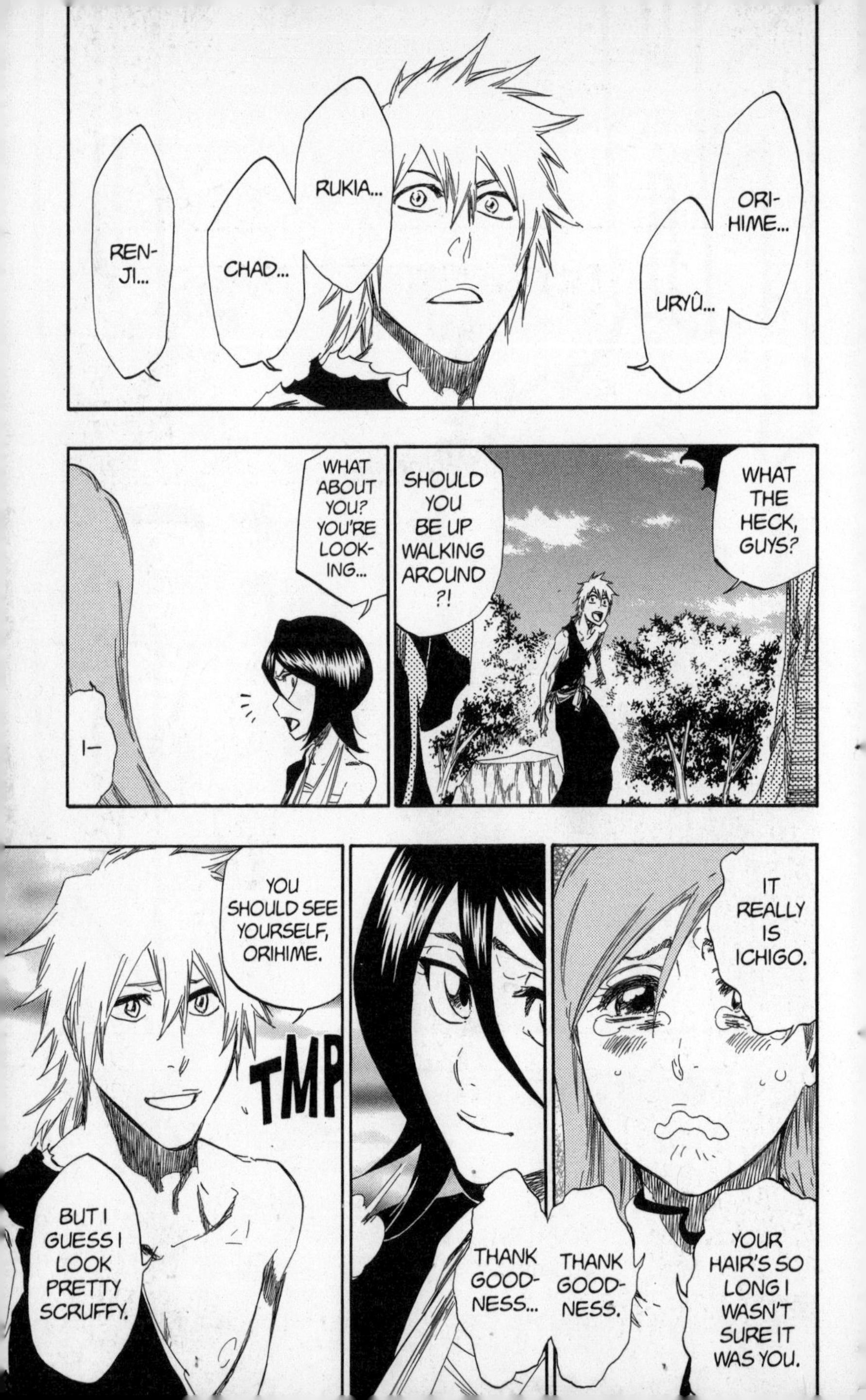
ORI-HIME...
URYÛ...
RUKIA...
CHAD...
REN-JI...
WHAT THE HECK, GUYS?
SHOULD YOU BE UP WALKING AROUND?!
WHAT ABOUT YOU? YOU'RE LOOK-ING...
I—
IT REALLY IS ICHIGO.
YOUR HAIR'S SO LONG I WASN'T SURE IT WAS YOU.
THANK GOOD-NESS.
THANK GOOD-NESS...
YOU SHOULD SEE YOURSELF, ORIHIME.
TMP
BUT I GUESS I LOOK PRETTY SCRUFFY.

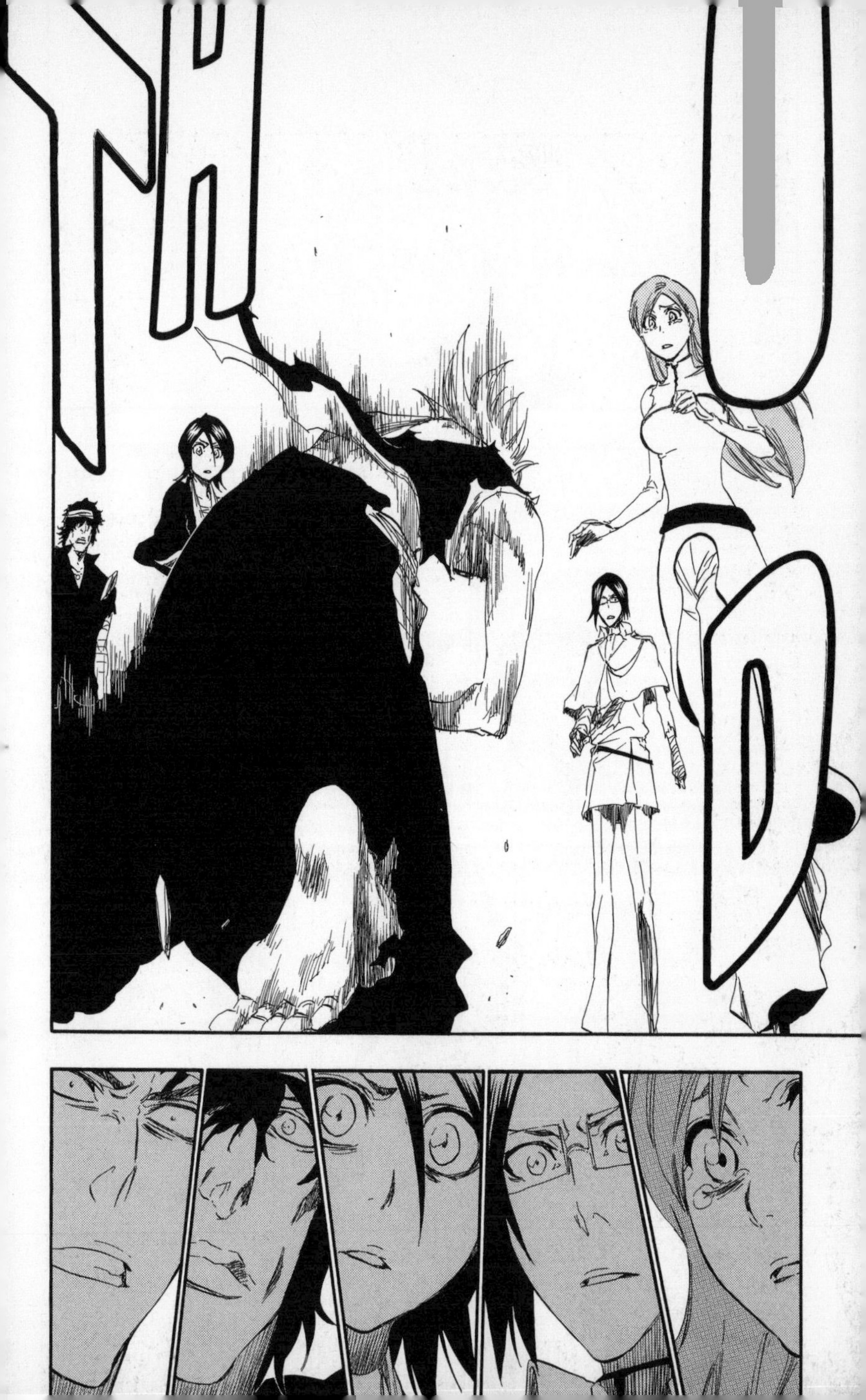
THUD

READ THIS WAY

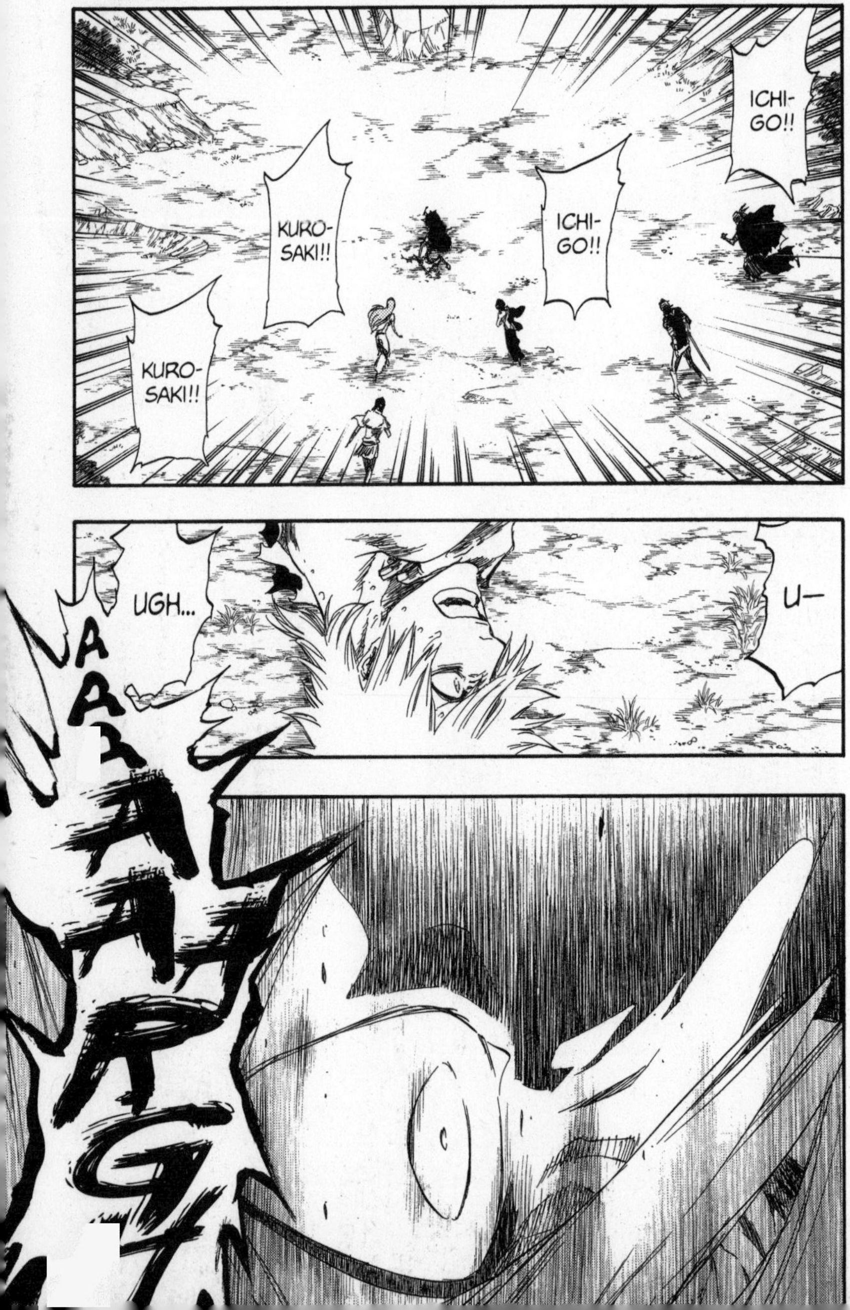

ICHI-GO!!
ICHI-GO!!
KURO-SAKI!!
KURO-SAKI!!
U—
UGH...

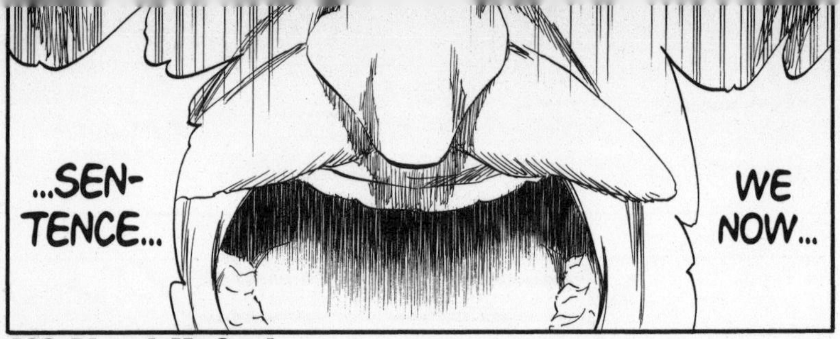
WE NOW...
...SEN-TENCE...

423. Bleach My Soul

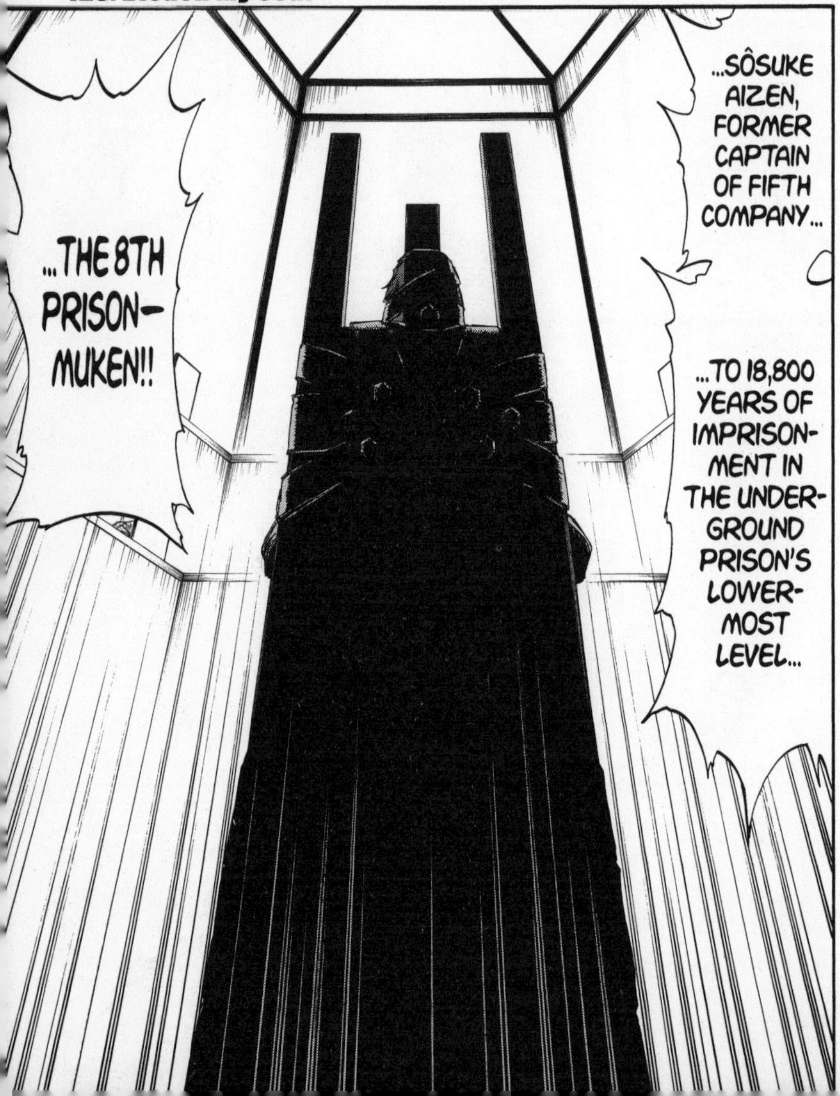
...SÔSUKE AIZEN, FORMER CAPTAIN OF FIFTH COMPANY...
...TO 18,800 YEARS OF IMPRISON-MENT IN THE UNDER-GROUND PRISON'S LOWER-MOST LEVEL...
...THE 8TH PRISON—MUKEN!!

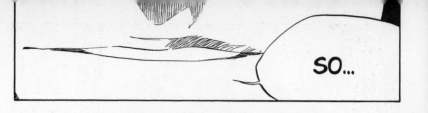

SO...

YOU PEOPLE ARE HANDING DOWN JUDGMENT ON ME, EH?

二十二

GRR...

...COMICAL.

RATHER...

TRAITOR!! DON'T PRESS YOUR LUCK JUST BECAUSE YOU'RE IMMORTAL!!
HURRY UP AND COVER HIS EYES AND MOUTH!!
三十五
EXTEND HIS SENTENCE TO 20,000 YEARS!!

BLEACH 423.

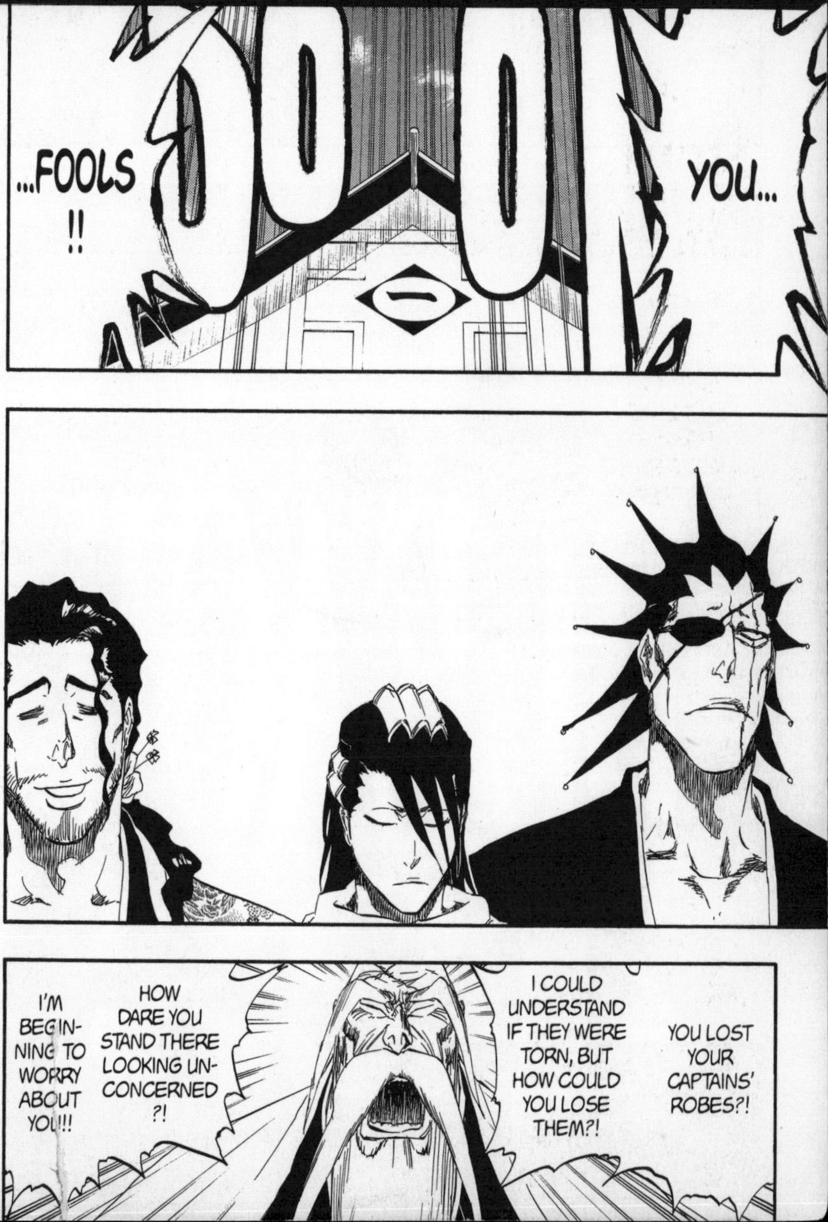
YOU...
...FOOLS !!
YOU LOST YOUR CAPTAINS' ROBES?!
I COULD UNDERSTAND IF THEY WERE TORN, BUT HOW COULD YOU LOSE THEM?!
HOW DARE YOU STAND THERE LOOKING UN-CONCERNED ?!
I'M BEGIN-NING TO WORRY ABOUT YOU!!!

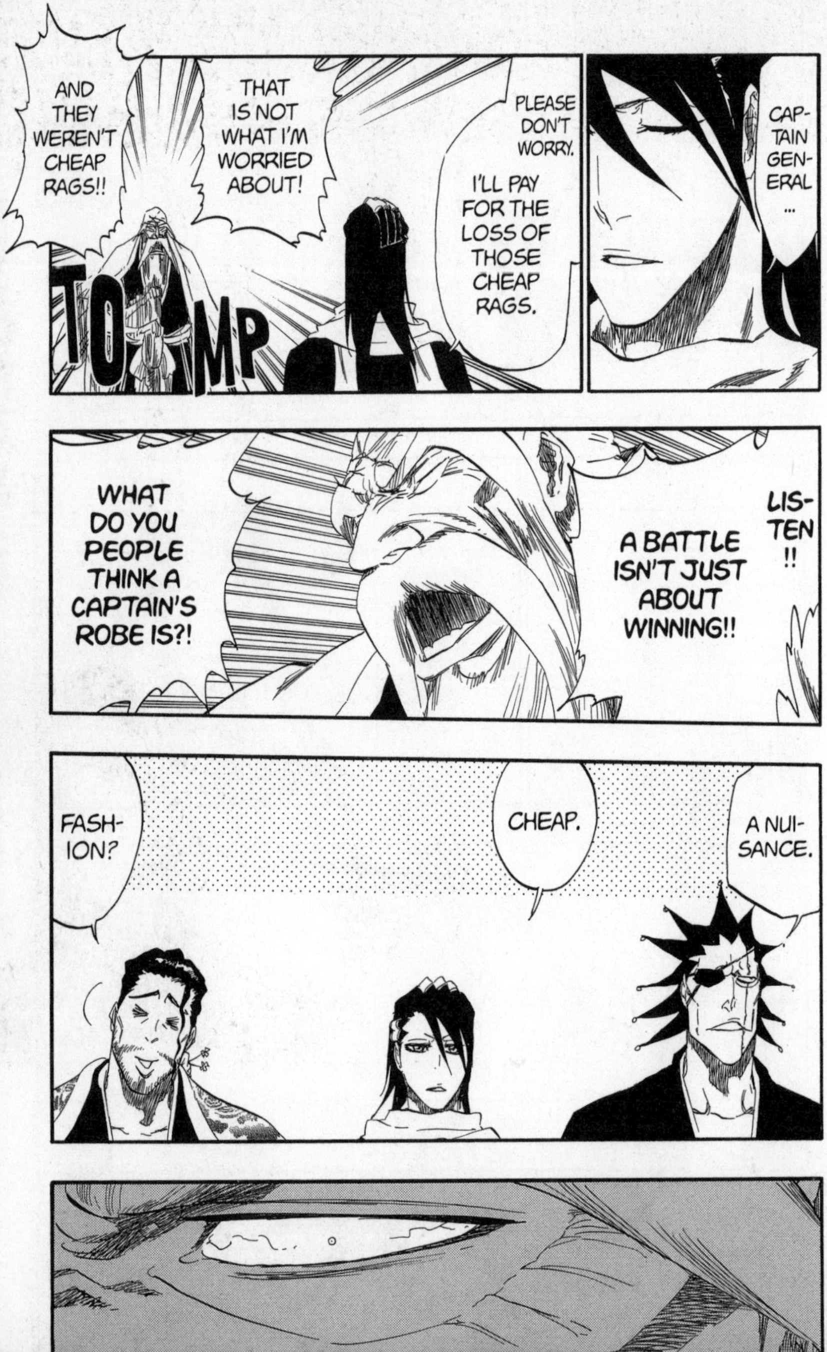

CAP-TAIN GEN-ERAL...
PLEASE DON'T WORRY.
I'LL PAY FOR THE LOSS OF THOSE CHEAP RAGS.
THAT IS NOT WHAT I'M WORRIED ABOUT!
AND THEY WEREN'T CHEAP RAGS!!
TOMP
LIS-TEN!!
A BATTLE ISN'T JUST ABOUT WINNING!!
WHAT DO YOU PEOPLE THINK A CAPTAIN'S ROBE IS?!
A NUI-SANCE.
CHEAP.
FASH-ION?

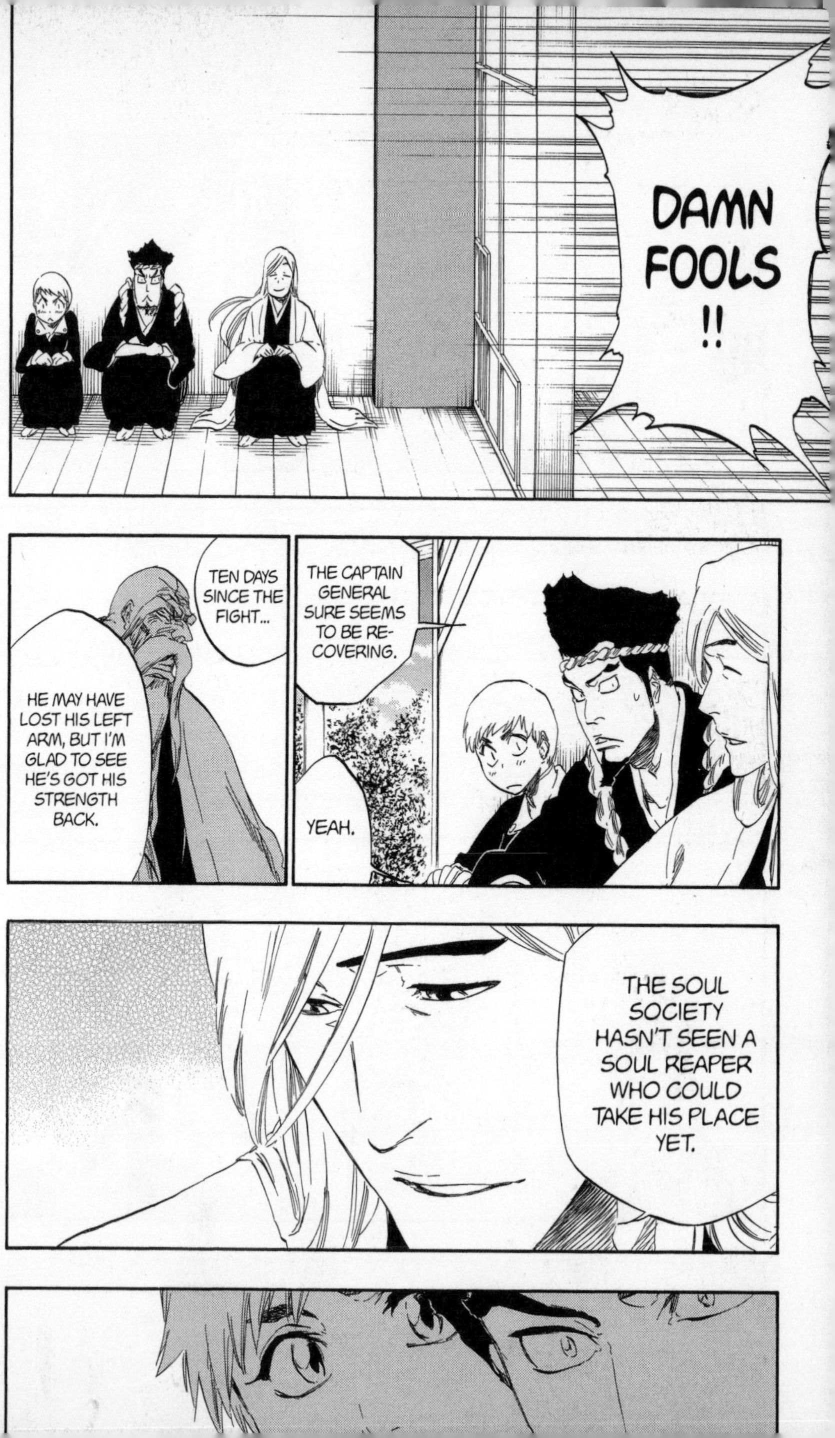
DAMN FOOLS !!
THE CAPTAIN GENERAL SURE SEEMS TO BE RE-COVERING.
YEAH.
TEN DAYS SINCE THE FIGHT...
HE MAY HAVE LOST HIS LEFT ARM, BUT I'M GLAD TO SEE HE'S GOT HIS STRENGTH BACK.
THE SOUL SOCIETY HASN'T SEEN A SOUL REAPER WHO COULD TAKE HIS PLACE YET.

READ THIS WAY

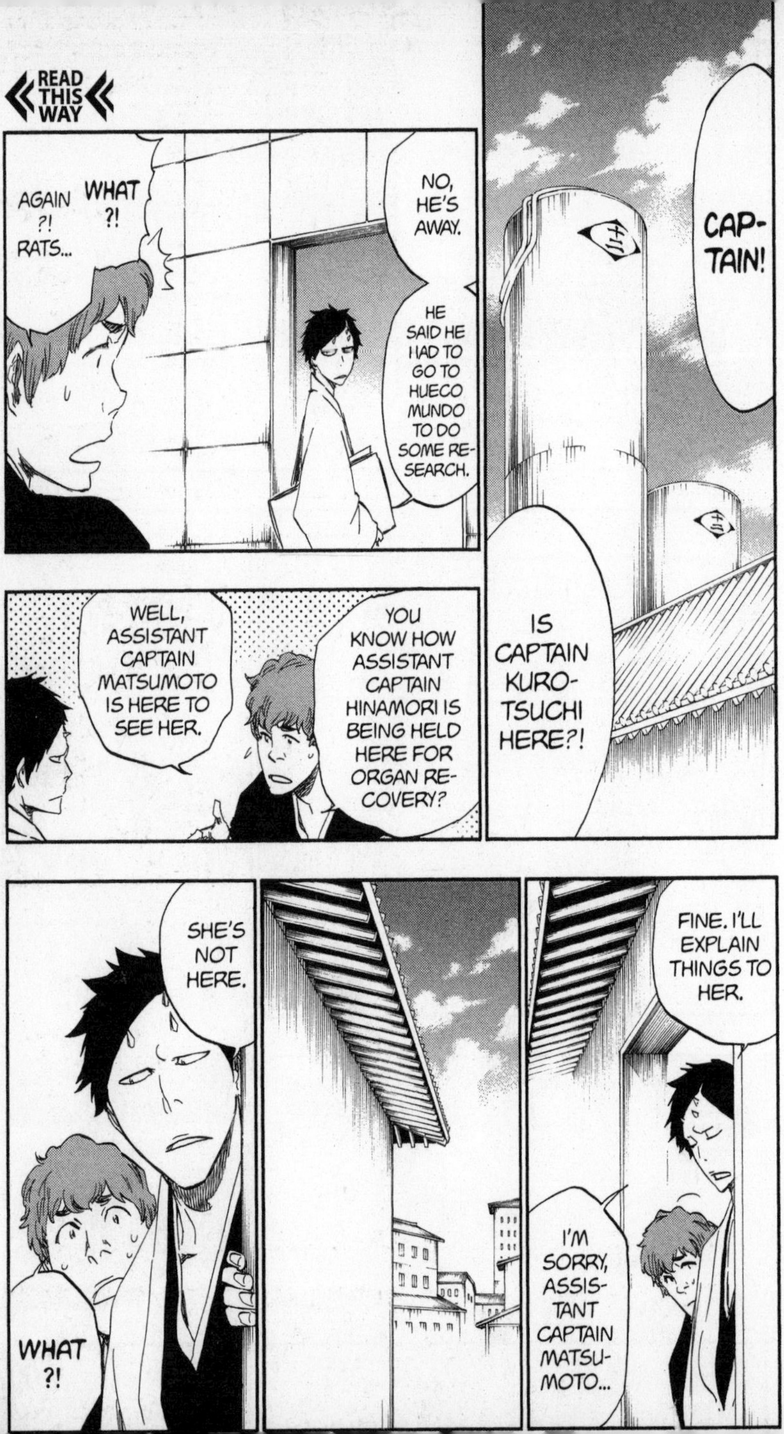
CAP-TAIN!
IS CAPTAIN KURO-TSUCHI HERE?!
NO, HE'S AWAY.
HE SAID HE HAD TO GO TO HUECO MUNDO TO DO SOME RE-SEARCH.
WHAT ?!
AGAIN ?! RATS...
YOU KNOW HOW ASSISTANT CAPTAIN HINAMORI IS BEING HELD HERE FOR ORGAN RE-COVERY?
WELL, ASSISTANT CAPTAIN MATSUMOTO IS HERE TO SEE HER.
FINE. I'LL EXPLAIN THINGS TO HER.
I'M SORRY, ASSIS-TANT CAPTAIN MATSU-MOTO...
SHE'S NOT HERE.
WHAT ?!

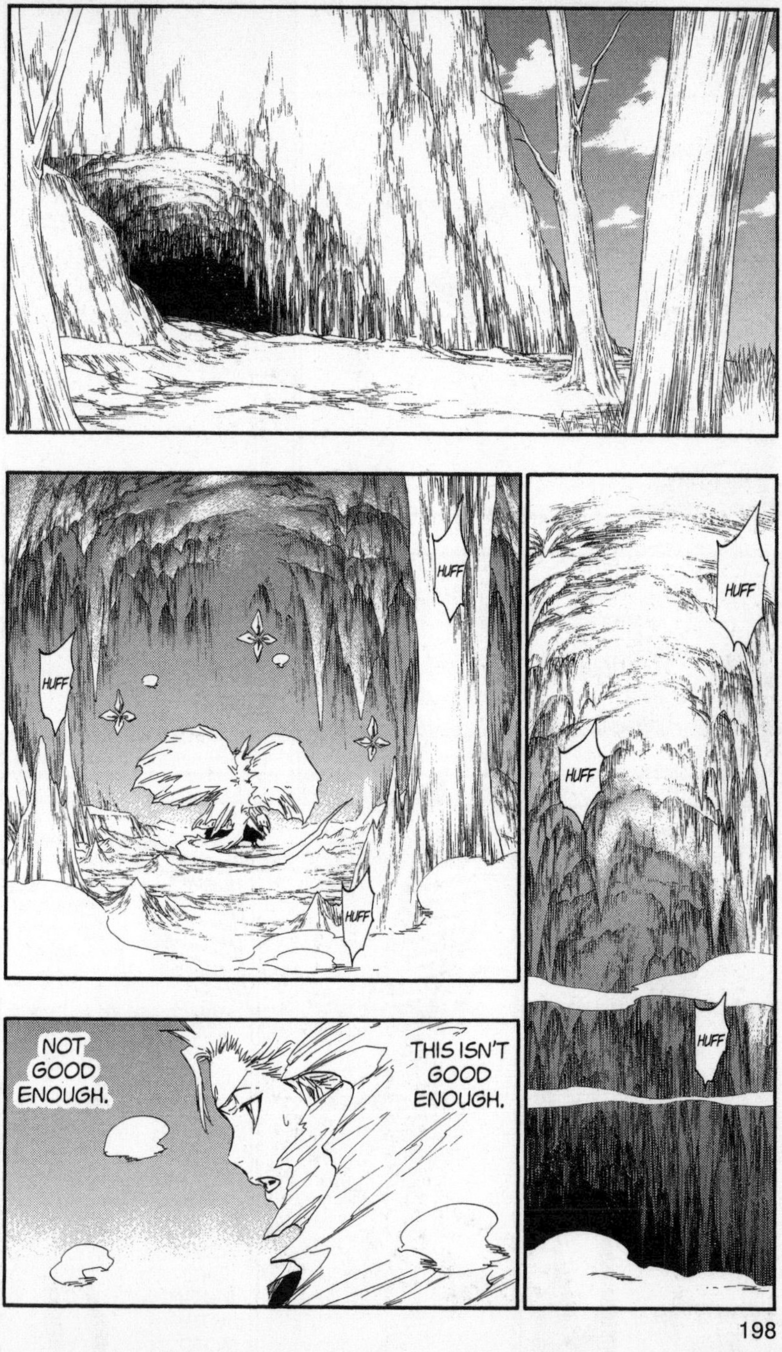
HUFF
HUFF
HUFF
HUFF
HUFF
HUFF
THIS ISN'T GOOD ENOUGH.
NOT GOOD ENOUGH.

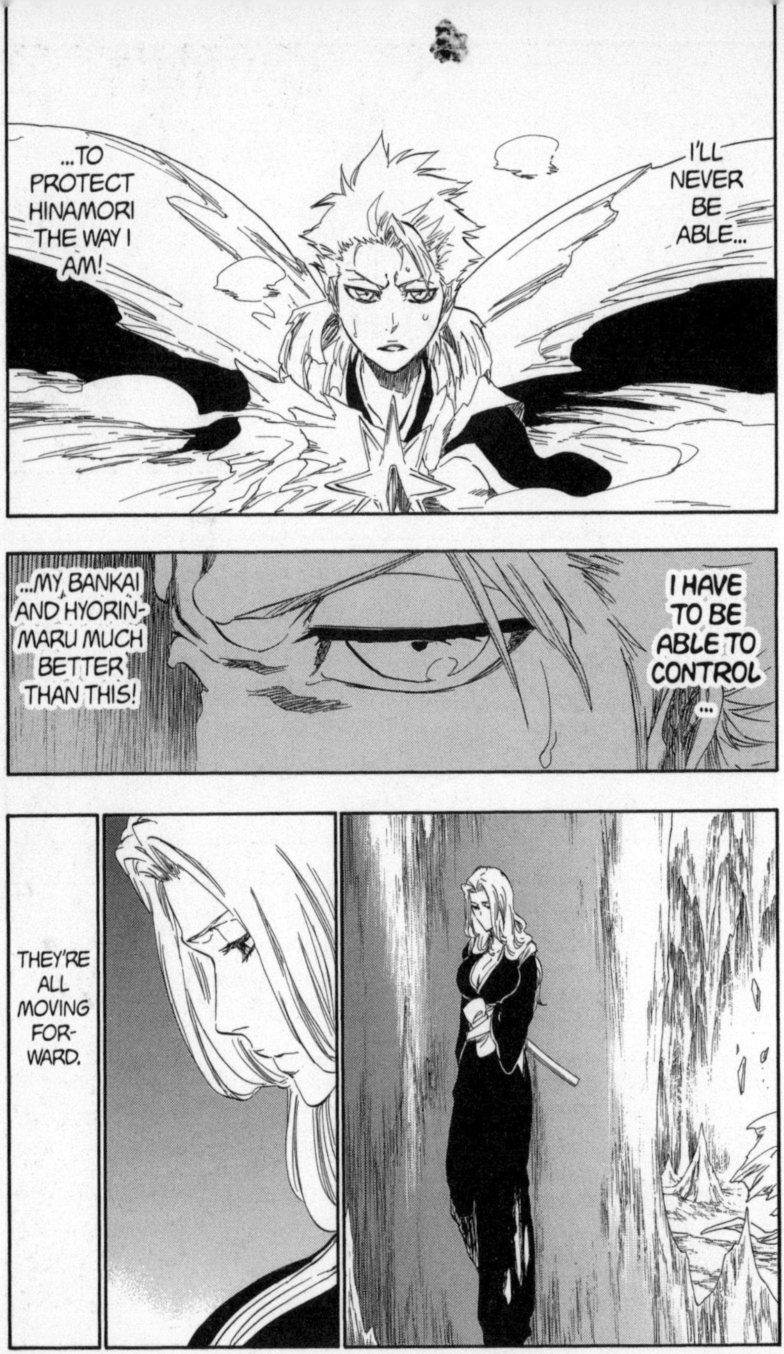
I'LL NEVER BE ABLE...
...TO PROTECT HINAMORI THE WAY I AM!
I HAVE TO BE ABLE TO CONTROL...
...MY BANKAI AND HYORIN-MARU MUCH BETTER THAN THIS!
THEY'RE ALL MOVING FOR-WARD.

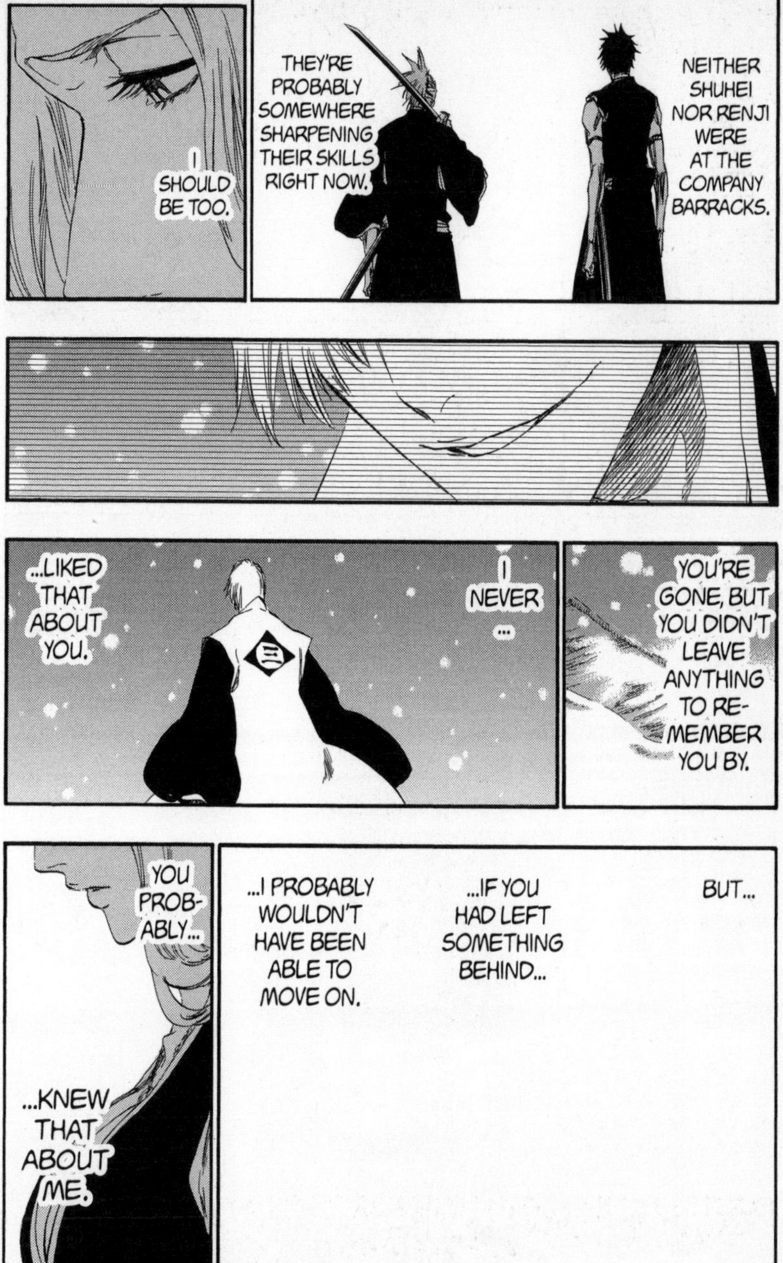
NEITHER SHUHEI NOR RENJI WERE AT THE COMPANY BARRACKS.
THEY'RE PROBABLY SOMEWHERE SHARPENING THEIR SKILLS RIGHT NOW.
I SHOULD BE TOO.
YOU'RE GONE, BUT YOU DIDN'T LEAVE ANYTHING TO RE-MEMBER YOU BY.
I NEVER ...
...LIKED THAT ABOUT YOU.
BUT...
...IF YOU HAD LEFT SOMETHING BEHIND...
...I PROBABLY WOULDN'T HAVE BEEN ABLE TO MOVE ON.
YOU PROB-ABLY...
...KNEW THAT ABOUT ME.

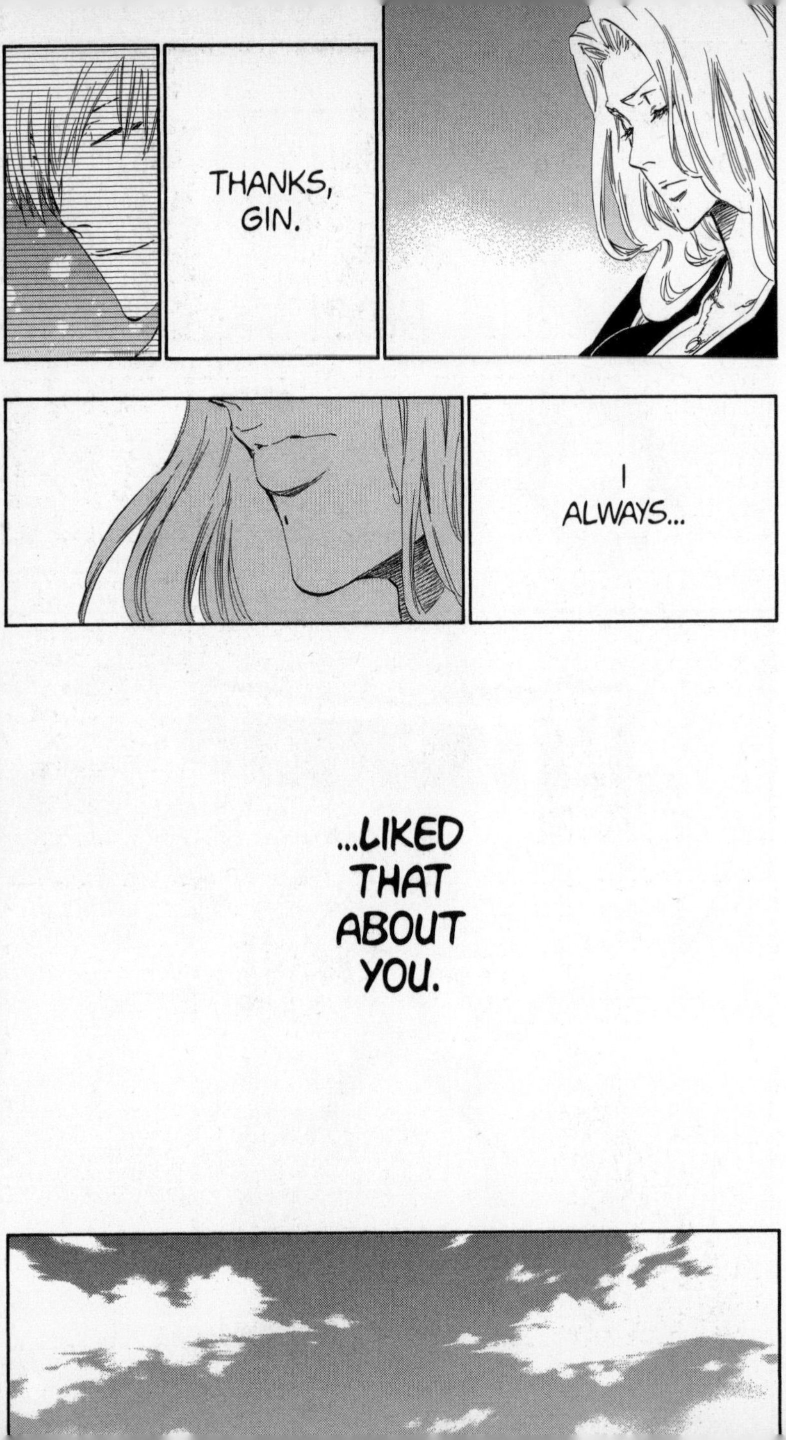
THANKS, GIN.
I ALWAYS...
...LIKED THAT ABOUT YOU.

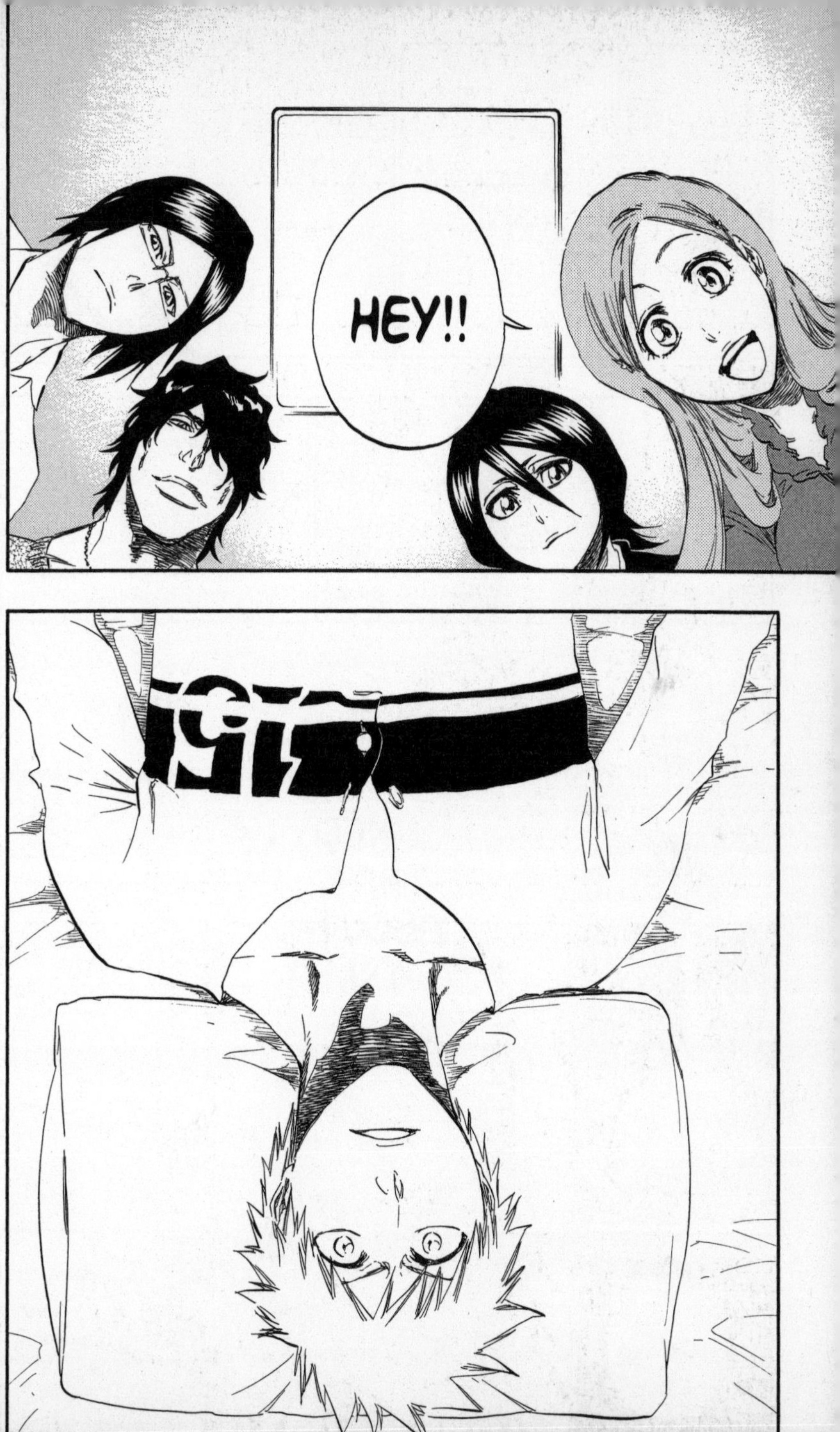
HEY!!

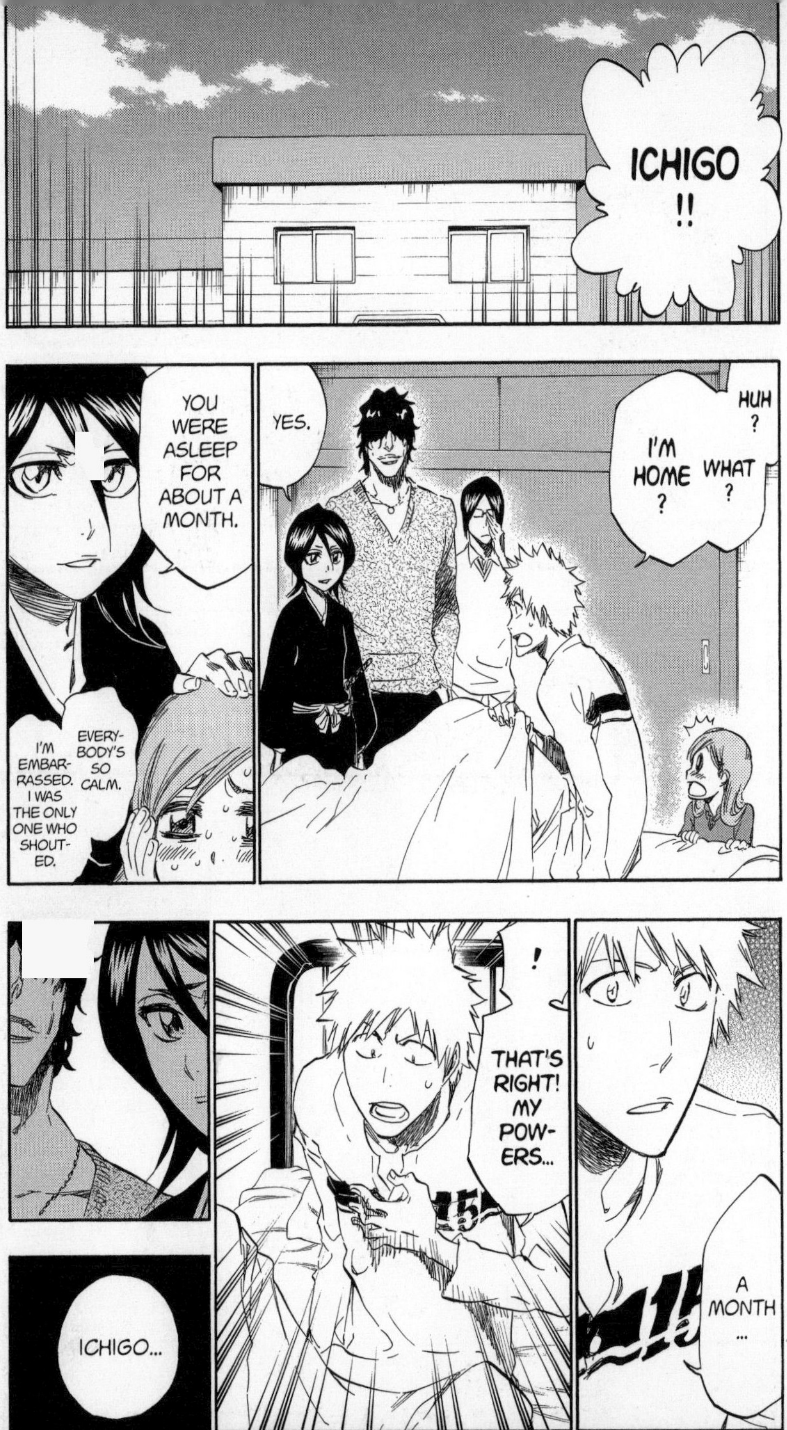
ICHIGO!!
HUH? WHAT?
I'M HOME?
YES.
YOU WERE ASLEEP FOR ABOUT A MONTH.
EVERY-BODY'S SO CALM.
I'M EMBAR-RASSED. I WAS THE ONLY ONE WHO SHOUT-ED.
A MONTH...
!
THAT'S RIGHT! MY POW-ERS...
ICHIGO...

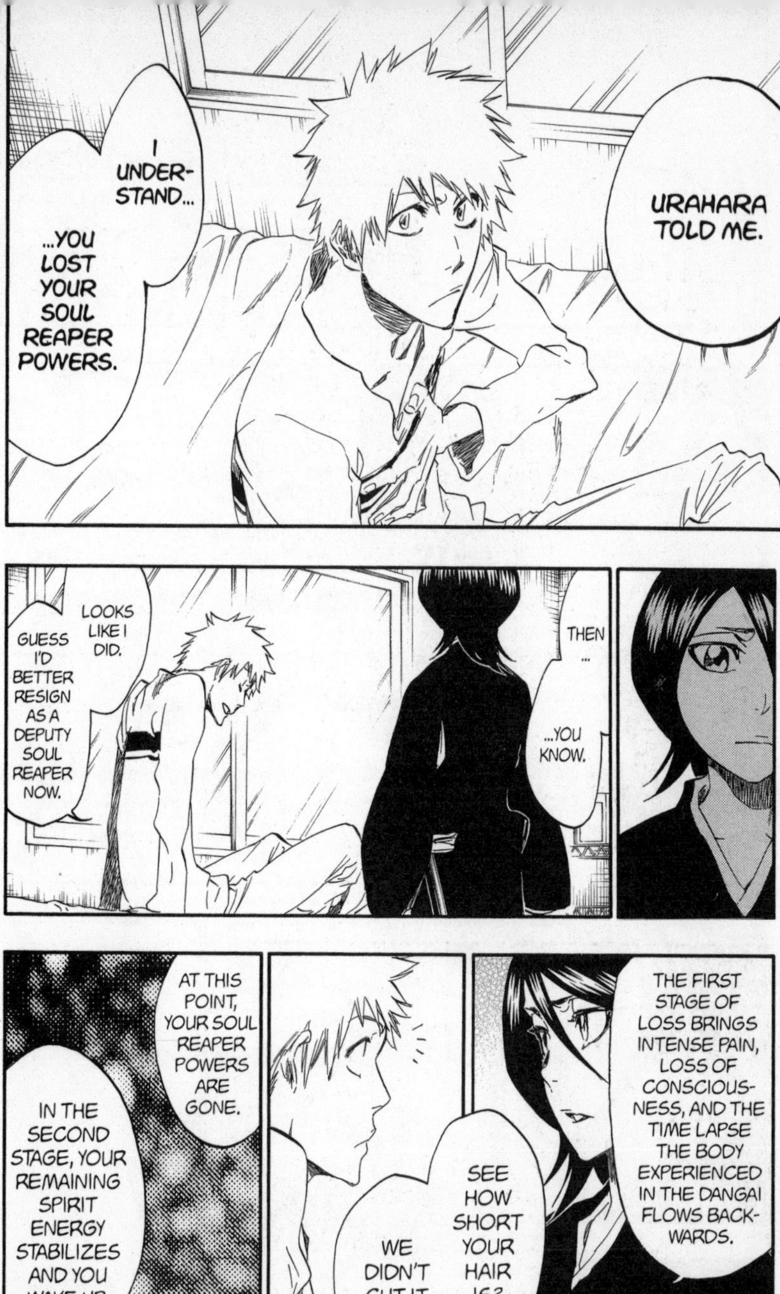
URAHARA TOLD ME.
I UNDER-STAND...
...YOU LOST YOUR SOUL REAPER POWERS.
THEN... ...YOU KNOW.
LOOKS LIKE I DID.
GUESS I'D BETTER RESIGN AS A DEPUTY SOUL REAPER NOW.
THE FIRST STAGE OF LOSS BRINGS INTENSE PAIN, LOSS OF CONSCIOUS-NESS, AND THE TIME LAPSE THE BODY EXPERIENCED IN THE DANGAI FLOWS BACK-WARDS.
SEE HOW SHORT YOUR HAIR IS?
WE DIDN'T CUT IT.
AT THIS POINT, YOUR SOUL REAPER POWERS ARE GONE.
IN THE SECOND STAGE, YOUR REMAINING SPIRIT ENERGY STABILIZES AND YOU WAKE UP.

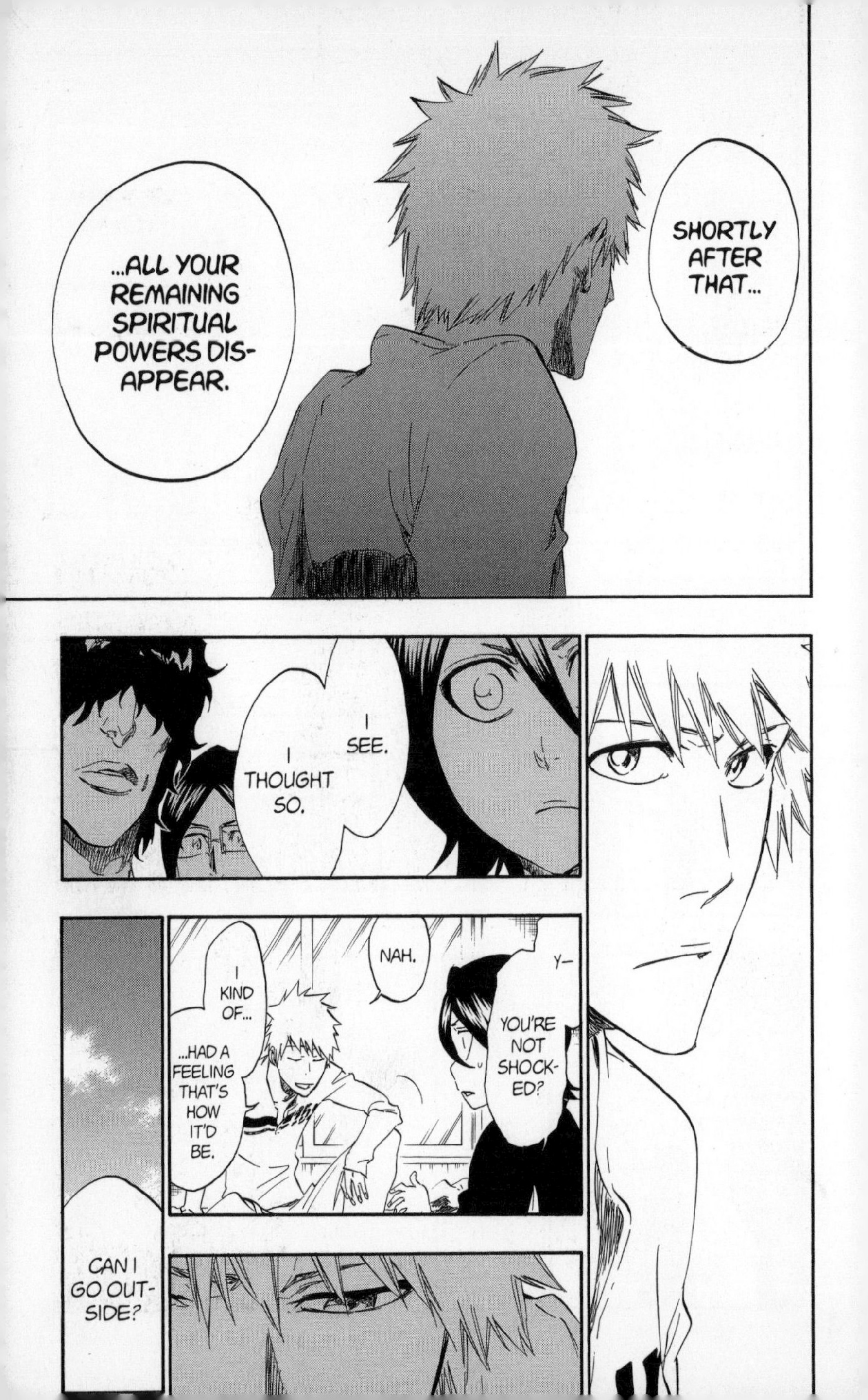
SHORTLY AFTER THAT...
...ALL YOUR REMAINING SPIRITUAL POWERS DIS- APPEAR.
I SEE.
I THOUGHT SO.
Y—
YOU'RE NOT SHOCK- ED?
NAH.
I KIND OF...
...HAD A FEELING THAT'S HOW IT'D BE.
CAN I GO OUT- SIDE?

KURO LINIC

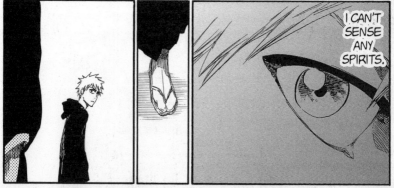

I CAN'T SENSE ANY SPIRITS.

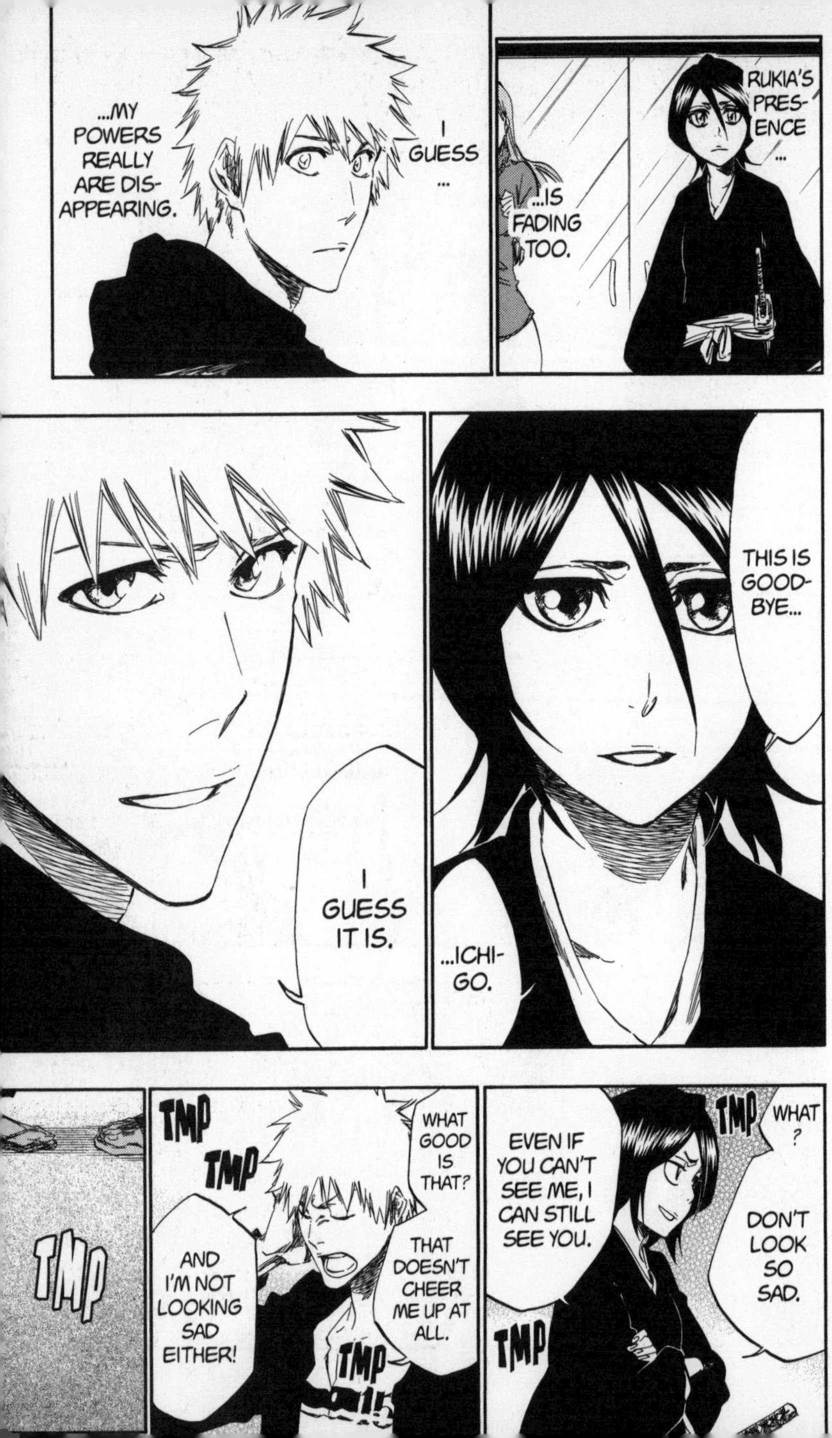
I GUESS ...
...MY POWERS REALLY ARE DIS-APPEARING.
RUKIA'S PRES-ENCE ...
...IS FADING TOO.
THIS IS GOOD-BYE...
...ICHI-GO.
I GUESS IT IS.
TMP
WHAT?
DON'T LOOK SO SAD.
EVEN IF YOU CAN'T SEE ME, I CAN STILL SEE YOU.
TMP
TMP
TMP
WHAT GOOD IS THAT?
THAT DOESN'T CHEER ME UP AT ALL.
AND I'M NOT LOOKING SAD EITHER!
TMP
TMP

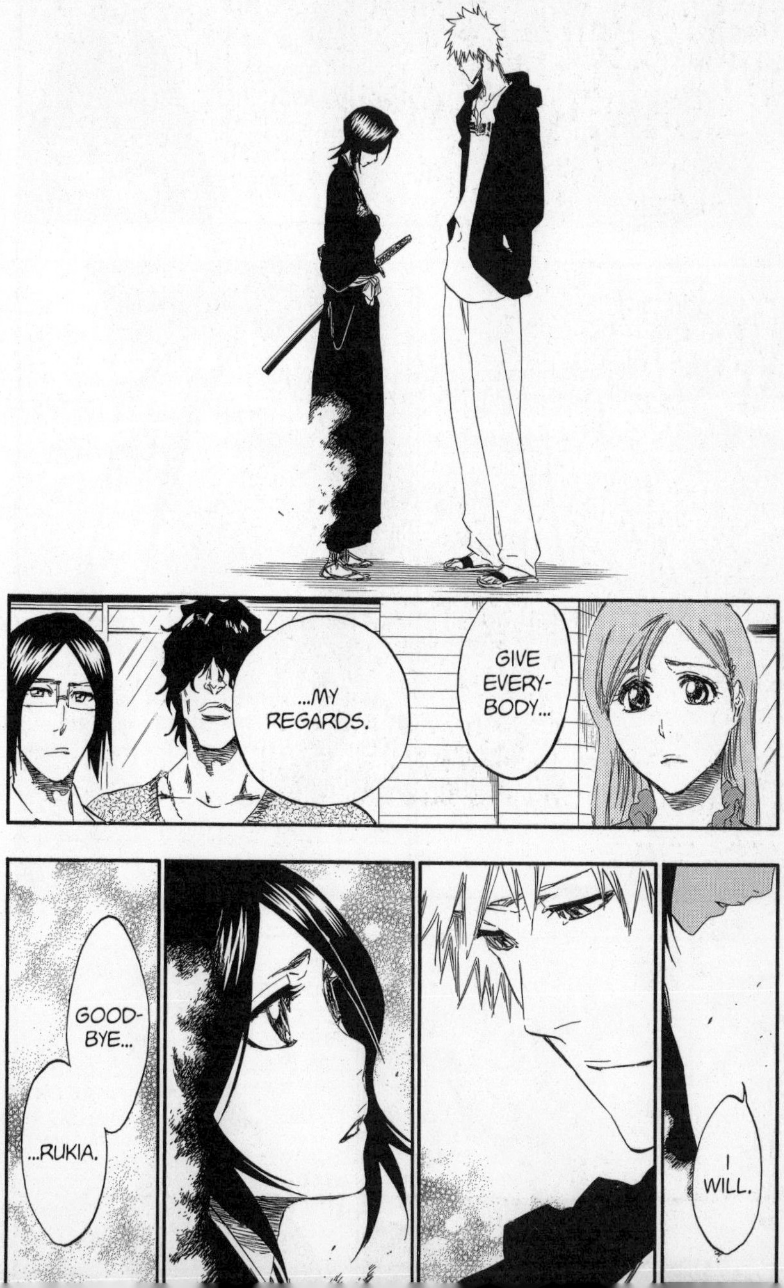
GIVE EVERY-BODY...
...MY REGARDS.
I WILL.
GOOD-BYE...
...RUKIA.

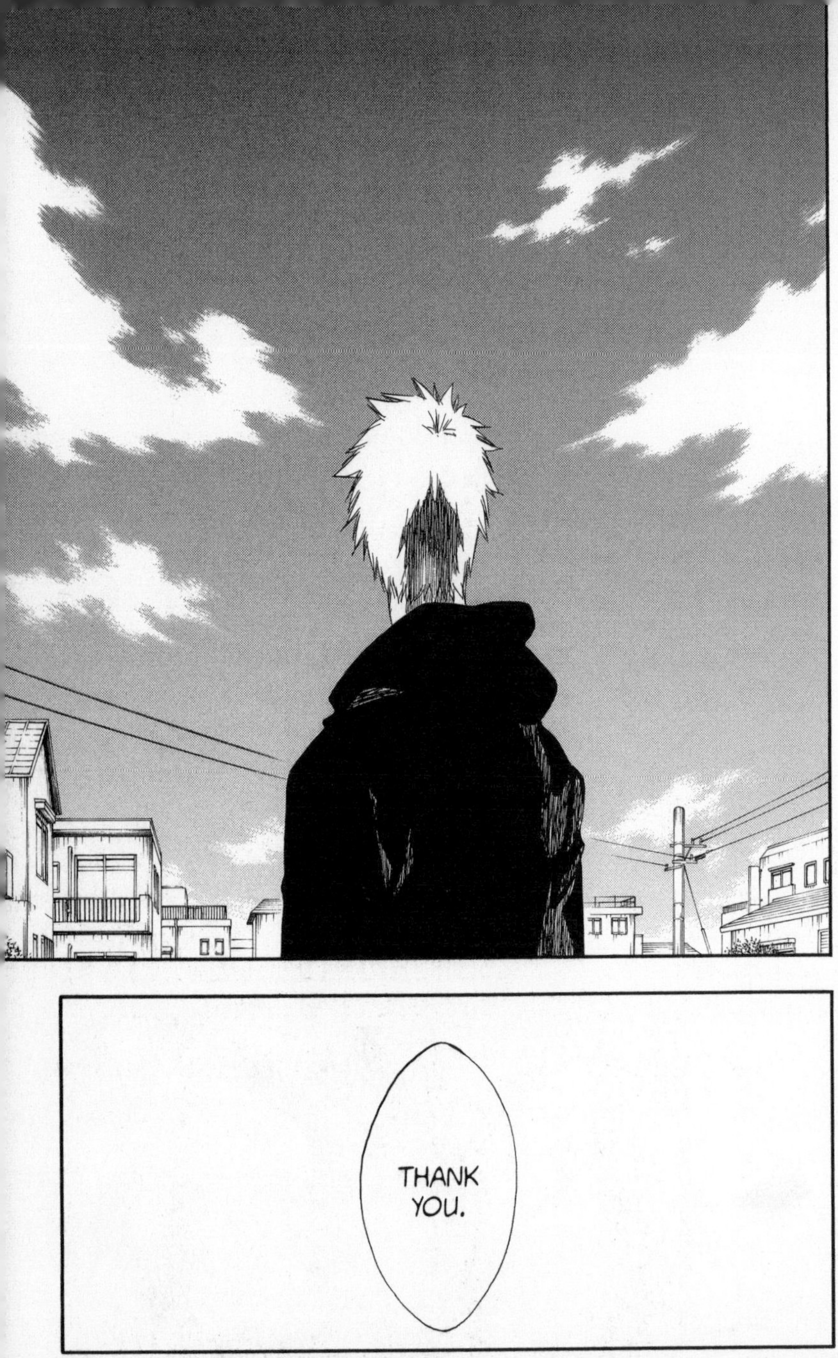
THANK YOU.

BLEACH

ARRANCAR ARC

●

THE END

VOLUME

AGENT ARC

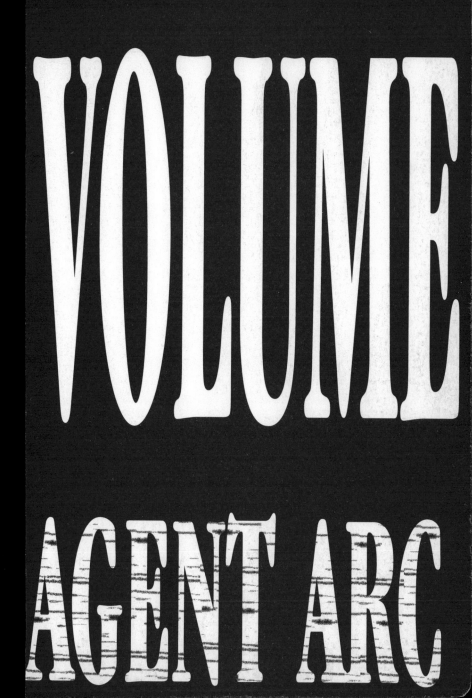

NEXT

THE LOST

CONTI
NUED
IN
BLEACH
49

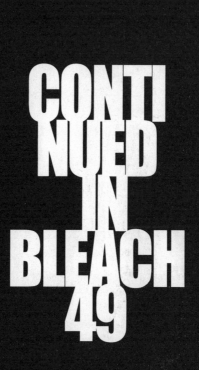